NINETEENTH-CENTURY ART

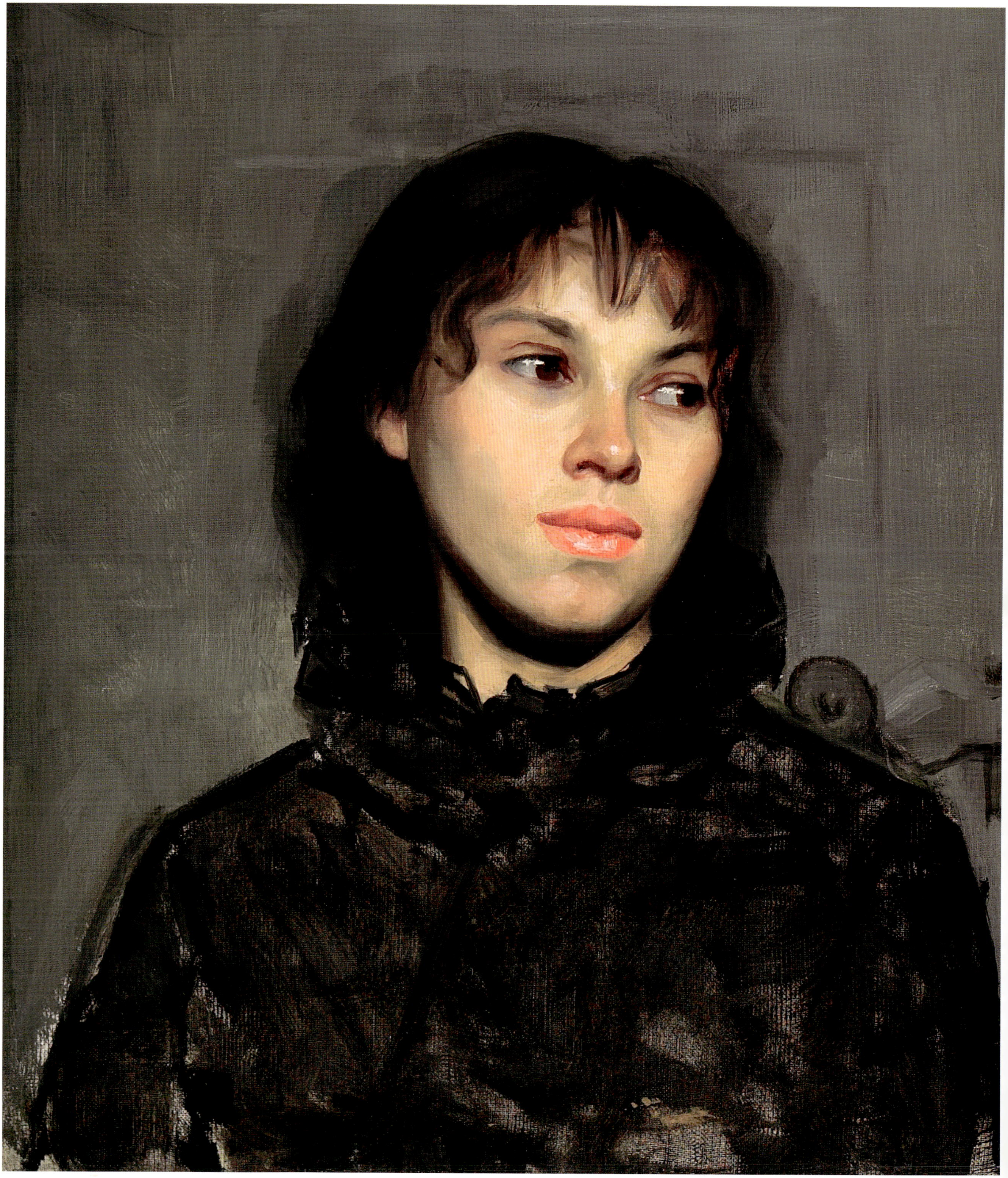

NINETEENTH-CENTURY ART

HIGHLIGHTS FROM THE TANENBAUM COLLECTION

AT THE ART GALLERY OF HAMILTON

ALISON McQUEEN

Joseph M. Tanenbaum
in association with D Giles Limited, London

First published jointly in 2015
by Mr. Joseph M. Tanenbaum
and GILES an imprint of
D Giles Limited
4 Crescent Stables
139 Upper Richmond Road
London SW15 2TN, UK
www.gilesltd.com

Library and Archives Canada
Cataloguing in Publication

McQueen, Alison, 1969-, author
Nineteenth-century art : highlights from the Tanenbaum Collection at the Art Gallery of Hamilton / Alison McQueen.

Includes index.
ISBN 978-1-897407-15-8 (pbk.)

1. Art, European--19th century--Catalogs. 2. Tanenbaum, Joey, 1932- -- Art collections--Catalogs. 3. Tanenbaum, Toby--Art collections--Catalogs. 4. Art Gallery of Hamilton--Catalogs. I. Art Gallery of Hamilton, issuing body II. Title. III. Title: 19th century art.

N6757.M36 2015

709.03'407471352
C2014-907121-3

ISBN (hardback): 978-1-907804-50-2
ISBN (paperback): 978-1-897407-15-8

For Mr. Joseph M. Tanenbaum:
Publisher: Joseph M. Tanenbaum
Author: Dr. Alison McQueen
Photography: Courtesy of Roy Timm, unless otherwise noted

For D Giles Limited:
Copyedited and proofread by Sarah Kane
Designed by Alfonso Iacurci
Produced by GILES, an imprint of D Giles Limited, London
Printed and bound in China
All measurements are in centimeters; height precedes width precedes depth.

Front cover:
Sophie Anderson (French, 1823–1903), *Toklihili: The Young Indian Princess*, 1863–71, oil on canvas, 103.3 × 66.5 cm, s.l.r.c. S. Anderson, Inv.2002.33.72

Page 2:
Mariya Bashkirtseva (Ukrainian, 1858–1884), *Portrait of a Woman*, 1882, oil on canvas, 55.5 × 46 cm, u.r. MB; s. verso, on stretcher, Marie Bashkirtseff and r. 1882 Paris, Inv.2002.33.78

List of Abbreviations

s.	signed
d.	dated
l.	lower
u.	upper
c.	center
cat.	catalogue
fig.	figure
l.l.	lower left
no.	number
r.	right
Inv.	Inventory number
AN	Archives Nationales de France

Page numbers in italics denote illustrations.

COLLECTORS' PREFACE

Collecting art has been an integral part of our married life. We started in the mid-1960s and we have never looked back. Looking at artworks and deciding which to acquire for our collection was something we always did together. We have been equal partners in all decisions regarding our art collection and our philanthropy. We have enjoyed a long-standing relationship with Hamilton that goes back to business connections in the 1970s and '80s through the Bridge and Tank Company. Many years ago now, a close friend, Susan Murray, recommended we get to know the Art Gallery of Hamilton better. The relationship we developed with the gallery and particularly with Louise Dompierre, who was director and CEO from 1998 to 2014, have been very important in our lives. Louise has been remarkable, and her enthusiasm for our nineteenth-century European collection meant that we began donating those works to the AGH. Since 2000, we have given over 210 European works and over ninety African and Oceanic artworks to the Art Gallery of Hamilton. With each gift we have enjoyed the feeling of supporting the arts community in Canada and of giving back to our wonderful country.

Joey's beloved paternal grandfather escaped from Poland in 1911 with only eight dollars in his pocket. When he found his way safely to Toronto, he started as a peddler with a push cart. He went on to create what by the third generation became one of the largest steel fabrication and distribution companies in Canada. Joey followed in his foosteps and was fortunate to continue operating the company, although it faced many difficulties when he took over the helm. Our love of artworks has helped us confront those difficulties and many of life's other challenges. The works in this book are highlights of the European art we have donated to the Art Galley of Hamilton. Each of the paintings, sculptures, and prints is impressive, beautiful, and stimulating in its own way. You will see, as we have, that the human spirit continues to be present through these works. They express passions and convey to us experiences and events from the past. We have enjoyed learning about the artists and the context in which they made their art. On many occasions, these works helped us surmount life events, both challenges in business and in human relationships. The works have appealed to both of us: they manifest passions and express emotions that have inspired and intrigued us. We are certain that you, our readers and fellow art lovers, will enjoy this book. We hope you will take pleasure in looking and learning, and that you will be inspired by these artworks as much as we have.

—

Joey and Toby Tanenbaum
Toronto, Ontario

Cat. 10

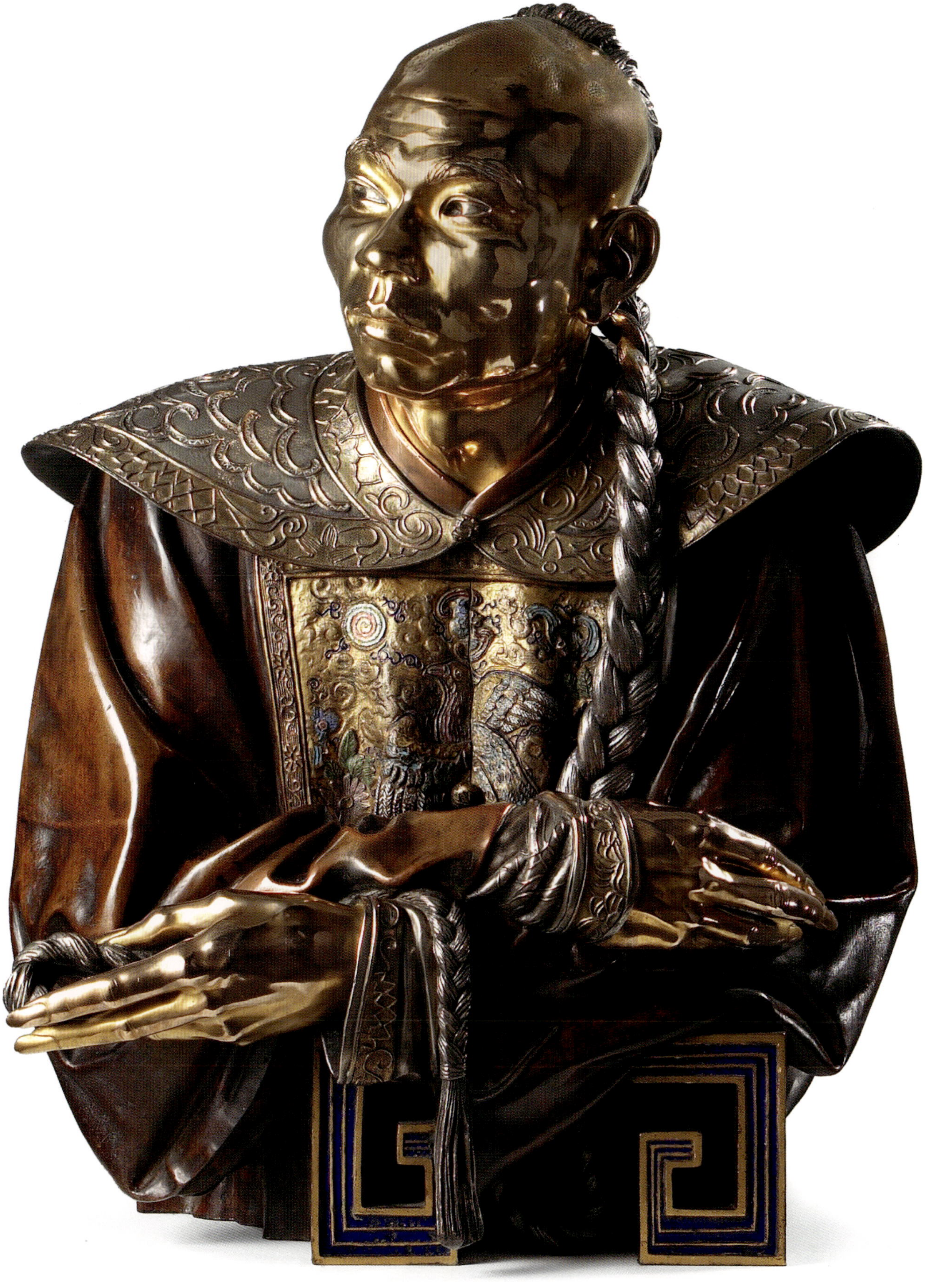

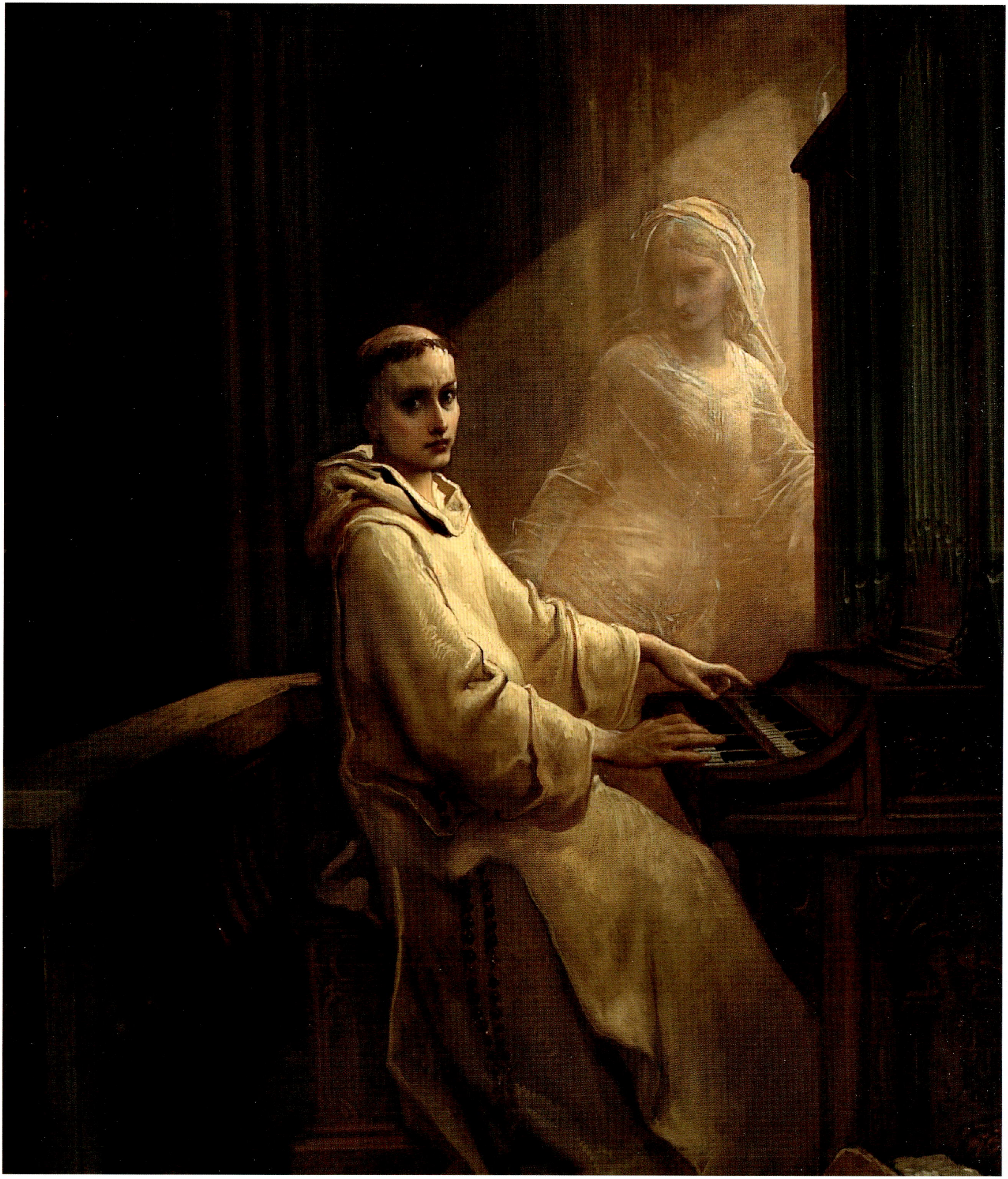

INTRODUCTION

In 2002, Joey and Toby Tanenbaum announced an unprecedented gift to the Art Gallery of Hamilton (AGH): over two hundred works of European art that span the "long" nineteenth century, the period from the later 1700s through the early 1900s. The AGH has been well recognized for its strong collection of Canadian historical art since its foundation in 1914. While the gallery had opportunities to acquire some European works over its hundred-year history, the Tanenbaums' generous gift transformed the AGH. Esteemed Louvre curator Jacques Foucart said of the gift, "As a whole, this Tanenbaum collection would, by itself, because of its diversity and originality, act as a foundation for a museum, a museum which, far from replicating what can be seen elsewhere, would provoke great and well-founded curiosity."[1] The European works from the Tanenbaum collection have indeed created a diverse and highly original collection. Joey and Toby have continued to contribute to the AGH, both financially and by the donation of artworks, including over ninety works of African and Oceanic art in 2010. With the support of the Tanenbaums and the leadership of Louise Dompierre, President and CEO from 1998 to 2014, the AGH has become one of the most important art museums in the country.

Joey and Toby Tanenbaum rank among Canada's most prominent art collectors. In addition to their impact on the AGH, their donations have had a profound effect on many of the leading cultural institutions in Canada including the National Gallery, the Royal Ontario Museum, the Art Gallery of Greater Victoria, and the Art Gallery of Ontario. In 2000 they were named Canada's "Outstanding Philanthropists of the Year," and in 2004 the Canadian Museums Association recognized the eminent nature of their patronage with the Award for Outstanding Achievement in Philanthropy. In 2011 and again in 2014 Joey and Toby were named among the "Top 200 collectors" in the world by *ARTnews* magazine.[2] While Joey has had a more public role than Toby, they have been equal participants in all decisions regarding their art purchases and donations. Joey was awarded the Order of Canada in 1996 in recognition of his lifetime of outstanding achievement and remarkable service to the nation. Toby's significant contributions were recognized by her appointment to the Order of Ontario in 2013. The motto of the Order of Canada, "Desiderantes meliorem patriam" (They desire a better country), underlines the extent to which they have both given back to their country. Joey has declared publicly the aspirations he and Toby have for their donations to Canadian art galleries and museums. He has sincerely and passionately quoted from the Torah, citing Hebrew prayers on how one should respond to good fortune, and he has spoken philosophically about the importance of making a public impact for the better.

At a personal level, Joey and Toby Tanenbaums' donations to the AGH provide genuine insight into their passionate collecting of art that evokes a strong human quality. This is conveyed particularly through the number of works that manifest emotional and dramatic representations of the human body, psyche, and spirit. The breadth and quality of the collection also testifies to their acumen. Their skills as connoisseurs were developed in part through their relationships with numerous dealers including the Shickman Gallery, Jack Kilgore, and Otto Nauman in New York, Peter Silverman in Paris, as well as the Bruton Gallery, Charles Jerdein, and Norman Leitman in London. While these knowledgeable dealers were the source of many important purchases, Joey and Toby also bought art at auction from Sotheby's and Christie's in Monaco, London, Rome, and New York.

Nothing in the upbringing of either Joey or Toby nurtured their interest in art. "I had no history whatsoever in art at all because we were a family brought up in the steel business," Joey recalls. "There was no art, period. [For] my late beloved grandfather, being an orthodox Jewish

Cat. 24 (Detail)

man, it was sinful to have the creation of people [represented in images], they always felt that it was against the wishes of G[-]d." Toby also grew up in an orthodox Jewish home but as a young girl she was drawn to strongly colored, finely made forms, in particular a cobalt blue basket with a silver filigree handle that sat on the piano in her family home.[3]

As a couple, their taste for collecting was fueled by an unusual experience: the negative response that their first acquisition elicited from Joey's family. In the early 1960s, after almost ten years of marriage, Joey and Toby moved into an English Tudor-style home in Toronto. They thought old English paintings would be the appropriate decor for the wood-paneled home, and they set out to Britnell's on Yonge Street, a company that at the time sold both books and art. They made their first purchase in July 1964 of an oil painting Joey can only vaguely recall today: "It was nothing. It was just a little girl, a little boy, playing with some bunny rabbits. It was absolutely nothing. What did we know?" They paid one hundred dollars and Joey wrote "Re: painting" at the bottom of the check. In those days, Joey's father reviewed his canceled checks on the first Friday of every month. At the end of the first week of August, Joey went to work at York Steel and was summoned into his father's office. His father Max closed the door and asked, "Joey, tell me something, are you my son?" Joey replied, "I think so Dad. I don't know. I mean, you should know more than I do, but I think so." Max then said, "Tell me, how could my son spend a hundred dollars for some *shmo-blo* to paint in oil?" To which Joey responded, "Dad, the painting talks to me." And Max fumed, "Talks to you, *schmalks* to you. Better you should invest in the stock market!" Joey and Toby then decided to prove his father wrong and they committed to developing an art collection.[4]

As a first step, the Tanenbaums began attending the Tom Phyfe auctions in Leaside, in east Toronto. At the time they thought that anything colorful was art. When friends saw the dozen works they had bought for their home, one of them took the couple aside, told them they lacked direction, and suggested they read *Apollo* and *Connoisseur* magazines. "We saw that we were really floundering, that we had to get proper advice," recalls Joey. Wide reading led them to Victorian art through dealers in London, England, but it was not until 1968, when a friend introduced them to David Brooke, then chief curator at the Art Gallery of Ontario, that they began to form a thoughtful collecting practice. Brooke was organizing an exhibition on Tissot and advised the Tanenbaums on their first major purchase: Tissot's *The Staircase* (1869). Today, the Tanenbaums consider this work their "first acquisition," and Tissot became one of their favored artists (cats. 44 and 45).[5] Joey has always approached art collecting as he does his business transactions. "Don't deal with the fringe element in the art world," he advises. "Don't go bargain hunting; and consult experts."[6]

The Tanenbaums began biweekly pilgrimages to New York to scour commercial art galleries including Shickman, Wildenstein, Schweitzer, and Shepherd. Building on their Tissot purchase, they started buying French art from the second half of the nineteenth century. Since works by the Impressionists were already priced beyond their reach, they focused on the teachers and contemporaries of the well-known artists. From there, they expanded their interests to include Old Master paintings, particularly of the Renaissance and Baroque periods. The Tanenbaums' affinity for the theatricality of much Baroque art can be seen in Luca Giordano's *The Suicide of Cato* (fig.1), a dramatic painting they donated to the AGH in 2000.

Despite the many public accolades Joey and Toby have received, their talents as art collectors were never fully recognized by Joey's father Max. Joey recalls an exchange between a developer and his father from 1973: "Max," said the developer, "I'm going to Joey and Toby's tomorrow night for dinner and I'm really looking forward to it"—to which Max replied, "When you go there you're gonna see the most expensive goddamn wallpaper in the whole world!" Compliments from Joey's father's remained indirect even after the Toronto showing of *The Other Nineteenth Century*, a traveling exhibition organized by the National Gallery of Canada in 1978–79.[7] When the head of the Israel Discount Bank commented, "Max, your son's collection is unbelievable!" Max responded, "Well, I'm going to tell you something. My son wasn't as stupid as I thought." Perhaps the greatest hurdle for Joey's father was his son's attraction to Christian subjects. A painting by Jean-Jacques Henner, *Christ on the Cross* (cat.56), once hung over Joey's desk in the Hamilton offices of the Bridge and Tank Company of Canada and aroused his father's ire. Max asked, "How could you have a picture of Christ on the cross hanging in your office? You're a good Jewish boy, how could you do that?" Joey replied. "Dad, don't you know, Christ was originally Jewish before he became Christian"—a response that appeased his father.

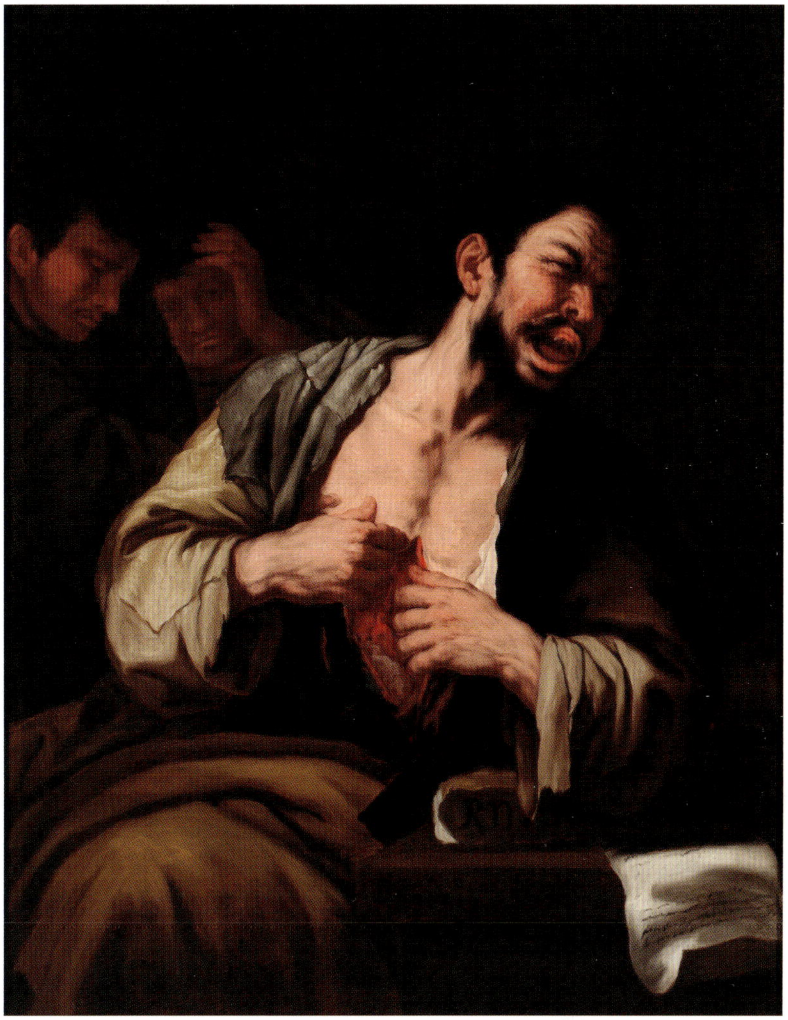

fig.1
Luca Giordano,
The Suicide of Cato,
c.1660. Oil on canvas,
49 × 38.2 cm. Art Gallery of Hamilton, Gift of Jenifer Lyn Tanenbaum from the Joey and Toby Tanenbaum Collection. Inv.2000.34.2. Photograph by Robert McNair

In their approach to nineteenth-century art, the Tanenbaums have been ambitious and intrepid collectors. While many collectors acquire works that can be readily hung and enjoyed in domestic spaces, the Tanenbaums have often bought large works, art that we are more accustomed to seeing in an institutional setting than in a private collection. Many of the works discussed in this catalogue, including works by Doré, Weeks, and Munkácsy, are vast in scale. Most private collectors would shy away from works of such size, and they would also follow established tastes or fashions.

The Tanenbaums have been bold and prescient. They acquired works that give us insight into a broad range of artistic production in the nineteenth century. Studying the art from their collection allows us to challenge what we know, or what we think we know, about nineteenth-century art and the oeuvre (body of works) of specific artists. Through this privileged experience, we learn a great deal. We come to a better understanding of how artists made a living from their works in various ways, how they traveled to seek out patrons, how they were innovative and shipped works to exhibitions, galleries, and collectors around the world, how their artistic practices related to their careers as teachers, and how their ideas sparked imaginations and intrigued their contemporaries. The reputation of most artists changes after their death. Some are lionized: their works are promoted by descendants, friends, art critics, and dealers—often individuals with vested interests. Works by other artists, those who might have enjoyed incredible success or even become celebrities at some point in their lives, can be forgotten posthumously, or for a period of time their work is perceived to be of marginal significance. Many are then the subject of renewed interest, sometimes beginning in the specific city, region, or national context from which they emerged. The reputations of other artists experience an incredible surge at some point, potentially a hundred or more years after their death, and it is only then that we have a better understanding of their contributions.

If art galleries and museums in our communities held in their care and displayed only those works that were already considered part of an established, canonical narrative we would never have an opportunity to challenge ourselves. We would think we understood everything about a particular artist, or that we knew all that is essential to art's history. When a significant private collection, such as that of the Tanenbaums, is donated to a public institution like the AGH, we have access to important works of art. Learning about those works means we can reflect critically on what we thought we knew about nineteenth-century art. And if we are open to it, we can come to think differently than we did before. Such an experience is an integral part of what studying art and its histories offers us.

Joey and Toby Tanenbaum looked beyond the spheres that defined the taste of most collectors of their time. And so their collection tells us fascinating stories, and gives us insight into the long nineteenth century in ways that few other collections can. The entries in this catalogue are written for all readers. They draw on the latest scholarship and seek to present that research so that it amplifies our understanding of individual objects. The catalogue is organized chronologically by the earliest known date for each entry—some examine multiple works by an artist—and they can be read or consulted as discrete parts, or larger sections of the book can be enjoyed in one sitting. Many connections that are internal to the catalogue are noted, such as when artists were associated through groups, exhibitions, or teacher–student relationships. For a reader interested in general biographical information on an artist, or a complete list of achievements and accolades, there are many readily available sources. Such information is included here when it enables readers to better understand the objects before them. This catalogue seeks to combine an in-depth study of the aesthetics of individual works with an analysis of their social and historical context. Readers are invited to look closely, and the full-color images will help make that a pleasurable and rewarding experience. For professionals in the field, this catalogue makes available a collection of works that will be of considerable interest. Some of the works, such as those by Doré and Cordier, have been loaned to recent retrospective exhibitions and are thus already known to experts. One of the aims of this book is to make it possible for many more works from the Tanenbaum collection to be available to scholars for their future research.

As a specialist in nineteenth-century art, it has been my great pleasure to work on the Tanenbaum collection. It has also been an intellectually enriching experience. I have had the opportunity to look at length at the works both in storage and on the walls at the AGH. I have drawn on research resources from around the world and have had an opportunity to consult with a number of specialists who are actively working on catalogues raisonnés (complete studies on specific artists), as well as provenance research. I would like to take this opportunity to thank those who helped make possible my work on this project. To begin, I thank Kim Pickett, and all the interlending staff of Mills Library at McMaster University, who enabled me to access rare resources from around the globe. Without their support and tenacity it would not have been possible to achieve the depth of research that was among the goals for this project. I thank the staff at the Art Gallery of Hamilton, and particularly Christine Braun, for graciously accommodating my many visits and patiently answering my questions. I also thank Benedict Leca, Director of Curatorial Affairs at the AGH (2012-2014), for his support of this project. For their advice, assistance, their insights or suggestions for specific resources I thank: Annette Amenta, Veronika Bebjak, Catherine Chambers, Erika Dolphin, Sandra Evoughlian, Libby Horner, Judy Major-Girardin, Dan Malan, Alexis Moline, Katharine Snider-McNair, and Adriaan

Verkelder. Several individuals were also generous in replying to my inquiries about exhibition and institutional histories and I thank: Beth Bahls, Jane-Coleman Harbison, Lucy Harper, Heather Lammers, Lisa Strong, and Peter Trepanier. I have sought to recognize the important scholarship that has been conducted on a number of the artists, and bibliographic references accompany each entry. I also want to recognize the research of Louise d'Argencourt and Patrick Shaw-Cable and their contributions, particularly at the time of the exhibition held in 2005 when the Tanenbaum donations were first shown at the AGH.[8] My thanks to everyone at D Giles Ltd who helped prepare this publication, particularly Allison McCormick and Sarah Kane.

I thank Joey and Toby Tanenbaum for entrusting me with the responsibility of authoring this book. I hope that my work does justice to their great contributions to Canada and to the Art Gallery of Hamilton. As an educator, I know the value of the resources they have given to Hamilton, how it contributes to the vibrant artistic life of the city, and to the cultural heritage of the nation. Many of the works in this catalogue have already traveled and been seen by people around the world. I hope that this book brings pleasure to those interested in the history of art and that it will continue to make it possible for the Tanenbaums' important donations to be appreciated around the globe.

—

Alison McQueen

Alison McQueen is Professor of Art History at McMaster University. Her book *Empress Eugénie and the Arts: Politics and Visual Culture in the Nineteenth Century* (2011) received a history prize from the Fondation Napoléon in Paris. Professor McQueen is also author of *The Rise of the Cult of Rembrandt: Reinventing an Old Master in Nineteenth-Century France* (2003). She is co-author of *Collecting in the Gilded Age: Art Patronage in Pittsburgh, 1890–1910* (1997) and *Félix Buhot: Peintre graveur entre romantisme et impressionisme, 1847–1898* (1998). Professor McQueen has undertaken research on the Tanenbaums' collection for over a decade. She contributed an essay to the exhibition catalogue *Heaven and Earth Unveiled: European Treasures from the Tanenbaum Collection* (2005) and authored *From Renaissance to Rodin: Celebrating the Tanenbaum Gift* (2012), on the family's donations to the Art Gallery of Ontario.

1 Translation of a letter from Jacques Foucart to Louise Dompierre, 6 November 2001.

2 Milton Esterow, "The ARTnews 200 Top Collectors," *ARTnews* (Summer 2011): 85–88, 90, 92–94, 96–98; Robin Cembalest, "The ARTnews 200 Top Collectors," *ARTnews* (Summer 2014): 51–54, 56, 58, 60, 62–63.

3 The author interviewed Toby Tanenbaum on 17 January 2001, 14 March 2001, and 21 June 2011.

4 Unless otherwise noted, all quotations of Joey Tanenbaum are taken from the author's interviews on 4 December 2000, 17 January 2001, 17 May 2011, and 13 October 2011.

5 Joey recalls purchasing the painting for $1,750 in 1968 and selling it to American-based collector Fred Koch for over $1 million in 1983.

6 Cited by Patricia Anderson in "The Education of an Art Collector," *The Financial Post* (14 July 1979).

7 Douglas Druick and Louise d'Argencourt. *The Other Nineteenth Century: Paintings and Sculpture in the Collection of Mr. and Mrs. Joseph M. Tanenbaum*. Ottawa: National Gallery of Canada, 1978.

8 Louise d'Argencourt et al. *Heaven and Earth Unveiled: European Treasures from the Tanenbaum Collection*. Hamilton: Art Gallery of Hamilton, 2005.

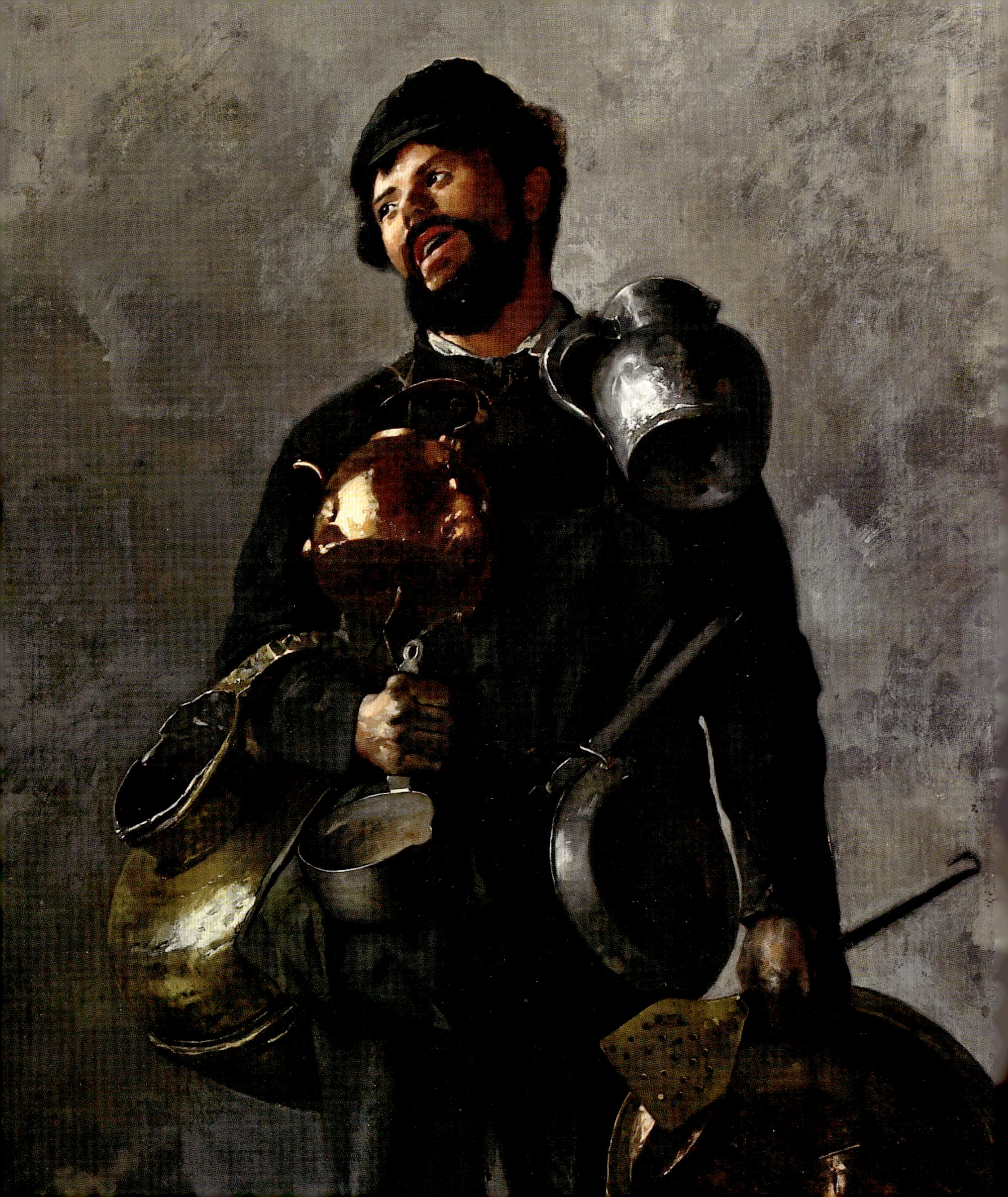

CATALOGUE

Jean-Antoine Houdon (French • 1741–1828)

1 — Flayed Man (L'Écorché)

1767 • plaster • 175 × 119.3 × 62.2 cm • s.base HOUDON F. • Inv.2002.33.44

Houdon was only twenty-five years of age and still a student at the Académie de France in Rome when he produced the *Flayed Man*, one of his most admired early works and certainly the most acclaimed anatomical sculpture in the history of art. The *Flayed Man*, or *L'Écorché* as it is best known, began as a preparatory work, but quickly came to be seen by contemporaries as both highly significant within Houdon's oeuvre, and as an important resource for art academies. Artists in western Europe had been studying from such casts since as early as the Renaissance period. Houdon started work on the *Flayed Man* in 1766 when he received a commission for two over-life-size sculptures for the church of Santa Maria degli Angeli. The church was the seat of the Carthusian order in Rome, and Houdon's commission came towards the end of extensive building renovations. The two sculptures were to be placed inside the church in niches that faced one another; they were to represent St. Bruno, founder of the order, and St. John the Baptist, whose life the reclusive monks sought to emulate. Houdon developed his *écorché* figure as he worked on his plans for the statue of St. John the Baptist.[1] Since the statue was to be placed high up in a niche, where it would be seen only from a frontal view and a low perspective, Houdon conceived of a figure with a tilted head, whose mouth was slightly open, as if speaking. Houdon also extended the figure's right arm as if he was blessing the monks who would gather and pass below.

The two statues were Houdon's first important commission, and he began his work by modeling the *écorché* figure in clay. According to the memoirs of Houdon's friend Johann Christian von Mannlich, a German painter visiting the Académie de France, students could attend anatomy lectures by a French professor of surgery. The artists had access to detailed instruction on the human muscular-skeletal structure and could also draw from the cadavers during their lessons. Mannlich recounted how few of the young artists attended the classes and that he and Houdon benefited greatly from their privileged instruction. Houdon set to work to study the position and form of each of the muscles of the human body, and to understand how different muscles responded when a figure shifted weight, tilted his head, or extended an extremity. He conceived of the St. John the Baptist figure in the classical Greek contrapposto pose, with the left leg bearing the majority of the body's weight and the right leg slightly bent and at rest. Thus, some leg muscles would be more attenuated than others, and they would intersect asymmetrically with the musculature of the figure's torso. The surgery professor came to see Houdon's work on the *Flayed Man* on several occasions, and gave his praise as well as suggestions. What started as a preparatory work in Houdon's studio also attracted considerable interest in the broader artistic community of the French academy in Rome. Many encouraged Houdon to transform his clay model into a plaster figure that could be used by his fellow students. The same year Houdon completed this work, the director of the academy, Charles Natoire, wrote of its potential significance for instructing art students more broadly. By 1775, less than eight years later, studying human anatomy from Houdon's plaster had become an integral part of the academy's curriculum in Rome. Houdon proved highly entrepreneurial, and when he returned to Paris he created a statue that could be cast in lightweight plaster, one that did not require additional support for the legs. He began selling the work and kept the plaster mold in his studio until his death in 1828. As his career developed, Houdon became best known for his portraits, full-figure and particularly busts of sitters including Voltaire, Diderot, Rousseau, George Washington, Thomas Jefferson, Emperor Napoleon I and Empress Josephine, among many other distinguished international figures. Houdon's commitment to close observation of his subjects meant that he often used life masks or, if necessary, death masks to help capture an accurate portrait. His portrait busts always evoked the complex connections between the exterior form of a head and face and the structure of bones and muscles hidden below the skin's surface. This *Flayed Man* is one of five known life-size plaster casts Houdon produced during his lifetime (without the tree trunk support). Three others survive and are in the collections of art academies in Philadelphia, Rouen, and Paris.

[1] Houdon executed *St. Bruno* in marble in 1766–67, and it remains in its niche in the church. Before Houdon left Rome in 1768, he completed the plaster of the St. John the Baptist figure; he never produced the marble, however, and the plaster was destroyed when it fell from its niche in 1894. A second plaster *St. John the Baptist* was discovered in Rome in 1921 and can be found today at the Galleria Borghese. Houdon produced a second *écorché* figure, with his right arm raised above his head, that he also cast in bronze and sold in various sizes.

Provenance
London, Daniel Katz Ltd.
Toronto, Joey and Toby Tanenbaum, 1998–2002

Exhibition History
Hamilton, Art Gallery of Hamilton, 28 May 2005–28 May 2006, *Heaven and Earth Unveiled: European Treasures from the Tanenbaum Collection*, cat.175; 180, *170*
Hamilton, Art Gallery of Hamilton, 28 August 2010–17 April 2011, *Conversations*
Hamilton, McMaster Museum of Art, 3 September–5 November 2011, *Enlightenment, Innovation and Revolution: The Long 18th Century*

Bibliography

Arnason, H.H. *The Sculptures of Houdon*. London: Phaidon, 1975, 13–15.

Postle, Martin. "Flayed for Art: The Écorché Figure in the English Art Academy," *The British Art Journal* vol.5 no.1 (Spring/Summer 2004): 55–63.

Poulet, Anne L. *Jean-Antoine Houdon: Sculptor of the Enlightenment*. Washington, D.C.: National Gallery of Art, 2003, 62–76.

Réau, Louis. *Houdon: Étude sur sa vie et sur son œuvre*. 2 vols. Paris: F. de Nobele, 1964, vol.1, 39–41.

Scherf, Guillaume, and Maraike Bückling. *Jean-Antoine Houdon: la sculpture sensible*. Paris: Somogy, 2010, 17.

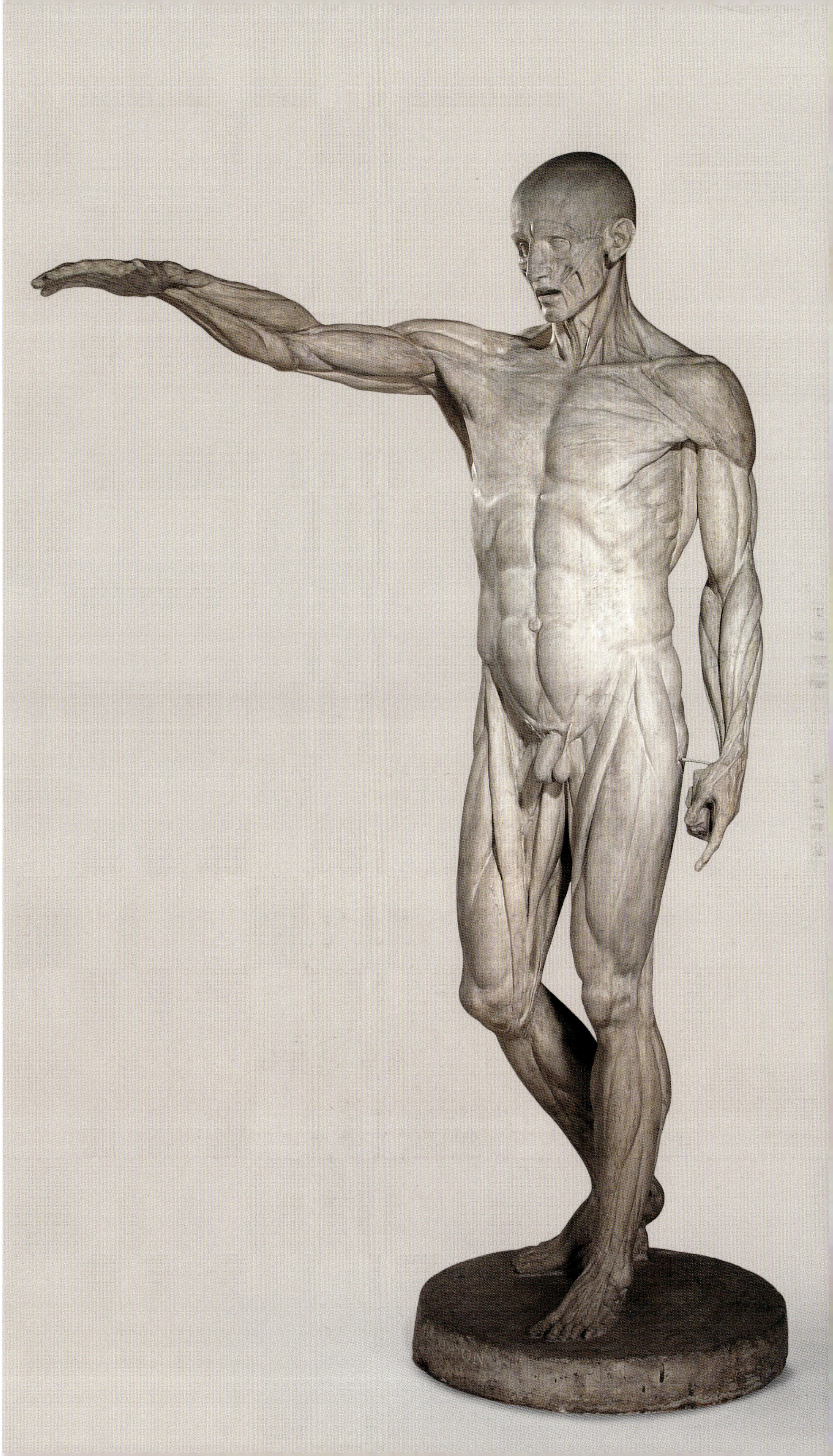

Henry Raeburn (Scottish • 1756–1823)

2 — Portrait of Anne Pringle

c.1795–1810 • oil on canvas • 76.5 × 63.7 cm • Inv.2002.33.43

When we perceive weightiness in this painting and feel its aura of sadness, we must also understand that our response is a sign of this portrait's success. Raeburn ranks among the most admired portraitists in Scottish history. He is particularly noted for his close study of each sitter's personality and his candid efforts to capture their appearance. What we know today of Raeburn's sitter Anne Pringle comes to us from the writings of her great-aunt Alison Cockburn (née Rutherford, 1713–1794), a notable Scottish poet and woman of letters. Cockburn's only son James fell in love with Anne, his second cousin. While Anne returned his affections and the two considered themselves betrothed, Anne's father would not condone their marriage. The specific reason was never recorded. It may have been the familial relationship, or that James had suffered serious physical ailments and was no longer able to work as captain in his regiment, or simply that Anne's father was attempting to hide the poor financial circumstances of his failing business. Regardless, Anne did not want to marry without her father's consent and thus felt forced to end the relationship. That decision had a profound impact on James, who died a short time later. The great-aunt and niece remained intimately connected, and at her death Cockburn bequeathed much of her property to Pringle. Cockburn had long admired Raeburn's paintings and in her letters recorded when she went to see his works, on one occasion accompanied by Anne's sister.

Whether the great-aunt commissioned this portrait from Raeburn, or whether it was executed with monies Anne inherited from her aunt, remains unclear. It is, however, necessary to understand the sad and convoluted family drama in order to appreciate the complex psychology Raeburn achieved in his *Portrait of Anne Pringle*. Raeburn spent time with his sitters. He worked from life and typically completed a canvas over a series of sittings. He did not undertake preparatory work, nor did he use underpainting. Raeburn combined the immediacy of his technique with an emotional sensitivity to his subjects. He worked up some areas, for example Pringle's face, with considerably more attention to detail than other areas, such as the blank backdrop. Raeburn also valued painting wet-on-wet, as is evident in the fluid strokes that undulate and define the edge of Pringle's ruffled neckline. The decisions that informed Raeburn's approach to each painting took place with the sitter present, and this allowed him the opportunity to experience his subject's personality and to bring her individuality to the canvas. Recent scholarship has argued that Raeburn's representations of women deserve much more attention than they have received to date. Works such as *Portrait of Anne Pringle* help us to see beyond the narrow nationalistic readings that have been constructed particularly around Raeburn's portraits of male sitters. Raeburn's empathy for his sitters and his impressive, bold handling of paint pervade his portraits and is integral to their success. The personal circumstances of a sitter such as Anne Pringle distinguish her from many of the fashionable figures of the Scottish Enlightenment, and this portrait thus affords valuable insights into the breadth of Raeburn's achievements.[1]

[1] An unwillingness to accept this unglamorous, middle-aged woman as one of Raeburn's sitters may have informed the decision to identify this portrait as "Circle of Sir Henry Raeburn" on one occasion. See New York, Christie's, 15 October 1998, lot 48.

Provenance

Selkirk, Professor A.S. Pringle-Pattison, by 1901
New York, Howard Young, 1930
St. Louis, Sydney M. Shoenberg
St. Louis, City Art Museum, 1948–84
New York, Sotheby's, 7 November 1984, lot 27 (as by Sir Henry Raeburn)
New York, John Levy Galleries
New York, Frederick J. Cummings, Inc.
Toronto, Joey and Toby Tanenbaum, 1986–2002

Exhibition History

Hamilton, Art Gallery of Hamilton, 28 May 2005–28 May 2006, *Heaven and Earth Unveiled: European Treasures from the Tanenbaum Collection*, cat.87 (as *Portrait, Anne Pringle*)

Bibliography

Armstrong, Sir Walter. *Sir Henry Raeburn*. London: W. Heinemann, 1901, 110.
Coltman, Viccy. "Henry Raeburn's Portraits of Distant Sons in the Global British Empire," *The Art Bulletin* vol.95 no.2 (June 2013): 294–311.
Greig, James. *Sir Henry Raeburn, R.A.: His Life and Works, with a Catalogue of His Pictures*. London: Otto Limited, 1911, 57.
Leonard, H. Stewart. "Sir Henry Raeburn's Portrait of Anne Pringle," *Bulletin of the City Art Museum of St. Louis* vol.37 no.1 (1952): 1–4.
Mearns, Jordan. "'Synonymous with Manly Portraits': Re-evaluating Raeburn's Women," in Viccy Coltman and Stephen Lloyd, eds. *Henry Raeburn: Context, Reception and Reputation*. Edinburgh: Edinburgh University Press, 2012, 314–34.
Rutherford (Cockburn), Alison. *Letters and Memoir of Her Own Life*. Edinburgh: David Douglas, 1900, 17–28, *facing 22*.
Stevenson, Lesley A. "The Technique of Sir Henry Raeburn Examined in the Context of Late Eighteenth-Century British Portraiture," in Ashok Roy and Perry Smith, eds. *Painting Techniques: History, Materials and Studio Practice. Contributions to the Dublin Congress 7–11 September 1998*. London: International Institute for Conservation of Historic and Artistic Works, 1998, 194–98.
Thomson, Duncan, et al. *Raeburn: The Art of Sir Henry Raeburn, 1756–1823*. Edinburgh: Scottish National Portrait Gallery, 1997.

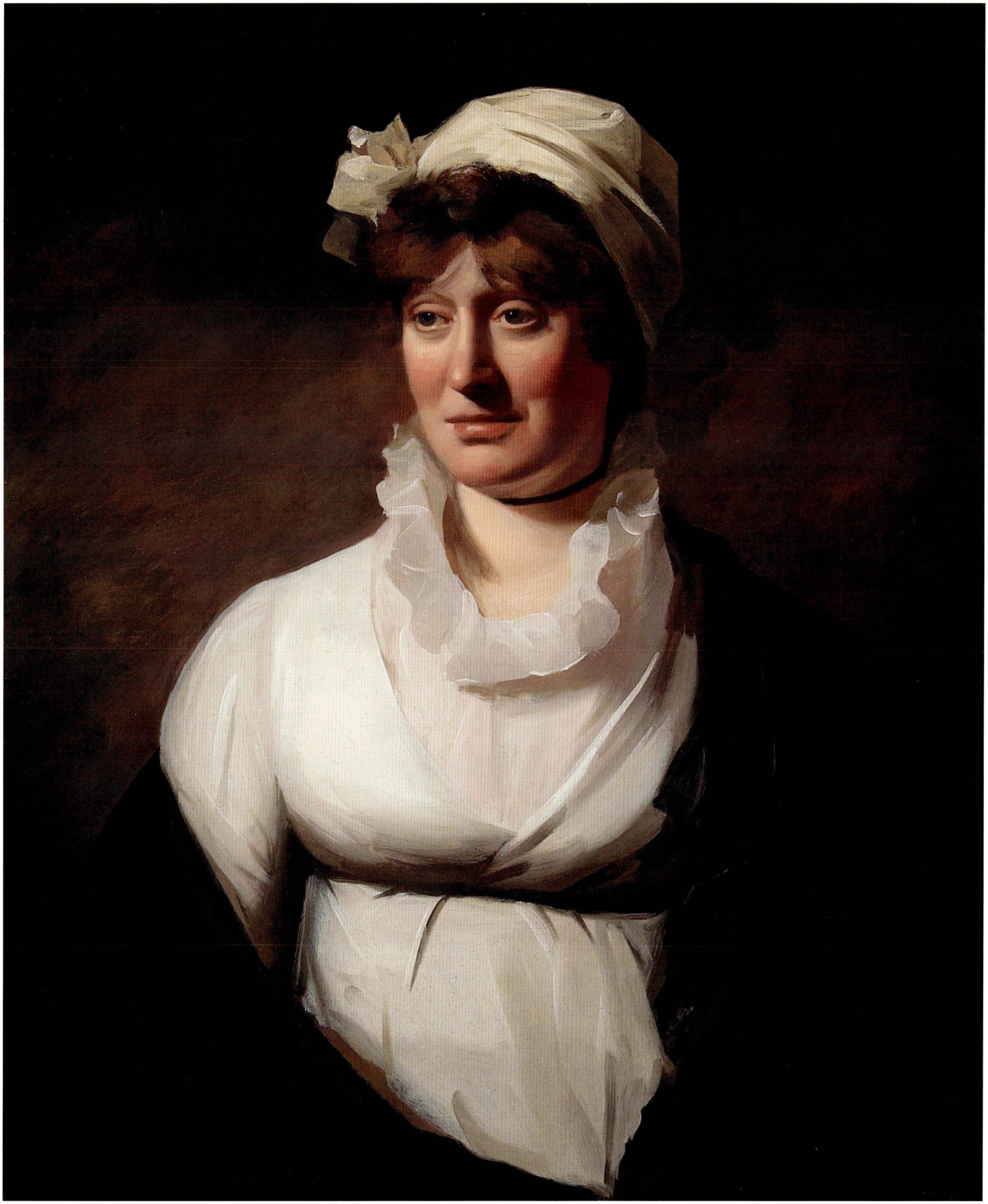

William Etty (English • 1787–1849)

3 — Reclining Male Nude

c.1825–28 • oil on millboard • 43.5 × 50.5 cm • inscribed on verso W.Etty R.A. • Inv.2002.33.110

Beginning in 1927, approximately 100 years after Etty painted this study, it was exhibited at the Tate Gallery in London on long-term loan from the collection of Sir Kenneth Clark, the internationally renowned British art historian. During the following decades, it hung as part of Clark's private collection at Saltwood Castle in Kent. There, it was among the works that inspired Clark's analysis of the nude body in the history of art, ideas that evolved into his landmark study *The Nude: A Study in Ideal Form* (1956). We can appreciate Clark's interest in Etty as an artist and his fascination with this particular painting when we consider how much it reveals about Etty's artistic practices. Etty focused this small-scale study on a male model posed with his torso raised and body directed away, receding into space. There is a strong three-dimensional quality to this figure, whose one arm extends languorously above his head while the other rests firmly on a block. A piece of white cloth serves to contrast with the tonalities of the man's skin. It highlights the model's right hand, drapes under his body, and encircles his upper left arm. Etty may also have planned to paint a layer of white over the section of red underpaint in the model's pubic area, where the cloth partially conceals yet still leaves much revealed. Red underpainting fills the background and also suggests a shadow cast across the middle of both thighs. The greater level of finish that we witness in the male model's torso is not unusual for Etty, who often executed extremities with less detail.

From 1807, when Etty first attended the Royal Academy Schools in London, he remained dedicated to studying the live model. Even after 1824, when he was elected an associate of the Royal Academy, Etty continued to attend life classes and remained committed to executing oil sketches on millboard, as he did with this *Reclining Male Nude*. Most academicians stopped attending the evening life classes as their careers advanced, but Etty continued even after he was made a full academician in 1828. His dedication to painting the nude body and his interest in remaining a life-long student did result in some criticism from contemporaries. For Etty such studies were important as the foundation of his work on large-scale history paintings and they were also significant as independent works in and of themselves. Both during and immediately after Etty's lifetime, it was his representations of the female nude that attracted the most negative attention and resulted in accusations his work was indecent and offensive. Today, scholars are particularly intrigued with his sensual representations of the male body and propose that for Etty it was more likely figures such as the *Reclining Male Nude* that held the most powerful erotic appeal.

Provenance

Saltwood Castle, Kent, Lord Kenneth Clark (by 1927)
London, Sotheby Parke Bernet, 5 July 1984, lot 199
Toronto, Joey and Toby Tanenbaum, 1984–2002

Exhibition History

London, Tate Gallery, 1927–29 (on long-term loan)
London, R.E.A. Wilson, November 1933, *Paintings by William Etty, R.A.*, cat.19
Oxford, Oxford Arts Club, April–May 1935, *Paintings by William Etty, R.A.*, cat.43
London, Oldham Art Gallery, Art Council of Great Britain, 23 April–14 May 1955, *An Exhibition of Painting by William Etty*, cat.40
Hamilton, Art Gallery of Hamilton, 28 May 2005–28 May 2006, *Heaven and Earth Unveiled: European Treasures from the Tanenbaum Collection*, cat.38; 13, *72*

Bibliography

Bignamini, Ilaria, and Martin Postle. *The Artist's Model: Its Role in British Art from Lely to Etty*. Nottingham: Nottingham University Art Gallery, 1991.
Edwards, Jason. "Queer and Now: On Etty's 'Autobiography' (1849) and 'Male Nude, with Arms Up-Stretched' (c.1830)," in Sarah Burnage et al., eds. *William Etty: Art and Controversy*. York: York Museum Trust, 2011, 91–102.
Farr, Denis. *William Etty*. London: Routledge & Kegan Paul, 1958, 176, no.242, pl.40.
Myrone, Martin. "William Etty, 'a child of the Royal Academy,'" in Sarah Monks et al., eds., *Living with the Royal Academy: Artistic Ideals and Experiences in England, 1768–1848*. Farnham: Ashgate Press, 2013, 171–94.
Postle, Martin, and William Vaughan. *The Artist's Model from Etty to Spencer*. London: Merrell Holberton, 1999, 20–21.
Robinson, Leonard. *William Etty: The Life and Art*. Jefferson: McFarland & Co., 2007, 263–66, 336.
Smith, Alison, ed. *Exposed: The Victorian Nude*. London: Tate Publishing, 2001, 61.

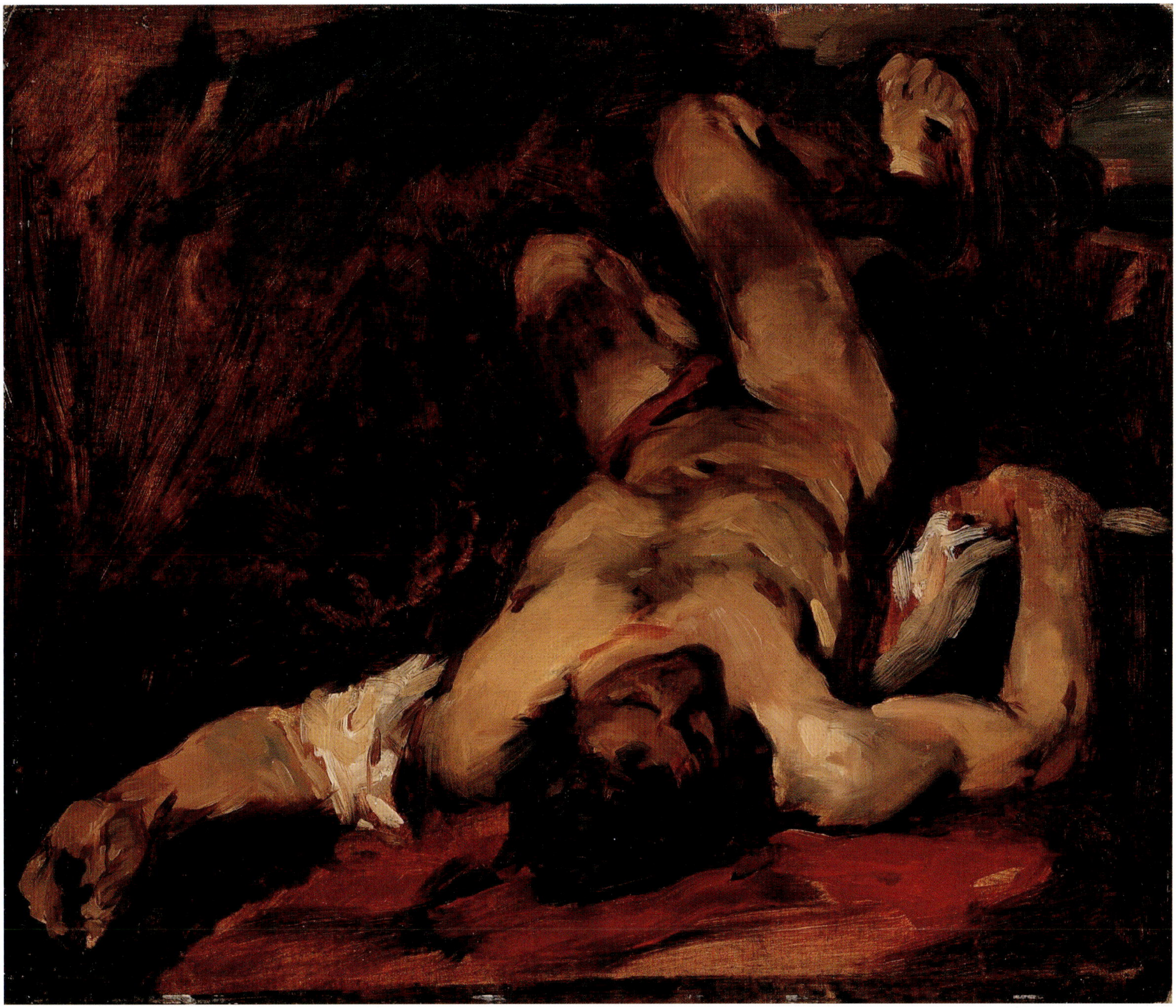

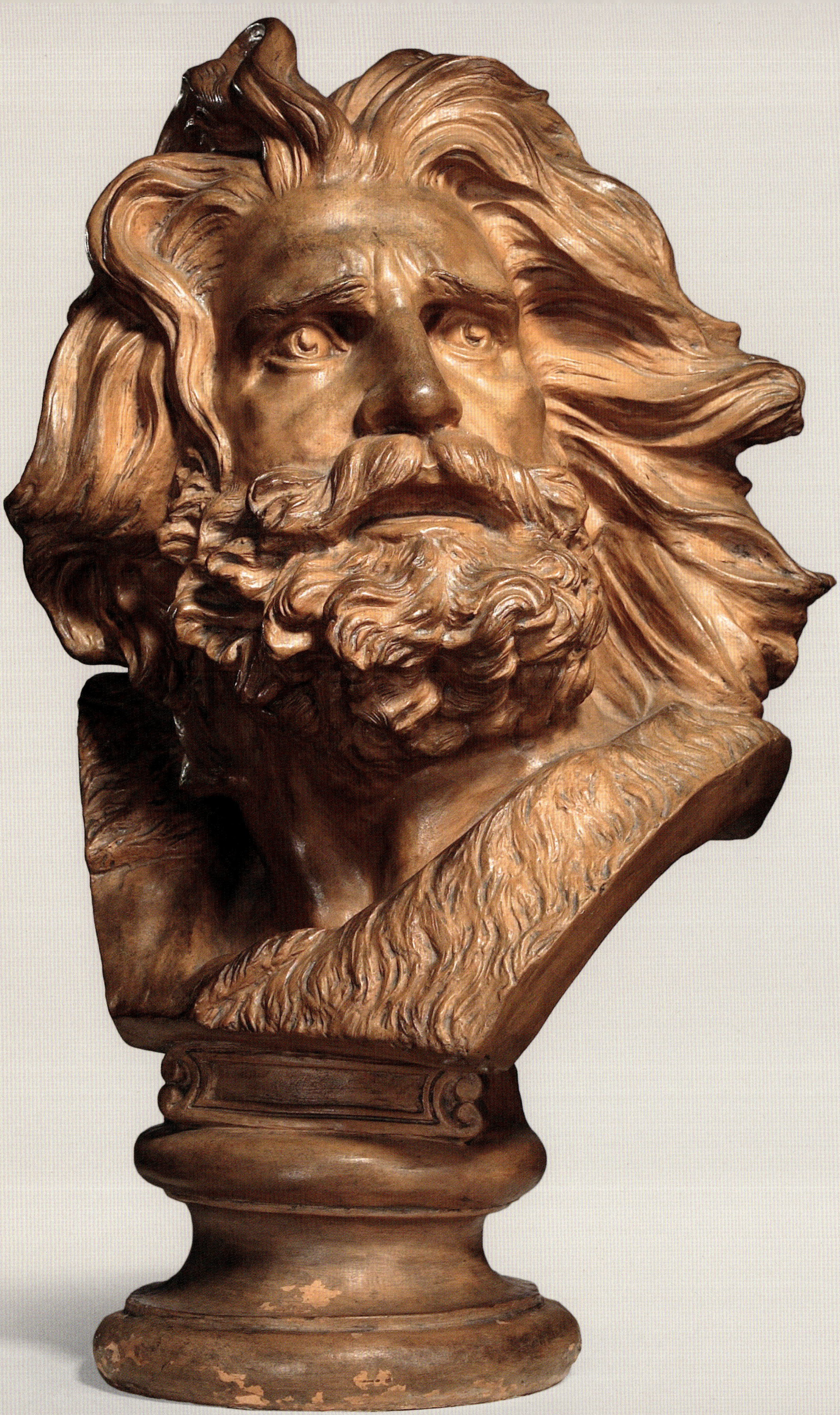

François Rude (French • 1784–1855)

4 — Head of a Warrior Gaul

1836 • terracotta with a thin wash of paint • 56 × 33 × 29 cm • Inv.2002.33.59

This work immediately evokes the subject's state of fear and anxiety. The dramatic lines of the man's tousled hair and the moving forms of his beard add to the psychological impact. His furrowed brow, deeply set eyes, and partially opened mouth all contribute to the momentary quality of the sculpture. This terracotta was chased before firing, and the surface was finished with a pigmented patina. Paint marks are particularly clear on the base and a gray-green hue emerges from crevices across the surface, adding a subtle coloration that enhances the work's impact. This expressive head relates to one of the central figures of Rude's most famous work, *Departure of the Volunteers in 1792*, best known as *La Marseillaise*, which he completed for the Arc de Triomphe in 1836. There, the muscular Gaul wears chain mail and decorative armor and stands astride at the center of six Revolutionary soldiers. They gather below the dramatic figure of a winged *Génie de la guerre* (Spirit of War, also identified as *Génie de la patrie*, Spirit of the Native Land) who unsheathes her sword and calls them to arms. The troops unite around the powerful figure of the Gaul, symbolic of the ancestry of French people prior to Roman conquest. The Gallic leader raises his helmet with outstretched arm and signals that it is time to unite and face the enemy. Rude's work continues to have the most significant impact of the four principal sculptures on the Arc de Triomphe and, after it was unveiled on the façade facing the Champs-Élysées, he found a market for individual sculptures of the Gaul. This terracotta is among those and was made in 1836 or later.[1] In the full sculpture on the Arc de Triomphe, the chin and beard are on a horizontal plane and, when seen within the larger context of the narrative, the Gaul's expression is transformed into one of confidence and determination. Taken in isolation, the terracotta and bronze heads suggest the subject's concern and uncertainty before something that remains unknown to the viewer. *Head of a Warrior Gaul* appears to truthfully describe its subject and yet Rude sought to capture the most dramatic moment possible, and thus aligned his work with romanticism.

Much earlier in Rude's career, in 1812, he won the prestigious Prix de Rome, but the financial challenges of the Académie de France meant he never enjoyed the multi-year fellowship to study in Italy. Instead, after the fall of the First Empire in 1815 he moved to Brussels with his Bonapartist protector and adopted father, Louis Fremiet. There, he married Louis's daughter, sculptor Sophie Fremiet. Rude received several prestigious commissions in Belgium and returned to Paris only in 1827. He was then awarded numerous commissions for public sculpture and, following the success particularly of *La Marseillaise*, he received the Legion of Honor and established his own studio which attracted several students.

[1] Another work, a posthumous bronze, was cast in 1857 by the Susse foundry and is now in the Musée des Beaux-Arts in Dijon (Inv.779; CA 1080).

Provenance

New York, Shepherd Gallery, 1973

Toronto, Joey and Toby Tanenbaum, 1973–2002

Exhibition History

Hamilton, Art Gallery of Hamilton, 28 May 2005–28 May 2006, *Heaven and Earth Unveiled: European Treasures from the Tanenbaum Collection*, cat.207; 181, *201* (as *Head of a Gaul*)

Hamilton, Art Gallery of Hamilton, 5 March 2011–19 August 2012, *From Rude to Rodin*

Bibliography

Aupetitallot, Yves. *François Rude, 1784–1855: présentation de la collection du musée pour le bi-centennaire de la naissance de Rude*. Dijon: Musée des Beaux-Arts, 1984, cat.8.

Barthélémy, Sophie, et al. *François & Sophie Rude: un couple d'artistes au XIXe siècle, citoyens de la liberté*. Paris: Somogy, 2012, 120–35, 251–52.

Feuillerat, Christophe. "François Rude: le haut-relief de l'Arc de triomphe de l'Étoile," Master's thesis, Université de Paris IV-Sorbonne, 1989.

Fourcaud, Louis de. *François Rude, sculpteur: ses œuvres et son temps (1784–1855)*. Paris: Librairie de l'art ancien et moderne, 1904.

Legrand, Maximien. *Rude: sa vie, ses œuvres, son enseignement. Considérations sur la sculpture*. Paris: Dentu, 1856.

Rouge-Ducos, Isabelle. *L'Arc de triomphe de l'Étoile: art et histoire*. Dijon: Faton, 2008.

-----. "Passions françaises autour de la Marseillaise de Rude: de l'utilisation de la sculpture à des fins politiques," *Revue de l'art* no.161 (2008): 33–42.

Alexandre-Gabriel Decamps (French • 1803–1860)

5 — Landscape (Evening Effect)

1846 • oil on canvas • 48.4 × 76.3 cm • s.d.l.r. DC/46/DECAMPS • Inv.2002.33.103

Decamps's career focused primarily on easel painting. He produced canvases on a range of topics including genre scenes, historical subjects and landscapes, all typically of a scale that could be displayed in domestic spaces. Decamps's works were popular with middle- and upper middle-class collectors from a range of professions, particularly during the July Monarchy (1830–48). During that period, Decamps often exhibited works at the Paris Salons. At the Salon of 1845, the year before he painted *Landscape (Evening Effect)*, Decamps exhibited nine drawings of the biblical story of Samson. Scholars of Decamps's work believe he aspired to promote his talents as a history painter so that he could attract attention from the state or elite collectors who would have the means to commission larger-scale canvases or perhaps a decorative cycle of paintings. Some have argued that Decamps, despite his considerable success, was still disappointed that he was never regarded as a painter in the "grand manner" like those who competed for the Prix de Rome (see cats.6 and 29). Decamps may have experienced some frustration but it never impeded him from exploring biblical themes and even returning to some of the orientalist subjects that had intrigued him since 1828 when he traveled to North Africa and the Middle East. From the mid-1840s, Decamps spent a significant amount of time in Chailly-en-Bière, a town southeast of Paris at the edge of the Fontainebleau forest. He enjoyed close ties with various artists of the Barbizon school, who were also interested in working directly from nature. Drawings and sketches were always an important part of Decamps's artistic process, and he spent much of his time working outdoors at various sites into the late 1840s.

The numerous elements Decamps included in *Landscape (Evening Effect)* reveal how the wooded landscape of the Fontainebleau forest was a place that inspired him to draw upon the full range of his artistic interests. Those aspects also suggest Decamps conceived of this particular landscape painting at least in part as a genre scene. On the far left, a shepherd guides a flock of sheep. In the center of the composition, nestled into the dense grouping of trees, is a woman dressed in a long red skirt who carries a large container on her head. On the far right of the canvas and more challenging for the eye to discern next to the horse's head, there is a cowherd with cattle. An abandoned piece of fence lies in the foreground and a rabbit darts off to the left. Each of the anecdotal details contributes to our sense that we are looking at a commonplace scene in the countryside. We could even interpret the two riders on horseback, the adult male with a child, as a reference to a real, lived experience. However, the mood Decamps captures in this painting goes beyond a simple representation of the sun setting in an everyday landscape. Decamps built his composition as a series of horizontal bands: ground, rolling tree-filled hills, and cloud-filled sky. He positioned the evening light to fall directly on the horse and riders, and to highlight the man as he gestures to the surrounding landscape. None of the details relates to specific historical or biblical narratives but they are also not incidental. Decamps successfully imbued the canvas with poetic qualities. Prominent critic Paul Mantz later wrote of Decamps that "he revealed a world, he had a spirit, fantasy, power and, as a poet, he rendered the mysterious struggles of light and shadow as if he was a grandson of Rembrandt." Decamps was held in such high regard by his contemporaries that he was one of four artists whose work was assigned a distinct space at the Exposition Universelle held in Paris in 1855. The other three artists— Delacroix, Ingres, and Vernet—were best known for their portraits, military subjects, and larger-scale history paintings. Decamps was thus the one artist whose predominantly smaller-scale works, including numerous landscapes and genre scenes, enjoyed a privileged space in that significant context.

Provenance

Paris, Amédée Susse sale, 11 February 1847

Paris, Galerie Fischer-Kiener, 1976–77

Toronto, Joey and Toby Tanenbaum, 1977–2002

Exhibition History

Ottawa, National Gallery of Canada, 26 May–10 September 1978; Victoria, Art Gallery of Greater Victoria, 19 October–3 December 1978; Edmonton, Edmonton Art Gallery, 15 December 1978–14 January 1979; Calgary, Glenbow-Alberta Institute, 3 February–22 March 1979; Montreal, Montreal Museum of Fine Arts, 5 April–13 May 1979; Toronto, Art Gallery of Ontario, 15 June–29 July 1979, *The Other Nineteenth Century: Paintings and Sculpture in the Collection of Mr. and Mrs. Joseph M. Tanenbaum*, cat.23, *83*

Hamilton, Art Gallery of Hamilton, 28 May 2005–28 May 2006, *Heaven and Earth Unveiled: European Treasures from the Tanenbaum Collection*, cat.29; 47, *110–11*

Hamilton, Art Gallery of Hamilton, 28 April–2 December 2007, *A Visual Bestiary*

Hamilton, Art Gallery of Hamilton, 24 September 2011–15 January 2012, *Masters of French Realism*

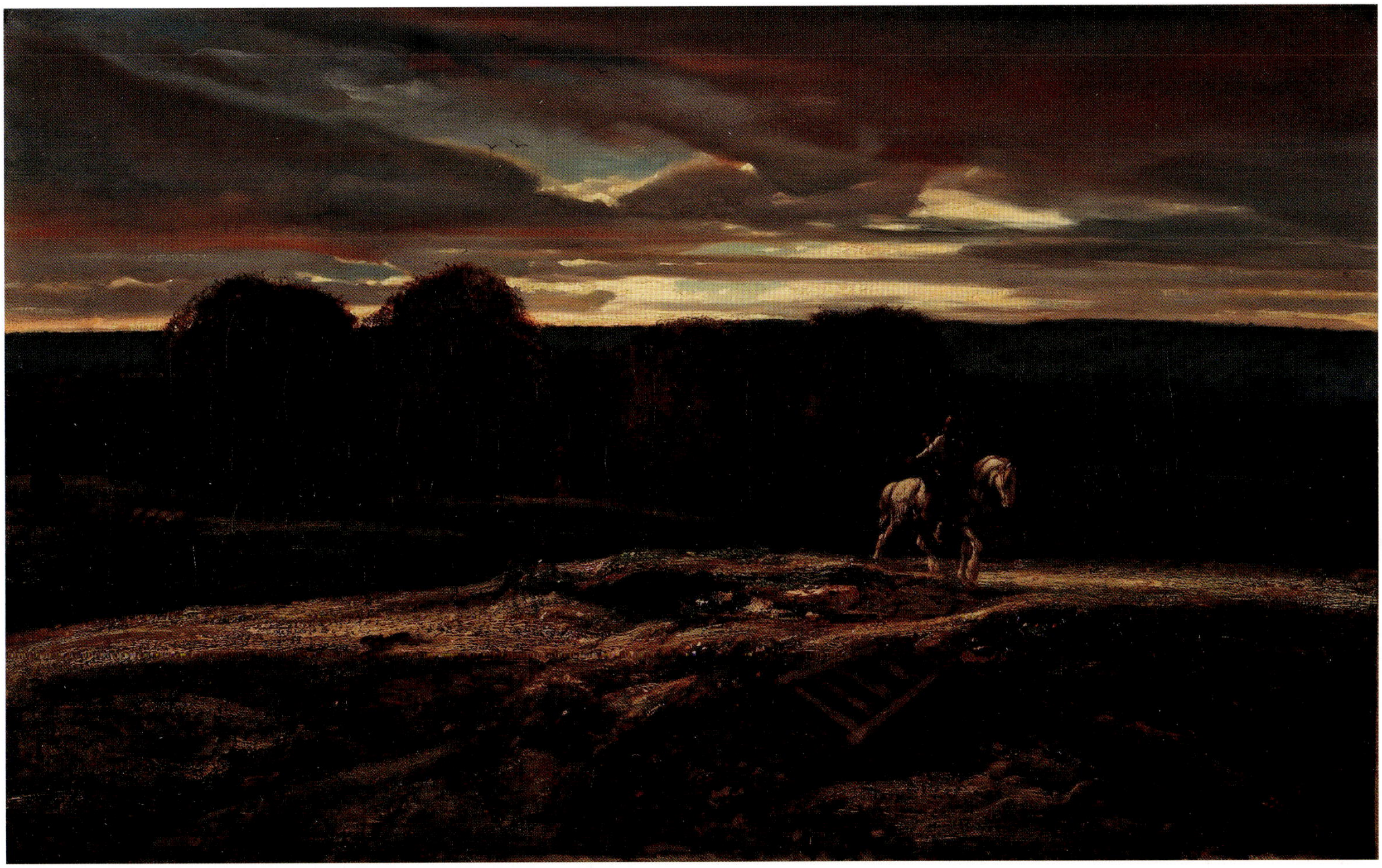

Bibliography

Bakhuÿs, Diederik. *Alexandre-Gabriel Decamps 1803–1860: peintures et dessins*. Rouen: Musée des Beaux-Arts, 2000, 4–12, 18.

Cass, David B. *Alexandre Gabriel Decamps, 1803–1860*. Williamstown, MA: Sterling and Francine Clark Art Institute, 1984.

Kelly, Simon. "The Early Collectors of the Barbizon School," *Journal of the History of Collections* vol.16 no.2 (2004): 161–72.

Mantz, Paul. "Decamps," *Gazette des Beaux-Arts* vol.12 (1 February 1862): 97–128 (128).

Miquel, Pierre. *Le paysage français au XIX siècle: 1824–1874, l'école de la nature*. 3 vols. Maurs-la-Jolie: Éditions de la Martinelle, 1975, vol.2, 158–93.

Moreau, Adolphe. *Decamps et son œuvre*. Paris: D. Jouaust, 1869, 210.

Mosby, Dewey F. *Alexandre-Gabriel Decamps, 1803–1860*. 2 vols. New York: Garland, 1977, vol.1, 181, 183, 202–33.

-----. "The Mature Years of Alexandre-Gabriel Decamps," *Minneapolis Institute of Arts Bulletin* vol.63 (1976–77): 97–109.

Alexandre Cabanel (French • 1823–1889)

6 — Portrait of Victor Massé

1847 • oil on canvas • 61 × 49.5 cm • s.d.l.l. A. CABANEL./ROMA/VILLA MEDICI/1847; verso c. à Mon ami/M.V. Massé/Paris • Inv. 2002.33.10

Victor (born Félix Marie) Massé (1822–1884) was a French composer and fellow *pensionnaire* at the Villa Medici (home of the Académie de France in Rome) when Cabanel painted this portrait. In 1844, Massé won the Prix de Rome, a national French competition for emerging artists, in the category of musical composition, and he held a three-year fellowship in Rome from 1845 to 1848. Cabanel ranked second in the painting competition for the Prix de Rome in 1845, but an additional vacancy from the previous year meant that two painters could now take up residence at the academy. When Cabanel arrived in 1846 he settled immediately into the vibrant artistic community. He had a great interest in music and often attended performances, particularly opera, during his time in Rome, becoming close friends with Massé. Capturing portrait likenesses was one of the principal ways the all-male network of *pensionnaires* (the Prix de Rome was closed to women) expressed their bonds of friendship. Another prizewinner, Félix Barrias, also painted a portrait of Massé in 1847 in an identical pose to Cabanel's work (Rome, Villa Medici), and Barrias included a commemorative inscription citing 1844, the year of Massé's success. The men were comfortable with the platonic homosociality of their intersecting artistic lives, and Cabanel showed his admiration for Massé both by painting his portrait and also giving it to him as a gift. Cabanel signed the painting above Massé's right shoulder "A. Cabanel./Roma/Villa Medici/1847" and thus clearly locates its creation during one of their two overlapping years in Rome. However, he also inscribed the work on the back "à Mon ami/ M.V. Massé/Paris," suggesting that Cabanel kept the painting after Massé returned to France, and only gave it to him later when they were both in Paris.

The oval form that frames the bust-length portrait of Massé is unusual within Cabanel's oeuvre. Much of the oval is edged with a border, and the four corners of the canvas were painted to suggest a frame. Cabanel painted the left edge of the letter V in "Villa Medici" partially eclipsed by the trompe l'oeil border, as if hidden by a frame that overlapped the surface of the real canvas. This visual play and the general appearance of the work suggest Cabanel hung the painting in Rome as a reminder of his now-absent friend, until they were later reunited. In Cabanel's quarters or studio, the direct and penetrating gaze, rosy flesh, and fine features would have made Massé seem quite present. The dark suit and cravat suggest an evening outing to an opera, with its attendant camaraderie. Massé went on to write nearly twenty operas and operettas, including *Galathée* (1852), *Les Noces de Jeanette* (1853), and *Paul et Virginie* (1876). He became chorus master at the Paris Opéra in 1860 and was also professor at the Paris Conservatoire (1866–80).

Cabanel studied in Rome until 1850, when he returned to Paris, his reputation growing significantly during the years of the Second Empire (1852–70). In Rome, Cabanel painted portraits for his own interest, and as he continued to refine his skills in following years he received many portrait commissions from prominent American and French sitters, including a full-length portrait of Emperor Napoleon III (1865; Château de Compiègne). From his early *Portrait of Victor Massé* to his later portrait of the emperor, Cabanel demonstrated his ability to depict a direct and psychologically penetrating gaze that conveyed a sitter's active intellectual life.

Provenance

London, Norman Leitman, 1986

Toronto, Joey and Toby Tanenbaum, 1986–2002

Exhibition History

Hamilton, Art Gallery of Hamilton, 28 May 2005–28 May 2006; Victoria, Art Gallery of Greater Victoria, 25 January–11 May 2008, *Heaven and Earth Unveiled: European Treasures from the Tanenbaum Collection*, cat.15; 15–17, *76* (as *Self-Portrait*).

Hamilton, Art Gallery of Hamilton, 10 February–13 May 2007, *Framed: The Art of the Portrait*

Hamilton, Art Gallery of Hamilton, 21 May–5 September 2011, *The French Connection*

Hamilton, Art Gallery of Hamilton, *The Painter Pictured: French Nineteenth-Century Paintings and Portrait Photographs*, 9 February 2013–9 February 2014

Bibliography

Amic, Sylvain, et al. *Alexandre Cabanel, 1823–1889: la tradition du beau.* Paris: Somogy, 2010, 25, 88–105, *104*, 454 (as *Portrait d'un pensionnaire de la Villa Médicis [Félix Massé]*).

Edidin, Stephen. *Training an Artist: Alexandre Cabanel and the Academic Process in 19th-Century France.* New York: Dahesh Musuem, 1998.

Nougaret, Jean. "Alexandre Cabanel. Sa vie, son œuvre, essai de catalogue," postgraduate diploma thesis, Université de Montpellier, 1962, 79, no.30.

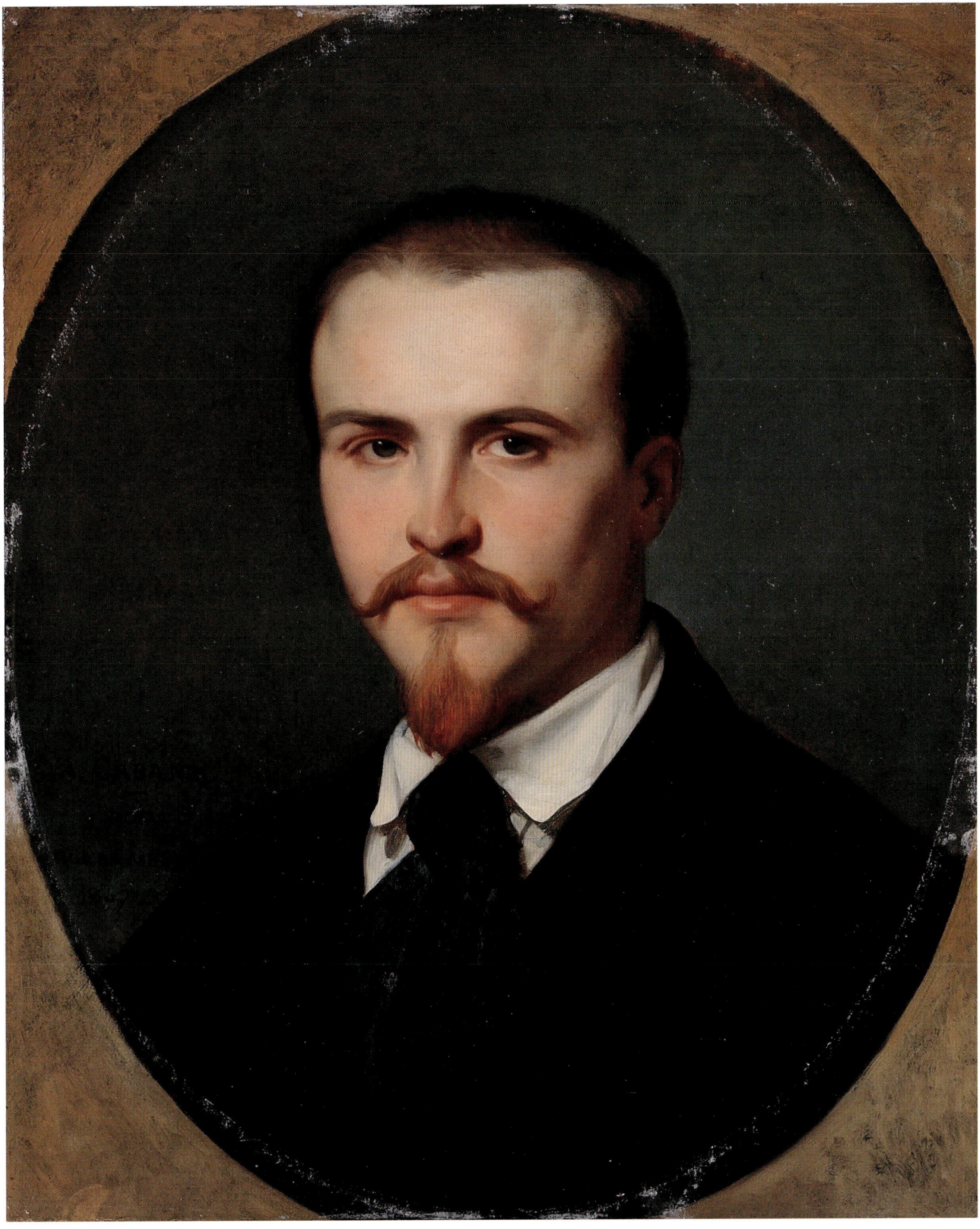

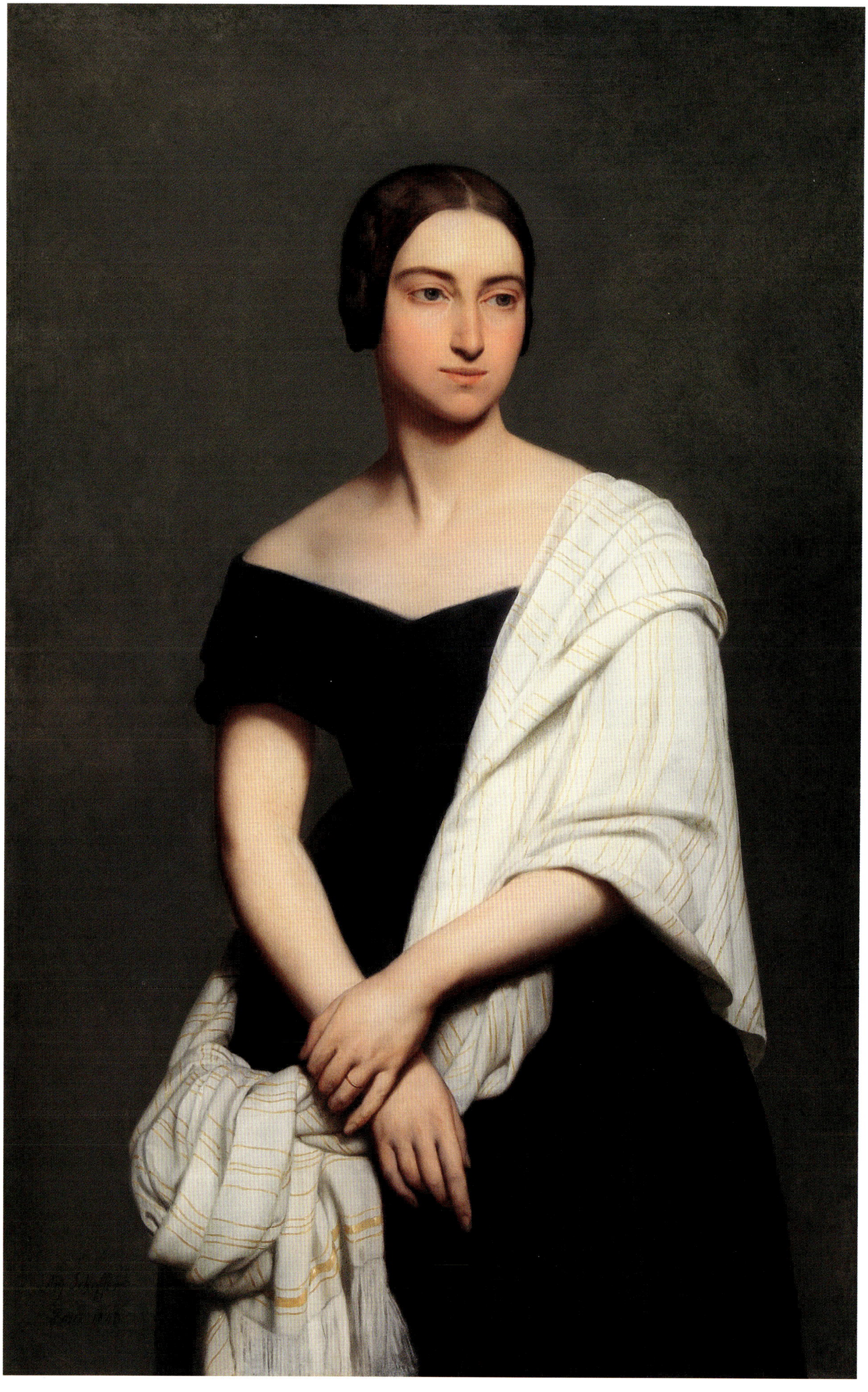

Ary Scheffer (Dutch • 1795–1858)

7 — Portrait of Mrs. Frederick Kent

1847 • oil on canvas • 119 × 74 cm • s.d.l.l. Ary Scheffer/Paris 1847 • Inv.2002.33.50

This portrait of Matilda Cotter (1824–1899) is traditionally entitled *Portrait of Mrs. Frederick Kent.* Cotter had married Kent two years earlier, in 1845, and she appears in this painting as an attractive, youthful, and demure twenty-three-year-old wife of a Protestant minister. Her only jewelry is one ring, a simple band, a symbol of her marriage. While the design of Cotter's dress adhered to the contemporary off-the-shoulder style then in fashion in Britain and continental Europe, the somber color of the silk suggests a gown suited to her social position. Scheffer also presents Cotter in a pose that exudes a sense of composure. The cream-colored shawl that drapes casually across Cotter's body contributes to the tonal harmony of the work. The material falls in gentle folds across her shoulder and forms a large knot next to Cotter's hands. The shawl's thin gold threads create subtle patterns and a play of line that add interest to the asymmetrical composition. The portrait radiates calm and projects an image of refined elegance. Cotter was one of five children born to Reverend James Lawrence Cotter and Matilda Sampayo, daughter of a Portuguese consul. Her parents met in the southern Irish town of Cork and she was named after her mother, who died shortly after her birth.

Scheffer was born in the Netherlands but spent most of his adult career based in Paris. It was there, in his large studio at 16 rue Chaptal, at the foot of Montmartre, that Cotter likely sat for her portrait. Scheffer was a mature artist in his early fifties when he received this commission. He had exhibited numerous works at the Paris Salons from 1812 until 1846, the year immediately prior to the portrait. He was acclaimed for his history painting, particularly his religious subjects, and received considerable support from the French government. While the state acquired a number of his works, like many of his contemporaries Scheffer also suffered from considerable negative press from art critics, who found fault with aspects of his technique. Scheffer's skill was, in fact, so highly regarded in the most elite French circles that he taught drawing lessons to the children of the duc d'Orléans from 1822. He also continued to enjoy a privileged relationship with the royal family both during and after King Louis-Philippe's reign (1830–48). Scheffer was very successful as a portraitist and, in addition to his portrait of King Louis-Philippe, his sitters included Queen Hortense (queen of the Netherlands, 1806–10), banker and politician Achille Fould, and writers Charles Dickens and Mme de Stäel. In 1847, the year of his portrait of Matilda Cotter, Scheffer also executed portraits of composer Frédéric Chopin and fellow painter Horace Vernet, with whom he was friends, as well as Austrian composer Sigismund von Neukomm and Irish novelist Sydney Owenson (Lady Morgan). Scheffer may well have reconnected with Cotter at an evening salon gathering hosted by one of the artist's numerous British friends and acquaintances. Scheffer had painted a smaller canvas of Cotter six years earlier, when she was seventeen. While the exact circumstances of both commissions remain unclear, there is no evidence that Scheffer ever painted a pendant portrait of Cotter's husband Frederick Kent (d.1885).

Provenance

Zurich, Mizrahi Kunst und Antiquitäten Inc.

Toronto, Joey and Toby Tanenbaum, 1987–2002

Exhibition History

Hamilton, Art Gallery of Hamilton, 28 May 2005–28 May 2006; Victoria, Art Gallery of Greater Victoria, 25 January–11 May 2008, *Heaven and Earth Unveiled: European Treasures from the Tanenbaum Collection*, cat.124; 37–38, *99*

Hamilton, Art Gallery of Hamilton, 28 August 2010–17 April 2011, *Conversations*

Hamilton, Art Gallery of Hamilton, 9 February 2013–9 February 2014, *The Painter Pictured: French Nineteenth-Century Paintings and Portrait Photographs*

Bibliography

Brem, Anne-Marie de. *L'Atelier d'Ary Scheffer.* Paris: Paris-Musées, 1991.

Ewals, Leo. *Ary Scheffer, 1795–1858.* Trans. Françoise Éveraars and Françoise Gaillard. Paris: Paris-Musées, 1996.

-----. "Ary Scheffer, sa vie et son œuvre," Ph.D. dissertation, Katholiek Universiteit Nijmegen, 1987, 382–83.

Morel, Dominique. "Rus in urbe: rue Chaptal, la maison et les ateliers d'Ary Scheffer," *Gazette des Beaux-Arts* vol.111 no.1432–33 (May–June 1988): 315–24.

Morris, Edward. "Ary Scheffer and his English Circle," *Oud Holland* vol.99 no.2 (1985): 294–323.

Six, E.W.C. *Museum Ary Scheffer: catalogueus der kunstwerken en andere voorwerpen.* Dordrecht: Uitgevers Maatschappij, 1934, 107–31.

Verhoogt, Robert. *Art in Reproduction: Nineteenth-Century Prints after Lawrence Alma-Tadema, Jozef Izraëls and Ary Scheffer.* Amsterdam: Amsterdam University Press, 2007.

Emmanuel Fremiet (French • 1824–1910)

8 — Wounded Bear

1850 • bronze • 27.6 × 17 × 14.5 cm • s.base next to hunter E. FREMIET • Inv.2002.33.118

9 — Wounded Bear

c.1893 • terracotta • 28.5 × 17 × 14.5 cm • s.base next to hunter E. FREMIET • Inv.2002.33.116

Fremiet received numerous medals at the Paris Salons for his work as an *animalier*, an artist who specialized in representing different types of animals. After he exhibited a large plaster *Wounded Bear* at the Salon of 1850 (no.3399), he intended smaller-scale bronze and terracotta works, such as those discussed here, for private art collectors. Such works were set on a table or mantle in a domestic setting where the coloration of the bronze and the clarity of the descriptive details could be appreciated up close. Fremiet later revisited the subject with another large-scale work for the Salon of 1885, *Bear and Man of the Stone Age*. Throughout his career, Fremiet returned to a subject that captured his imagination and that of many of his contemporaries: how the earliest documented humans negotiated their survival with the largest of animals, particularly those that could stand on two legs. At first the title and form of this work appear to emphasize the bear's impending death: the bear cries out in anger and pain as blood pours from a wound and cascades down, intersecting with a net between the man's legs. The network of broken lines creates a textured surface, like that of the bear's fur, that contrasts with the man's smooth, muscular form. We soon realize, though, that despite this frozen moment of action, both man and bear will die. The man's lungs deflate and he hangs limp, as the bear presses both paws into his chest. This battle was one that featured prominently in contemporary French anthropological studies, and texts emphasized how "primitive" man developed weapons to fight "ferocious animals." Fremiet took liberties to make his narrative clear, and turned the Stone Age hunter into a gladiator-type figure wielding a dagger. The only one to survive will be the soon-to-be orphaned baby bear, her nose and paws visible as she tries to help and climbs her parent's leg. Fremiet suggests that life cycles and therefore battles between humans and nature will continue.

Among the leading *animaliers* of his time, Fremiet received numerous commissions for large-scale sculptures for public spaces. From 1854 to 1866 he also produced over fifty works for the private collection of Emperor Napoleon III. Fremiet exhibited many of these works publicly, and imperial patronage bolstered his reputation. Imperial patronage likely helped him in 1859 when the Salon jury refused to exhibit his controversial *Gorilla Abducting a Young Negress*. In the end, the work was presented behind a protective and provocative curtain. Fremiet remained closely connected to the study of nature and prehistory throughout his career. In the early 1840s he worked as an illustrator at the Muséum National d'Histoire Naturelle, and in 1875 he returned as professor of animal drawing. The terracotta *Wounded Bear* (cat.9) may date to 1850 like the bronze (cat.8), although it has been dated as late as the 1890s.[1] The proposed later date connects the ongoing interest in Fremiet's work on this theme to a commission he received in 1893 for a relief sculpture on the exterior of what is today the gallery of comparative anatomy and paleontology in the southern part of the Jardin des Plantes.

[1] A related terracotta in the collection of the Metropolitan Museum of Art is dated c.1850 and was cast from an example without the dagger (Inv.1990.108).

Provenance

Bronze
Louveciennes, Marie-Jose Ambrogi
Toronto, Joey and Toby Tanenbaum, 1981–2002

Terracotta
New York, Shepherd Gallery
Toronto, Joey and Toby Tanenbaum, 1972–2002 (purchased from Galerie Osten-Kaschey Ltd.)

Exhibition History

Bronze
Hamilton, Art Gallery of Hamilton, 28 May 2005–28 May 2006, *Heaven and Earth Unveiled: European Treasures from the Tanenbaum Collection*, cat.171; *163*, 184
Hamilton, Art Gallery of Hamilton, 9 February 2013–9 February 2014, *The Painter Pictured: French Nineteenth-Century Paintings and Portrait Photographs*

Terracotta
Louisville, J.B. Speed Art Museum, 2 November–5 December 1971, *Nineteenth-Century French Sculpture: Monuments for the Middle Class*, cat.70, *183*
New York, Shepherd Gallery, 1973, *Western European Bronzes of the Nineteenth Century: A Survey*, cat.35b (reproduced)
Ottawa, National Gallery of Canada, 26 May–10 September 1978; Victoria, Art Gallery of Greater Victoria, 19 October–3 December 1978; Edmonton, Edmonton Art Gallery, 15 December 1978–14 January 1979; Calgary, Glenbow-Alberta Institute, 3 February–22 March 1979; Montreal, Montreal Museum of Fine Arts, 5 April–13 May 1979; Toronto, Art Gallery of Ontario, 15 June–29 July 1979, *The Other Nineteenth Century: Paintings and Sculpture in the Collection of Mr. and Mrs. Joseph M. Tanenbaum*, cat.82, *223* (as *Bear and Gladiator*)
Los Angeles, Los Angeles County Museum of Art, 4 March–25 May 1980; Minneapolis, Minneapolis Institute of Arts, 25 June–21 September 1980; Detroit, Detroit Institute of Arts, 27 October 1980–4 January, 1981; Indianapolis, Indianapolis Museum of Art, 22 February–29 April 1981, *The Romantics to Rodin: French Nineteenth-Century Sculpture from North American Collections*, cat.147, *279* (as *Bear and Gladiator*)
Hamilton, Art Gallery of Hamilton, 28 May 2005–28 May 2006, *Heaven and Earth Unveiled: European Treasures from the Tanenbaum Collection*, cat.172; 184
Hamilton, Art Gallery of Hamilton, 5 March 2011–19 August 2012, *From Rude to Rodin*
Hamilton, Art Gallery of Hamilton, 9 February 2013–9 February 2014, *The Painter Pictured: French Nineteenth-Century Paintings and Portrait Photographs*

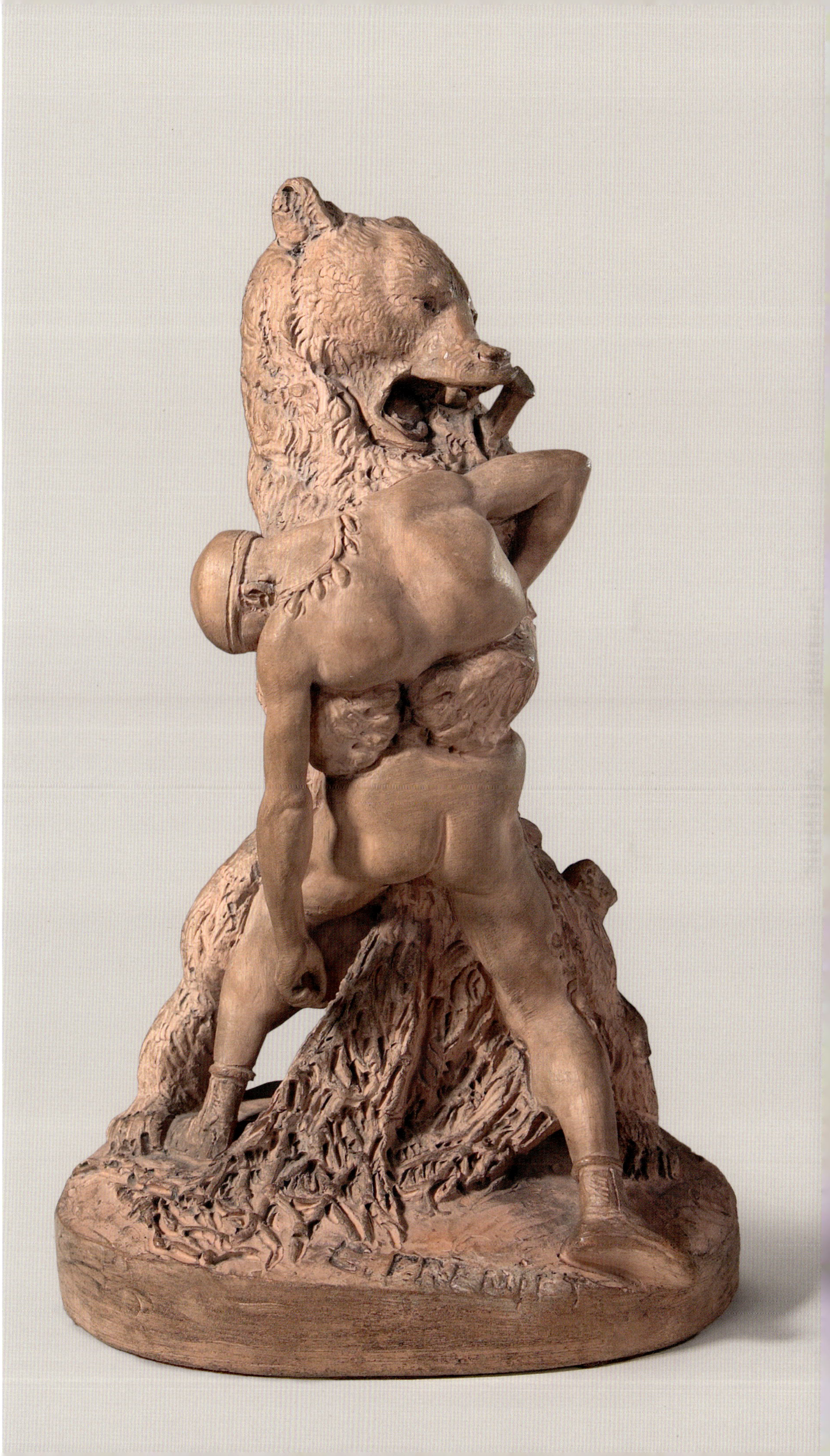

Bibliography

Chevillot, Catherine. *Emmanuel Fremiet, 1824–1910: la main et le multiple.* Dijon: Musée des Beaux-Arts, 1988, 98, 105.

Draper, James. "French Terracottas," *Metropolitan Museum of Art Bulletin* vol.49 no.3 (Winter 1991/1992): 1–57 (49).

Ducros, Jacqueline, and Albert Ducros. "'Gare au Gorille': l'audace de Fremiet," *Bulletins et mémoirs de la Société d'anthropologie de Paris* vol.4 nos.3–4 (1992): 269–72.

Figuier, Louis. *L'Homme primitif: tableau de nature.* Paris: L. Hachette, 1870, 37–60.

Granger, Catherine. *L'Empereur et les arts: la liste civile de Napoléon III.* Paris: École des Chartes, 2005, 204–5, 733–38.

Kemp, Martin. "Fremiet's frenzy," *Nature* vol.397 no.6713 (1998): 727.

Weissberg, Liliane. "Monkey Business," *Kunstforum international* no.114 (July–August 1991): 237–52.

Zgórniak, Marek. "Fremiet's 'Gorillas': Why Do they Carry off Women?," *Artibus et Historiae* vol.27 no.54 (2006): 218–37.

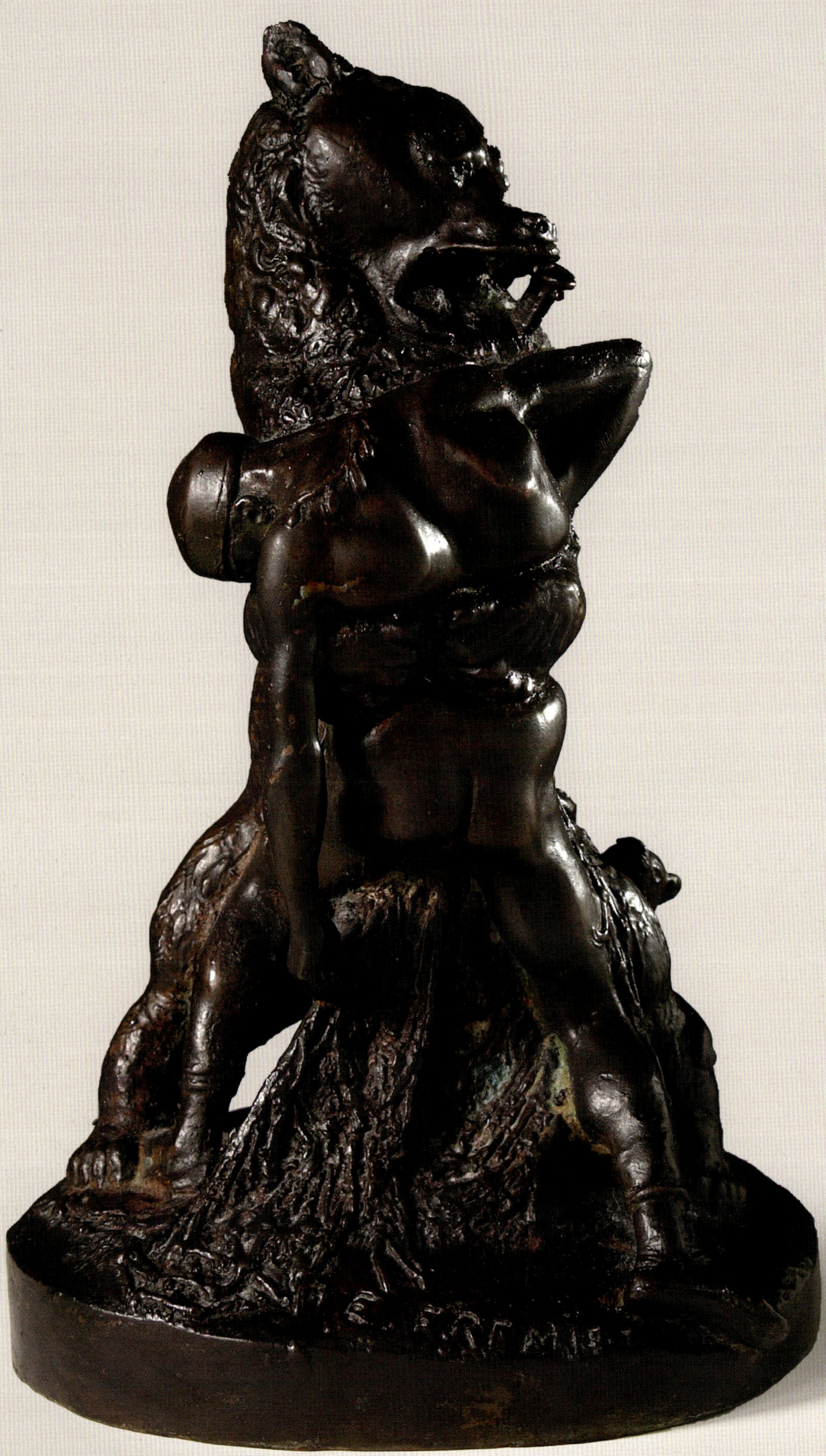

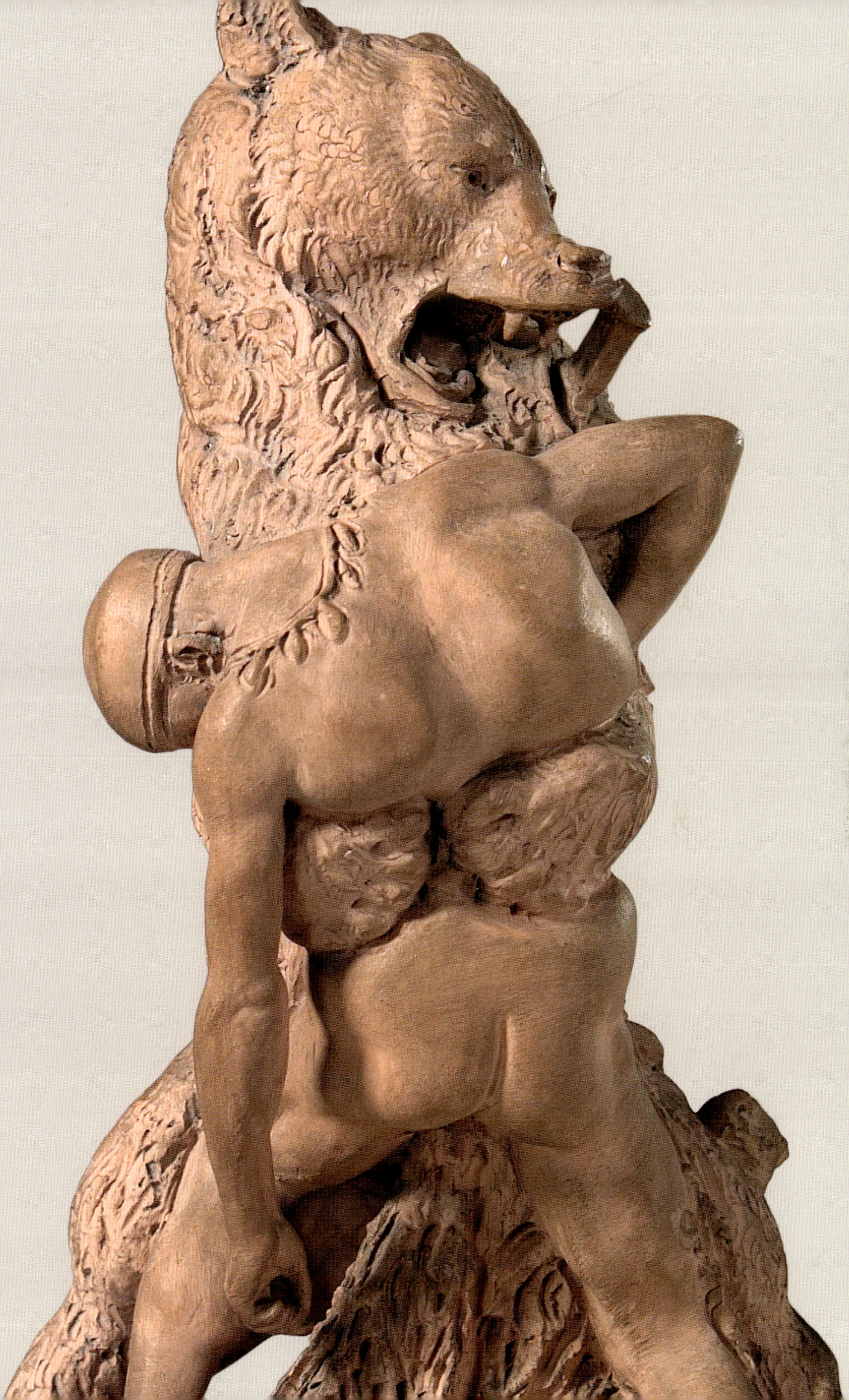

Charles Henri Joseph Cordier (French • 1827–1905)

10 — Chinese Man

1853 • gilt, silvered, enameled bronze bust; red patina for the clothing and enamels • 69 × 50 × 45 cm • s.d.l.r. side of scroll C. CORDIER/sculp & pinx/1853 • inscribed l.l. side of scroll Simonet/pere et fils/fondeurs • Inv.2002.33.92

This sculpture exemplifies the high quality of Cordier's work when he emerged as one of the leading sculptors of mid-nineteenth-century France. Cordier combined technologies at the forefront of contemporary practice with his inquisitive interest in non-European subjects and created works that continue to amaze and impress. When Cordier first exhibited a *Chinese Man* at the Salon of 1852, he presented it as part of a pair in plaster, the pendant of *Chinese Woman*, and entitled the group *Chinese Couple* (no.1338). Cordier sought out this couple, Chung-Ataï and Suen-Ahupor Yung-Achoy, to be his sitters while they were traveling in Paris. It was not unusual for a sculptor like Cordier to show works first in plaster form at the Salon. One hoped a patron would commission the work in marble or bronze, and few artists could finance such an expensive undertaking independently. Cordier met with success and received a commission from the Ministry of Fine Arts for a pair cast in bronze for the anthropology gallery at the Jardin des Plantes in Paris.[1] The 5,000 francs Cordier received was intended both for his own income and to cover all the costs of the materials and expertise of the Simonet foundry.

Cordier also speculated on his rising status. He was confident in his abilities and had won a third-class medal in sculpture following the Salon of 1850, where he exhibited an impressive display of nine works in plaster, marble, and bronze. Cordier wanted to promote his career and secured the funds necessary to cast the Chinese couple again in bronze, but this time he added gold, silver, and blue enamel details. He patinated the clothing and enamel with a layer of red, and exhibited the works together but as separate submissions at the Salon of 1853, where they were identified as Mongolian (nos.1279, 1280). Visitors to the Salon experienced Cordier's polychrome works in a large gallery space dominated by white marble and plaster as well as bronze sculpture, and the impact of the luminous surfaces of the skin and finely detailed decorations of the dress was immediate. Cordier achieved the reflective areas of flesh by using galvanoplasty, a process of electroplating metal patented in 1842 by the silversmiths of the house of Christofle.

Chinese Man and *Chinese Woman* were controversial and, while some critics defended Cordier's work, others claimed such work was not art. One critic, Claude Vignon (Noémie Constant), argued that the plaster busts Cordier showed in 1852 were like "characters of Chinese screens" and "simply ugly for the sake of ugliness." Cordier rose above the polemics and cast variations that included an openwork architectural corner behind the man, a pagoda behind the woman, and smaller-scale reductions with the figures placed on openwork wooden bases. In each version of the *Chinese Man*, the essential features remained the same: he rests his arms gently on a stylized scroll motif that serves as a small table, his long braid hangs down between the scrolls, twists in his right hand and ends hanging gently over one wrist. He turns to his right so that in the original pendant he looked towards the woman. In other versions he holds a long pipe in his left hand. In 1853 Cordier described his work as an *essai* or "test" in polychrome sculpture. He promoted an uncommon approach for the mid-nineteenth century, but one that had been popular in previous centuries, particularly in Italy.

Cordier exhibited the full-scale polychrome bronze pair again in Paris at the Exposition Universelle of 1855 (nos.4286, 4287). They were also among the subjects for twenty-three photographs he had Charles Marville undertake for an album of "ethnographic sculpture" that Cordier created in his studio in 1858. He may have used the album to attract further commissions, and indeed Cordier enjoyed considerable state patronage. He was the official sculptor of the Muséum National d'Histoire Naturelle from 1851 to 1866 and went on government-sponsored artistic missions to Algeria (1856), Greece (1858–59), and Egypt (1865). Cordier also enjoyed the patronage of prominent private collectors including Empress Eugénie, who displayed her set of the pendant busts, *Chinese Man* and *Chinese Woman*, in her private quarters at the Tuileries palace. While some believe the works may have been among those destroyed during the fires of the Paris Commune in 1871, Eugénie arranged to have many objects removed from both her private and the Louvre collections in late August 1870 during the Franco-Prussian War. The early history of the sculpture illustrated here remains unknown, and thus one can only speculate on whether it might have been part of an imperial collection during Cordier's lifetime.

[1] AN F21/72. The works were transferred to the Muséum National d'Histoire Naturelle around 1854.

Provenance

New York, Armin B. Allen Inc., 1985

Toronto, Joey and Toby Tanenbaum, 1985–2002

Exhibition History

Paris, Musée d'Orsay, 2 February–2 May 2004; Quebec City, Musée National des Beaux-Arts du Québec, 10 June–6 September 2004; New York, Dahesh Museum of Art, 21 October 2004–9 January 2005, *Charles Cordier (1827–1905), l'autre et l'ailleurs*, cat.80

Hamilton, Art Gallery of Hamilton, 28 May 2005–28 May 2006, *Heaven and Earth Unveiled: European Treasures from the Tanenbaum Collection*, cat.154; 183, *161*

Hamilton, Art Gallery of Hamilton, 10 February–13 May 2007, *Framed: The Art of the Portrait*
Hamilton, Art Gallery of Hamilton, 22 May–6 September 2010, *Europe's Exoticized East*

Bibliography

Blühm, Andreas. *The Color of Sculpture, 1840–1910*. Zwolle: Waanders, 1996, 35–36.
Boström, Antonia. "Charles Cordier," in Roberta Panzanelli et al. *The Color of Life: Polychromy in Sculpture from Antiquity to the Present*. Los Angeles: J. Paul Getty Museum, 2008, 160–63.
Cordier, Charles. *Sculptures ethnographiques: marbres et bronzes d'après divers types de races humaines*. Photographs by Charles Marville. Paris: l'auteur, 1858.
Deyasi, Marco. "Ethnographic Sculpture and the Complexities of Race: The Cultural Politics of Charles Cordier, Théodore Rivière and Auguste Rodin," paper presented at the College Art Association Conference, Chicago, 12 February 2010.
Durand-Révillon, Jeannine. "Un promoteur de la sculpture polychrome sous le Second Empire, Charles-Henri-Joseph Cordier (1827–1905)," *Bulletin de la Société de l'histoire de l'art français* vol.29 (1982): 181–98.
Granger, Catherine. *L'Empereur et les arts: la liste civile de Napoléon III*. Paris: École des Chartes, 2005, 726.
Larson, Barbara. "The Artist as Ethnographer: Charles Cordier and Race in Mid-Nineteenth-Century France," *The Art Bulletin* vol.87 no.4 (December 2005): 714–22.
Margerie, Laure de, et al. *Facing the Other: Charles Cordier (1827–1905), Ethnographic Sculptor*. New York: Harry N. Abrams, 2004, 21, *60–61*, 155–58.
McQueen, Alison. *Empress Eugénie and the Arts: Politics and Visual Culture in the Nineteenth Century*. Aldershot: Ashgate, 2011, 174, 219 fn.76.
Vignon, Claude. *Le Salon de 1852*. Paris: E. Dentu, 1852.

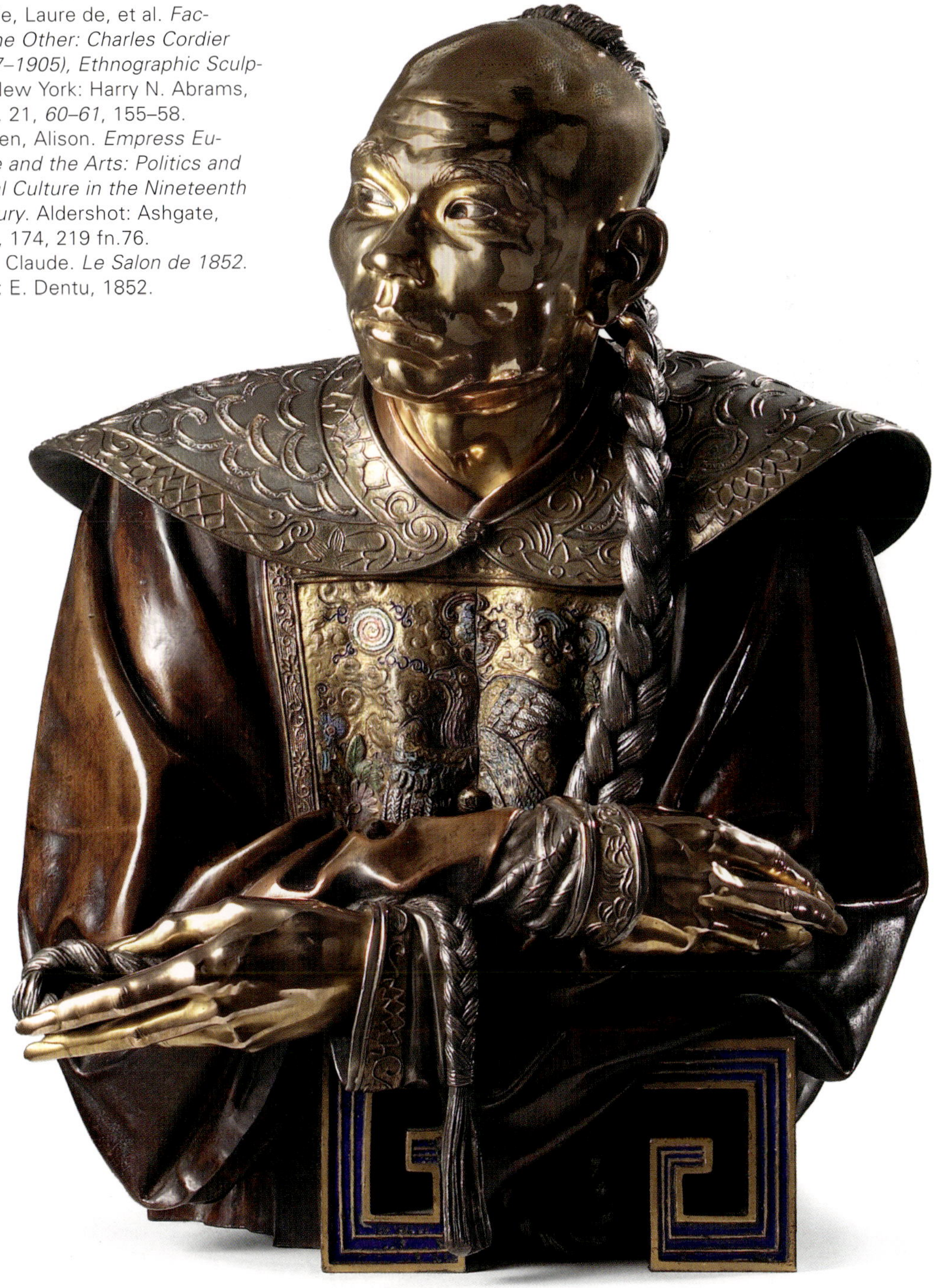

Jean-Léon Gérôme (French • 1824–1904)

11 — Portrait of Mademoiselle Durand

1853 • oil on canvas • 126.1 × 86.4 cm • s.d.l.l.c. J.L. GEROME/1853 • Inv.2002.33.130

12 — Portrait of an African Woman

c.1880 • oil on canvas • 41 × 32.2 cm • s.l.l. J.L. GEROME • Inv.2002.33.26

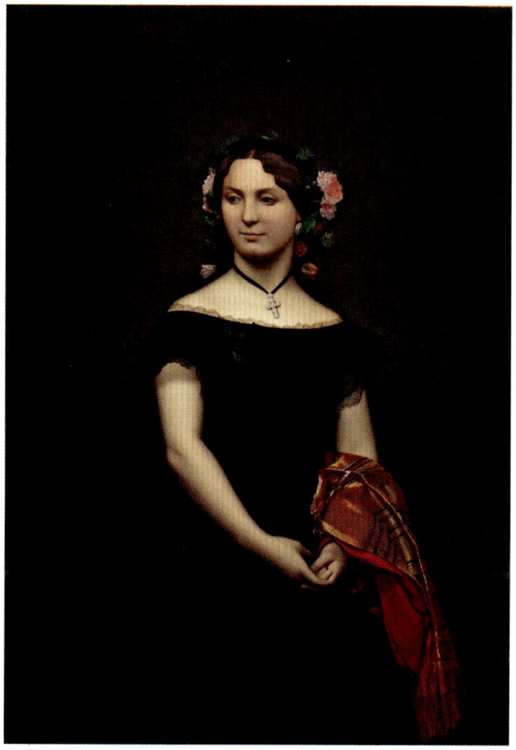

11

In 1863, Gérôme was one of three artists selected as the first professors of painting at the recently restructured École des Beaux-Arts. It was a prestigious appointment that recognized Gérôme's status as a sought-after teacher and gave him a secure, high-profile position from which he could promote his work for the rest of his career. Painted during the decades before and after this appointment, *Portrait of Mademoiselle Durand* and *Portrait of an African Woman* demonstrate how Gérôme studied his sitters closely and over an extended period of time. He was so exacting of himself, and sought to capture likeness to such a degree, that it sometimes took quite a while for him to be satisfied that a work was indeed complete and ready to leave his studio. What we now interpret visually as a high level of surface detail was, in fact, only one part of Gérôme's rigorous artistic process. Both of these works are fascinating within the history of portraiture and neither were commissions in the conventional sense.

It was Gérôme who sought out Mlle Durand, an actress at the Palais-Royal theater, and convinced her to "sit" for him (cat.11). Serving as Gérôme's model meant, in fact, standing for long periods, and Durand loaned him one of her gowns, a scarf, and headdress so that he could work on these elements without her present. Ultimately, the dress and accessories were the most successful passages of the composition. The wool-lined scarf appears to fall casually from Durand's left forearm, but Gérôme reveals his own attentiveness to this sumptuous area of paint: a precise fold defines the centerline of the fabric, linear bands appear and disappear across its width, and the silk facing shimmers as it reflects the light. Durand seems to stand quite still, but the diagonal position of her upper body and gentle turn of her head and neck animate the pose. Durand's necklace was very important within the composition, despite its small size. Gérôme's careful choice was that this cross, with its seven individual diamond-like gems, would not lie straight but rather hang casually from a black ribbon and add a subtle liveliness to the entire composition.

Gérôme and Durand each had a markedly different understanding of this collaboration. Durand tired of the long studio visits and stopped coming, thinking they were no longer pursuing the project. But Gérôme completed the painting expecting he was going to be paid 2,000 francs, then a competitive fee for a portrait commission of this scale. Durand refused, stating she had never agreed to such a high figure and that only a modest sum had ever been discussed. Quite unusual for the time, their case went before the Tribunal of the Seine in November 1854. The painting was presented to the judges who determined "it was impossible to recognize Mlle Durand in the person Gérôme has represented," that she did not have to accept it, and was required only to pay an indemnity of 200 francs.[1] Gérôme was likely frustrated with this outcome but it certainly did not have a negative impact on his reputation. He received prestigious commissions for both individual and group portraits including *Madame la baronne Nathaniel de Rothschild (née Charlotte de Rothschild)* (1866; Paris, Musée d'Orsay) and *The Reception of the Siamese Ambassadors at Fontainebleau* (1861–64, Château de Versailles). While he painted these works on a much smaller scale than *Portrait of Mademoiselle Durand*, he continued to employ a labor-intensive process and often prepared portraits of individual sitters as he worked towards a larger composition, as was the case for his four years of work on the over eighty portraits required for the reception at Fontainebleau.

The interplay between precise study, portrait likeness, and larger figural compositions offers considerable insight into how *Portrait of an African Woman* (cat.12) fits within the context of Gérôme's painting practice. Unlike the portrait of Durand, the surface of this work is not inscribed with a date and the context of its creation deserves attention. The painting has been published as a product of circa 1872, although no justification

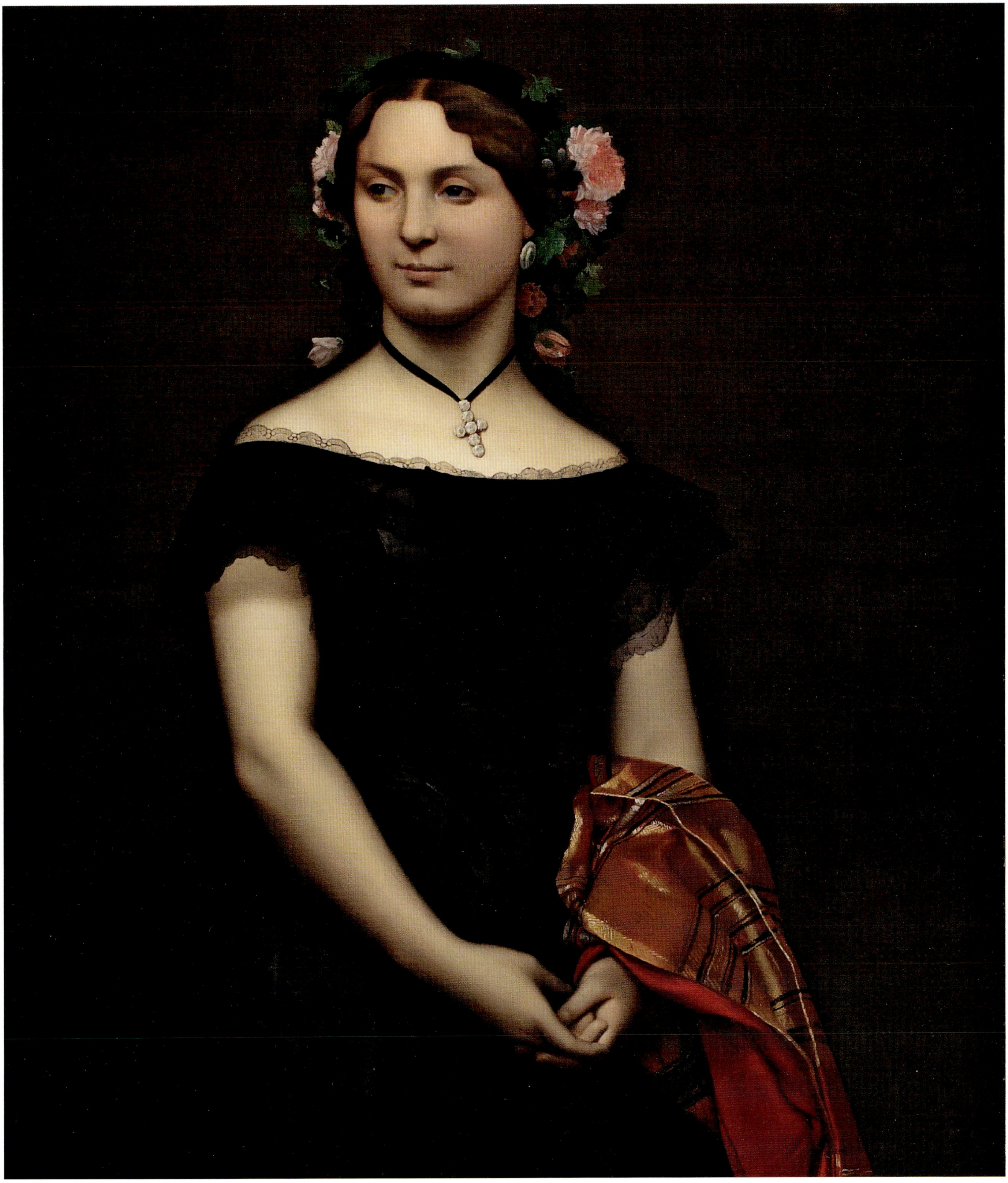

has ever been given for assigning that date. Indeed this sitter reappears in a modified pose in a Turkish bath scene dated 1886 (*The Terrace of the Seraglio*; private collection), where she is a full-length figure with her face even more shrouded in blue scarves. She carries a hookah and a long-stemmed *chibouk* pipe, the upper half of which appears in this work. Gérôme produced Middle Eastern bath scenes in 1872, but the close connection with the later composition, and his practice of producing individual portraits as he prepared multi-figure compositions, suggests a later date. Gérôme traveled to Constantinople for the first time in 1853 and returned to the Ottoman capital in 1871, 1875, and 1879. He traveled to Egypt six times between 1856 and 1880.

Gérôme painted *Portrait of an African Woman* with such attention to the sitter's physiognomy she may have been a Nubian woman he hired as a model while he was in Egypt. The precise lines Gérôme used to define the woman's eyelids, nose, and mouth, the glow of her left cheek, and the peach and pink highlights of her skin and lips all reveal his interest in an evocative likeness. Four layers of more freely painted scarves frame her face, with the fabric at the top of her head only loosely formed by green and white brushstrokes. For Gérôme this was a portrait he needed to complete, not to submit to a public exhibition, but as an integral part of his meticulous studio process. In the context of Gérôme's numerous bath scenes, female African figures were often positioned as attendants working for Caucasian women. While such scenes were popular within the contemporary art market, when Gérôme depicted the African woman in isolation, as he does here, we should consider her as the subject of the work rather than as any artificial construction of his imagination.

[1] *Gazette des Tribunaux*, no.8545.

Provenance

Portrait of Mademoiselle Durand
Paris, Galerie Boussod-Valadon
Paris, J.N. Streep
New York, Hammer Gallery
New York, H. Shickman Gallery, 1970–72
Toronto, Joey and Toby Tanenbaum, 1972–2002

Portrait of an African Woman
New York, H. Shickman Gallery, 1973
Toronto, Joey and Toby Tanenbaum, 1973–2002

Exhibition History

Portrait of Mademoiselle Durand
New York, H. Shickman Gallery, February 1970, *The Neglected 19th Century: An Exhibition of French Paintings*, cat.21 (reproduced)
Dayton, Dayton Art Institute, 10 November–30 December 1972; Minneapolis, Minneapolis Institute of Arts, 26 January–11 March 1973; Baltimore, Walters Art Gallery, 6 April–20 May 1973, *Jean-Léon Gérôme*, cat.3, *32* (as *Portrait of Mlle Duvergier*)
Ottawa, National Gallery of Canada, 26 May–10 September 1978; Victoria, Art Gallery of Greater Victoria, 19 October–3 December 1978; Edmonton, Edmonton Art Gallery, 15 December 1978–14 January 1979; Calgary, Glenbow-Alberta Institute, 3 February–22 March 1979; Montreal, Montreal Museum of Fine Arts, 5 April–13 May 1979; Toronto, Art Gallery of Ontario, 15 June–29 July 1979, *The Other Nineteenth Century: Paintings and Sculpture in the Collection of Mr. and Mrs. Joseph M. Tanenbaum*, cat.30, *103* (as *Portrait of a Lady*)
Hamilton, Art Gallery of Hamilton, 28 May 2005–28 May 2006, *Heaven and Earth Unveiled: European Treasures from the Tanenbaum Collection*, cat.48; 36–37, *98* (as *Portrait, Mademoiselle Durand*)
Hamilton, Art Gallery of Hamilton, 10 February–13 May 2007, *Framed: The Art of the Portrait*
Toronto, Art Gallery of Toronto, *Drama and Desire: Artists and the Theatre*, 19 June–26 September 2010 (hors catalogue)
Hamilton, Art Gallery of Hamilton, 21 May–5 September 2011, *The French Connection*
Hamilton, Art Gallery of Hamilton, 9 February 2013–9 February 2014, *The Painter Pictured: French Nineteenth-Century Paintings and Portrait Photographs*

Portrait of an African Woman
Hamilton, Art Gallery of Hamilton, 28 May 2005–28 May 2006; Victoria, Art Gallery of Greater Victoria, 25 January–11 May 2008, *Heaven and Earth Unveiled: European Treasures from the Tanenbaum Collection*, cat.47; 55, *127* (as *Black Servant Girl*).
Hamilton, Art Gallery of Hamilton, 22 May–6 September 2010, *Europe's Exoticized East*
Hamilton, Art Gallery of Hamilton, 21 May–5 September 2011, *The French Connection*
Hamilton, Art Gallery of Hamilton, 9 February 2013–9 February 2014, *The Painter Pictured: French Nineteenth-Century Paintings and Portrait Photographs*

Bibliography

Ackerman, Gerald. *The Life and Work of Jean-Léon Gérôme with a Catalogue Raisonné*. New York: Sotheby's Publications, 1986, cat.54, 39–40, *40*, 194, *195* (*Portrait of Mlle Durand*), 336 fn.111; cat.226, *233* (identified as panel and entitled *The Black Servant Girl*; 2000 rev. ed. cited as canvas and Studio of Gérôme).
Boime, Albert. "À la Mode and Haute Couture," *Burlington Magazine* vol.112 no.810 (September 1970): 645–51 (*645*, 646).
Dierden, Roger. *From Homer to the Harem: The Art of Jean Lecomte du Nouÿ*. New York: Dahesh Museum of Art, 2004, *30*, 31.
Lanes, Jerrold. "The Neglected 19th Century, H. Shickman Gallery," *Artforum* (April 1970): 79–81, *79*.
Makariou, Sophie, and Charlotte Maury. "The Paradox of Realism: Gérôme in the Orient," trans. Jonathan Sly in *The Spectacular Art of Jean-Léon Gérôme (1824–1904)*. Paris: Skira Flammarion, 2010, 259–65.
Moreau-Vauthier, Charles. *Gérôme peintre et sculpteur. L'homme et l'artiste d'après sa correspondance, ses notes, les souvenirs de ses élèves et de ses amis*. Paris: Hachette, 1906.
Nochlin, Linda. "The Imaginary Orient," in *The Politics of Vision: Essays on Nineteenth-Century Art and Society*. New York: Harper & Row, 1989, 33–59.
Miller, Peter Benson. "Gérôme and Ethnographic Realism at the Salon of 1857," and Mary Roberts, "Gérôme in Istanbul," in Scott Allan and Mary Morton, eds. *Reconsidering Gérôme*. Los Angeles: J. Paul Getty Museum, 2010, 106–18, 119–34.
Said, Edward W. *Orientalism*. New York: Vintage Books, 1978.

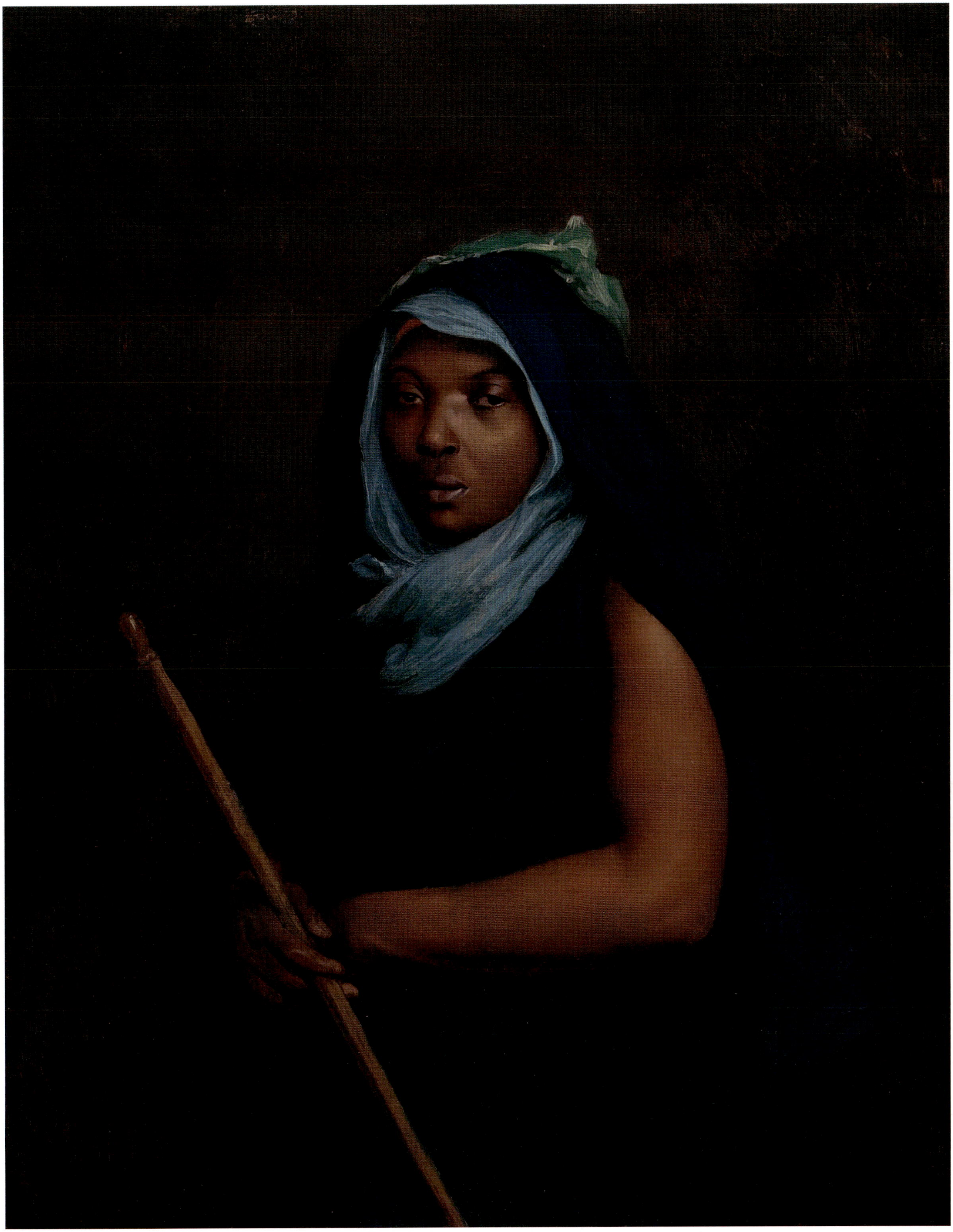

Alfred Dehodencq (French • 1822–1882)

13 — Execution of a Jewish Woman in Morocco

c.1861 • oil on canvas • 216 × 165 cm • s.l.r. alfred Dehodencq • Inv.2002.33.104

This painting presents the viewer with a challenging scene: a large crowd has gathered to witness a public execution in a square in Tangier, the most northern coastal city of Morocco. Tensions build as the decisive moment draws closer. Armed men, dressed in red and gold, struggle to control bodies that press forward and closer to the central wooden stage. Dehodencq portrays a scene wrought with divisions that are both evocative and symbolic. A woman is about to be killed, and, although there appears to be a small group of female observers on a distant rooftop, the masses closest to the execution are all men. These men are also divided in two distinct realms by their clothing, accessories, emotional responses, and the structure of the composition. In the foreground, two men look across the shadowy divide that demarcates the separate spaces. The scene revolves around religious conflict between Jews and Muslims in mid-nineteenth-century Morocco, and this specific disagreement is about to play out on the body of a young, innocent woman. It is a dramatic painting, layered with palpable tensions, and yet intentionally artificial. The viewer hovers somewhere between standing within the crowd's energy and raised up, with a privileged view of the platform. Dehodencq does not make it entirely clear how he advocates spectators respond, and this is integral to his success with this unsettling scene. Two extant preparatory drawings indicate how Dehodencq worked through his ideas; he considered a scene with several horses in a larger cityscape, and ultimately settled on this powerful, vertically oriented and crowd-focused composition.[1]

Dehodencq was an active artist-traveler who worked in both Spain and Morocco between 1850 and 1863. While he did not witness this public execution, Dehodencq's extensive work in Morocco and the success of the painting generated two erroneous legends: that he had actually been present and that his painting proved so politically controversial the first version had been destroyed by angry Moroccans. Neither was true. In fact, Dehodencq addresses events from 1834: the controversial treatment and ultimate death of Sol (Suleika) Hachuel. In the decades following Sol's execution, many versions of her story circulated in Jewish and European languages, but there were only two historically accurate accounts of her martyrdom that drew on primary sources from her family. These document tensions within her Jewish home that led Sol to turn to her Muslim neighbors, who then notified Muslim judges that Sol had converted to Islam. She denied the conversion, was charged with renunciation, and imprisoned. Sol was executed after numerous failed efforts to convince her to convert, and she became a potent symbol of Jewish minority status in Morocco. Dehodencq assigned Sol the ultimate revenge—she looks indignantly to the executor who pulls back her long hair and exposes her neck—and yet he suggestively exposes her chest. The body of the female martyr Sol becomes a contested site for negotiating religious tensions and the colonial politics of North Africa. When Dehodencq exhibited *Execution of a Jewish Woman in Morocco* at the Salon of 1861, he displayed it with a second painting, *Jewish Bride in Tangiers* (no.820). Records indicate that the French government initially planned to buy the execution scene but ultimately purchased his other work.[2] That painting presented a culturally charged moment in a Moroccan Jewish woman's life, when she closes her eyes and is guided through the streets to her fiancée's home. It was a subject that brought Dehodencq a level of commercial success, and he returned to it numerous times over the following two decades. While more challenging for his contemporaries, Dehodencq's *Execution of a Jewish Woman in Morocco* is a historically significant work and a rare visual record of the life of Sol Hachuel.

1 Musée du Louvre RF 3776, 3777.

2 AN F/21/131; Musée des Beaux-Arts, Dunkirk.

Provenance

Charles Paix-Séailles, 1906
London, Sotheby's, 24 June 1981, lot 197
London, Timothy Hobart Fine Art
Toronto, Joey and Toby Tanenbaum, 1982–2002

Exhibition History

Paris, Salon, 1861, no.819
Marseille, Exposition Nationale Coloniale, 1906, no.19
Hamilton, Art Gallery of Hamilton, 28 May 2005–28 May 2006, *Heaven and Earth Unveiled: European Treasures from the Tanenbaum Collection*, cat.31; 54–55, *126*
Hamilton, Art Gallery of Hamilton, 22 May–6 September 2010, *Europe's Exoticized East*
Montreal, Museum of Fine Arts, 26 January–7 June 2015, *Marvels and Mirages of Orientalism: Benjamin Constant in his Time*, cat.

Bibliography

Laskier, Michael M., and Yaacov Lev. "The Martyrdom of Sol Hachuel," in *The Convergence of Judaism and Islam: Religious, Scientific, and Cultural Dimensions*. Gainesville: University of Florida Press, 2011, 109–21.
Martinière, Henri de la. *Souvenirs du Maroc*. Paris: Plon, 1919, 8.
Prat, Véronique. "Alfred Dehodencq: 1822–1882." 2 vols. Ph.D. dissertation, Université de Paris IV, 1977.
Schroeter, Daniel J. "The Shifting Boundaries of Moroccan Jewish

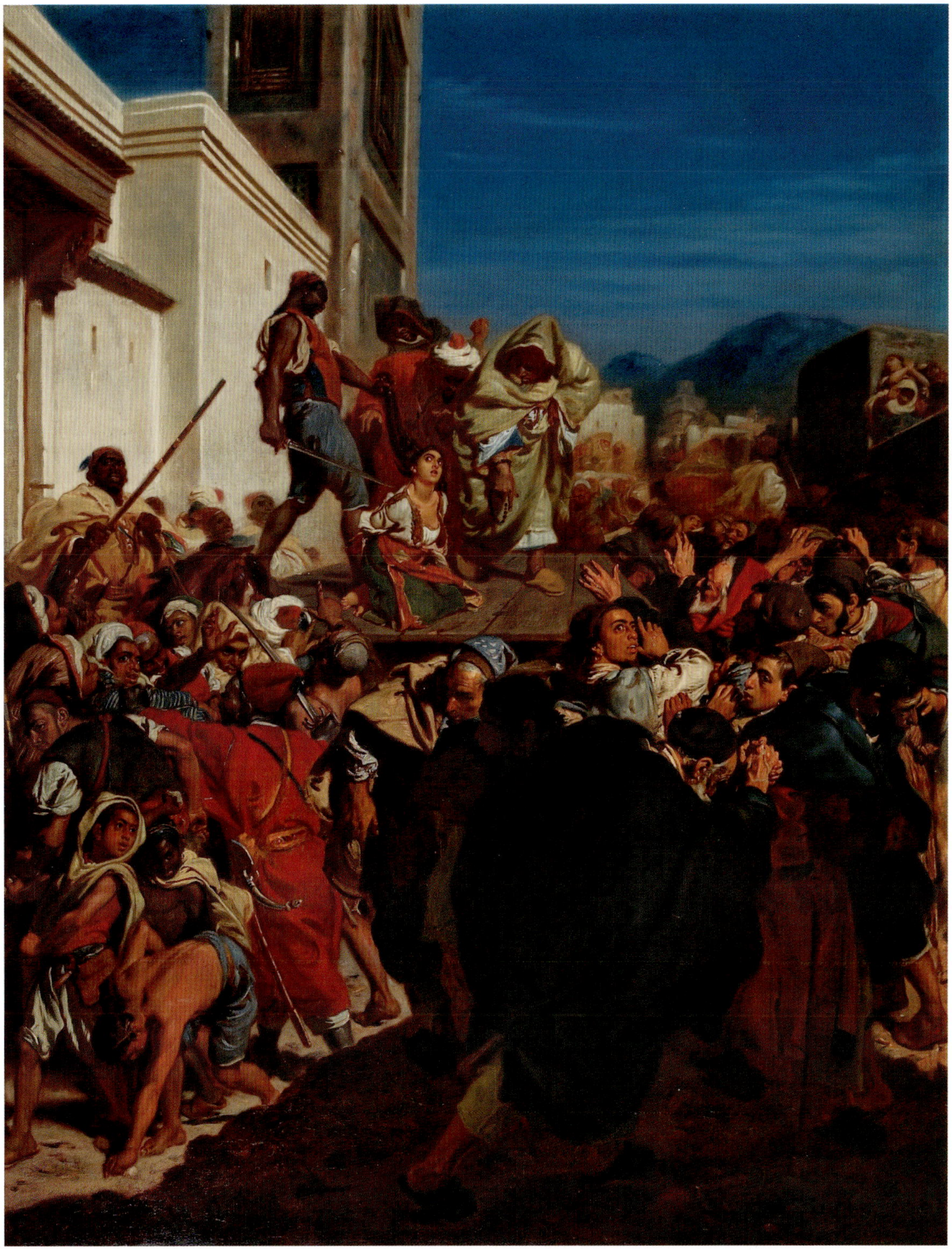

Identities," *Jewish Social Studies* vol.15 no.1 new series (Fall 2008): 145–64.
Séailles, Gabriel. *Alfred Dehodencq: l'homme et l'artiste*. Paris: Société de Propagation des Livres d'Art, 1910, 112–16, *facing page 112*.
-----. *Alfred Dehodencq: histoire d'un coloriste*. Paris: Paul Ollendorff, 1885, 145–51.
Vance, Sharon. *The Martyrdom of a Moroccan Jewish Saint*. Leiden: Brill, 2011.
-----. "Sol Hachuel, 'Heroine of the Nineteenth Century': Gender, the Jewish Question and Colonial Discourse," in Emily Benichou Gottreich and Daniel J. Schroeter, eds. *Jewish Culture and Society in North Africa*. Indiana: Indiana University Press, 2011, 201–25.

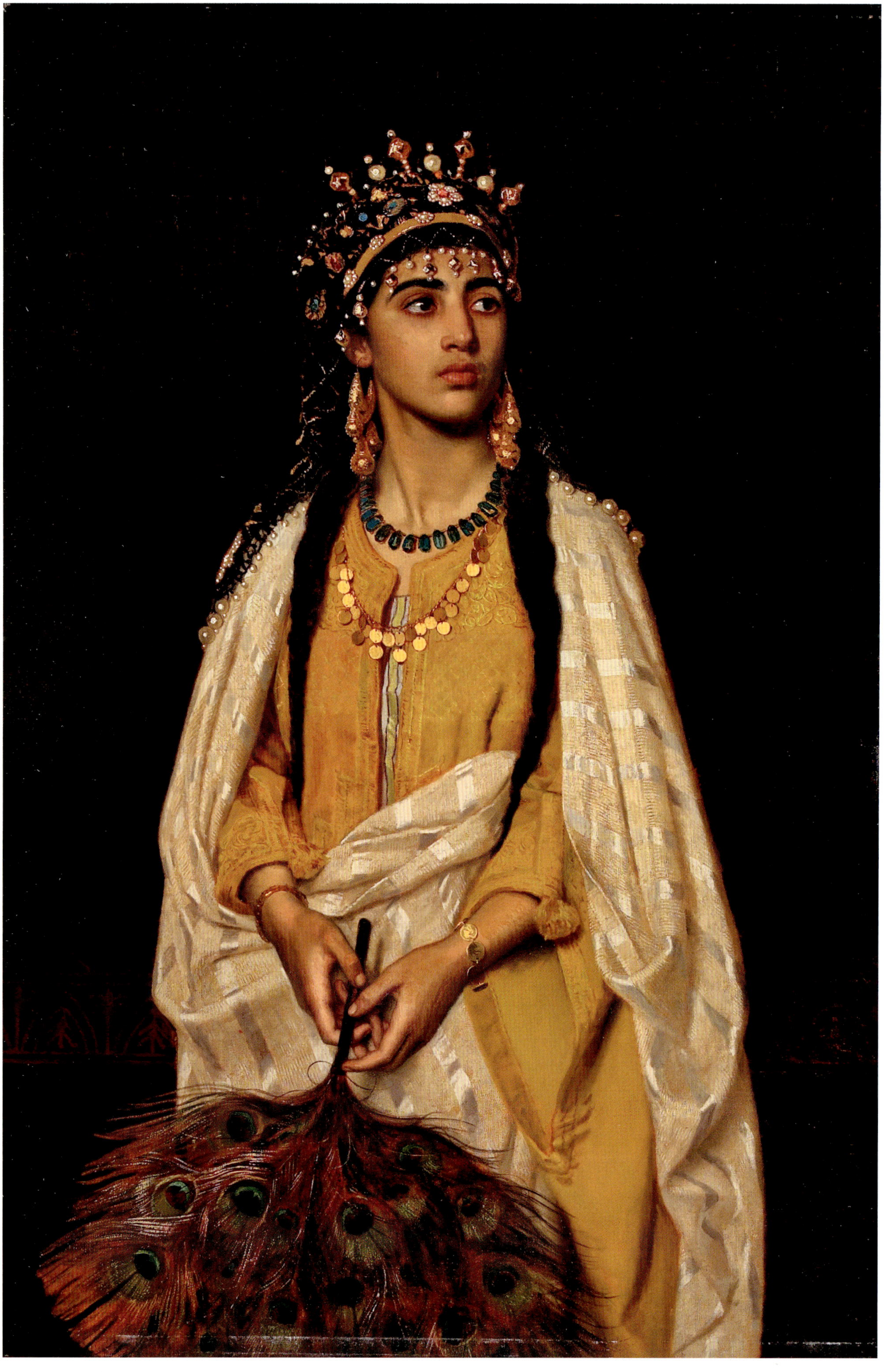

Sophie Anderson (French • 1823–1903)

14 — Toklihili: The Young Indian Princess

1863–71 • oil on canvas • 103.3 × 66.5 cm • s.l.r.c. S. Anderson • Inv.2002.33.72

Anderson (née Gengembre) painted this large-scale, three-quarter-length figure as a form of imaginary portraiture. She also designed the painting to appeal to the contemporary market for exotic subject matter, particularly of physically attractive women. Anderson's rendering of the face and neck suggest she worked from the live model, one likely dressed in elements of this costume and to which the artist added some of the more ornate accessories. The title for the work implies, however, that this is an actual portrait, one of a specific south Asian princess named Toklihili.[1] Anderson's elaboration of a fictive realm is central to her success with this painting. The heavily jeweled princess stands proudly, upright and turned to look off into the distance, following a well-established convention within the traditions of British and European portraiture. She is positioned in a shallow interior space, set against a wall embellished with a narrow, low-lying decorative band. In the upper left-hand corner an obscure hieroglyphic-like symbol floats on the gridded wall covering. This dark backdrop sets off Toklihili's glowing skin and the layers of luminous silk fabrics that adorn her body. Anderson assigned the figure a regal identity and thus, appropriately for her subject, she does not pose Toklihili in an overtly sexual or provocative way. There are, nonetheless, notable details that emphasize this princess as a sensual being. Anderson draws attention to the taut sinews and indentation at the nape of Toklihili's neck, to her well-modeled hands and forearms that peek out from unlined sleeves, and most notably to the lines of two braids of hair that frame and suggest the curve of her breasts. The design and embroidered details of Toklihili's clothing and the peacock feather fan suggest a cultural context in a purely generalized manner. To this, Anderson added an elaborate headdress, encrusted with multi-colored gems and pearls that cascade down the sitter's shoulders, and this offers the clearest enunciation of Toklihili's social status. Within the context of colonial rule in the nineteenth century, Anderson's romanticized image of Indian resources—textiles, mining, and populace—would have held considerable appeal for its British audience.

Anderson used the same model for *Toklihili* as she did in at least two other works. In one, *Scheherazade* (Walsall, The New Art Gallery), the sitter assumes the guise of the legendary Persian queen and famed storyteller of *One Thousand and One Nights*. In the other work, entitled *In the Harem, Tunis* (current location unknown), she appears lounging on a divan in an odalisque-like pose. In each of these works Anderson used fabrics, gold coin-like jewelry, and other details such as peacock feathers and headscarves to transform her model into a North African or Middle Eastern subject. For Anderson, the model was a malleable form that could be dressed up, accessorized, and placed in a range of orientalizing guises. There is no evidence Anderson traveled to any of the exotic locales she evoked in these paintings, although she did live and work in a number of international venues in Britain, Europe, and the United States. Anderson often signed her works but she did not include dates on *Toklihili* or the other extant canvases that depict the same model. *Toklihili: The Young Indian Princess* likely dates to between 1863 and 1871, when Anderson was based in London for an extended period. Between 1858 and 1860 Anderson exhibited over twenty works at the Royal Academy and the Society of British Artists. She also showed works at the Grosvenor Gallery between 1878 and 1887, during a period when she had moved to Italy for health reasons and was actively involved in the artistic community in Capri.

[1] An inscription on the back of the canvas, "Toklihili: La jeune princesse/Indienne par S. Mishmani," is of unknown origin and cannot be identified as the hand of the artist. Efforts to identify Mishmani as the author of a particular literary text have not proved fruitful.

Provenance

London, Christie's, 5 November 1982, lot 114

London, Sotheby's, 16 March 1988, lot 158

Toronto, Joey and Toby Tanenbaum, 1988–2002

Exhibition History

Hamilton, Art Gallery of Hamilton, 28 May 2005–28 May 2006, *Heaven and Earth Unveiled: European Treasures from the Tanenbaum Collection*, cat.1; 57, *133*

Hamilton, Art Gallery of Hamilton, 10 February–13 May 2007, *Framed: The Art of the Portrait*

Hamilton, Art Gallery of Hamilton, 22 May–6 September 2010, *Europe's Exoticized East*

Bibliography

Casteras, Susan P., and Coleen Denney, eds. *The Grosvenor Gallery: A Palace of Art in Victorian England.* New Haven: Yale University Press, 1999, 86.

Denney, Colleen. *At the Temple of Art: The Grosvenor Gallery, 1877–1890.* Madison, NJ: Fairleigh Dickinson University Press, 2000, 130, 140.

Graves, Algernon. *A Dictionary of Artists who have exhibited works in the principal London exhibitions of oil paintings from 1760 to 1880.* London: George Bell and Sons, 1884, 5.

Marshall, Peter. "British-India Connections c.1780 to c.1830: The Empire of the Officials," in Michael J. Franklin, ed. *Romantic Representations of British India.* London: Routledge, 2006, 45–64.

Lewis, Reina. *Gendering Orientalism: Race, Femininity and Orientalism.* New York: Routledge, 1996, 119–20, pl.28.

-----. "Women Orientalist Artists: Diversity, Ethnography, Interpretation," *Women: A Cultural Review* vol.6 no.1 (1995): 91–106.

Eugène Isabey (French • 1803–1886)

15 — Trawlers at Sea

c.1865 • oil on canvas • 62.2 × 94.8 cm • s.l.l. E. Isabey • Inv.2002.33.129

In this scene, three men have joined forces in the stern of a boat, each pulling on the cords of a fishing net. They have lowered their masts and repositioned ballast in an effort to balance out their weight. In the foreground, the boat is surrounded by waves that roil and churn and, just a short distance away, a second boat seems to fare no better. While there are few openings in the ominous, dark, and cloud-filled sky, a shaft of light falls directly on the fishers, their net, and the whitecaps in the sea. That play of light is no coincidence as Isabey used this traditional device to highlight areas of the composition and to elicit particular responses from the viewer. We are likely to empathize with the three men as they exert considerable effort to fulfill the tasks that are the basis of their livelihood. We are also encouraged to feel compassionate since the men confront seemingly insurmountable conditions. Isabey was among the most well regarded marine and seascape painters of his time, and *Trawlers at Sea* exemplifies his interest in romantic traditions, specifically the struggle of humans against the powerful forces of nature.

Throughout his long career, Isabey's primary interest was to depict the coastlines and sea views of Normandy and Brittany. He filled numerous albums with drawings that focused on ships and water. He did countless studies of parts of ships, sketches that focused on a mast, sails, or the shape of a prow. He also sketched ports at low tide, and ships marooned on a beach or caught in turbulent, agitated water. Many of Isabey's pencil drawings, particularly of ships at sea, look like they were completed at a feverish pace, and few include details that connect them with a particular place. With his watercolors, however, it is often possible to relate a work with a specific geographic location such as the rocky cliffs at Saint-Malo or Étretat. Isabey's seascapes were praised from the very first time he submitted his work and received a medal at the Salon in 1824. During the July Monarchy Isabey was also commissioned by the government to produce works that commemorated significant contemporary events in a marine or sea context. These included *King Louis-Philippe Disembarking at Portsmouth, 6 October 1844* (1844) and *King Louis-Philippe Escorting Queen Victoria on Board the Yacht "Victoria and Albert" docked at Le Tréport, 7 September 1843* (1845; both now in the Château at Versailles). Works such as these relied on Isabey's ability to present complex compositions that included numerous ships and figures, specific weather conditions, and a particular historical event.

Isabey painted smaller canvases, such as *Trawlers at Sea*, for an entirely different market. He undoubtedly hoped the painting would sell in the growing market of private collectors who were hanging landscapes and seascapes in their domestic settings with increasing regularity. Before the end of the century the painting was acquired by British collector Sir James Bell who in turn loaned it to a large exhibition of French works mounted at Guildhall Art Gallery in London in 1898.[1] Isabey made numerous trips to Britain from as early as 1821 and developed close relations with British artists including Richard Parkes Bonington. Like a number of other French artists, he also took refuge in England for a longer period in 1870–71 (see cats.28, 34, and 35). Isabey also maintained strong connections with French artists including Delacroix and Boudin, as well as Jongkind who was his pupil (see cat.17).

[1] A second work by Isabey, *Return to Port, Honfleur*, was loaned by British collector Reginald Vaile (cat.99 in the Guildhall catalogue).

Provenance

Collection of Sir James Bell, by 1898
New York, Shickman Gallery, 1970
Toronto, Joey and Toby Tanenbaum, 1970–2002

Exhibition History

London, Corporation of London Art Gallery (Guildhall), 6 June–31 August 1898, *Loan Collection of Pictures by Painters of the French School*, cat.88 (as *Hauling in the Nets*)
Glasgow, International Exhibition, 1901, cat.1399 (as *Night Trawlers*)
New York, H. Shickman Gallery, February 1970, *The Neglected 19th Century: An Exhibition of French Paintings*, cat.24 (as *Night Fishermen*; reproduced)
Toronto, Art Gallery of Ontario, 15 June–29 July 1979, *The Other Nineteenth Century: Paintings and Sculpture in the Collection of Mr. and Mrs. Joseph M. Tanenbaum* (as *Night Fishermen*; hors catalogue)
Hamilton, Art Gallery of Hamilton, 28 May 2005–28 May 2006, *Heaven and Earth Unveiled: European Treasures from the Tanenbaum Collection*, cat.62; 47, *114*

Bibliography

Bazin, Pierre. *Eugène Isabey, 1803–1886*. Dieppe: Musée de Dieppe, 1966.
Cunningham, Charles C., Susan D. Peters, and Kathleen Zimmerer. *Jongkind and the Pre-Impressionists: Painters of the Ecole Saint-Siméon*. Williamstown, MA: Sterling and Francine Clark Art Institute, 1976, 115–21.
Leribault, Christophe. *Eugène Isabey: cabinet des dessins*. Paris: Musée du Louvre, 2012.
Miquel, Pierre. *Eugène Isabey, 1803–1886. la marine au XIXe siècle*. 2 vols. Maurs-la-Jolie: Martinelle, 1980.
Noon, Patrick, and Stephen Bann. *Crossing the Channel: British and French Painting in the Age of Romanticism*. London: Tate Publishing, 2003, 192–97, 217, 257.
Schabacker, P.H., and K.H. Spencer. *Eugène Isabey: Paintings, Watercolors, Drawings, Lithographs*. Cambridge, MA: Fogg Art Museum, 1967.

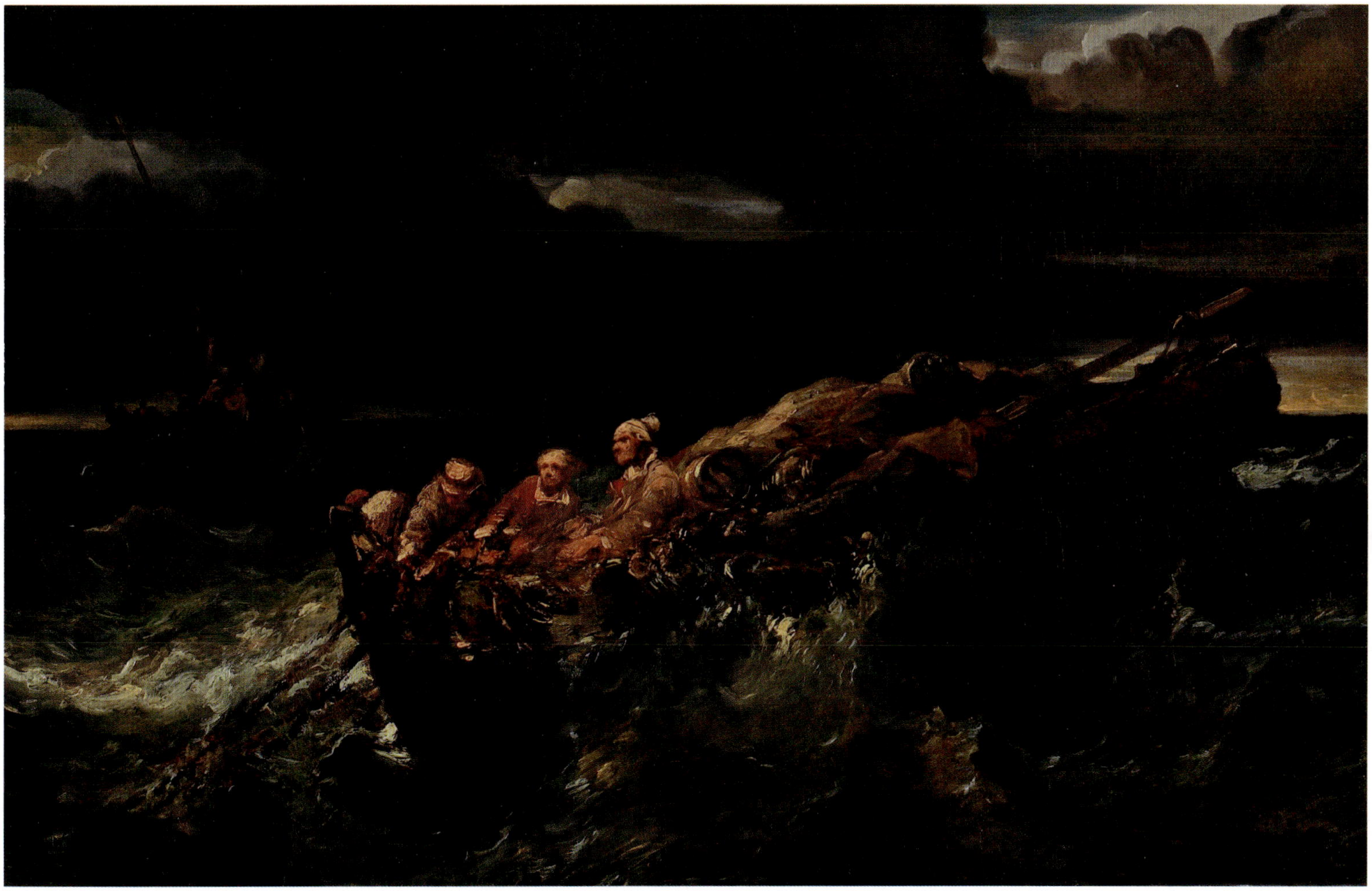

Félicien Joseph Victor Rops (Belgian • 1833–1898)

16 — Country Road

c.1865–75 • oil on canvas laid on wood panel • 23.1 × 35.8 cm • s.l.r. Felix [Felÿ] Rops à l'ami Anton • Inv.2002.33.177

Rops is best known today for his prolific work as a printmaker. He is also famous, and in the view of some notorious, for the erotic content of many of his prints. *Country Road* offers us insight into another aspect of Rops's oeuvre, one that has been somewhat eclipsed over time by the level of interest in his more provocative subject matter. Landscapes were a meaningful subject for Rops from the first decades of his life when he lived largely in his native Belgium, and that interest continued through to the later decades when he was based in France (he lived in Paris from 1874). In Brussels in 1868, Rops, Meunier (see cats.54 and 55), and Charles de Groux, father of Henry de Groux (see cat.67), were among the founders of the Société Libre des Beaux-Arts, the "Free Society" that challenged academicism, and promoted realist practices in Belgian art, as well as exhibition spaces outside the official Salon exhibitions. Through that group Rops also became close with Belgian landscape painters Louis Artan and Louis Dubois. Rops often spent time traveling with these and other artist friends. One of his favorite areas to relax and paint nature was in the Dinant region of southern Belgium, particularly around Anseremme, a village south of Namur where he was born. Rops also spent time just west of Anseremme, near Mettet, where his in-laws owned property. There is nothing that identifies *Country Road* specifically as Anseremme or Mettet, but the painting likely depicts a small village in the Dinant region. Rops liked to escape from city life, whether Brussels or later Paris, and enjoyed returning to his painting practice through rural subject matter. When painting landscapes he typically worked on a quite small scale, as he did with *Country Road*. He used oil paint either on paper or on canvas that he then adhered to another support, usually a wood panel. These were not works that he ever planned to exhibit. Rather they were small-format paintings, works he did for personal pleasure and that he often gave to friends as gifts. Rops's inscription "to my friend Anton" in the lower right-hand corner means that *Country Road* survives as a testimony of gift-giving in the supportive artistic community Rops treasured.[1] It also reveals a less familiar aspect of Rops's artistic output, one that was not tied to or motivated by commercial interests.

Country Road shows Rops's direct and spontaneous approach to *plein air* subjects. He offers a perspective with two roads intersecting and forming an asymmetrical composition, which adds visual interest within a scene that is imbued with calm. Rops captures the essentials and includes only those details that are necessary to convey the subject. He treats many forms as flat areas of paint, such as the planks of wood that make up the dilapidated fences, and he surrounds those with a darker contour line. A series of single loose brushstrokes come together to form a figure and, for Rops, it never seems necessary to add details to a face or body. The figures are not incidental as they suggest anecdotal elements, but their main role is to help the viewer identify with the placid environs. Underpainting appears on the far left, on the road, and in the houses that dissolve into the background. Sections of the canvas also emerge and seem as integral to the composition as any section of paint. Critics who knew of such works by Rops praised his abilities, and saw the tension between this and his often sexually charged representations of women. Well-known critic Arsène Alexandre later wrote, "There is a whole part of his oeuvre that escapes Satan. It's the part where he studies nature attentively, imbues it with strong rustic sensations and depicts country people with a simplicity of means and a vigor of expression that one finds only in [the work of French artist Jean-François] Millet."[2]

[1] To date, there is no conclusive evidence that supports identifying Dutch arist Anton Mauve (1838–88) as the recipient of this gift.

[2] Arsène Alexandre, "Rops, rustique, satirique et luxurieux," *La Plume* no.172 (15 June 1896): 454–55.

Provenance

New York, Schweitzer Gallery, 1975

Toronto, Joey and Toby Tanenbaum, 1975–2002

Exhibition History

Hamilton, Art Gallery of Hamilton, 28 May 2005–28 May 2006, *Heaven and Earth Unveiled: European Treasures from the Tanenbaum Collection*, cat.114

Bibliography

Basseporte, Gérald. *Regards sur Félicien Rops, peintre à Essonnes.* Paris: Les presses du Management, L.P.M., 1998.

Bonnier, Bernadette. *Le Musée provincial Félicien Rops, Namur.* Brussels: Fonds Mercator, 2005, 77–78, 80–81, 152, 154, 190–95.

Carrette, Francis, et al. *Natures de peintres / Schildersignatuur: Boulenger, Artan, Rops, De Braekeleer, Vogels, Ensor.* Brussels: Bruxelles-Musées-Exposition, 2005, 96–119.

Hoozee, Robert. "Le paysage," in Anne Pingeot et al. *Paris-Bruxelles, Bruxelles-Paris: réalisme, impressionnisme, symbolisme, art nouveau: les relations artistiques entre la France et la Belgique, 1848–1914.* Paris: Réunion des musées nationaux, 1997, 140–50.

Hoozee, Robert, et al. *Het landschap in de Belgische kunst, 1830–1914.* Ghent: Museum voor Schone Kunsten, 1980.

Mascha, Ottokar. *Félicien Rops und sein Werk: Katalog seiner Gemälde, Originalzeichnungen, Lithographien, Radierungen, Vernismous, Kaltnadelblätter, Heliogravüren.* Munich: A. Langen, 1910, 6, 18–19.

Mattart, Astrid, et al. *Félicien Rops, 1833–1898.* Paris: Flammarion, 1985, 80–94.

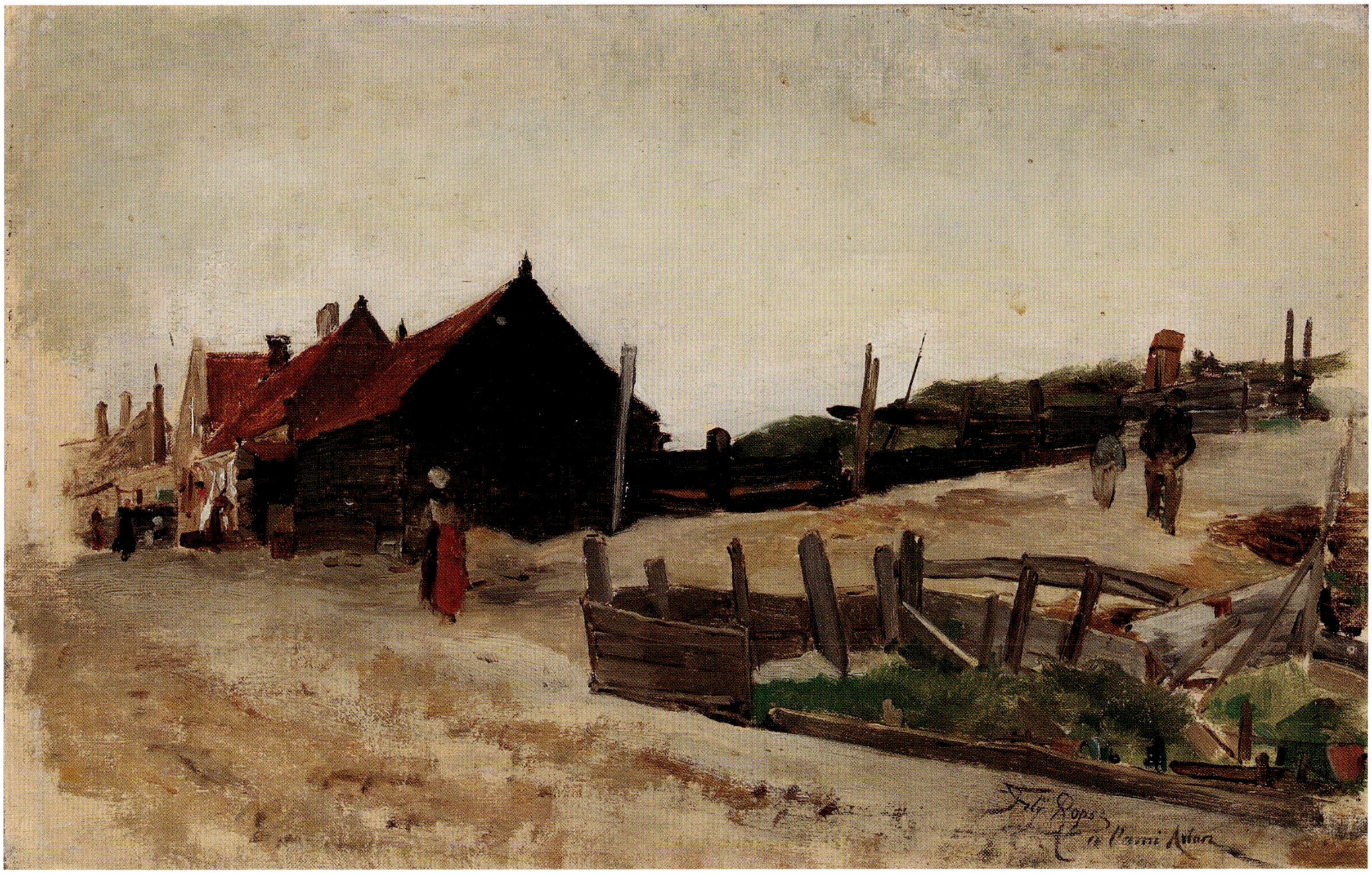

Johan Barthold Jongkind (Dutch • 1819–1891)

17 — Moonlight Scene

1866 • oil on canvas • 33.2 × 47.3 cm • s.d.l.r. Jongkind 1866 • Inv.2002.33.132

Jongkind focused his attention on intersections of land and water, where nature and culture meet at harbors, rivers, and coastlines in the Netherlands and northern France. In his *Moonlight Scene*, brushwork both clearly delineates forms and creates a loose network of strokes that animate the entire composition. He conveys gentle movement in the clouds, leaves, and surface of the water, yet imbues the scene with a sense of calm. Jongkind was an early exponent of working *en plein air*, in oil and watercolor, and drew upon that work for his etchings. *Moonlight Scene* exemplifies Jongkind's experimental, inter-media approach, particularly in his use of *contre jour*, a compositional strategy with dark forms placed against a light background that was of particular interest to printmakers. The sky is bathed by the diffused light of the low moon, its reflection a glowing concentration of peach, yellow, and white paint that notably predates Monet's *Impression, Sunrise* (1872; Paris, Musée d'Orsay) by six years. The bright night sky allows Jongkind to emphasize the forms that anchor his composition: the two boats, a row of trees, and particularly the four windmills—one of which is largely contained by the mast and stays of the sailboat. This work appears spontaneous yet Jongkind used structuring devices. The windmills decrease in scale at regular intervals, and their perspectival line plays off both the row of trees and the small gate in the lower left-hand corner. Every aspect of this work draws the viewer to the luminous moon.

In the mid-1860s when Jongkind painted *Moonlight Scene* he was actively involved in two different artistic networks to disseminate his work to the public. He exhibited both paintings and etchings at the Salon exhibitions, and he also published his etchings in each of the five volumes of *Eaux-fortes modernes* produced by the Société des Aquafortistes (Society of Etchers) between 1862 and 1867. Jongkind's use of *contre jour* and his interest in depicting the landscape as a *croquis* or sketch comes through in both his oil paintings and his etched plates. Like many artists involved in the innovative Société des Aquafortistes, Jongkind was inspired by Rembrandt's etchings, particularly the *contre jour* effect of *The Three Trees* (1643), one of the most revered works among painter-printmakers in nineteenth-century France. Dutch by birth, Jongkind went to Paris first in 1846 and started exhibiting at the Salon in 1848. He spent a large portion of his professional life in France, based in part in Paris and often working in northern coastal towns, including Honfleur, Sainte-Adresse, and Le Havre. Jongkind did, however, return to the Netherlands, most notably from 1855 to 1860 when he was based in Rotterdam. He produced *Moonlight Scene* during one of his annual trips to his native country between 1861 and 1869, possibly near Rotterdam, although Jongkind worked along various canals in 1866. Jongkind drew inspiration from works by artists of the Barbizon school, many of whom were his friends from when he first moved to France. Jongkind's own works were, in turn, a source of considerable interest among artists in the "Anonymous Society" that later took on the name impressionists. Although Jongkind chose not to exhibit with the impressionists, and preferred to reach his prospective patrons through Salon exhibitions, in 1920 Monet wrote to his friend, the art critic Gustave Geffroy, "Jongkind, along with Corot, is at the origin of what one called impressionism."[1]

[1] Unpublished letter, Documentation Center, Musée d'Orsay.

Provenance

New York, H. Shickman Gallery, 1971

Toronto, Joey and Toby Tanenbaum, 1971–2002

Exhibition History

New York, H. Shickman Gallery, February 1970, *The Neglected 19th Century: An Exhibition of French Paintings*, cat.28 (reproduced)

Toronto, Art Gallery of Ontario, 1974, *Opening Exhibition* (label on verso of painting)

Ottawa, National Gallery of Canada, 26 May–10 September 1978; Victoria, Art Gallery of Greater Victoria, 19 October–3 December 1978; Edmonton, Edmonton Art Gallery, 15 December 1978–14 January 1979; Calgary, Glenbow-Alberta Institute, 3 February–22 March 1979; Montreal, Montreal Museum of Fine Arts, 5 April–13 May 1979; Toronto, Art Gallery of Ontario, 15 June–29 July 1979, *The Other Nineteenth Century: Paintings and Sculpture in the Collection of Mr. and Mrs. Joseph M. Tanenbaum*, cat.42, *131*

Hamilton, Art Gallery of Hamilton, 28 May 2005–28 May 2006; Victoria, Art Gallery of Greater Victoria, 25 January–11 May 2008, *Heaven and Earth Unveiled: European Treasures from the Tanenbaum Collection*, cat.66, *283*

Bibliography

Cunningham, Charles C., Susan D. Peters, and Kathleen Zimmerer. *Jongkind and the Pre-Impressionists: Painters of the Ecole Saint-Siméon*. Williamstown, MA: Sterling and Francine Clark Art Institute, 1976, 25–31.

Hefting, Victorine. *Jongkind: sa vie, son œuvre, son époque*. Paris: Arts et métiers graphiques, 1975.

-----. *Jongkind d'après sa correspondance*. Utrecht: Haentjens Dekker & Gumbert, 1969.

McQueen, Alison. *The Rise of the Cult of Rembrandt: Reinventing an Old Master in Nineteenth-Century France*. Amsterdam: Amsterdam University Press, 2003, 160–73.

Patin, Sylvie, John Sillevis, and Götz Czymmek. *Johan Barthold Jongkind*. Paris: Réunion des musées nationaux, 2004.

Société des Aquafortistes. *Eaux-fortes modernes*. 5 vols. Paris: Cadart & Luquet, 1862–67.

Stein, Adolphe, et al. *Jongkind: catalogue critique de l'œuvre, peintures*. Vol.1. Paris: Brame & Lorenceau, 2003, cat.412 (as *Port near Rotterdam, Full Moon*).

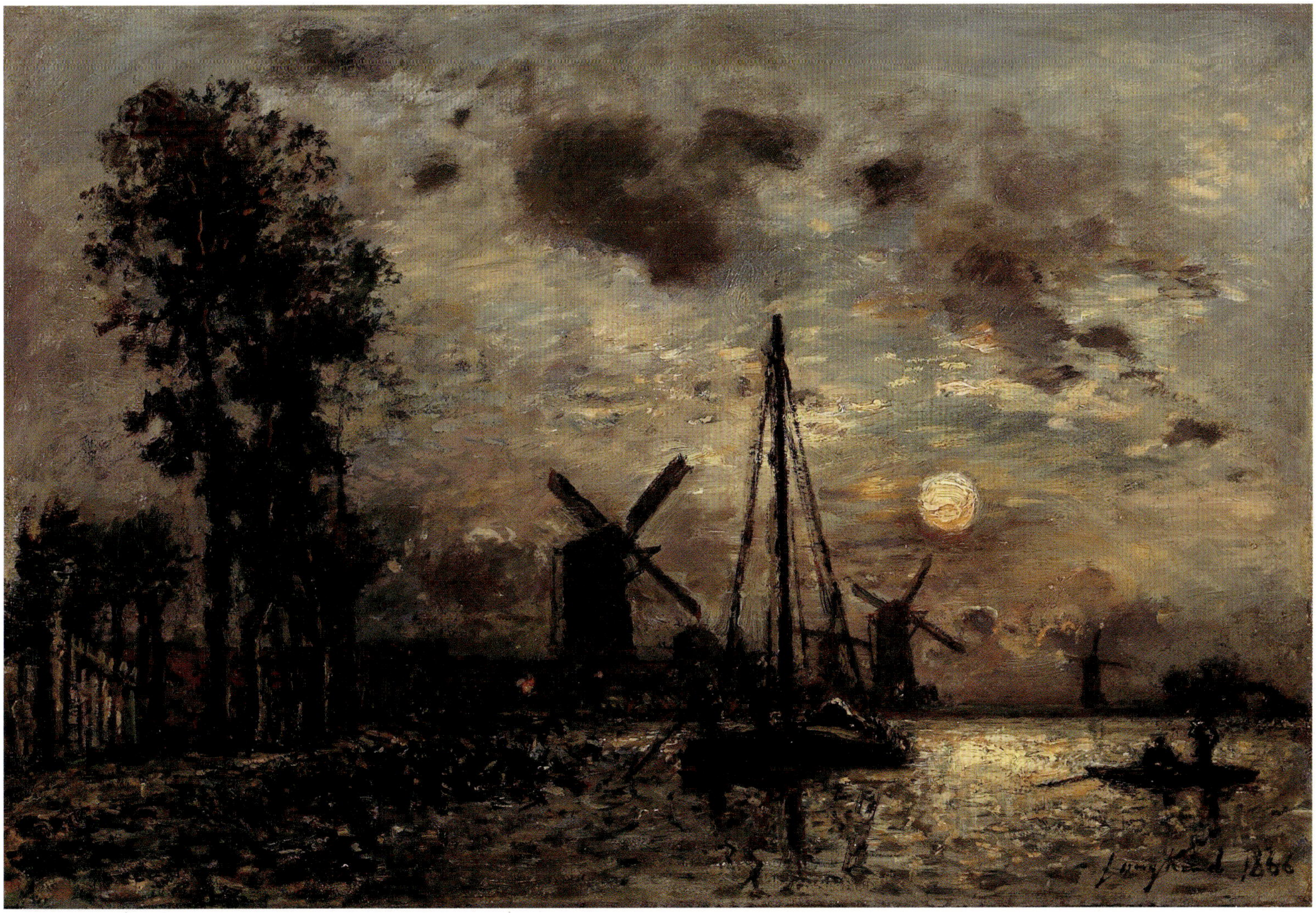

Wissman, Fronia E. "Johan Barthold Jongkind, *Frigates*," in Sarah Lees, ed. *Nineteenth-Century European Paintings at the Sterling and Francine Clark Art Institute.* Vol.1. New Haven: Yale University Press, 2012, 438–39.
Zarobell, John. "Johan Barthold Jongkind," in Juliet Wilson-Bareau and David Degener, eds. *Manet and the Sea.* Philadelphia: Philadelphia Museum of Art, 2004, 173–77.

Théodule Augustin Ribot (French • 1823–1891)

18 — The Musicians

c.1860–70 • oil on canvas • 128 × 93 cm • s.l.r. t. Ribot • Inv.2002.33.170

19 — Geometer

c.1870–80 • oil on canvas • 73.7 × 60 cm • s.l.r. t. Ribot • Inv.2002.33.165

20 — Death of a Saint

1867 • Oil on canvas • 60 × 73.4 cm • s.d.l.r. t. Ribot 1867 • Inv.2002.33.46

Ribot was a central figure of the realist movement in mid-nineteenth-century France. He received the respect and support of his fellow artists and also enjoyed numerous accolades from the government. The state awarded him two medals for his paintings in 1864 and 1865, and acquired a number of his works for provincial museums as well as the Musée du Luxembourg in Paris, then the nation's principal gallery for contemporary art. *The Musicians*, *Geometer*, and *Death of a Saint* exemplify important elements of Ribot's larger body of work and help us to understand the appeal of his oeuvre. Whether he was depicting an erudite mathematician, a holy martyr, or humble street musicians, Ribot had the ability to make his figures feel authentic and accessible to a broad audience. Characteristic of his style, Ribot painted within a narrow range of earthy tones, and also used light sparingly. He was adept at presenting the materiality and solidity of objects as well as the three-dimensional volume of figures. And he did so in ways that were outside the dominant visual practices of his time.

As Ribot was developing his own style, he turned to seventeenth-century Spanish art for inspiration. His works suggest his interest particularly in the paintings of Jusepe de Ribera, and contemporary art critics were quick to note the connection. Ribot's finances were quite limited and there is no evidence he was able to travel to Spain. Since Ribot only moved to Paris in 1845 and returned to the capital in 1851, after working for three years in Algeria, it is unlikely that the "Spanish Museum" mounted at the Louvre from 1838 to 1848 had a significant impact on him. Spanish art figured in a number of private collections in mid-nineteenth-century Paris, but the most accessible resource for Ribot was the art on display at the Louvre from the early 1850s. The small but notable national collection of Spanish works then included fifteen paintings by Murillo, Ribera, and Velázquez, although Murillo's large *Holy Family* hung in the palace at Saint-Cloud from 1855. As we understand the availability of Spanish art for Ribot, we can appreciate the challenge he set for himself when he chose to emulate art that was outside the mainstream. Much later in his career, after he was awarded the Legion of Honor and a medal at the Paris world's fair of 1878, several of his artist friends had their own medal cast for him that read "For Théodule Ribot, the independent painter." Ribot was inspired by alternative models, and his contemporaries valued this original aspect of his work. He also found ways to respond to the prototypes he admired and used loose brushwork for details such as the hair and hands of his *Geometer* (cat.19). He subtly varied his technique to suit different subjects. For example, the central figure in *Death of a Saint* (cat.20), dated 1867, reworked the clearly delineated nude male body Ribot presented at the Salon that year (*Torture by Wedges*; Rouen, Musée des Beaux-Arts), as well as in 1865 (*St. Sebastian*; Paris, Musée d'Orsay).

Active as both a painter and printmaker, Ribot promoted his career in a variety of venues. In addition to the acclaim his paintings received at the Salons (he also exhibited etchings in the print section), he showed his work at commercial galleries in Paris and contributed etchings to several albums published by the Société des Aquafortistes (1862–67). Ribot exhibited regularly with the Sociétés des Amis des Arts in various cities in the French provinces and sent his works to shows in international centers including Amsterdam (1865), Munich (1869), and Vienna (1873).

Provenance

The Musicians
Paris, Munkácsy studio sale, 4 June 1898, lot 24
London, Christie's, 23 April 1971, lot 144
Paris, Galerie André Watteau
Munich, G. Heineman
New York, H. Shickman Gallery
Toronto, Joey and Toby Tanenbaum, 1973–2002

Geometer
Paris, Hôtel Drouot, estate sale of Théodule Ribot's widow, 30 May 1896
Saint-Cloud, Princess Marie de Grace
New York, H. Shickman Gallery
Toronto, Joey and Toby Tanenbaum, 1970–2002

Death of a Saint
London, Williams Gallery
Paris, Galerie André Watteau
Toronto, Joey and Toby Tanenbaum, 1974–2002

Exhibition History

The Musicians
New York, H. Shickman Gallery, October 1971, *The Neglected 19th Century: An Exhibition of French Paintings, Part II* (reproduced)
Ottawa, National Gallery of Canada, 26 May–10 September 1978; Victoria, Art Gallery of Greater Victoria, 19 October–3 December 1978; Edmonton, Edmonton Art Gallery, 15 December 1978–14 January 1979; Calgary, Glenbow-Alberta Institute, 3 February–22 March 1979; Montreal, Montreal Museum of Fine Arts, 5 April–13 May 1979; Toronto, Art Gallery of Ontario, 15 June–29 July 1979, *The Other Nineteenth Century: Paintings and Sculpture in the Collection of Mr. and Mrs. Joseph M. Tanenbaum*, cat.55, *165*
Washington, D.C., National Gallery of Art, 5 December 1982–6 March 1983, *Manet and Modern Paris*, cat.71
Hamilton, Art Gallery of Hamilton, 28 May 2005–28 May 2006, *Heaven*

18

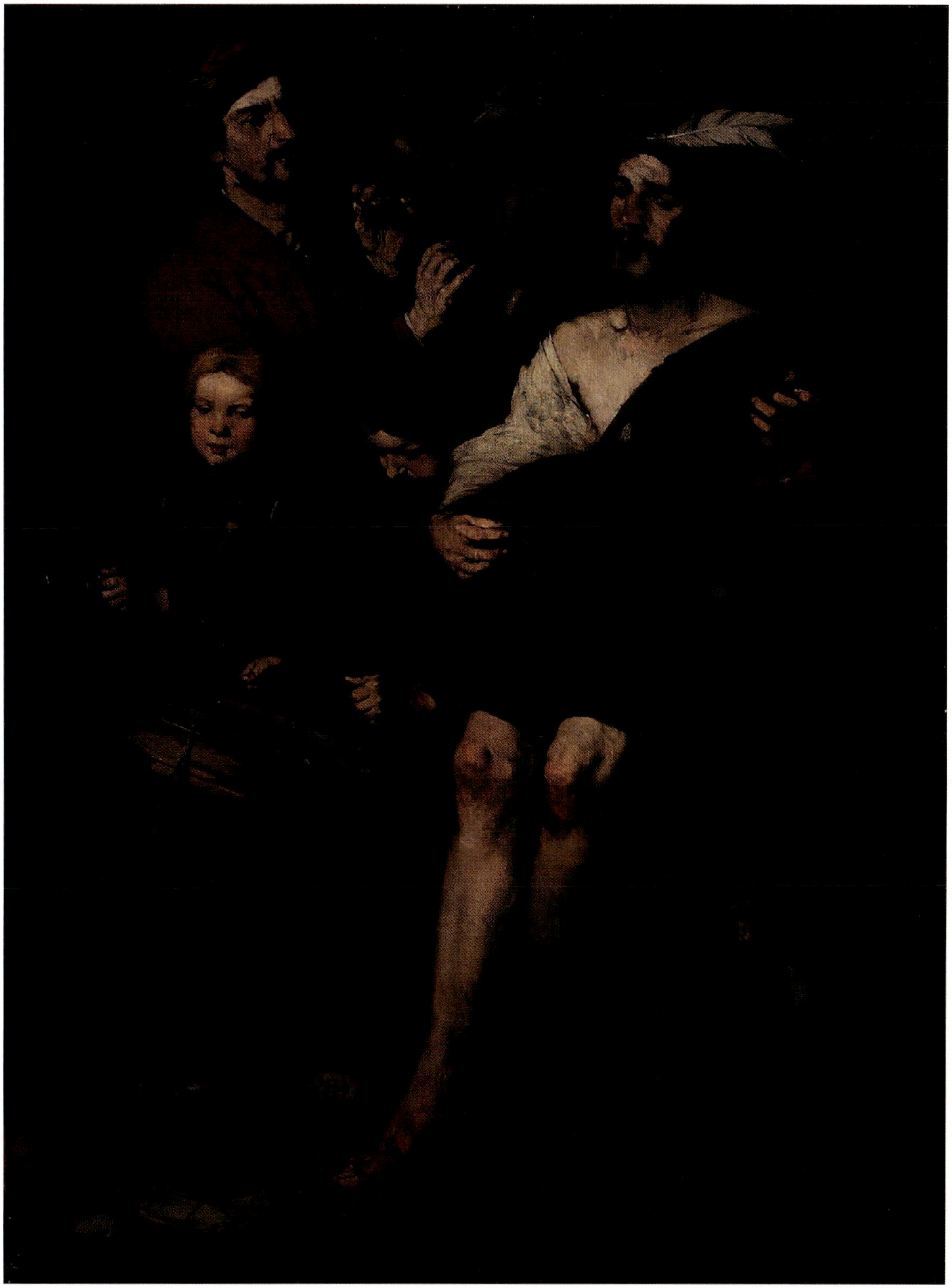

and Earth Unveiled: European Treasures from the Tanenbaum Collection*, cat.102; 51, *122*
Hamilton, Art Gallery of Hamilton, 24 September 2011–15 January 2012, *Masters of French Realism*
Hamilton, Art Gallery of Hamilton, 9 February 2013–9 February 2014, *The Painter Pictured: French Nineteenth-Century Paintings and Portrait Photographs*

Geometer
Paris, Galerie Bernheim Jeune, 1890, *Exposition T. Ribot*, cat.165
Paris, Bernheim Jeune & Cie, 1911, *Exposition Ribot*, cat.5
Hamilton, Art Gallery of Hamilton, 28 May 2005–28 May 2006, *Heaven and Earth Unveiled: European Treasures from the Tanenbaum Collection*, cat.98; 51, *121*
Hamilton, Art Gallery of Hamilton, 24 September 2011–15 January 2012, *Masters of French Realism*

Death of a Saint
Paris, École des Beaux-Arts, 1892, *Exposition Th. Ribot*, cat.40 (? *Le Lapidé*, 57 × 72 cm)
Hamilton, Art Gallery of Hamilton, 28 May 2005–28 May 2006, *Heaven and Earth Unveiled: European Treasures from the Tanenbaum Collection*, cat.96; 59, *85*
Hamilton, Art Gallery of Hamilton, 15 December 2007–21 September 2008, *The Word Made Flesh: Images of Devotion*
Hamilton, Art Gallery of Hamilton, 24 September 2011–15 January 2012, *Masters of French Realism*

Bibliography

Coutu, Jean. "Théodule Ribot, peintre," 2 vols. Ph.D. dissertation, Université de Paris, 1965.
Fourcaud, Louis de. *Théodule Ribot, sa vie et ses œuvres*. Paris: L. Baschet, 1885.
Luxenberg, Alisa. *The Galerie Espagnole and the Museo Nacional 1838–1853: Saving Spanish Art, or the Politics of Patrimony*. Aldershot: Ashgate, 2008.
Sertat, Raoul. *Exposition Théodule Ribot*. Paris: E. Ménard, 1892.
Villot, Frédéric. *Notice des tableaux exposés dans les galeries du Musée national du Louvre. 1ère partie: École d'Italie et d'Espagne.* Paris: Vinchon, 1852, 257–64.
Weisberg, Gabriel P. "Théodule Ribot: Popular Imagery and *The Little Milkmaid*," *Bulletin of the Cleveland Museum of Art* vol.63 (October 1976): 253–63.
-----. *The Realist Tradition: French Painting and Drawing, 1830–1900*. Cleveland: Cleveland Museum of Art, 1980, 49, 122–25, 309.

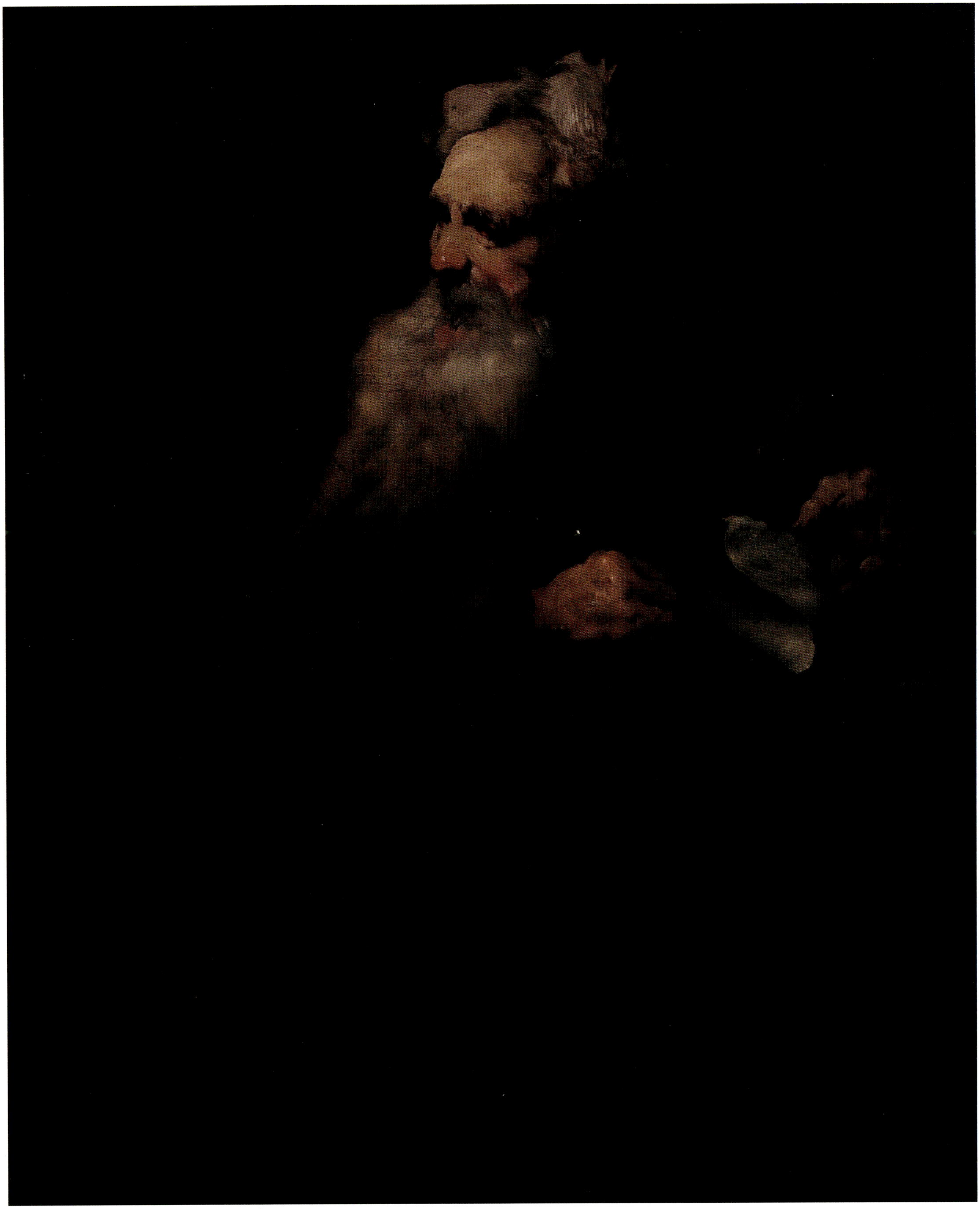

19

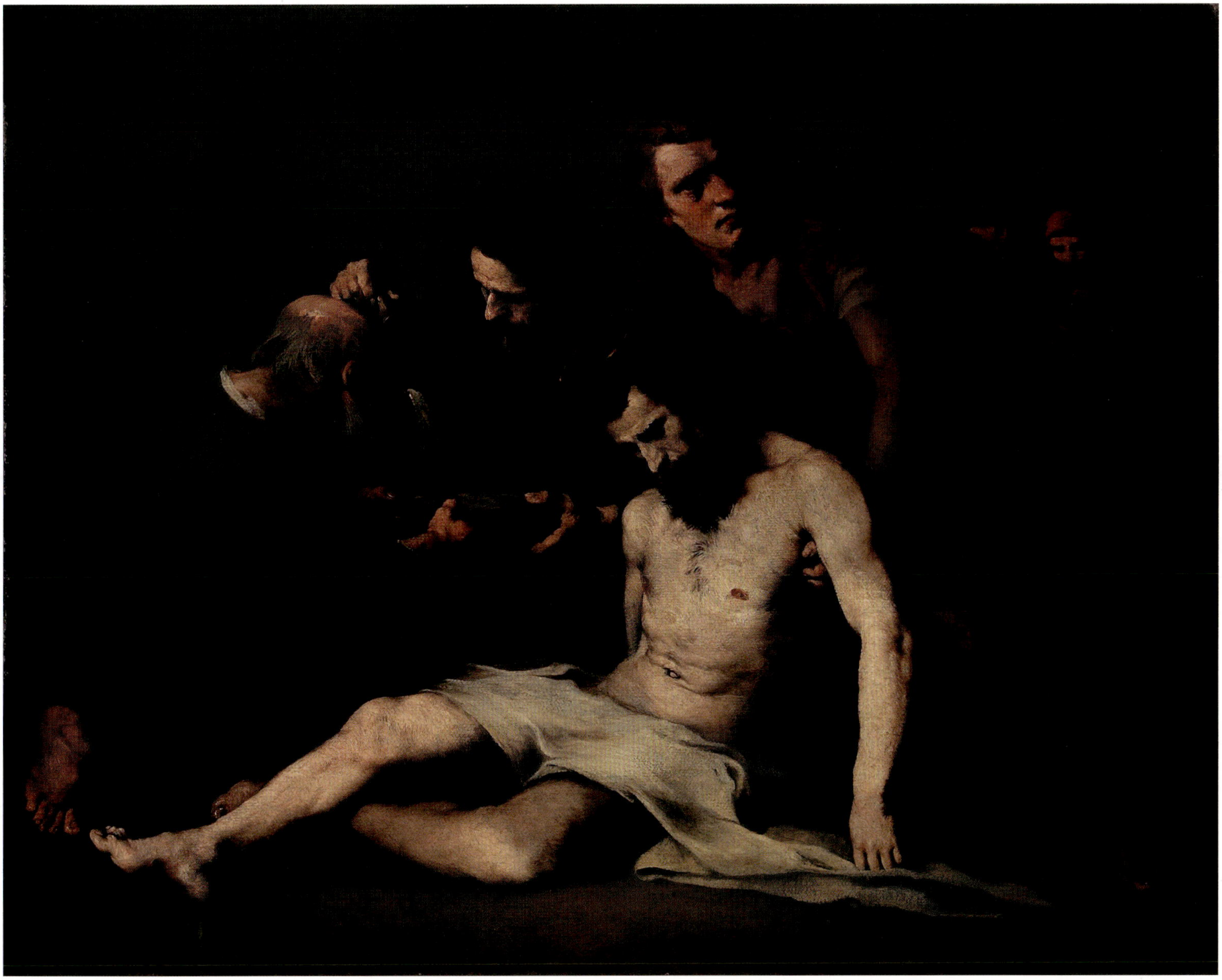

20

Gustave Doré (French • 1832–1883)

21 — The Triumph of Christianity over Paganism

1868 • oil on canvas • 300 × 200 cm • s.d.l.l. Gv Doré/1868 • Inv.2002.33.18

22 — Spanish Street Scene

c.1869 • oil on canvas • 129.5 × 194 cm • s.l.l. Gv Doré • Inv.2002.33.16

23 — Terror

1879 • bronze • 58.4 × 12 × 12 cm • s.base below snake G. Dore • Inv.2002.33.107

24 — The Monk's Dream

1880 • oil on canvas • 241.5 × 303 cm • s.d.l.l. Gv Doré/1880 • Inv.2002.33.19

Doré was a prolific printmaker, an ambitious painter, and a productive sculptor. The three paintings and one sculpture discussed here give insight into the religious subject matter that dominated his output, as well as the Spanish subjects that attracted his attention for decades. At one point in their history, the two religious paintings were also exhibited at the Doré Gallery, an exhibition space the artist cofounded in London in 1867. Doré attracted considerable international interest for his book illustrations, and from 1848 he regularly exhibited paintings at Salon exhibitions. He was in such high demand as an artist that two London-based entrepreneurs offered him an exclusive contract for his works. James Liddle Fairless and George Lord Beeforth set up an agreement with Doré, and *The Triumph of Christianity over Paganism* (cat.21) was the first of many works they commissioned. Fairless and Beeforth showed the painting first at the German Gallery in London, and then at the gallery named for Doré. *The Triumph of Christianity* remained on view at the gallery on a regular basis, and it attracted a broad viewing and paying public. In the following years, Doré executed a number of other large-scale religious works that also went on exhibition in London, including *The Monk's Dream* (cat.24), which was displayed at the Doré Gallery for the first time in 1881 and entitled *The Day Dream*. The paintings were also reproduced in engravings and the gallery managed the robust sales of such prints. The market value of Doré's name and oeuvre was such that his paintings remained on view in London well after his death in 1883, and an estimated 2.5 million people went to see the approximately fifty-nine of his works that were displayed at the gallery until it closed in 1892.

The possibilities of seeing Doré's large-scale works did not end there. By October 1892, *The Triumph of Christianity over Paganism* and *The Monk's Dream* were on tour in the United States as part of the "Doré Gallery" mounted first in the basement at Carnegie Music Hall in New York City and then at the Art Institute in Chicago. Some of the works were then shown in Boston, again in New York, and after the venue closed in Philadelphia only sixteen of the works were shipped back to London. *The Triumph of Christianity* and *The Monk's Dream* were among those that remained in the United States, where they were placed in storage. The works were effectively the possession of the U.S. Import Company that managed first their transportation and then storage until 1927 when the company stopped paying the bills. As tastes changed and there was renewed interest in Doré's work, in 1947 his paintings were "rediscovered" in storage in Manhattan and then sold to various collections.

Significant for the appeal of Doré's work during his lifetime was his ability to offer viewers a personal connection with his subject matter, whether he was depicting a commonplace scene in a Spanish town, or the challenges of a monk's life, or a dramatic scene of judgment. As spectators we are invited to ask ourselves how we would respond to the spiritual and moral decisions Doré presents. In *The Triumph of Christianity over Paganism*, Christ appears surrounded by an aureole of light and hundreds of angels. The archangel Michael, with his sword and shield, mediates between the realm of heaven and the sphere of pagan deities below. The most prominent figure is Zeus with his lightning bolt, and he is surrounded by figures from Celtic, Egyptian, Greco-Roman, Babylonian, and other cultures. Zeus's gold crown falls into the dark abyss that is also closest to the spectator standing before the large painting. Deities from a range of global traditions have been judged and found wanting. They will follow the plight of the crown into the dark unknown. Doré asks viewers to decide for themselves what path they choose to follow. *The Monk's Dream* invites the spectator to identify with a similar question. Doré presents the monk as a life-size figure, with darkened, hollowed-out eyes and veins pulsing in his forehead. He sits apart from the other monks, playing music that accompanies their procession. But he is distracted by either a wish or a memory that appears as a woman in diaphanous clothes. The monk looks out to the viewer and seems to ask what we suggest he do in response to the dilemma before him.[1]

Doré's works combined a theatrical use of light with the strong graphic abilities he developed throughout his successful career in book illustration. The dramatic power of a moment of decision comes into play also in his secular subjects such as *Spanish Street Scene* (cat.22). As two well-dressed young women enter a church, they walk past numerous figures of all ages and abilities that request their help. Doré appears to present us with

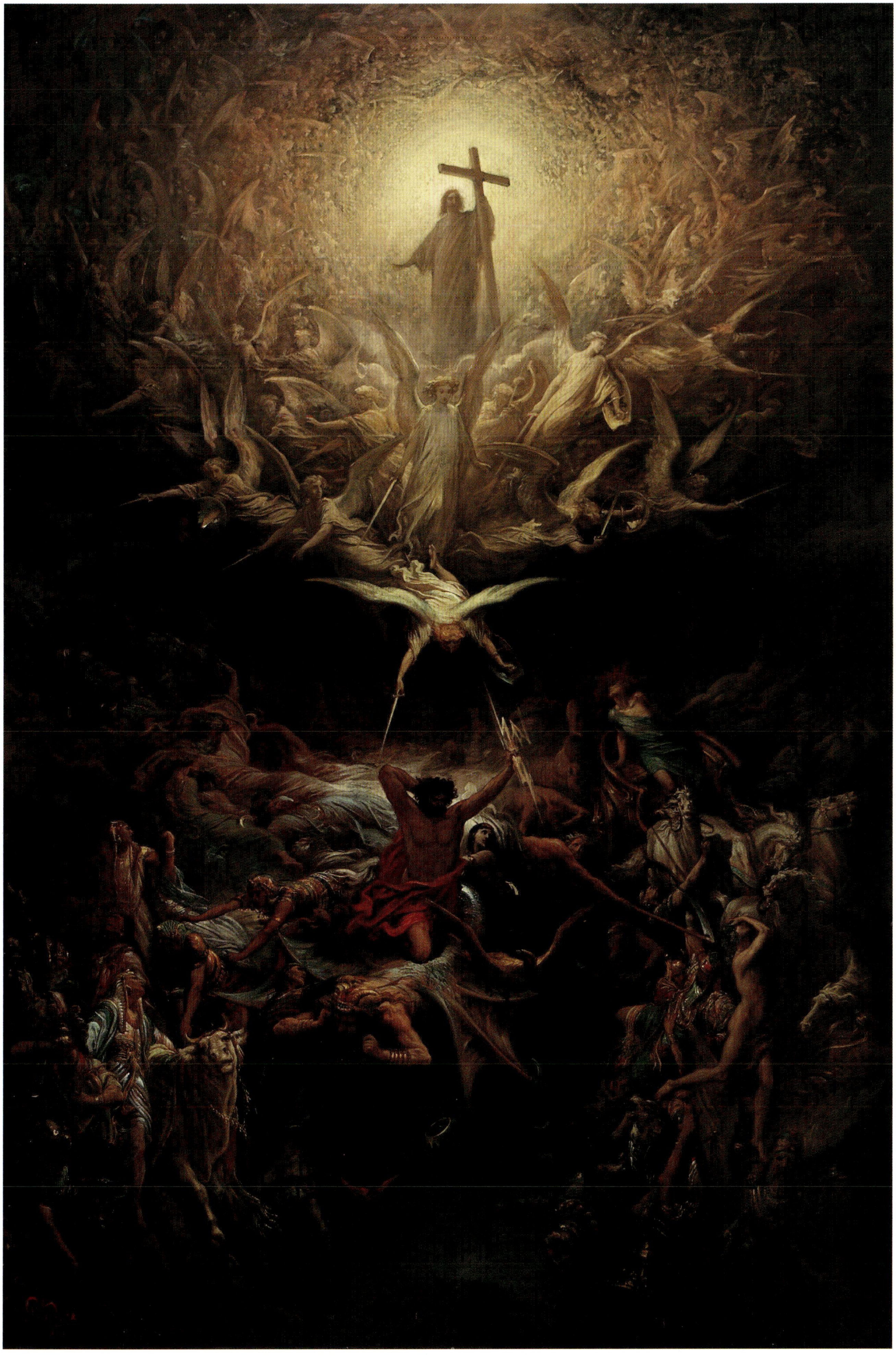

a genre scene that draws upon his first-hand experiences during two trips to Spain in 1855 and 1861–62. Implicit in Doré's scene of everyday life, though, is a larger moral question, one that asks whether the two women will help those in need in their surrounding community. A dramatic and decisive moment is also significant for Doré's sculpture *Terror* (cat.23), a work he first exhibited in plaster at the Salon of 1879. His subject for this work has been variously interpreted and may represent the religious story of Hagar, an Egyptian woman who served Sarah and who gave birth to a son, Ishmael, fathered by Sarah's husband Abraham. Mother and child were cast out of their community, and Doré presents Hagar's efforts to protect her son from a predatory snake. Scriptures narrate the role of divine intervention assisting Hagar and Ishmael in their plight, and again Doré's engaging, theatrical approach to a subject invites viewers to reflect on the moral choices in their own lives.

[1] Doré painted a second work, *The Neophyte* (c.1880–83), as a pendant subject to *The Monk's Dream*; both paintings were inspired by Frère Angel, a figure in George Sand's novel *Spiridon* (1839). *The Neophyte* is now in the City Art Collection, Department of Cultural Affairs, City of Los Angeles (P-420).

Provenance

The Triumph of Christianity over Paganism
London, Messrs. Fairless/Beeforth, Doré Gallery, 1868
U.S. Import Company, c.1898
New York, Manhattan Storage and Warehouse Co., 28 October 1947, lot 20
San Francisco, Albert F. Roller, by 1947
San Francisco, George Whitney Jr.
San Francisco, Chester Helms
New York, Sotheby's, 30 October 1980, lot 40
Toronto, Joey and Toby Tanenbaum, 1980–2002

Spanish Street Scene
New York, H. Shickman Gallery
Toronto, Joey and Toby Tanenbaum, 1970–2002

Terror
London, Anthony Roth Fine Arts
Toronto, Joey and Toby Tanenbaum, 1985–2002

The Monk's Dream
London, Messrs. Fairless/Beeforth, Doré Gallery, 1880–81
U.S. Import Company, c.1898
New York, Manhattan Storage and Warehouse Co., 28 October 1947, lot 19
London, Christie's, 29 November 1991, lot 51
Toronto, Joey and Toby Tanenbaum, 1991–2002

Exhibition History

The Triumph of Christianity over Paganism
London, German Gallery, 1868, *Doré Exhibition*
London, Doré Gallery, 1869–92, cat.23
New York, Carnegie Music Hall, October 1892–March 1893; New York, Old Armory, 1893–94; Chicago, Art Institute of Chicago, 21 January–4 October 1896, *Doré Gallery*, cat.8
Hamilton, Art Gallery of Hamilton, 28 May 2005–28 May 2006, *Heaven and Earth Unveiled: European Treasures from the Tanenbaum Collection*, cat.37; 31, *93* (as *Triumph of Christianity*)
Hamilton, Art Gallery of Hamilton, 9 February 2013–9 February 2014, *The Painter Pictured: French Nineteenth-Century Paintings and Portrait Photographs*
Ottawa, National Gallery of Canada, 13 June–14 September 2014, *Gustave Doré (1832–1883): Master of Imagination*, cat.238; *273*

Spanish Street Scene
New York, H. Shickman Gallery, February 1970, *The Neglected 19th Century: An Exhibition of French Paintings*, cat.11 (reproduced)
Ottawa, National Gallery of Canada, 26 May–10 September 1978; Victoria, Art Gallery of Greater Victoria, 19 October–3 December 1978; Edmonton, Edmonton Art Gallery, 15 December 1978–14 January 1979; Calgary, Glenbow-Alberta Institute, 3 February–22 March 1979; Montreal, Montreal Museum of Fine Arts, 5 April–13 May 1979; Toronto, Art Gallery of Ontario, 15 June–29 July 1979, *The Other Nineteenth Century: Paintings and Sculpture in the Collection of Mr. and Mrs. Joseph M. Tanenbaum*, cat.24, *87*
Hamilton, Art Gallery of Hamilton, 28 May 2005–28 May 2006; Victoria, Art Gallery of Greater Victoria, 25 January–11 May 2008, *Heaven and Earth Unveiled: European Treasures from the Tanenbaum Collection*, cat.36; 55–56, *130–31*

Terror
Hamilton, Art Gallery of Hamilton, 28 May 2005–28 May 2006, *Heaven and Earth Unveiled: European Treasures from the Tanenbaum Collection*, cat.165
Hamilton, Art Gallery of Hamilton, 9 February 2013–9 February 2014, *The Painter Pictured: French Nineteenth-Century Paintings and Portrait Photographs*

The Monk's Dream
London, Doré Gallery, 1881, cat.18 (as *Day Dream*)
New York, Carnegie Music Hall, October 1892–March 1893; New York, Old Armory, 1893–94; Chicago, Art Institute of Chicago, 21 January–4 October 1896, *Doré Gallery*, cat.10 (as *Day Dream*)
Hamilton, Art Gallery of Hamilton, 28 May 2005–28 May 2006, *Heaven and Earth Unveiled: European Treasures from the Tanenbaum Collection*, cat.34; 31–32, *94*
Hamilton, Art Gallery of Hamilton, 15 December 2007–21 September 2008, *The Word Made Flesh: Images of Devotion*
Hamilton, Art Gallery of Hamilton, 9 February 2013–9 February 2014, *The Painter Pictured: French Nineteenth-Century Paintings and Portrait Photographs*
Ottawa, National Gallery of Canada, 13 June–14 September 2014, *Gustave Doré (1832–1883): Master of Imagination*, cat.230; *263*

Bibliography

Clapp, Samuel F., and Nadine Lehni. "Une introduction à la sculpture de Gustave Doré," *Bulletin de la Société de l'histoire de l'art français* (1991): 219–53 (229, 245–46).
Descriptive Catalogue of the Great Pictures by Gustave Doré. London: Doré Gallery, 1891, 6, 42–44, 61–68.
Fusco, Peter. "Gustave Doré," in Peter Fusco and H.W. Janson, eds. *The Romantics to Rodin: French Nineteenth-Century Sculpture from North American Collections*. New York: G. Braziller, 1980, 238–39.
Haskell, Francis. "Doré's London," in *Past and Present in Art and Taste: Selected Essays*. New Haven: Yale University Press, 1987, 129–40.
Kaenel, Philippe. *Gustave Doré (1832–1883): Master of Imagination*. Ottawa: National Gallery of Canada, 2014, 242, 262–65, 272–73.
Renonciat, Annie. *La Vie et l'œuvre de Gustave Doré*. Paris: ACR Édition, 1983.
Roosevelt, Blanche. *Life and*

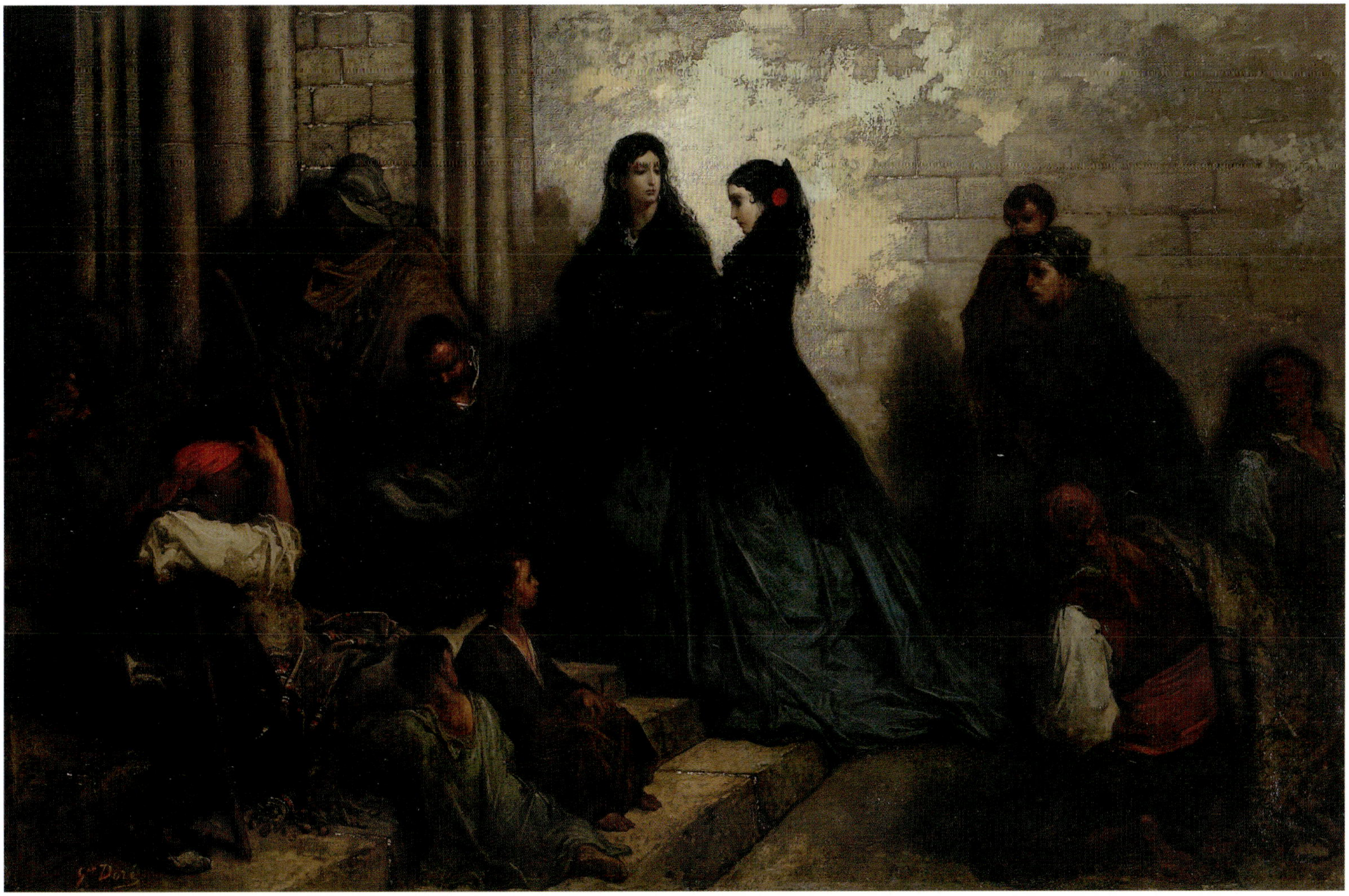

22

Reminiscences of Gustave Doré. New York: Cassel and Company, 1885, 346.
Zafran, Eric, Robert Rosenblum, and Lisa Small. *Fantasy and Faith: The Art of Gustave Doré*. New York: Dahesh Museum of Art, 2007, 65–89, 139, 169–70.

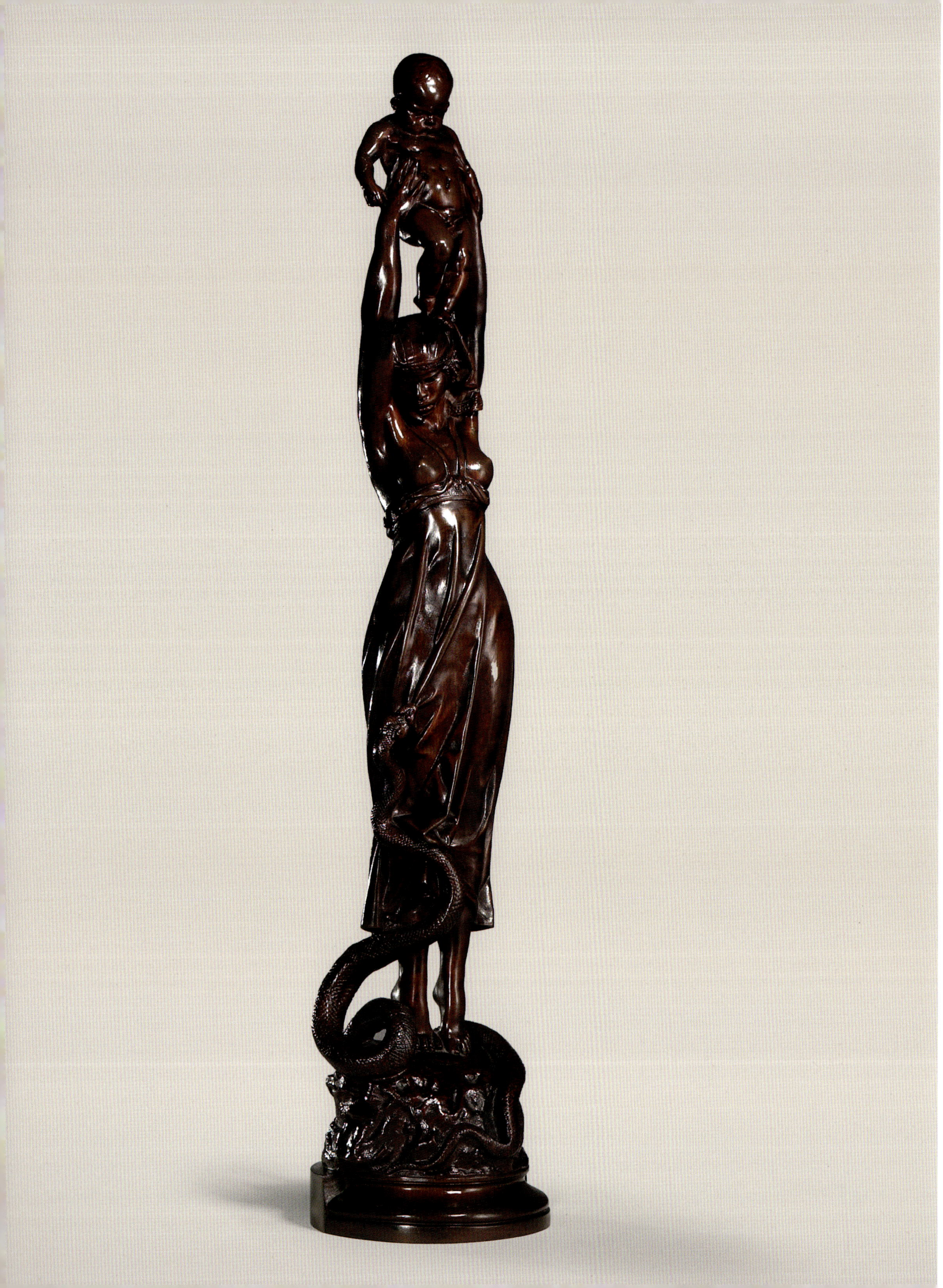

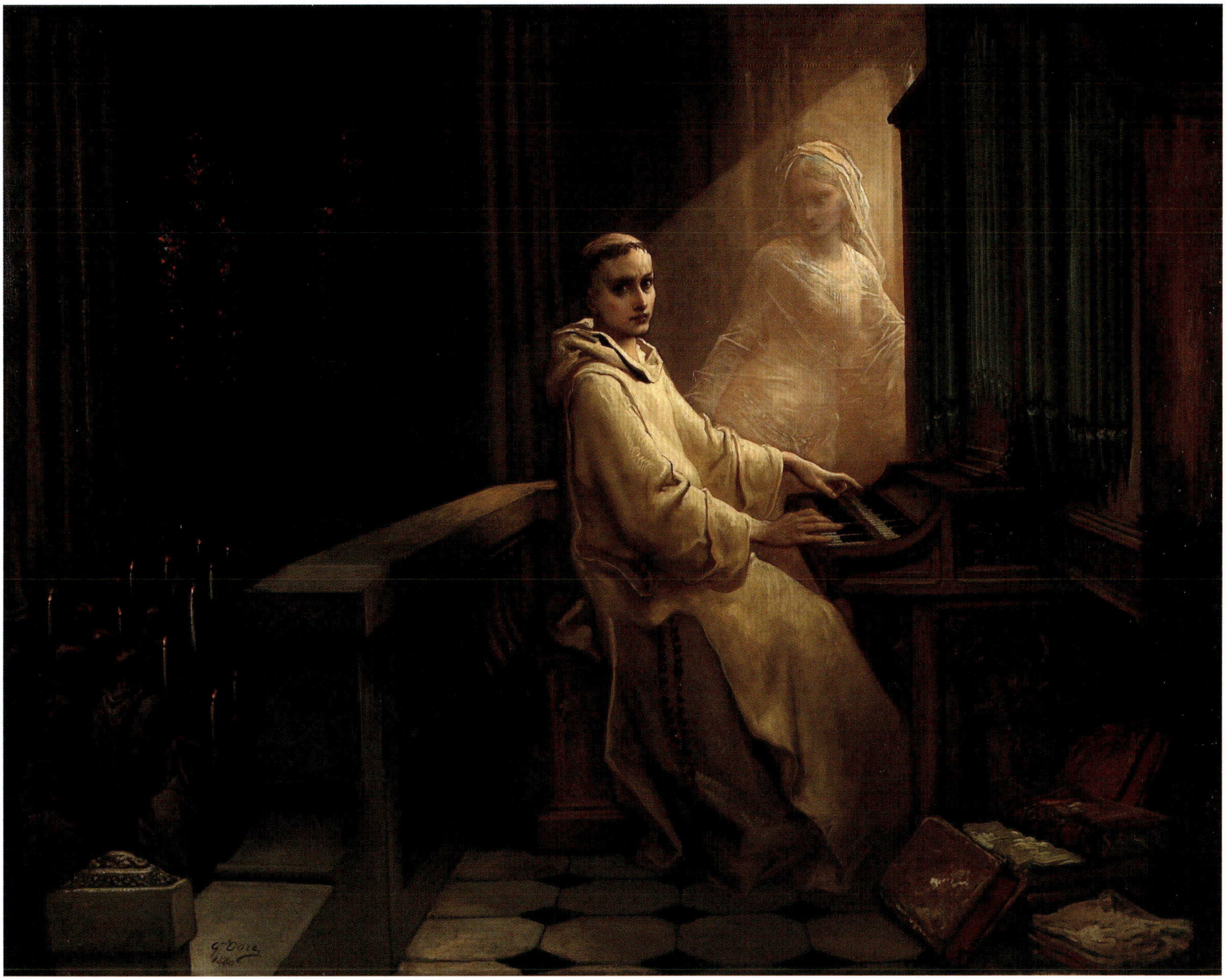

24

Alphonse Legros (English • 1837–1911)

25 — Spanish Cantors

1870 • oil on canvas • 176 × 216.2 cm • s.d.l.l. A. Legros 1870 • Inv.2002.33.35

When Legros was at work on this painting in England in 1870, his studio practice brought together two principles that, at least on the surface, would seem to be in tension with one another. He undertook both a close study of live models and also emphasized the role of memory. Legros's interest in descriptive details—the architectural elements of a religious space, the fabrics of liturgical vestments, the expressive physiognomy of his sitters—have often led people to assume his paintings present a particular historical moment or at least the more generalized cultural context that his own title for a work would imply. Legros posed this very challenge to his audience when he entitled this painting *Spanish Cantors* and exhibited it in London at the Royal Academy in 1871. The nine men present a range of social types, dress, and accessories. The three figures in the center of the composition appear in lay clothing, another man appears as a tonsured cleric, one man wears a black cap, and the two in front wear miters, the liturgical headdresses typically worn by bishops on formal occasions. The cello leaning casually to the left of the composition implies music, and the man on the far right holds a wand loosely in his hand. This could be a baton to lead a musical performance, but neither of the two books that are visible seems to be the appropriate scale for religious songbooks. If the men were singing in habit we would expect to see them in a choir, but they appear neither in choir stalls nor behind an altar. Rather the pulpit on the far left suggests they are seated in the high tribune. When Legros developed this composition he drew upon his experiences traveling in Spain a decade earlier, in the fall of 1860. In the year immediately following that trip he captured many of his impressions of Spanish masses in a series of etchings.[1] In those works Legros was far more literal in his presentation of liturgical practices within the well-defined spaces of religious architecture. His early artistic education at the "Petite École" in Paris, however, placed a strong emphasis on visual memory as a source of individual expression, and Legros continued to foster these skills for the rest of his career.

It may well have been Legros's ambiguous merging of secular figures and religious subject matter that appealed to the British collectors Martha Mary Smith (1835–1919) and her husband Thomas Eustace Smith (1831–1903), as *Spanish Cantors* was one of three works they bought directly from the artist. They also acquired a landscape (current location unknown) and *Blessing the Sea*, which Legros exhibited at the Royal Academy in 1873 (Sheffield, Graves Art Gallery). Eustacia, as Martha was commonly known to contemporaries, was the one principally responsible for selecting works for the couple's art collection, which included works by prominent British artists of the period, including Watts, Leighton, and Burne-Jones. By the mid-1870s, Legros's *Spanish Cantors* hung in the Smiths' new home at 52 Princes Gate, across from Hyde Park, where it was set within an elaborate interior decorative scheme that Whistler viewed as the benchmark for his own achievement, the "Peacock Room," commissioned by collector Frederick Leyland for his own house just footsteps away at number 49. From 1863, when Legros first moved from Paris to London, he was well regarded by contemporary British collectors and artists. The acquisition of *Spanish Cantors* for the notable Smith collection indicates the status of his reputation, which continued to grow after 1876 when he was appointed as a professor at the Slade School of Art.

[1] Frances Seymour Haden acquired early states of Legros's etchings *Procession in a Spanish Church* and *Spanish Cantors* in December 1860 (Poulet-Malassis 1877, nos.49 and 59).

Provenance

London, Thomas Eustace Smith and Martha Mary [Eustacia] Smith (née Dalrymple)

London, Sotheby's, 13 June 1934, Alexander Henderson, 1st Lord Faringdon sale

London, Sotheby's, 22 June 1988, lot 370 (as *Emile Bougaud, Bishop of Laval, Leading a Meeting of Other Bishops*)

Toronto, Joey and Toby Tanenbaum, 1988–2002

Exhibition History

London, Royal Academy of Arts, 1871, cat.187

Hamilton, Art Gallery of Hamilton, 28 May 2005–28 May 2006, *Heaven and Earth Unveiled: European Treasures from the Tanenbaum Collection*, cat.73; 58–59, *136*.

Hamilton, Art Gallery of Hamilton, 15 December 2007–21 September 2008, *The Word Made Flesh: Images of Devotion*

Bibliography

Geiger, Monique, ed. *Alphonse Legros, peintre et graveur, 1837–1911*. Dijon: Musée des Beaux-Arts, 1957.

McConkey, Kenneth. *Impressionism in Britain*. London: Barbican Art Gallery, 1995, 14.

Poulet-Malassis, Auguste, and Alphonse Wyatt Thibaudeau. *Catalogue raisonné de l'œuvre gravé de M. Alphonse Legros, 1855–1877*. Paris: J. Baur, 1877.

Selzer, Andrew. "Alphonse Legros: The Development of an Archaic Visual Vocabulary in Nineteenth-Century Art," Ph.D. dissertation, State University of New York at Binghamton, 1980.

Weisberg, Gabriel P. *The Realist Tradition: French Painting and Drawing, 1830–1900*. Cleveland: Cleveland Museum of Art, 1980, 115–17, 298–99.

Wilcox, Timothy. "The Aesthete Expunged: The Career and Collection of T. Eustace Smith, M.P." *Journal of the History of Collecting* vol.5 no.1 (1993): 43–57.

-----. *Alphonse Legros, 1837–1911*. Dijon: Musée des Beaux-Arts, 1988.

-----. "Alphonse Legros (1837–1911): Aspects of His Life and Work," Ph.D. dissertation, University of London, 1980.

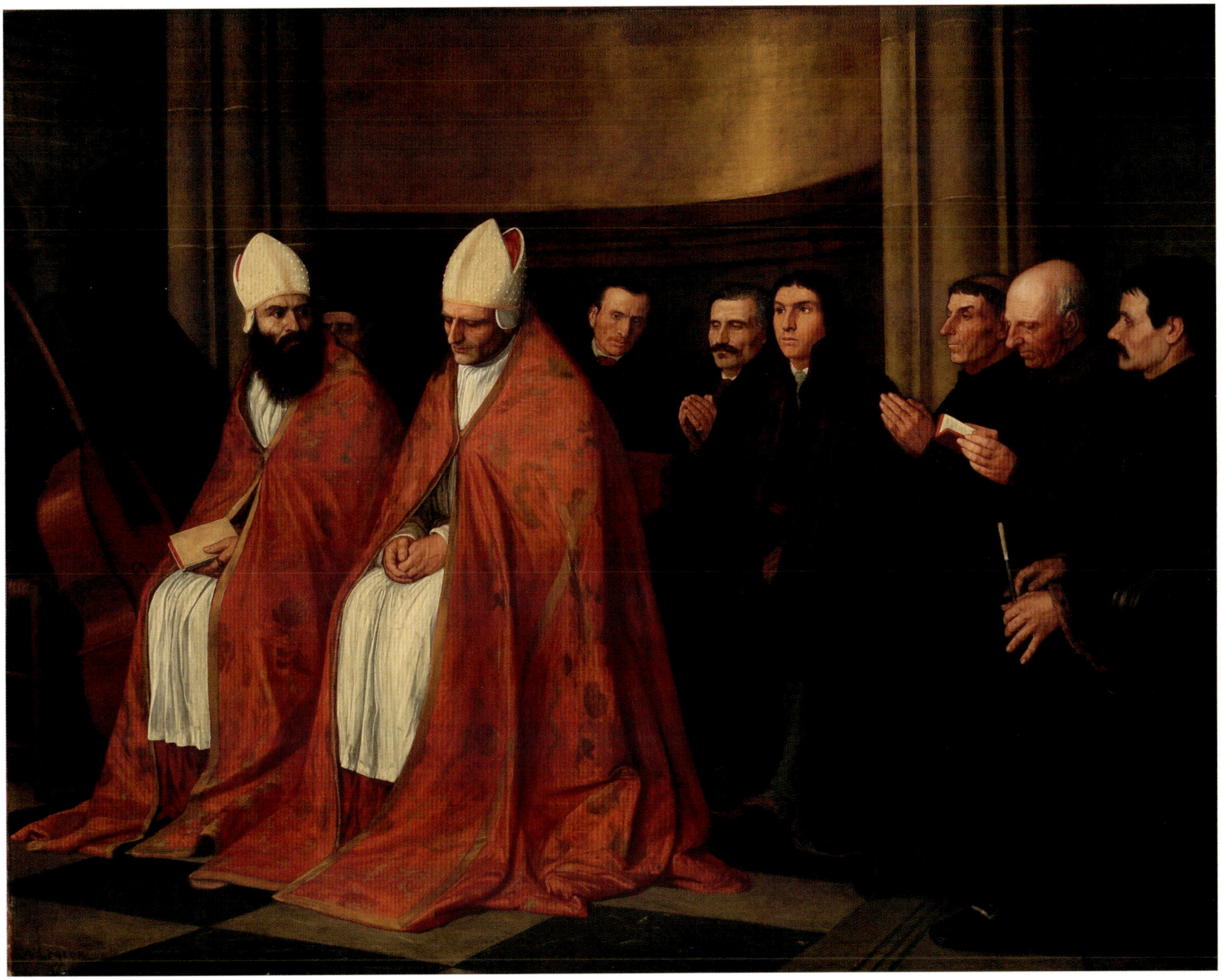

Antonio Ciseri (Swiss • 1821–1891)

26 — Transport of the Body of Christ

after 1870 • oil on canvas • 104 × 152.4 cm • s.l.r. A. Ciseri f. • Inv.2002.33.11

This painting relates to one of the commissions Ciseri received for churches in his native Switzerland. Ciseri moved to Florence in 1833 and began studies at the Accademia di Belle Arti the following year. He honed his skills over the following decade, won the triennial competition in 1843, and had developed a solid reputation by the end of the 1840s. Ciseri then began receiving commissions for religious works that would hang in churches in the Swiss canton of Ticino where he was born. He painted a *Pietà* for the church of Magadino (1850–51) and *St. Anthony Abbot* for the church in Ronco sopra Ascona (1859–60). Ciseri maintained a studio in Florence, where he also received a commission for *The Martyrdom of the Maccabees* (1852–63) for the Florentine church of Santa Felicità. With each of these commissions, Ciseri's work is often connected with a veristic approach. Rather than follow heroic traditions, he presented sacred subjects in a direct manner that engaged his contemporaries. In 1864, Ciseri received a commission from lawyer Bartolomeo Rusca and began work on *Transport of the Body of Christ*, a painting that would occupy his attention for the following six years. It was to hang in the Santuario della Madonna del Sasso in Locarno, an old town at the north end of Lake Maggiore. Set at a high elevation of 1148 ft (350 m), the church was famed both for its majestic panoramas and its art, including a *Flight into Egypt* (1520) by Italian architect and painter Bramantino (c.1465–1530). Ciseri's aim was that his own religious paintings would rival the achievements of such previous artists. He took his time completing *Transport of the Body of Christ*, and executed numerous preparatory works, including *bozzetti* (oil sketches), compositional drawings, and studies of individual figures, some of which are now in the prints and drawings department of the Uffizi gallery in Florence. In his careful preparatory work, Ciseri explored various possibilities for how he might present his subject.

The bearing or transportation of Christ's body is part of the Passion, the events leading up to and following the Crucifixion. The episode follows the Deposition or Descent from the Cross, and precedes the Entombment, with which it is sometimes confused. In all of Ciseri's preparatory work it is clear that his interest (and likely the terms of his commission) focused on how Christ's body was carried to the site of the tomb. The grave itself does not appear in his composition, which emphasizes movement across a horizontal plane. The seven figures that accompany Christ traverse a dry and rocky elevated pass. To the left of the composition and above Christ's body are glimpses of the architecture below. Ciseri presents lower sunlight in the later afternoon, light that he uses to emphasize particular areas of the work. These include the emotional expressions of Christ's companions and the Savior's own body. At the foot of that body, Ciseri presents Joseph of Arimathea and Nicodemus carrying the majority of Christ's weight. It was Joseph of Arimathea who secured permission from Pilate to remove Christ from the Cross, and he brought the linen shroud that was used to carry the body. Nicodemus provided the aloes and myrrh that were used to preserve Christ's body. Ciseri's composition emphasizes the significant roles of Joseph of Arimathea and Nicodemus, both of whom were secret followers of Christ and members of the Sanhedrin, the Jewish legislative council in Jerusalem. Ciseri positions St. John the Evangelist as the sole support at Christ's head and, seemingly unaffected by the weight he carries, St. John's primary purpose is to engage the viewer with his plaintive expression. Ciseri depicts the female companions with the greatest emotional responses. This and his use of light, rhetorical gestures, and classicizing drapery, all reveal Ciseri's interest in connecting his work with previous artistic traditions. The Virgin Mary motions to Christ's body as she looks imploringly to heaven. Mary Magdalene is so overwhelmed by emotion she can hardly stand upright and her hair eclipses her face. Ciseri staged the scene carefully and composed each detail, but he always created a sense of immediacy and consistently made historical, religious subjects feel accessible to his viewers. Even before *Transport of the Body of Christ* left Ciseri's studio in Florence, the painting was already attracting attention. Ciseri received several commissions to paint smaller-scale versions, including the one illustrated here that is approximately one half its size.[1]

[1] Another version is in the collection of the Galleria d'Arte Moderna di Palazzo Pitti (after 1868, oil on panel, 80 × 136 cm, Inv. com.358). London-based Italian restorer Raffaello Pinti commmissioned a replica, which was completed in the early 1870s, and the Doré Gallery in London commissioned a replica in 1882. Before he shipped the first painting to Locarno, Ciseri also received a visit from printmaker Charles Cattermole (1832–1900) who came to discuss the production of an engraving.

Provenance

London, Sotheby's, 12 February 1986, lot 53 (as *The Entombment of Christ*)

Toronto, Joey and Toby Tanenbaum, 1986–2002

Exhibition History

Hamilton, Art Gallery of Hamilton, 28 May 2005–28 May 2006; Victoria, Art Gallery of Greater Victoria, 25 January–11 May 2008, *Heaven and Earth Unveiled: European Treasures from the Tanenbaum Collection*, cat.24; 28, *88–89* (as *The Entombment*)

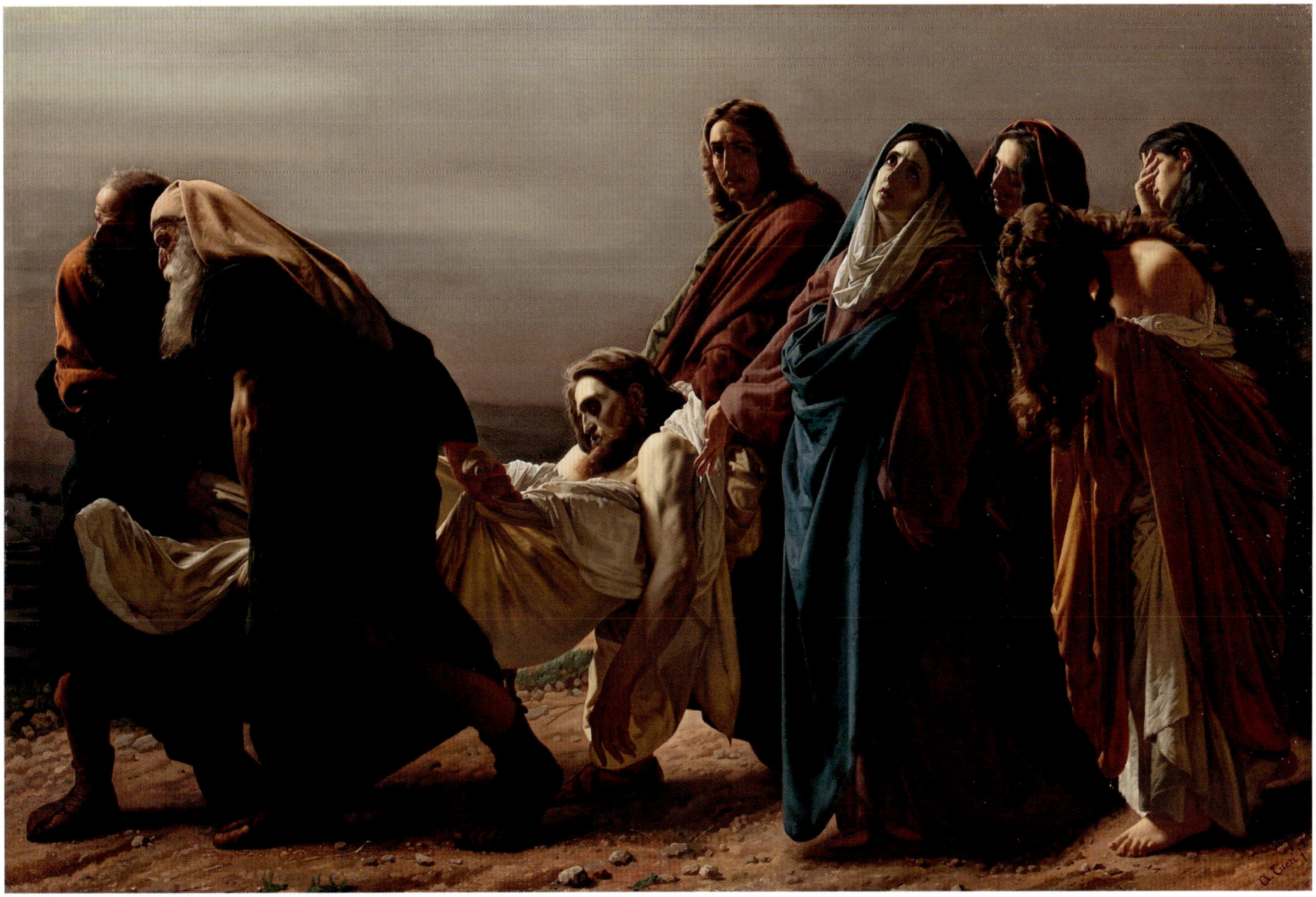

Bibliography

Basignana, L. "Ciseri, Antonio," in Enrico Castelnuovo and Gioacchino Barbera, eds. *La pittura in Italia: l'ottocento*. 2 vols. Milan: Electa, 1991, vol.1, 343, 353.

Bietoletti, Silvestra. "Antonio Ciseri, sensibile interprete della società toscana nella seconda metà dell'ottocento," *Gazzetta antiquaria* vol.10 (1991): 59–64.

Ciseri, Ilaria. "Il volto di Firenze: la città vissuta da Antonio Ciseri," *Arte & storia* vol.11 no.48 (2010): 386–91.

Olson, Roberta J.M. *Ottocento: Romanticism and Revolution in 19th-Century Italian Painting*. New York: American Federation of Arts, 1992, 177.

Spalletti, Ettore. "Antonio Ciseri: da Ronco sopra Ascona a Firenze," *Arte & storia* vol.11 no.48 (2010): 358–85.

-----, and Carlo Sissi. *Omaggio ad Antonio Ciseri, 1821–1891*. Florence: Centro Di, 1991, 66–84.

Vasta, Daniela. *La pittura sacra in Italia nell'ottocento: dal Neoclassicismo al Simbolismo*. Rome: Gangemi, 2012, 94–95, 105.

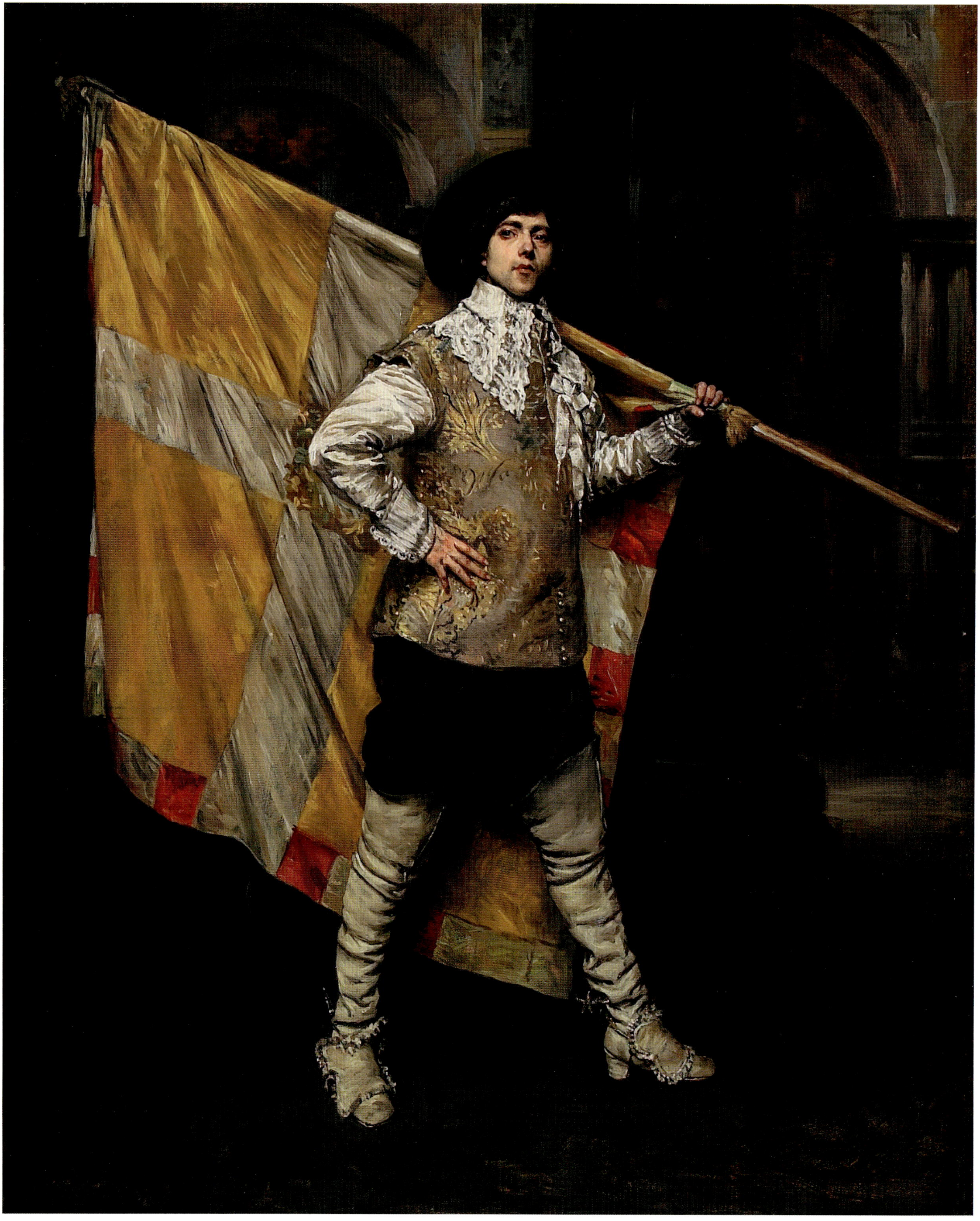

Ferdinand Roybet (French • 1840–1920)

27 — Standard Bearer

c.1870–80 • Oil on wood panel • 81 × 65 cm • s.l.r. F.Roybet • Inv.2002.33.181

A standard bearer was an officer of an army, navy, or militia company who carried the flag or ensign of his group. In Roybet's *Standard Bearer*, the artist isolated the figure, dressed him in finery, and positioned him with legs astride. The group's colorful banner rests easily on his shoulder. This is a figure who is proud of his symbolic role and awaits instructions to march forth in a procession. Roybet's work attracted considerable attention from the first time he exhibited his paintings and etchings at the Paris Salons in the mid-1860s. He dedicated much of his time to historically inspired subjects from 1866 when he received a medal for his painting of a man from the sixteenth century, during the time of King Henri III.[1] Roybet's ability to depict historical dress—as is evident in the silk vest, lace collar, and cuffs in this *Standard Bearer*—was such that contemporaries readily connected his work with the Dutch seventeenth-century artist Frans Hals. Critic Georges Lafenestre wrote in his review of a *Standard Bearer* Roybet exhibited at the Salon of 1897 that one would presume the painting to be an unknown work by Hals if it were not for the modern-looking head.

Roybet quickly became one of the most commercially successful artists of his time, and the popular appeal of his figures in fancy dress was the source of both great acclaim and considerable challenges in the artist's life. Roybet was an admirer of Rembrandt and ultimately emulated much more than the Dutch master's techniques as an etcher. Like Rembrandt, Roybet was an avid collector of furnishings for his home, acquiring an extensive collection of props for his studio. To support his lifestyle, or perhaps because of the standard of living to which Roybet aspired, he negotiated agreements with various dealers that required him to produce a set number of works a month in exchange for a regular stipend. Roybet worked first with the dealers Basset and Moureaux, then developed a longer-term arrangement with Hector Brame (1831–1899), and later worked with Georges Petit (1856–1920). Roybet racked up such considerable debts that in 1877 he had to sell much of his personal collection. He then went bankrupt and in 1884 was evicted from the home he rented from Brame. These personal challenges, like those of Rembrandt who also experienced bankruptcy, in no way inhibited Roybet's artistic success. His skill as a painter, his "extraordinary technique" as Lefenestre had referred to it, meant Roybet was ranked *hors concours*. Beginning in 1868, he had the right to exhibit at Salon exhibitions without submitting his works to the jury. Despite this privileged status, Roybet simply chose not to show his work at the Salon from 1869 until 1892. When he returned, his work was awarded the Salon's medal of honor and he was made a chevalier of the Legion of Honor. During his lifetime, Roybet enjoyed critical acclaim, official recognition from the state, and international attention from private collectors who valued his abilities as a colorist and the facility of his technique, particularly in his paintings of figures in historical costume.

[1] *Un fou sous Henri III* (Salon of 1866, no.1702) is often cited as Roybet's painting of a jester that is in the Musée de Grenoble (Inv.MG1483), but that canvas is signed and dated 1867. The painting from 1866 is in the Musée des Beaux-Arts, Rouen, and currently entitled *Head of a Young Man in Henri III Costume* (Inv.866.11).

Provenance

New York, Schweitzer Gallery

Toronto, Frederick Thom Gallery, 1968

Toronto, Joey and Toby Tanenbaum, 1968–2002

Exhibition History

Hempstead, New York, Emily Lowe Gallery, Hofstra University, *Art Pompier, Anti-Impressionism: 19th Century French Salon Painting*, 22 October–15 December 1974, cat.77, *73*

Ottawa, National Gallery of Canada, 26 May–10 September 1978; Victoria, Art Gallery of Greater Victoria, 19 October–3 December 1978; Edmonton, Edmonton Art Gallery, 15 December 1978–14 January 1979; Calgary, Glenbow-Alberta Institute, 3 February–22 March 1979; Montreal, Montreal Museum of Fine Arts, 5 April–13 May 1979; Toronto, Art Gallery of Ontario, 15 June–29 July 1979, *The Other Nineteenth Century: Paintings and Sculpture in the Collection of Mr. and Mrs. Joseph M. Tanenbaum*, cat.61, *177*

Hamilton, Art Gallery of Hamilton, 28 May 2005–28 May 2006, *Heaven and Earth Unveiled: European Treasures from the Tanenbaum Collection*, cat.122

Bibliography

Burgan, J.P. "F. Roybet," *L'Œuvre d'art* vol.11 (February 1903).

La Chronique des Arts (30 December 1866): 310.

Delannoy, Agnès. *Hommage aux fondateurs: Ferdinand Roybet et Consuelo Fould.* Courbevoie: Musée Roybet-Fould, 1992, 28–32, 46.

Estève, Jean. "La vie et l'œuvre de Ferdinand Roybet 1840–1920," Master's thesis, Université de Paris IV, 1979.

Honoré, Léopold. "Ferdinand Roybet," *Revue du midi* (15 November 1910): 1–16.

Hungerford, Constance Cain. *Ernest Meissonier: Master in his Genre.* New York: Cambridge University Press, 1999.

Lafenestre, Georges. "Les salons de 1897," *Revue des deux mondes* vol.141 (1897): 669–70.

McQueen, Alison. *The Rise of the Cult of Rembrandt: Reinventing an Old Master in Nineteenth-Century France.* Amsterdam: Amsterdam University Press, 2003, 187–89.

Yeide, Nancy. "Hector Brame: An Art Dealer in Nineteenth-Century Paris," *Apollo* vol.433 (March 1998): 40–47.

François Bonvin (French • 1817–1887)

28 — The Indiscreet Servant

1871 • oil on canvas • 52.8 × 35 cm • s.d.l.r. F. Bonvin 1871 • Inv.2002.33.81

Bonvin painted this canvas in London, where he lived in self-imposed exile during the Franco-Prussian War and Commune. He was there among many contemporary French artists, including Carpeaux (see cat.36), Dalou (cats.34 and 35), Monet, and Pissarro, who established themselves in England in 1870-71. Some stayed for a longer period while for others it was the first of a series of visits. Many artists, like Puvis, Manet, Fantin-Latour, and Degas stayed behind in Paris. Some served as soldiers in the National Guard during the Siege while others remained almost entirely sequestered in their studios. London offered Bonvin a welcome reprieve from this tumultuous period in his homeland and afforded him a more stable context to pursue his studio practice. During this time Bonvin developed a connection with art dealer and fellow émigré Paul Durand-Ruel to whom he sold a few paintings. Although the principal figure in *The Indiscreet Servant* is a young woman, Bonvin has intentionally coded the interior domestic space as a masculine domain. A pair of leather boots, placed neatly between the legs of a simple chair, stand in for the absent male, as does the white collar hanging above a discarded shirt and the top hat, the dark form of which rests on the chest of drawers and nearly merges into the back wall. Bonvin emphasizes private correspondence as the key element of this intrusion on intimate space: the letter has been taken from a drawer filled with personal papers, while its protective envelope lies on the floor. Although Bonvin foregrounds "London" as an integral part of his signature and thus reminds us of his own unusual circumstances, he does not posit the scene as a literal depiction of his own experiences. Bonvin first developed his ideas for this painting in an extant watercolor dated January 1871, adding the man's clothing and accessories only in this final composition. Bonvin and his companion Louison Köhler (1850–1935) traveled to England together, and he staged her as his model for this fictive scene. Her features are clearly recognizable from other works, such as *Young Woman with a Mandolin* (1873–74; Cleveland Museum of Art). Köhler stands in as a transgressive young female servant; her open mouth gives voice to the intimate text that breaks the monotony of her domestic work.

In this painting, as in many by Bonvin, we witness his interest in earlier traditions of still-life and genre painting. As early as the Salon of 1849, critics compared Bonvin's works to those of eighteenth-century French artist Chardin. Bonvin had studied and admired the work of Chardin and many Dutch seventeenth-century artists in the Louvre collection. He visited Holland for the first time in 1867 and continued to be inspired by Dutch scenes of everyday life throughout his career. Bonvin found his own means to explore the subject of domestic staff breaching their duties, a subject that appeared in the work of Nicholas Maes and other Dutch artists in the seventeenth century. Bonvin's still lifes, genre scenes, and portraits met with considerable success at the Salons of the 1850s and 1860s, and he was a central figure of the realist movement. He received state commissions and was awarded third- and second-class medals for earlier works in 1849 and 1850. Bonvin was also made a chevalier of the Legion of Honor in June 1870, just weeks prior to the outbreak of war. The timing of this accolade, and his departure for England in late August, makes the challenging circumstances in which he painted *The Indiscreet Servant* that much more poignant. The following year, in August 1871, Bonvin and Köhler returned to France and settled in her hometown of Saint-Germain-en-Laye to the west of Paris.

Provenance

Paris, Galerie Georges Petit, Alexandre Blanc sale, 3–4 December 1906

Paris, Hôtel Drouot, 30 June 1950

London, Sotheby's, 19 June 1963

London, Sotheby's, 2 December 1971

London, Charles Jerdein, 1976

Toronto, Joey and Toby Tanenbaum, 1976–2002

Exhibition History

Ottawa, National Gallery of Canada, 26 May–10 September 1978; Victoria, Art Gallery of Greater Victoria, 19 October–3 December 1978; Edmonton, Edmonton Art Gallery, 15 December 1978–14 January 1979; Calgary, Glenbow-Alberta Institute, 3 February–22 March 1979; Montreal, Montreal Museum of Fine Arts, 5 April–13 May 1979; Toronto, Art Gallery of Ontario, 15 June–29 July 1979, *The Other Nineteenth Century: Paintings and Sculpture in the Collection of Mr. and Mrs. Joseph M. Tanenbaum*, cat.9, *51*

New York, Wheelock Whitney and Company, 26 April–24 May 1984, *François Bonvin, 1817–1887: An Exhibition of Painting*, cat.16

Hamilton, Art Gallery of Hamilton, 28 May 2005–28 May 2006, *Heaven and Earth Unveiled: European Treasures from the Tanenbaum Collection*, cat.13; 66, *147*

Hamilton, Art Gallery of Hamilton, 13 September 2008–4 January 2009, *Blood, Sweat and Tears: Labour in Art*

Hamilton, Art Gallery of Hamilton, 24 September 2011–15 January 2012, *Masters of French Realism*

Bibliography

Denney, Colleen. "Exhibitions in Artist Studios: François Bonvin's 1859 Salon des Refusés," *Gazette des Beaux-Arts* vol.122 (September 1993): 97–108.

Moreau-Nélaton, Étienne. *Bonvin raconté par lui-même.* Paris: H. Laurens, 1927, 78, fig.57.

Weisberg, Gabriel P. *The Realist*

Tradition: French Painting and Drawing, 1830–1900. Cleveland: Cleveland Museum of Art, 1980, 246–47, 273–74.
-----. "François Bonvin's Woman Reading," *Bulletin of the Detroit Institute of Arts* vol.60 nos.3–4 (Winter 1982): 92–99.
-----. *François Bonvin*. Paris: Éditions Geoffroy-Dechaume, 1979.
-----. "The Traditional Realism of François Bonvin," *The Bulletin of the Cleveland Museum of Art* vol.65 no.9 (November 1978): 281–98.
-----. *François Bonvin and the Critics of His Art*. London: Apollo Press, 1974.
-----. "The Paintings of François Bonvin in the Wadsworth Atheneum," *Wadsworth Atheneum Bulletin* vol.6 no.3 (Winter 1970): 40–48.
-----. "François Bonvin and an Interest in Several Painters of the Seventeenth and Eighteenth Centuries," *Gazette des Beaux-Arts* vol.76 (December 1970): 359–66.

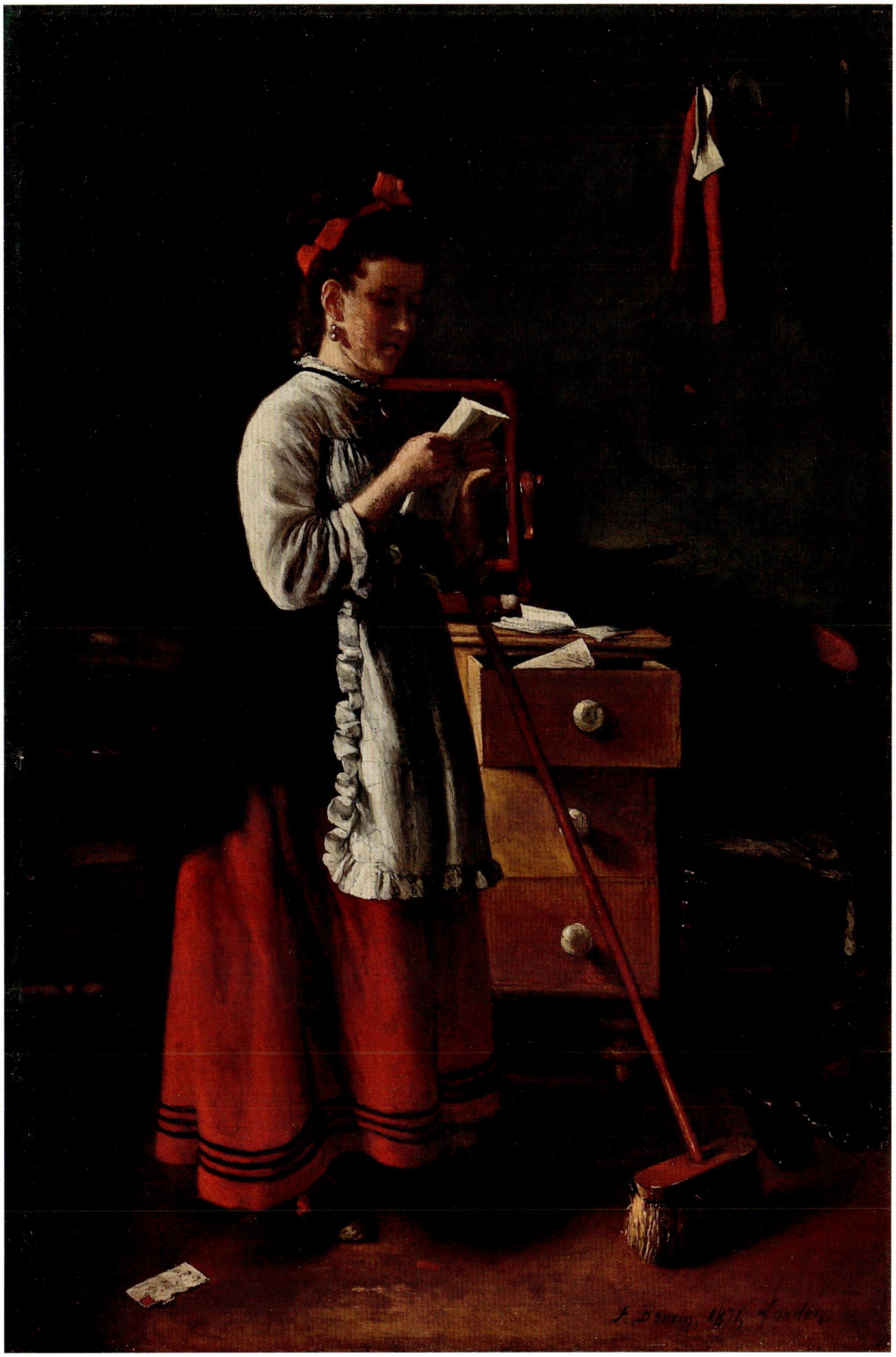

Théobald Chartran (French • 1849–1907)

29 — Oedipus's Farewell to the Corpses of His Wife and Sons

1871 • oil on canvas • 146.5 × 114.8 cm • s.d.l.l. TH. CHARTRAN 1871 • Inv.2002.33.9

For an aspiring history painter in nineteenth-century France, the Prix de Rome was the most sought-after award. The prize was established in 1663 as a Prix Royal, with the first group of artists heading out to the Académie de France in Rome for a period of study that ranged from two to five years. Chartran worked hard to be among the artists honored by the national École des Beaux-Arts, and his *Oedipus's Farewell* gives us rare insight into an artist's experiences in this competition. When he produced this work Chartran was twenty-two years old, and it was the third time he had entered the competition. He had started early knowing that he was only eligible to compete until he was thirty. In 1871 Chartran made it to the third and final round. He had passed the preliminary exams that involved a small-scale sketch of a historical subject painted in a single day, followed by a larger-scale male nude painted over four seven-hour sessions. Chartran was then selected as one of ten artists in the final competition. Each faced the same complex historical narrative and the same scale of canvas as well as paper for their preparatory work. Each also had a limit of twelve hours to produce the drawing followed by seventy-two hours to paint in an individual cell-like studio space. These were very intense circumstances for the young candidates and challenged not only their artistic abilities but also their emotional fortitude. Intuition also played an important role, and when faced with the decision of how to position the canvas—vertically or horizontally—Chartran committed himself to develop his composition on a vertical plane.

Chartran then set to work to present the full range of his skills. The tragic Greek hero Oedipus became a vehicle for Chartran to present his abilities as a draftsman and to show how well he could present the male body, expression, and rhetorical gesture. The emotive power of Oedipus's hand as it hovers over the dead body of his wife (and mother) Jocasta creates the most charged area of the composition. Chartran adhered to the requirements and presented the figures in a shallow space outside the palace in Thebes. He capitalized on his thorough knowledge of ancient Greek polychrome architecture and the ornamentation of shrines. Although Chartran's *Oedipus's Farewell* successfully captured the essence of emotional and physical composure in the face of tragedy, the award that year went to Édouard Troudouze (1848–1907), who presented a less architecturally complex setting and used a horizontal picture plane. Nonetheless, Chartran benefited considerably from this experience and went on to win the Prix de Rome in 1877 for his work *The Sack of Rome by the Gauls*. After Chartran completed his artistic education, he developed an international career, and his abilities as a portraitist attracted notable patrons. While Chartran worked a portion of the year in the United States to fulfill commissions from his growing American clientele, he did not put aside his investment in history painting as some have claimed. He continued to produce history paintings late in his career, and his opinion was much sought after in 1894 during the debate over the Prix de Rome's future (it was not suppressed until 1968). At the same time, Chartran responded to a changing patronage base and developed the rigorous training we witness in *Oedipus's Farewell* into a highly successful career that united portraiture with scenes of contemporary history, such as *The Signing of the Protocol of Peace between the United States and Spain on August 12, 1898* (1899; Washington, D.C., The White House, Gift of Henry Clay Frick).

Provenance

London, Whitford and Hughes Fine Paintings

Toronto, Joey and Toby Tanenbaum, 1984–2002

Exhibition History

Hamilton, Art Gallery of Hamilton, 28 May 2005–28 May 2006, *Heaven and Earth Unveiled: European Treasures from the Tanenbaum Collection*, cat.23; 14–15, *75* (as *The Farewell of Oedipus to the Corpses of His Wife and Sons*)

Toronto, Art Gallery of Toronto, *Drama and Desire: Artists and the Theatre*, 19 June–26 September 2010 (hors catalogue)

Hamilton, Art Gallery of Hamilton, 21 May–5 September 2011, *The French Connection*

Bibliography

Grunchec, Philippe. *Les Concours des prix de Rome de 1797 à 1863*. 2 vols. Paris: École Nationale Supérieure des Beaux-Arts, 1986–89, vol.1, 27–31.

Gsell, Paul. "La suppression du prix de Rome et les opinions de M.M. Chartran, Besnard et Rodin," *La Vie contemporaine et Revue parisienne réunies* vol.4 (1894): 496–516.

Weisberg, Gabriel P. *Against the Modern: Dagnan-Bouveret and the Transformation of the Academic Tradition*. New York: Dahesh Museum of Art, 2002, 39–41.

-----, et al. *Collecting in the Gilded Age: Art Patronage in Pittsburgh, 1890–1910*. Pittsburgh: Frick Art and Historical Center, 1997, 212–24.

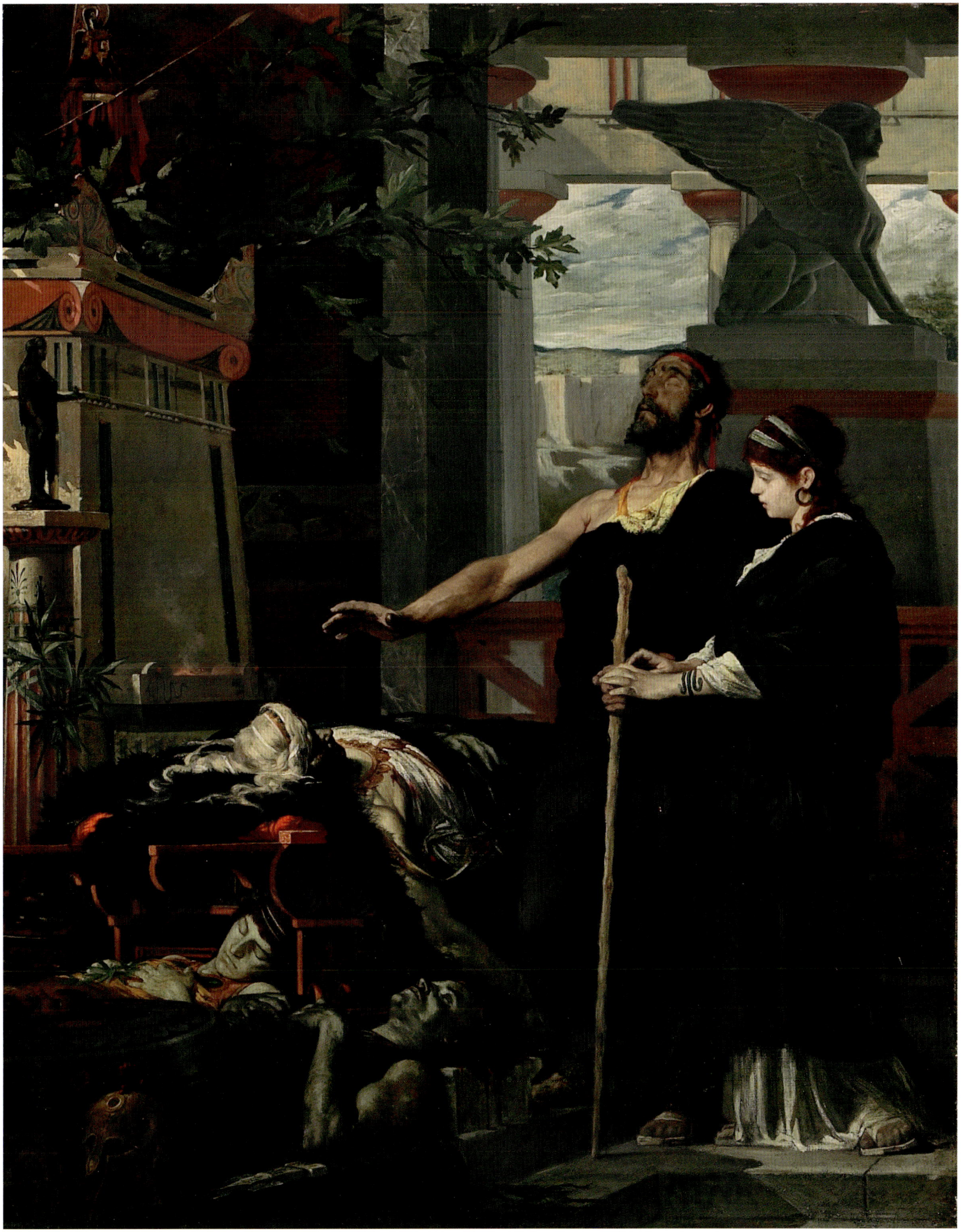

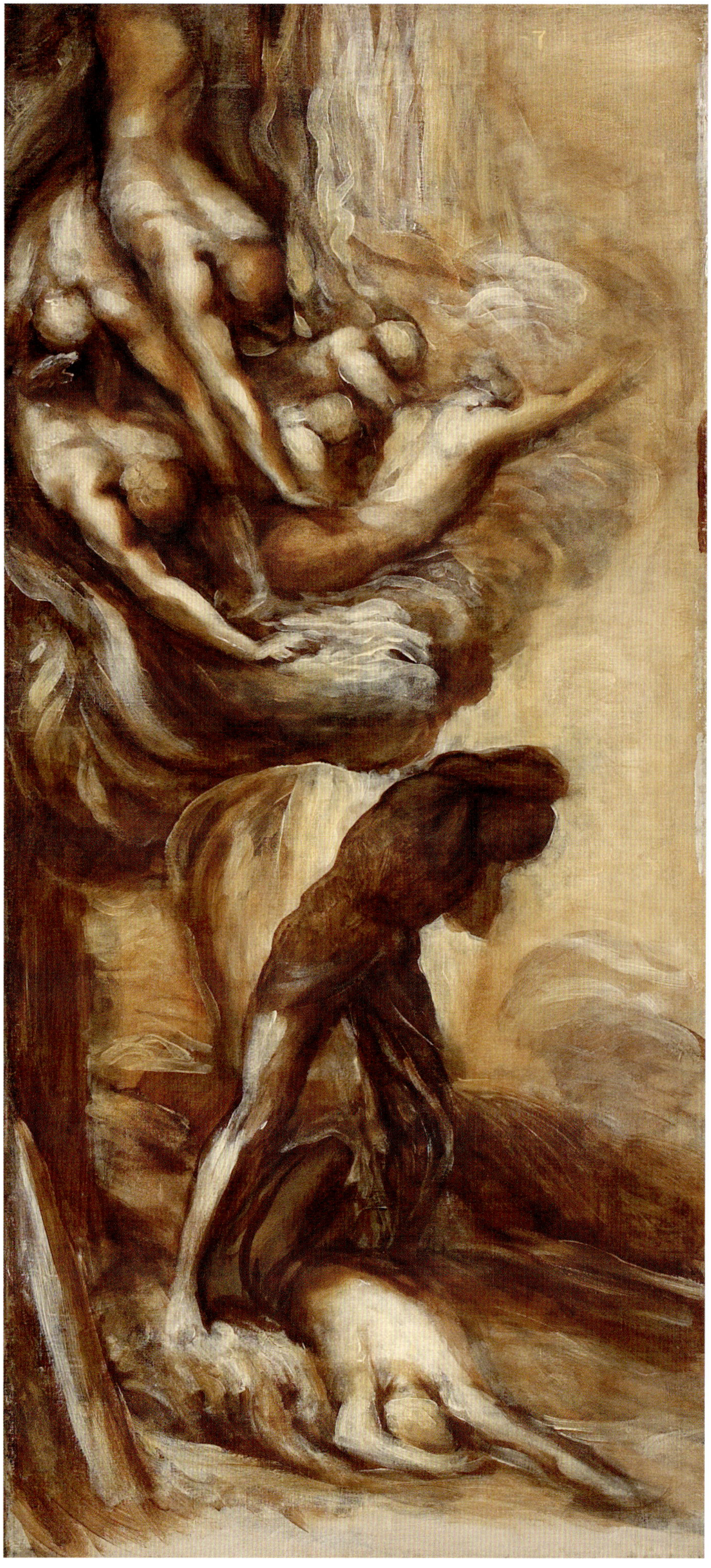

George Frederick Watts (English • 1817–1904)

30 — Sketch for "The Denunciation of Cain"

1871–72 • oil on canvas • 150.1 x 69 cm • Inv.2002.33.53

This is a preliminary sketch for a large-scale painting Watts presented to the Royal Academy as part of his diploma work. It also relates to a larger scheme of six paintings Watts had developed on the subject of Adam and Eve, their expulsion from paradise, and the fate of their sons Cain and Abel. Watts had begun work on the series by the mid-1860s and designed his cycle to include three single-figure compositions, known as *The Eve Trilogy*, and three multi-figure narratives, *The Creation of Eve*, *After the Transgression*, and *The Denunciation of Cain*. While Watts never realized his desire to see the works installed as one large cycle in a public space—his preference was a building in Manchester—he maintained a clear vision of how the group should evolve as a whole. During Watts's lifetime the cycle became known as *The House of Life*, and he exhibited several of the versions together in Europe, including in Paris at the Galerie Georges Petit in 1883. Throughout his career Watts was fascinated with how the Old Testament story of Creation related to his own views on evolution and the human spirit.

According to his wife, the Scottish artist Mary Fraser-Tyler, Watts often worked simultaneously on monochromatic and colored schemes. He completed this *Sketch for "The Denunciation of Cain"* in *camaïeu*, a monochromatic technique of painting in two or three tints of a single pigment. As with his canvases *The Creation of Eve* and *After the Transgression*, Watts developed the composition for *The Denunciation of Cain* in a vertical format and designed two figural groups that connect the realms of heaven and earth. Six muscular spirits descend like messengers from heaven. They approach and then retreat from Cain, who stands upright over the dead body of his brother. Watts chose to present the dramatic moment that follows after Cain killed Abel, when Cain receives God's curse for his violent act. Cain covers his ears and arcs his body but he cannot escape his fate. Watts said he intended this scene to symbolize "reckless, selfish humanity." God's curse appears in abstracted form: rays of light fall from heaven and illuminate Cain's figure. The landscape suggests the spaces where both brothers labored, Cain as a farmer and Abel as a shepherd. It also stands in for the expansive terrain in which Cain was destined to spend the rest of his life as a nomad and outcast. As a leading figure of the British symbolist movement, Watts was elected an associate of the Royal Academy in January 1867 and, quite unusually, he was promoted to full academician before the end of the same year. Following the established custom, Watts was to present the academy with an example of his work. In a short four-month period, Watts moved from small-scale sketch to the final large-scale version of this subject. He exhibited it for the first time in London in 1872 and entitled the work *My Punishment is Greater Than I Can Bear*, as a direct reference to Scripture (Genesis 4:11–13). When Watts presented the painting to the Royal Academy he assigned it a new title, *The Denunciation of Cain*.[1] A colored version that is of comparable scale to this sketch is in the collection of the Watts Gallery in Guildford, Surrey.[2]

1 Royal Academy, London, 427.5 x 202.5 cm, Inv.03/1313.

2 180 x 99 cm, COMWG.76.

Provenance

Thomas Esmond Lowinsky, 1892–1947

Mrs. Thomas Esmond Lowinsky, 1947–after 1954

London, Sotheby's, 9 April 1980, lot 54

Toronto, Joey and Toby Tanenbaum, 1980–2002

Exhibition History

London, Tate Gallery, 9 December 1954–16 January 1855, *George Frederic Watts*, cat.57

Hamilton, Art Gallery of Hamilton, 28 May 2005–28 May 2006, *Heaven and Earth Unveiled: European Treasures from the Tanenbaum Collection*, cat.135; 13, *73*

Hamilton, Art Gallery of Hamilton, 15 December 2007–21 September 2008, *The Word Made Flesh: Images of Devotion*

Bibliography

Barlow, Paul. "The Pointless Meaningfulness of Watts's Work," in Colin Trodd and Stephanie Brown, eds. *Representations of G.F. Watts: Art Making in Victorian Culture*. Aldershot: Ashgate Press, 2004, 29–47.

Bills, Mark, and Barbara Bryant. *G.F. Watts: Victorian Visionary*. New Haven: Yale University Press, 2008, 162–70.

Gould, Veronica Franklin. *G.F. Watts: The Last Great Victorian*. New Haven: Yale University Press, 2004, 106, 112, 170.

-----, ed. *The Vision of G.F. Watts OM RA (1817–1904)*. Guildford: Watts Gallery, 2004, 68.

Stewart, David Alan. "G.F. Watts: The Social and Religious Themes," Ph.D. dissertation, Boston University, 1988.

Watts, Mary S. Fraser-Tytler. *George Frederick Watts*. 3 vols. London: Macmillan, 1912, vol.1, 257–62.

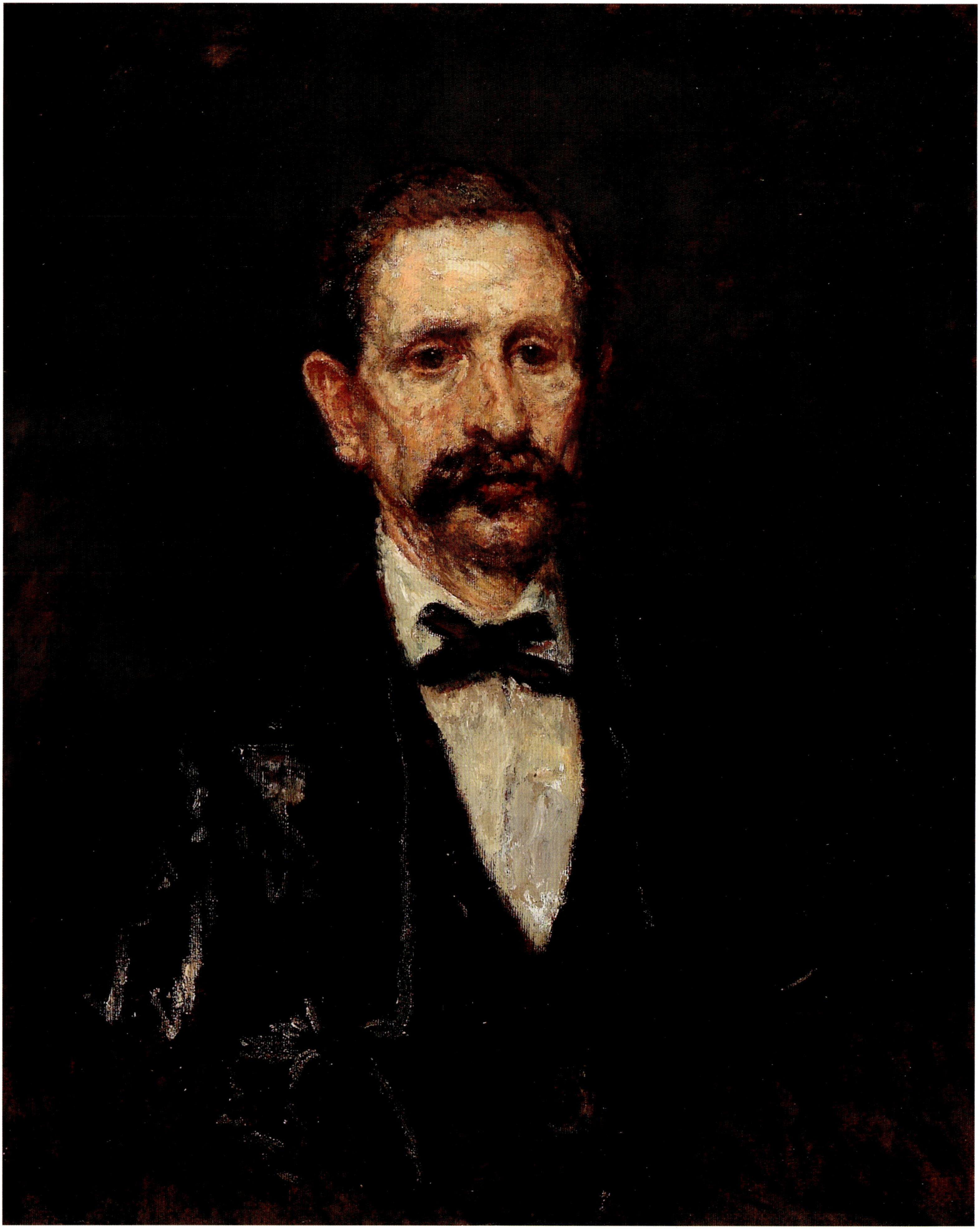

Adolphe Monticelli (French • 1824–1886)

31 — Portrait of a Man with a Bow Necktie

c.1872 • oil on canvas mounted on wood • 65.8 × 52.7 cm • Inv.2002.33.38

This sitter wears formal day dress; throughout the 1870s and into the 1880s men donned white ties for formal evening events. Fashionable for the day, the man's collar is pressed high into wings above a narrow black ribbon necktie that lies with surprising symmetry. Monticelli assigned the bow tie a significant position within the composition: its meticulous x-shape form balances the sitter's thick, downward-turning moustache and stands out against the gray, ochre (orange-yellow), and viridian (blue-green) areas of paint. The viewer's eye reads these pigments as a white shirt. Monticelli created the glowing red tone of this work by first covering the surface of the canvas with a red ground. In areas where he applied viridian on top of red, he created gray. Where he mixed ochre with viridian he achieved a stronger green tonality. To create the large button on the man's vest, he removed paint layers to reveal the red underpainting. Monticelli is well known for his thick application of paint, and on this canvas his heaviest brushwork is in the man's face, shirt, and tie. By comparison, there is noticeably less surface texture in the man's vest and jacket, which nearly dissolve into the background. Some feverishly rendered white and pink lines appear on the man's jacket, a few of which define the lapel, but they are largely detached from any descriptive role. Monticelli focuses our attention on the man's deep-set, almost sad eyes, which look out directly to the viewer.

This work likely dates to after the Franco-Prussian War (1870–71), when Monticelli had settled back in his hometown of Marseille. After studying art in Paris for a year beginning in 1846, Monticelli returned to the capital in the mid-1850s, and again from 1863 to 1870. He developed close friendships with artists associated with the earlier Barbizon school and the emerging impressionists, and engaged in a close study of Delacroix's work. By the mid-1860s, Monticelli had developed his innovative technique to combine close observation with loose brushwork and a thick, often impastoed application of paint. Monticelli benefited from a supportive network of friends, including Diaz, Guigou, and Cézanne, and enjoyed painting expeditions with those friends, although he remained quite independent and never affiliated himself with a particular group. In 1886, the year of Monticelli's death, Vincent van Gogh discovered his work in Paris at the Galerie Delarebeyrette. Four years later, Vincent's brother Theo organized a subscription to raise the necessary funds to finance the first book published about Monticelli's work, which included lithographs reproducing twenty paintings. Guigou wrote the text for this book, and argued that Monticelli was both an innovative colorist and that he was not insane. Monticelli had heard this claim during his lifetime and responded to it with characteristic equanimity. He was conscious of how unusual his style of painting was for the time, and understood his contemporaries found it difficult to respond to his works. The van Gogh brothers collected six paintings by Monticelli, and Vincent wrote of his work in many letters, stating specifically how much his own technique was indebted to Monticelli. During the final fifteen years of his life, when Monticelli had returned to Provence, he supported himself by painting both still lifes and portraits. While the sitter of *Portrait of a Man with a Bow Necktie* remains unidentified, the shape of his face, and the distinctive features of his ears, eyes, nose, and moustache all suggest how Monticelli sought to capture his sitter's likeness while at the same time remaining engaged in his own highly original technique.

Provenance

Marseille, Léon Chave
Paris, Henri Rouart (Paris, Galerie Manzi-Joyant sale, 1912, lot 257)
Paris, George Viau; New York, Paul Rosenberg & Co.
New York, Eugene Victor Thaw
New York, Sotheby's, 24 October 1989, lot 19
Toronto, Joey and Toby Tanenbaum, 1989–2002

Exhibition History

Marseille, Musée Cantini, 1936, *Monticelli: Exposition du Cinquantenaire*, no.159
Paris, Galerie Jacques Dubourg, 1942, *Monticelli*, no.15
Hartford, Wadsworth Atheneum, 15 October–30 November 1952, *The Romantic Circle*, no.60
Pittsburgh, Carnegie Institute, 27 October 1978–7 January 1979; Amsterdam, Rijksmuseum Vincent van Gogh, 28 June–2 September 1979, *Monticelli: His Contemporaries, His Influences*, cat. 75, *213*
Marseille, Centre de la Vieille Charité, 12 October 1986–4 January 1987, *Adolphe Monticelli (1824–1886)*, 166, *166*
Hamilton, Art Gallery of Hamilton, 28 May 2005–28 May 2006, *Heaven and Earth Unveiled: European Treasures from the Tanenbaum Collection*, cat.79, *144* (as *Man Wearing a Bowknotted Cravat*)
Hamilton, Art Gallery of Hamilton, 10 February–13 May 2007, *Framed: The Art of the Portrait*

Bibliography

Alauzen, André M., and Pierre Ripert. *Monticelli: sa vie et son œuvre*. Paris: Bibliothèque des arts, 1969, 355, 367.
Gouirand, André. *Les Peintres provençaux: Monticelli*. Paris: L.H. Hay, 1900.
Guigou, Paul, and A.M. Lauzet. *Adolphe Monticelli*. Paris: Boussod, Valadon & Cie., 1890.
Guinand, Louis, and G. Guinand. *La Vie et les œuvres de Monticelli*. Marseille: Imprimerie Marseillaise, 1931.
Raillard, Georges. *Monticelli l'étrange*. Marseille: André Dimanche, 2008.
Sheon, Aaron. *Monticelli: His Contemporaries, His Influence*. Pittsburgh: Carnegie Museum of Art, 1978.
-----. "Monticelli and Van Gogh," *Apollo* vol.85 (1967): 444–48.
Stammégna, Sauveur. *Catalogue des œuvres de Monticelli*. 2 vols. Marseille: S. Stammégna, 1986, vol.2, 40, pl.451.
Stoner, Kate, and Rachel Morrison. "Adolphe Monticelli: The Materials and Techniques of an Unfashionable Artist," *National Gallery Technical Bulletin* vol.33 (2012): 50–72.
Taylor, Max Fielding. "Monticelli: A Forerunner of Van Gogh," Master's thesis, University of Iowa, 1956.
Vial, Marie-Paule. *Van Gogh—Monticelli*. Paris: Réunion des musées nationaux, 2008, 20, 40–42.

Antoine Vollon (French • 1833–1900)

32 — Kitchen Interior

1870s • oil on wood panel • 26.7 × 34.9 cm • s.l.r. A. Vollon • Inv.2002.33.193

33 — The Pig

1874 • oil on canvas • 89 × 66.5 cm • s.d.u.l. A.Vollon 74 • Inv.2002.33.51

Vollon modified his technique, and adjusted how he built up layers of paint to suit varied surfaces. In *The Pig* (cat.33), long, unmodulated strokes delineate the shape of the hanging carcass. Swirls of paint loosely form viscous organs, and broad areas of tone intersect to convey the crumbling exterior wall of a butcher shop. Vollon frames our view of the quiet interior space with anecdotal details of a mop and bucket. Someone will come to clean up the drops that fall from the dense network of red, yellow, and white patches of paint Vollon uses to suggest blood concentrated high in the chest. Vollon implies human presence also in *Kitchen Interior* (cat.32): someone swept debris into one area of the floor and then put down their broom. Such details allow Vollon to convey a momentary quality to both compositions. He then turns our attention to the weightiness, the physical presence of objects and their captivating surfaces. In both works Vollon invites us to consider the play between interior and exterior. In *Kitchen Interior*, light reflects off the inner linings of a large copper pot and small brass-lined skillet. Highlights of paint subtly suggest the exterior form of a glass pitcher and also emphasize the elegant shape of the copper kettle. With Vollon, paint goes beyond simply a way to describe form and surface texture and becomes a means of creating a meditative visual experience. In studying these two works, we quickly come to understand how Vollon was among the most acclaimed still-life painters of his time.

Vollon was well respected by his fellow artists and received increasing attention from a broader public when his work was acquired by the state at the Salon of 1864 and then awarded a medal the following year. Indeed his reputation soared to such an extent that by 1868 he was ranked exempt and could exhibit paintings at the Salon without having them reviewed by the jury. In the 1870s he was a regular member of the jury. Critics praised his work and compared it to that of Chardin, the celebrated French eighteenth-century still-life painter. Contemporaries also recognized connections between Vollon's paintings and that of Dutch artists of the seventeenth century. When Vollon exhibited *The Pig* in 1875 critics immediately connected it with Rembrandt's *The Slaughtered Ox* (1655), which was acquired for the Louvre museum in 1857 and attracted considerable interest from French artists in the following decades. When Vollon showed *The Pig* at the Salon, it was hung in the very last room of an alphabetically organized exhibition. It did not languish in that space, rather it was praised as the most important work in the room. A critic writing for *Le Figaro* newspaper extolled Vollon's touch and made a direct comparison between the "energetic effect" of his "forceful strokes" and Rembrandt's painting. Another art critic and writer, Albert Wolff, who had already recognized the work's merit, acquired it for his private art collection, and loaned it to the Salon of 1875. Wolff valued detailed descriptions in his own writing and appreciated Vollon's significance among realist painters. Vollon had the impressive ability to focus the viewer's attention on the sumptuous physical presence of even the most banal of objects. In the pictorial spaces of *Kitchen Interior* and *The Pig* he demonstrates how a commonplace visual experience can assume poetic form.

Provenance

Kitchen Interior

Paris, Hôtel Drouot, Dussol sale, 17 March 1884, lot 103 (as *Nature morte, Le Cellier*)

Rotterdam, Vendu Notarishuis, 12–13 November 1981, lot 40 (as *Nature Morte, cellier*)

London, Christie's, 17 November 1995, lot 93

London, Christie's, 14 March 1996, lot 10

Toronto, Joey and Toby Tanenbaum, 1996–2002

The Pig

Paris, Albert Wolff

Paris, Alexandre Dumas, fils

Paris, Hôtel Drouot, 16 February 1882, lot 88 (as *Intérieur de boucherie*)

Paris, Hôtel Drouot, 12–13 May 1892

Paris, A. Diot

Paris, Hôtel Drouot, Diot sale, 8–9 March 1897, lot 130 (as *Le cochon*)

Paris, Galerie Bernheim-Jeune

Paris, Galerie André Watteau, 1967 (purchased in New York)

New York, H. Shickman Gallery, 1969

Toronto, Joey and Toby Tanenbaum, 1971–2002

Exhibition History

Kitchen Interior

Amsterdam, Huinck & Scherjon, 23 December 1936, no.40 (? as *Nature morte, Les cuivres*, 27 × 35 cm)

Hamilton, Art Gallery of Hamilton, 28 May 2005–28 May 2006, *Heaven and Earth Unveiled: European Treasures from the Tanenbaum Collection*, cat.131; 63–64, *141*

Hamilton, Art Gallery of Hamilton, 28 August 2010–17 April 2011, *Conversations*

Hamilton, Art Gallery of Hamilton, 24 September 2011–15 January 2012, *Masters of French Realism*

The Pig

Paris, Salon of 1875, no.1974 (collection of A. Wolff)

New York, H. Shickman Gallery, October 1971, *The Neglected 19th Century: An Exhibition of French Paintings, Part II* (as *A Side of Beef*; reproduced)

Ottawa, National Gallery of Canada, 26 May–10 September 1978; Victoria, Art Gallery of Greater Victoria, 19 October–3 December 1978; Edmonton, Edmonton Art Gallery, 15 December 1978–14 January 1979; Calgary, Glenbow-Alberta Institute, 3 February–22 March 1979; Montreal, Montreal Museum of Fine Arts, 5 April–13 May 1979; Toronto, Art Gallery of Ontario, 15 June–29 July 1979, *The Other Nineteenth Century: Paintings and Sculpture in the Collection of Mr. and Mrs. Joseph M. Tanenbaum*, cat.70, *195*

Hamilton, Art Gallery of Hamilton, 28 May 2005–28 May 2006; Victoria, Art Gallery of Greater Victoria, 25 January–11 May 2008, *Heaven and Earth Unveiled: European Treasures from the Tanenbaum Collection*, cat.132; 62–63, *140*

Hamilton, Art Gallery of Hamilton, 24 September 2011–15 January 2012, *Masters of French Realism*

Bibliography

Chu, Petra ten Doesschate. *French Realism and the Dutch Masters.* Utrecht: Haentjens Dekker & Gumbert, 1974, 64, fig.127.

Martin, Étienne. *Antoine Vollon: peintre, 1833–1900.* Marseille: Académie des Lettres, Sciences, et Arts, 1923.

Rousseau, Jean. "Le Salon de 1875, fin de la peinture," *Le Figaro* (17 May 1875): 1–2.

Savill, Rosalind. "Vollon's 'Curiosités', the comte de Nieuwerkerke and the Wallace Collection," *Burlington Magazine* vol.122 no.932 (November 1980): 767–70.

Tabler, Carol Forman. *Antoine Vollon (1833–1900): "A painter's painter."* New York: Wildenstein, 2004, 13, fig.2.

-----. "Antoine Vollon and his Smashing Pumpkin: On Media Hype and and the Meanings of Still Life," *Nineteenth-Century Art Worldwide* vol.1 no.2 (Autumn 2002).

-----. "Vollon's Curiosités and the comte de Nieuwerkerke: Official Patronage and Private Pleasure," *Burlington Magazine* vol.124 no.953 (August 1982): 505–7.

Weisberg, Gabriel P. *The Realist Tradition: French Painting and Drawing, 1830–1900.* Cleveland: Cleveland Museum of Art, 1980, 154–55, 238–40, 312.

-----. "A Still Life by Antoine Vollon, Painter of Two Traditions," *Bulletin of the Detroit Institute of Art* vol.56 no.4 (1978): 222–29.

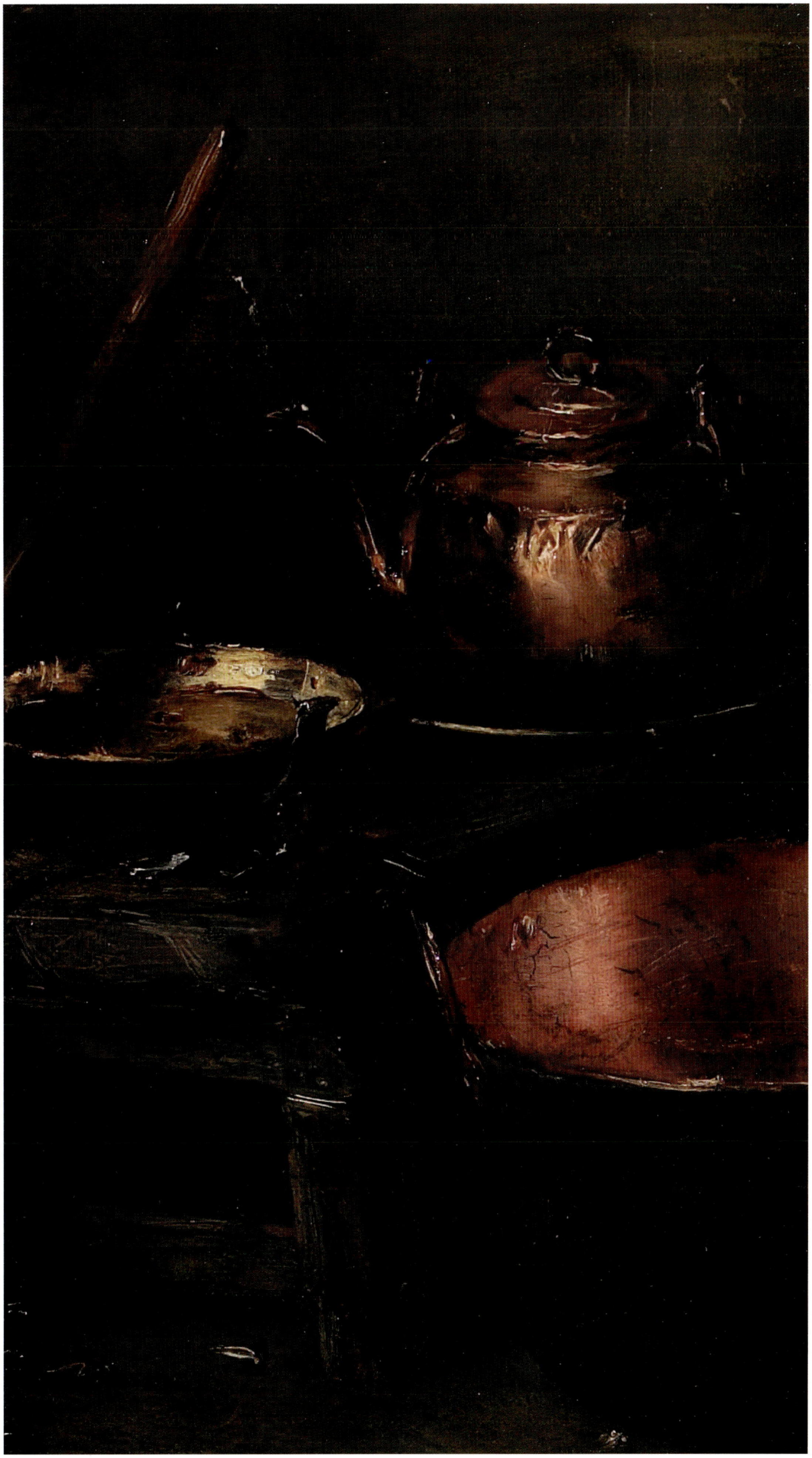

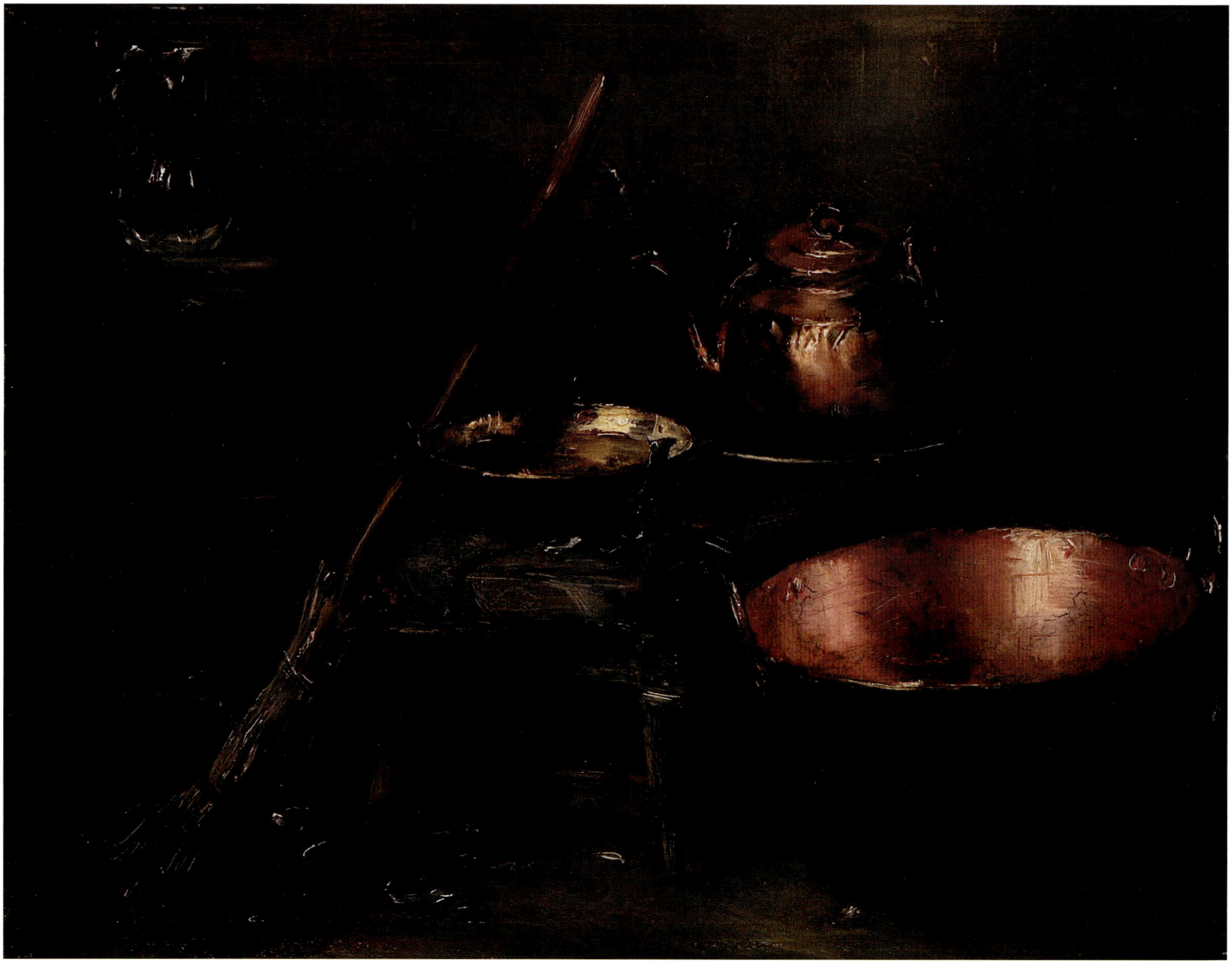

32

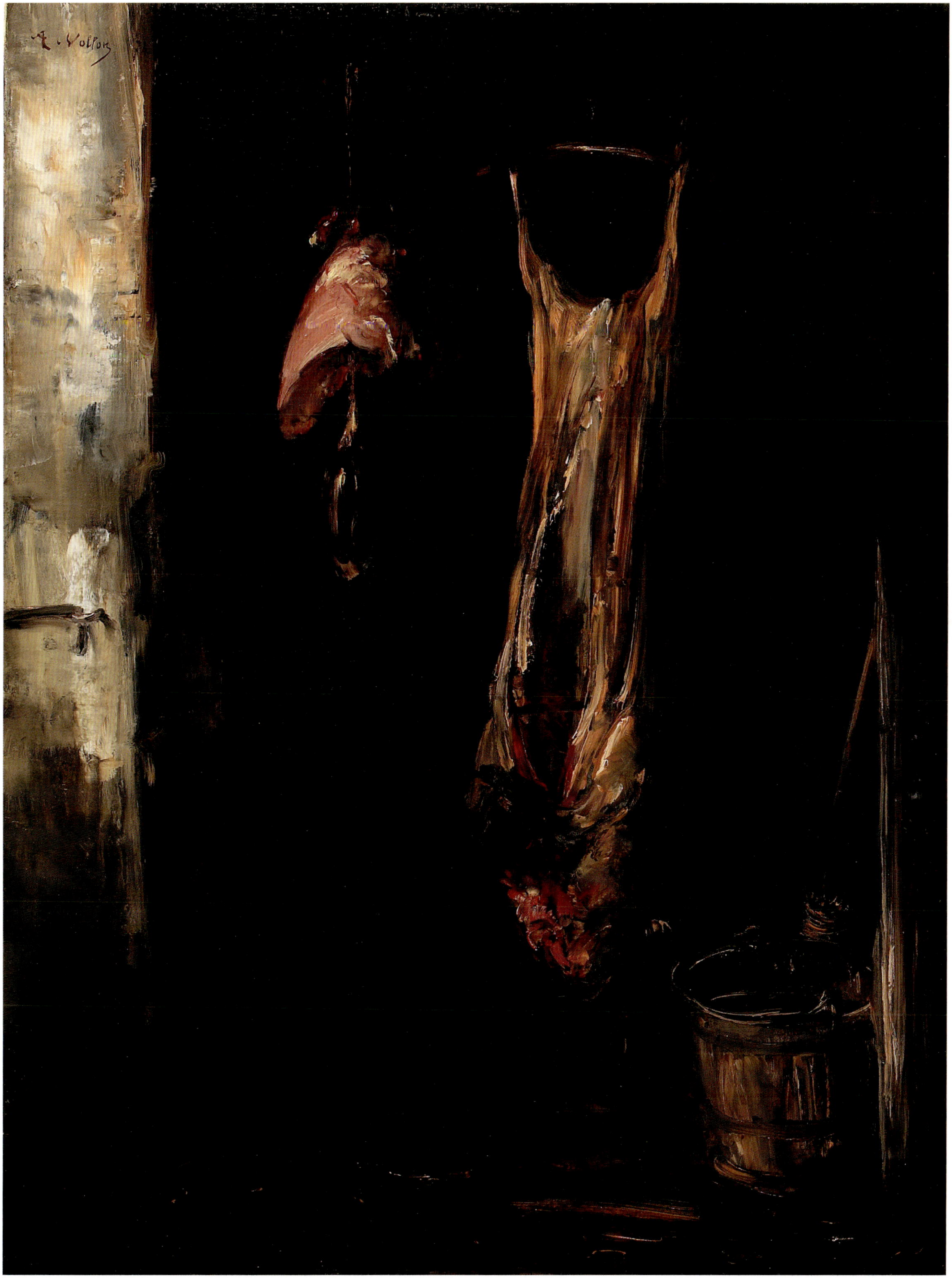

Jules Dalou (French • 1838–1902)

34 — Parisian Woman Nursing Her Child

1874 • plaster • 47 × 23.5 × 36.2 cm • s.d.l.base DALOU/1874 • Inv.2002.33.66

35 — Woman Reading in an Armchair

1877–78 • terracotta • 18.3 × 14.1 × 16.4 cm • Inv.2002.33.99

Dalou created both of these works in London, where he was based from mid-1871 until 1879. He sought exile in Britain after participating in the Federation of Artists that had supported the elected Council of Paris's right of self-governance, and then efforts to expand its authority and replace the existing state power with a new form of national governance. During this brief yet historic period of the Paris Commune (18 March–28 May 1871), Dalou was appointed as a curator, protecting works at the Louvre beginning May 16. When the Commune was suppressed, Dalou escaped to England with his wife and daughter and successfully reestablished his artistic career in London. He became a sculpture professor at the South Kensington School of Art and attracted considerable attention from British collectors. While some of his patrons commissioned portraits, many were drawn to his intimate domestic subjects. Dalou had declared his interest in depicting everyday life while he was still in France. In 1870 he exhibited a plaster *Embroiderer* (no.4401), an ambitious life-size figure, at what turned out to be the last Salon of the Second Empire. He received the competitive sum of 3,000 francs from the government to produce it as a smaller-scale marble; however, circumstances meant he was never able to complete that commission.[1]

Based in London, Dalou continued in the same vein. He examined women who were actively engaged in domestic activities and he often worked through his ideas in terracotta *ébauches*, rough sculpted studies like *Woman Reading in an Armchair* (cat.35). Dalou adapted the scale of his work in response to his circumstances and prospective market. The active surface of this sculpture revealed his thinking process: he pressed and shaped small pieces of clay, positioning the figure in a relaxed pose with a distinct s-curve from head to foot. The woman is Irma Dalou, the artist's wife, whom a contemporary admirer said loved to read. Jules made several drawings of Irma reading, in a small notebook, on loose paper, and even on a page taken from an agenda (printed date July 1877). He studied his model closely over an extended period and made another terracotta of Irma nude other than her shoes, her arms carefully poised to hold an absent book.[2] When Dalou moved to his final iteration of this subject in terracotta, and later in plaster, he seated Irma more upright, with a smaller book held close to her body. Constantine Alexander Ionides, an active British collector of Dalou's work, acquired that version as a terracotta dated 1877.[3]

Dalou's work attracted British art collectors from when he first exhibited *Maternal Joy* at the Royal Academy in London in 1872. *Parisian Woman Nursing Her Child* (cat.34) is among the variations Dalou produced, in smaller scale, in response to that public interest. From 1872 to 1877 Dalou explored this subject through three discrete social identities: a woman from Boulogne, a more generalized French peasant, and a bourgeois Parisian. Each woman holds a child to her breast and the child either actively feeds or has fallen asleep. Although perhaps inspired by his own domestic life, Dalou does not depict their daughter Georgette, who was then five years old. Dalou exhibited these works at the Royal Academy exhibitions, in terracotta, plaster, and marble, and they generated numerous sales and two major commissions. In 1877, the City of London commissioned a marble group *Charity* for a fountain behind the Royal Stock Exchange.[4] Also in 1877, Queen Victoria commissioned Dalou to create a terracotta sculpture in memory of her five male grandchildren who had not survived into adulthood. He was given the dimensions for a specific niche, and the work is now in a different location, set into the right wall of the Private Chapel at Windsor Castle. *Parisian Woman Nursing Her Child* and *Woman Reading in an Armchair* were part of Dalou's productive and successful period in England, where he was valued for his ability to convey emotion and sentiment. Dalou and his family returned to France in 1879 after the Third Republic government announced an amnesty for Communards and rescinded the life sentence of hard labor that he had been assigned in absentia in 1873.

1 AN F/21/130.

2 Petit Palais, Paris.

3 Manchester Art Gallery.

4 Bronze in situ since 1897.

Provenance

Parisian Woman Nursing Her Child
Paris, Galerie Delestre
Toronto, Joey and Toby Tanenbaum, 1981–2002 (purchased through Norman Leitman, London)

Woman Reading in an Armchair
Paris, Galerie Delestre
Toronto, Joey and Toby Tanenbaum 1979–2002

Exhibition History

Parisian Woman Nursing Her Child
Paris, Galerie Delestre, December 1978, *Dalou inédit*, cat.2 (reproduced)
Hamilton, Art Gallery of Hamilton, 28 May 2005–28 May 2006, *Heaven and Earth Unveiled: European Treasures from the Tanenbaum Collection*, cat.159, *166*
Hamilton, Art Gallery of Hamilton, 5 March 2011–19 August 2012, *From Rude to Rodin*

Woman Reading in an Armchair
Toronto, Art Gallery of Ontario, 15 June–29 July 1979, *The Other Nineteenth Century: Paintings and Sculpture in the Collection of Mr. and Mrs. Joseph M. Tanenbaum* (hors catalogue)

Hamilton, Art Gallery of Hamilton, 28 May 2005–28 May 2006, *Heaven and Earth Unveiled: European Treasures from the Tanenbaum Collection*, cat.164; 184–85, *166*
Hamilton, Art Gallery of Hamilton, 5 March 2011–19 August 2012, *From Rude to Rodin*

Bibliography

Cadet, Pierre. "L'Édition des œuvres de Dalou par la maison Susse," *Gazette des Beaux-Arts* vol.123 no.1501 (February 1994): 97–110.

Caillaux, Henriette. 'L'intimité," in *Aimé-Jules Dalou (1838–1902)*. Pref. Henry Vitry. Paris: Librairie Delagrave, 1935, 77–85.

Hargrove, June. "Carrier-Belleuse, Clésinger and Dalou: French Nineteenth Century Sculptors," *Minneapolis Institute of Arts Bulletin* vol.61 (1974): 28–43.

Hunisak, John M. "Jules Dalou," in Peter Fusco and H.W. Janson, eds., *The Romantics to Rodin: French Nineteenth-Century Sculpture from North American Collections*. New York: G. Braziller, 1980, 185–89.

-----. *The Sculptor Jules Dalou: Studies in His Style and Imagery*. New York: Garland Publishing Inc., 1977, 70–81.

Simier, Amélie. "Maternités," and "Liseuses," in Amélie Simier and Marine Kisiel, *Jules Dalou, le sculpteur de la République: catalogue des sculptures de Jules Dalou conservées au Petit Palais*. Paris: Paris musées, 2013, 346–57, 366–70.

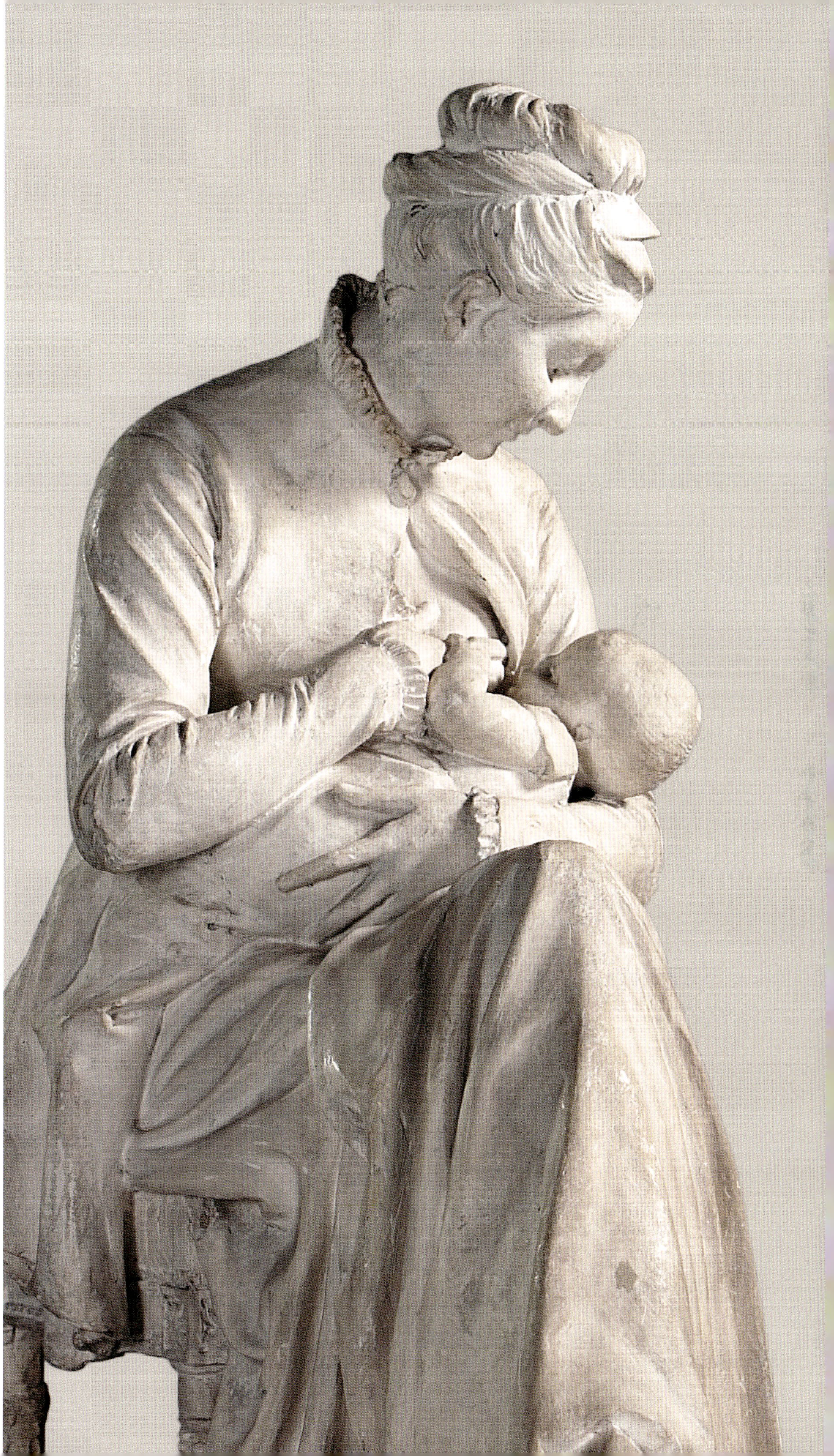

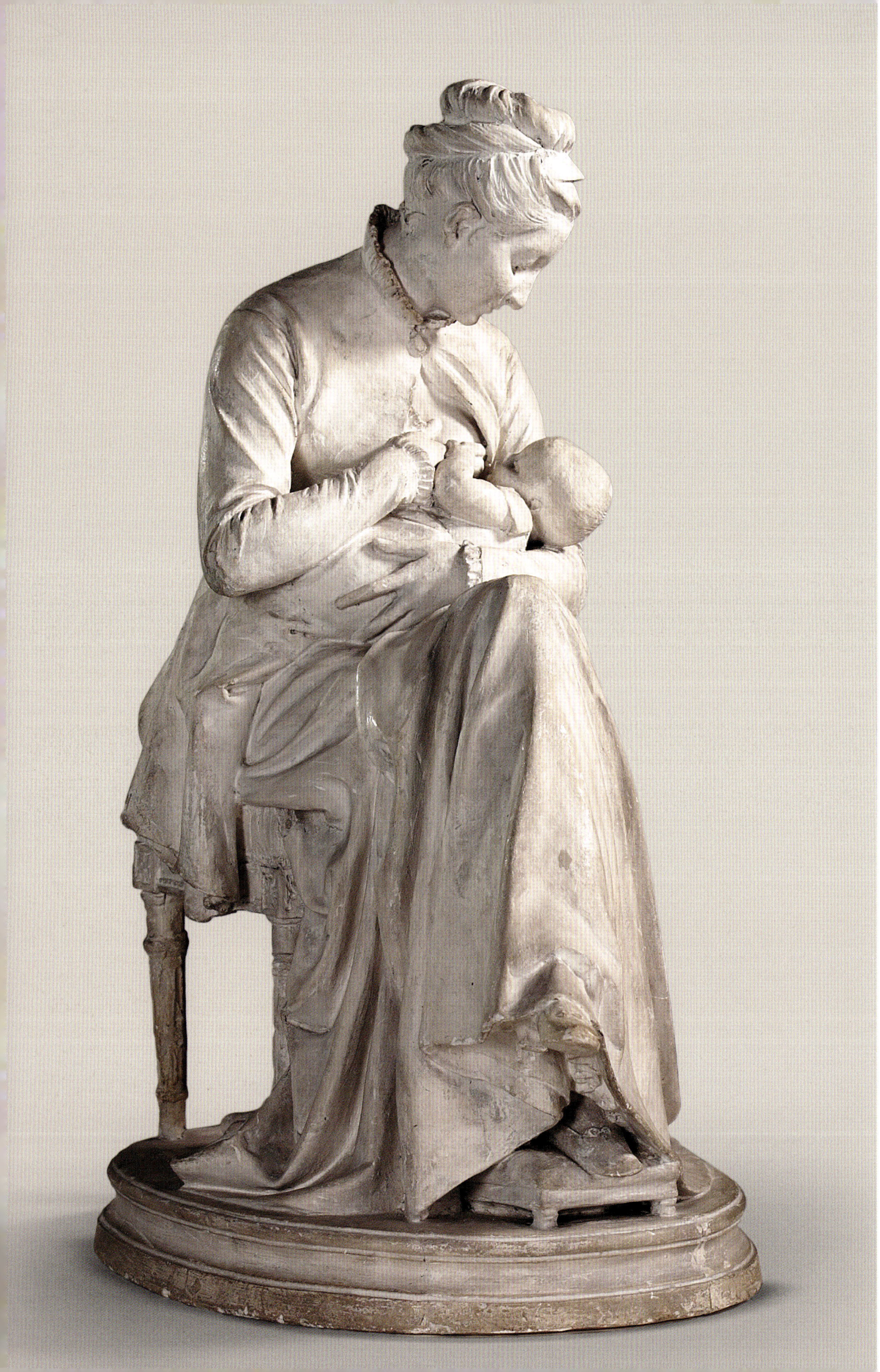

35

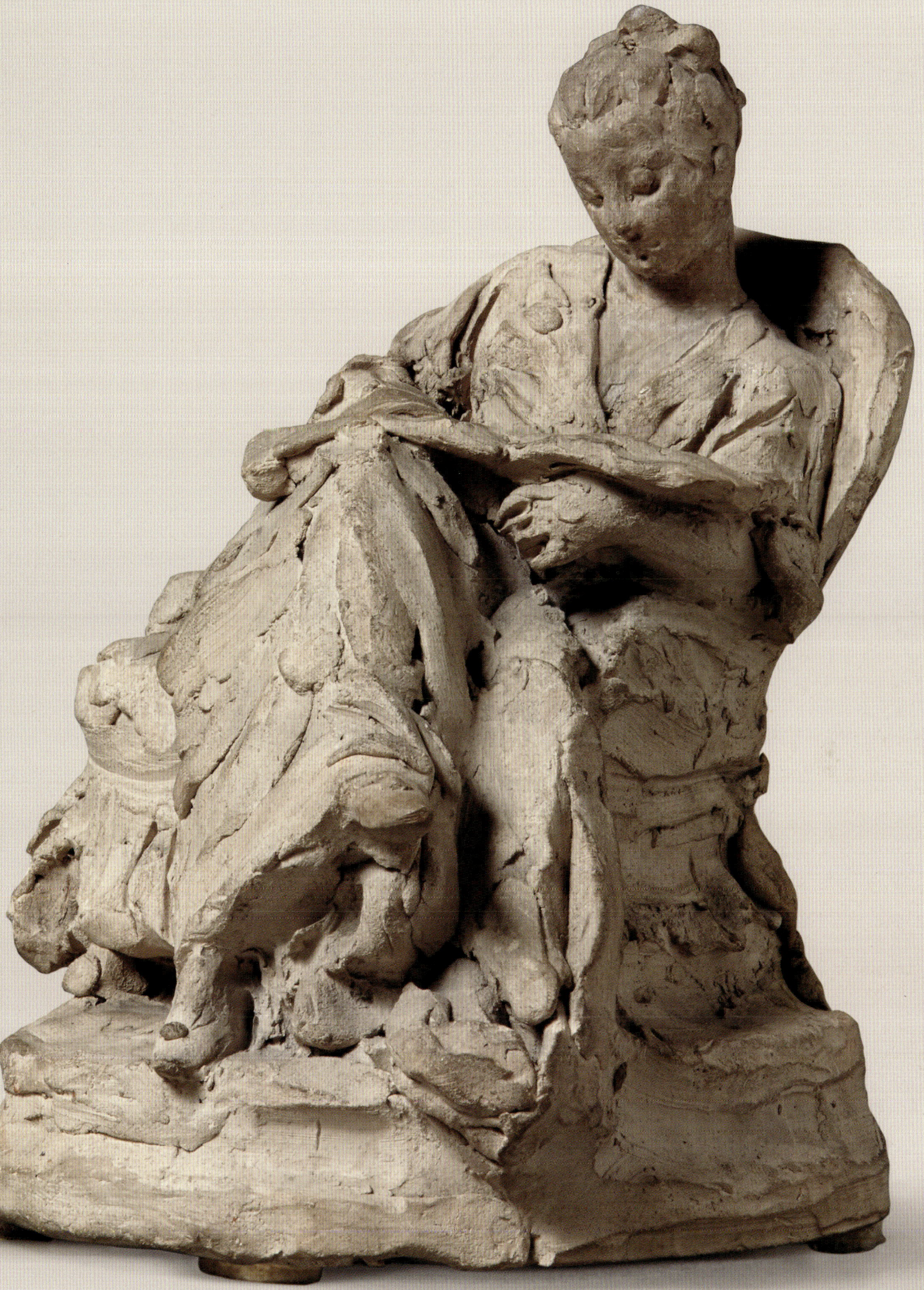

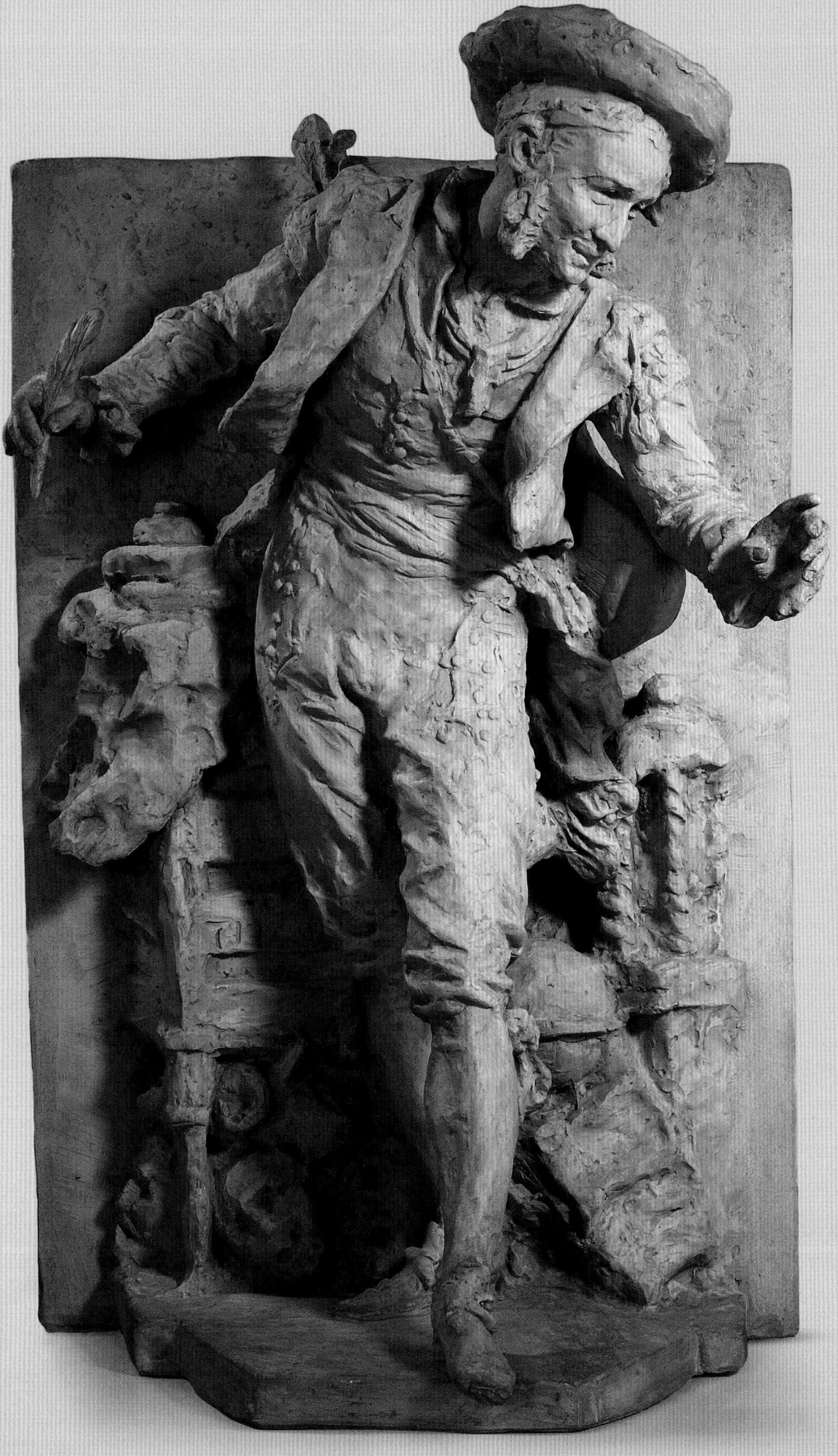

Jean-Baptiste Carpeaux (French • 1827–1875)

36 — Figaro

1874 • Terracotta • 81.7 × 50 × 38.5 cm • s.d.back r. B. Carpeaux. 1874. Preceded by an eagle stamp PROPRIETE CARPEAUX; on base at left ATELIER DEPOT/71 RUE BOILEAUX/AUTEUIL, PARIS

When the French newspaper *Le Figaro* moved from weekly to daily distribution in 1866, it was the newspaper with the largest circulation in the country. As a result of this growth, in 1874 the newspaper also relocated to a state-of-the-art building at 26 rue Drouot, in the heart of Paris's publishing district. Carpeaux was asked to be part of a jury to select a sculpture for the front façade of the new headquarters, a highly ornate, neo-baroque building.[1] The newspaper sought to promote the talent of emerging artists, and two young sculptors Amy and Boisseau received the commission. Before the jury convened for the competition, Carpeaux explored his own ideas, and it was in this context that he created the terracotta *Figaro*. Although Carpeaux sculpted the work purely for his own interest, he still adhered to many of the terms laid out by the newspaper. He envisaged a full-length figure set on a pedestal protruding from the second floor of the building, jutting out over the sidewalk and connecting with passers-by below.

Carpeaux presented a dynamic, open-form pose: he extended Figaro's foot and particularly arm well beyond the confines of the podium, and with a playful smile and tilt of the head Figaro directs his gaze to imaginary spectators at street level.[2] With *Figaro*, Carpeaux returned to many of the ideas he explored in the central male figure of his sculpture *Dance* commissioned for the front of Garnier's new opera house. Polemical when it was first unveiled in 1869, *Dance* enjoyed considerable acclaim by the time Carpeaux was at work on *Figaro*. Carpeaux sought to capture the spirit of the protagonist from Pierre Beaumarchais's play *The Marriage of Figaro* (1778), from whom the newspaper took its name. Beaumarchais finished writing the comedy by 1778 but it was first performed publicly only in 1784, following revisions and careful review by censors, and it was incredibly popular. Figaro, a former barber turned count's valet, had to work hard to curb his employer's romantic interest in his fiancé. Figaro was soon interpreted as an embodiment of anti-aristocratic and pro-republican sentiments in the pre-Revolutionary period. Carpeaux suggests Figaro's energetic and irreverent character through the pliable and expressive surface of his terracotta. The quill in Figaro's hand, guitar slung across his back, and theatrical masks piled at his feet refer to the original context of the play and its props, and also allude to various modes of expression. Free expression of ideas remained a challenge in France until 1881 when the government relaxed all laws restricting the press in both image and text. From its origins, *Le Figaro* newspaper took its motto from Beaumarchais's play: "Without the freedom to criticize, there is no true praise."

1 For views of the building see A.P. Martial's etching *Figaro* (1877) and the glass negative *L'Hôtel du Figaro, 26 rue Drouot, Paris, 9e* produced by Agence Roll (1921), both in the Cabinet des Estampes et de la Photographie, Bibliothèque Nationale de France.

2 This sculpture was produced during Carpeaux's lifetime and carries the stamp of his studio at 71 rue Boileau in Auteuil, near the southern part of the Bois de Boulogne. Another lifetime terracotta is in the Musée des Arts Décoratifs in Paris (Inv.18348), and a related drawing is in the prints and drawings department at the Louvre (RF 8885). The work was also cast in bronze posthumously by Carpeaux's family, and a terracotta dated 1876 is in the collection of the Petit Palais (PPS 1564).

Provenance

Paris, Fabius Frères
Toronto, Joey and Toby Tanenbaum, 1985–2002 (purchased through Alain Lesieutre, Paris)

Exhibition History

Hamilton, Art Gallery of Hamilton, 28 May 2005–28 May 2006, *Heaven and Earth Unveiled: European Treasures from the Tanenbaum Collection*, cat.148
Hamilton, Art Gallery of Hamilton, 9 February 2013–9 February 2014, *The Painter Pictured: French Nineteenth-Century Paintings and Portrait Photographs*

Bibliography

Carpeaux, Louise Clément. *La Vérité sur l'œuvre et la vie de J.B. Carpeaux*. Pref. Camille Mauclair. 2 vols. Paris: Dousset et Bigerelle, 1934–35, vol.1, 375.
Draper, James, et al. *The Passions of Jean-Baptiste Carpeaux*. New Haven: Yale University Press, 2014.
Poletti, Michel. *Jean-Baptiste Carpeaux: l'homme qui faisait danser les pierres*. Montreuil: Gourcuff-Gradenigo, 2012.
-----, and Alain Richarme. *Jean-Baptiste Carpeaux, sculpteur: catalogue raisonné de l'œuvre édité*. Paris: Éditions de l'amateur, 2003, 84–85.
Wagner, Anne Middleton. *Jean-Baptiste Carpeaux: Sculptor of the Second Empire*. New Haven: Yale University Press, 1986.

Louis Robert Carrier-Belleuse (French • 1848–1913)

37 — The Tinker

1875 • oil on canvas • 197.5 × 108.5 cm • s.d.l.l. LOUIS. CARRIER-BELLEUSE/1875 • Inv.2002.33.84

The subject of this work is one of the most visible of the *petits métiers*, the self-employed small tradespeople who worked in the streets of French cities. Popular prints known as *images d'Épinal* document how men and women specialized in particular trades in the nineteenth century.[1] Men cleaned windows, sharpened knives, posted advertising, and sold hot chocolate from metal containers worn on their backs. Women sold bread and prepared cooked food, such as sausages, on portable stoves. In this painting Carrier-Belleuse depicts a tinker, someone who specializes in repairs of a broad range of metal objects, such as pots, kettles, and utensils. In nineteenth-century France the tinker was known as the *rétameur* or, in more common slang, *étameur*. This was a specifically masculine trade offering services that were among the highest in demand from both private dwellings and small businesses such as restaurants and bars. Since urban streets, and particularly those in central Paris, were filled with different tradespeople competing for attention, each of the *petits métiers* developed distinct ways of announcing their presence. They uttered calls or cries that the public could readily identify with their respective field. The call of the *rétameur* was identifiable as a short recitative, one often accompanied by the sound of a utensil striking against a metal pot. Ranging over at most three different musical notes, the distinctive cry of the tinker was simple and to the point: "Étameur, voilà étameur, étameur des cass'rol."

Carrier-Belleuse sought to convey an authentic representation of the *rétameur* in the life-size figure that dominates this canvas. He depicted the tinker standing on a cobblestone street with his head tilted back and mouth partially open, suggesting this worker is in the midst of calling out to proclaim his presence. Carrier-Belleuse has posed the tinker with no less than seven different metal objects that serve a dual purpose. They advertize the tinker's ability to repair cookware as well as fireplace implements and suggest he is capable of restoring numerous types of metals including brass, copper, and pewter. This work is also carefully staged to display Carrier-Belleuse's own talents as a painter. The artist shows his ability to render reflective metallic surfaces and to suggest the three-dimensionality of different objects from a range of perspectives. The pitcher, saucepan, kettle, small brazier pan, large vessel, utensil, and lid either hang from his body or are held at every possible angle. Carrier-Belleuse studied with his father Albert-Ernest Carrier-Belleuse (see cat.46) and at the École des Beaux-Arts with Boulanger and Cabanel (see cat.6). He exhibited a number of paintings at the Salons that focused on urban male workers. Some of these are multi-figure scenes that can still be traced today, including men melting tar for street repairs in *A Bitumen Team* and men unloading flour to a boulangerie in *Les Forts des Halles* (*Flour Carriers, Parisian Scene*).[2] In each of these paintings Carrier-Belleuse conveys aspects of the challenging life of the urban working poor. These were men who struggled for subsistence living. Some were hired as day laborers and others, like the *rétameur*, were self-employed and literally carrying on their backs the infrastructure of their mobile business.

[1] *Les petits métiers de Paris*, no.179, 1864, wood engraving in *Images d'Épinal de la Maison Pellerin*, vol.7. Cabinet des Estampes et de la Photographie, Bibilothèque Nationale de France.

[2] *A Bitumen Team* was exhibited at the Salon of 1883 and is now on deposit at the Musée des Beaux-Arts, Arras (from the collection of the Musée d'Orsay, VBA-S-D00A46-0001). *Flour Carriers, Parisian Scene* was exhibited at the Salon of 1885 and is now in the Petit Palais, Paris (PP-PDUT01445).

Provenance

London, Christie's, 18 November 1994, lot 164 (as *Le Rétameur*)
Toronto, Joey and Toby Tanenbaum, 1994–2002

Exhibition History

Hamilton, Art Gallery of Hamilton, 28 May 2005–28 May 2006, *Heaven and Earth Unveiled: European Treasures from the Tanenbaum Collection*, cat.16; 50, 119 (as *Copper Polisher*)
Hamilton, Art Gallery of Hamilton, 13 September 2008–4 January 2009, *Blood, Sweat and Tears: Labour in Art*
Hamilton, Art Gallery of Hamilton, 21 May–5 September 2011, *The French Connection*

Bibliography

Kastner, Jean-Georges. *Les Voix de Paris: essai d'une histoire littéraire et musicale des cris populaires de la capitale depuis le Moyen Age jusqu'à nos jours.* Paris: G. Brandus, Dufour et Cie, 1857, 102, score plate 26.

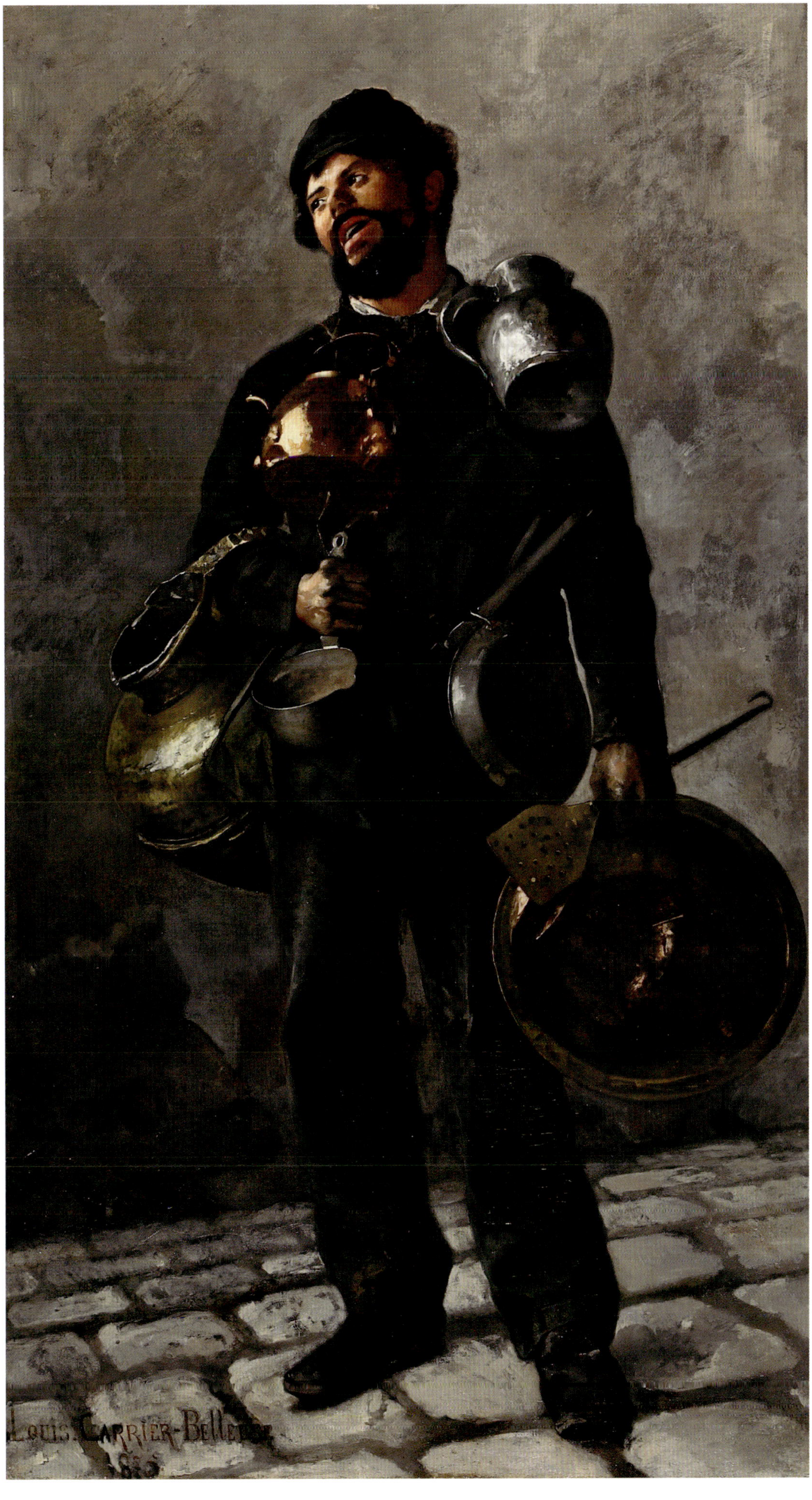
Louis Carrier-Belleuse

Charles Bargue (French • c.1826/27–1883)

38 — Seated Bashi-Bazouk

c.1875–77 • oil on canvas • 46.4 × 32.7 cm • Inv.2002.33.75

39 — Muslims at Prayer

c.1875–80 • oil on wood panel • 35.2 × 26.8 cm • Inv.2002.33.76

A few years before Bargue painted *Seated Bashi-Bazouk* and *Muslims at Prayer*, he published a drawing course that became one of the most successful of its kind and brought him considerable renown. Bargue brought out his three-volume *Cours de dessin* with the prominent art dealer and publisher Adolphe Goupil between 1868 and 1873. He collaborated on the first two volumes with Gérôme (see cats.11 and 12) who, in 1863, was one of three artists chosen for the École des Beaux-Arts' new positions for painting professors. The collaboration brought together 200 lithographs by Bargue that reproduced plaster casts, paintings, and drawings after old master and contemporary artists, as well as drawings of male nudes in a range of positions.[1] It offered material that aspiring artists could use to develop their skills, under the direction of a private instructor, before seeking admission to the competitive national art school. While there were several such published art courses in nineteenth-century France, Bargue's was particularly well regarded and, to this day, the "Bargue method" continues to be the basis of teaching at Academies of Realist Art in Canada, the United States, and Britain.

In *Seated Bashi-Bazouk* (cat.38), Bargue used a strong contour line to define the figure of a Turkish soldier at rest. During the Crimean War (1854–56) and the later Russo-Turkish War (1877–78), bashi-bazouk were independent, mercenary officers who were part of the military reserve. They were hired primarily as sentinels and worked on reconaissance missions. Bargue presented this soldier off duty, lounging on a long divan, with one arm pulled back to reveal the butts and stocks of his two pistols. The armaments serve as reminders of the man's military position, Bargue focusing however on the bashi-bazouk's leisure time. Cradled in the well-defined musculature of the soldier's calves is a water pipe, the hookah or *narghile* that has brought on the detached state of reverie that is apparent on his face. Bargue presented the soldier's dress and the setting with sufficient detail to invite spectators into the composition. We are to imagine ourselves reclining across from this man, perhaps about to take up the mouthpiece of the water pipe that sits on the floor and awaits our use. Bargue painted a number of such scenes of individual sentinels, seated and standing, which can be traced today.[2] Given the precise application of paint in Bargue's other known works, *Seated Bashi-Bazouk* was likely a sketch for a related composition of comparable scale. Bargue is believed to have made an undocumented visit to North Africa, either Egypt or Algeria, between 1871 and 1872. Extant drawings suggest Bargue worked extensively from the live model and then continued to stage orientalizing scenes in his studio. The figure in *Seated Bashi-Bazouk* also appears in a drawing by Gérôme, suggesting that the two artists sketched from the same model.[3] Bargue's colorful *Muslims at Prayer* (cat.39) also appears to have been a sketch for a larger-scale painting that remains untraced today. A number of extant related drawings reveal Bargue's desire to create an authentic presentation of the four different Muslim men, who are made distinctive through their detailed dress and musculature while at the same time being united in the cyclical, physical movements of their prayer.[4] Traces of underdrawing are apparent in the lower left-hand corner, where Bargue carefully laid down lines that recede into the composition and demarcate the positions of both the figures and their prayer carpets.

1 Bargue exhibited a collection of ten of his lithographs after works by Michelangelo, Holbein, Raphael, Andrea del Sarto, Flandrin, Bonnat, Gérôme, Dubois, and Gleyre at the Salons of 1867 (no.2717) and 1868 (no.4166).

2 For example *Bashi-Bazouk* (1875, oil on canvas, 46.4 × 33.3 cm; New York, Metropolitan Museum of Art, Inv.87.15.102) and *Turkish Sentinel* (1877, oil on panel, 28 × 21 cm; Boston, Museum of Fine Arts, Inv.03.601).

3 Jean-Léon Gérôme, *Bashi-Bazouk* (1882; private collection), illustrated Ackerman 2003, 279.

4 *Two Studies of a Man at Prayer* (Boston, Fogg Art Museum, 1940.102), as well as four drawings in the Walters Art Museum, Baltimore: *Moslem Prostrating Himself on a Prayer Rug* (37.1222), *Moslem at Prayer* (37.1339), and two entitled *Arab Kneeling in Prayer* (37.1328 and 37.1338). The related grisaille painting is *Arabs at Prayer* (lost; illustrated Ackerman 2003, 305).

Provenance

Seated Bashi-Bazouk
New York, Schweitzer Gallery
Toronto, Joey and Toby Tanenbaum, 1972–2002

Muslims at Prayer
New York, Blakeslee and Co.
Montreal, Sir William Van Horne, 1891–1915
Montreal, Van Horne estate
New York, Parke-Bernet, 24 January 1946, lot 20
New York, Schweitzer Gallery
Toronto, Joey and Toby Tanenbaum, 1972–2002

Exhibition History

Seated Bashi-Bazouk
Hempstead, New York, Emily Lowe Gallery, Hofstra University, *Art Pompier, Anti-Impressionism: 19th Century French Salon Painting*, 22 October–15 December 1974, cat.2, *23*
Ottawa, National Gallery of Canada, 26 May–10 September 1978; Victoria, Art Gallery of Greater Victoria, 19 October–3 December 1978; Edmonton, Edmonton Art Gallery, 15 December 1978–14 January 1979; Calgary, Glenbow-Alberta Institute, 3 February–22 March 1979; Montreal, Montreal Museum of Fine Arts, 5 April–13 May 1979; Toronto, Art Gallery of Ontario, 15 June–29 July 1979, *The Other Nineteenth Century: Paintings and Sculpture in the Collection of Mr. and Mrs. Joseph M. Tanenbaum*, cat.4, *41*

Hamilton, Art Gallery of Hamilton, 28 May 2005–28 May 2006; Victoria, Art Gallery of Greater Victoria, 25 January–11 May 2008, *Heaven and Earth Unveiled: European Treasures from the Tanenbaum Collection*, cat.6; 55, *128*
Hamilton, Art Gallery of Hamilton, 22 May–6 September 2010, *Europe's Exoticized East*

Muslims at Prayer
Montreal, Art Association, 1891, no.2
Montreal, Art Association, 1933, no.112 (Van Horne collection)
Ottawa, National Gallery of Canada, 26 May–10 September 1978; Victoria, Art Gallery of Greater Victoria, 19 October–3 December 1978; Edmonton, Edmonton Art Gallery, 15 December 1978–14 January 1979; Calgary, Glenbow-Alberta Institute, 3 February–22 March 1979; Montreal, Montreal Museum of Fine Arts, 5 April–13 May 1979; Toronto, Art Gallery of Ontario, 15 June–29 July 1979, *The Other Nineteenth Century: Paintings and Sculpture in the Collection of Mr. and Mrs. Joseph M. Tanenbaum*, cat.5, *43*
Hamilton, Art Gallery of Hamilton, 28 May 2005–28 May 2006, *Heaven and Earth Unveiled: European Treasures from the Tanenbaum Collection*, cat.5; 55, *129* (as *Prayer in the Mosque*)
Hamilton, Art Gallery of Hamilton, 22 May–6 September 2010, *Europe's Exoticized East*

Bibliography

Ackerman, Gerald M., with Graydon Parrish. *Charles Bargue Drawing Course: With the Collaboration of Jean-Léon Gérôme*. Paris: ACR Édition, 2003.
Bargue, Charles, and Jean-Léon Gérôme. *Cours de dessin*. 3 vols. Paris: Goupil, 1868–71.
Freitas, Fernando. "The Bargue Method: Learning to Draw the Traditional Way," *Drawing* (Fall 2013): 78–85.
Kelly, Simon. "Charles Bargue (1825–1883), *Arab Kneeling in Prayer*, c.1875," in Jay McKean Fisher et al. *The Essence of Line: French Drawings from Ingres to Degas*. Baltimore: Walters Art Museum, 2005, 88–91.
Sterling, Charles, and Margaretta M. Salinger. *French Paintings: A Catalogue of the Collection of the Metropolitan Museum of Art*. 3 vols. New York: Metropolitan Museum of Art, 1966, vol.2, 175–76.

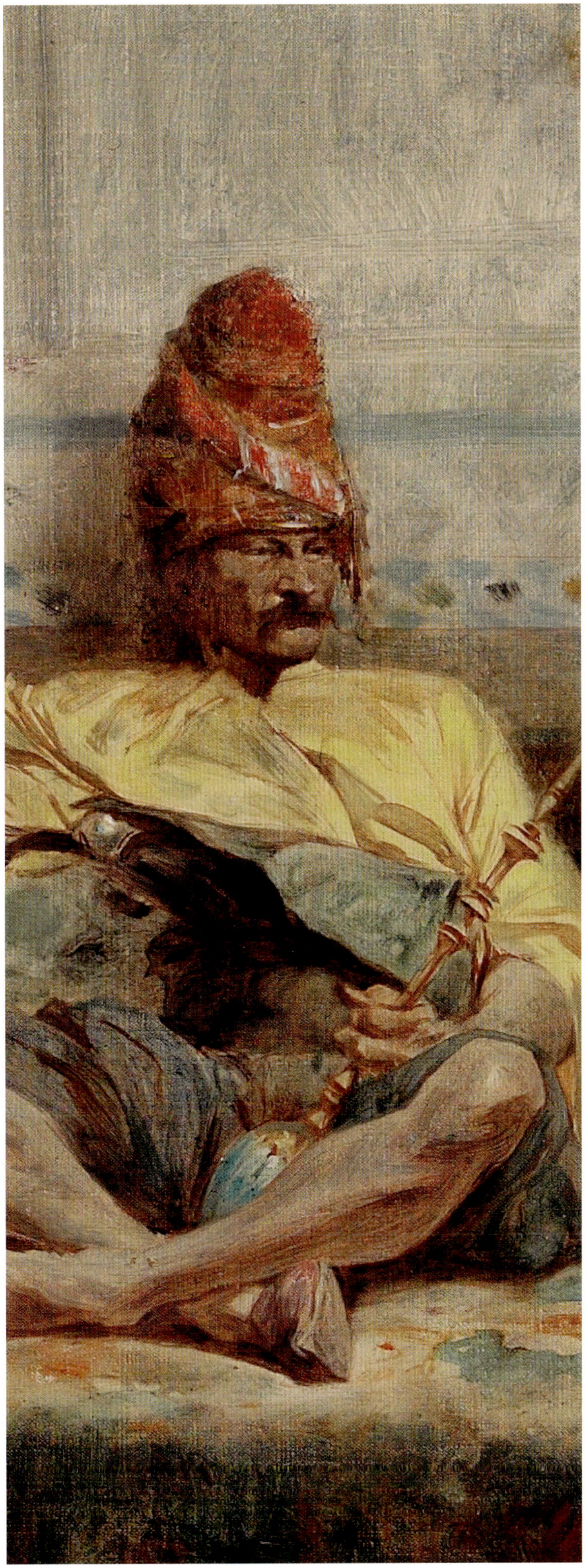

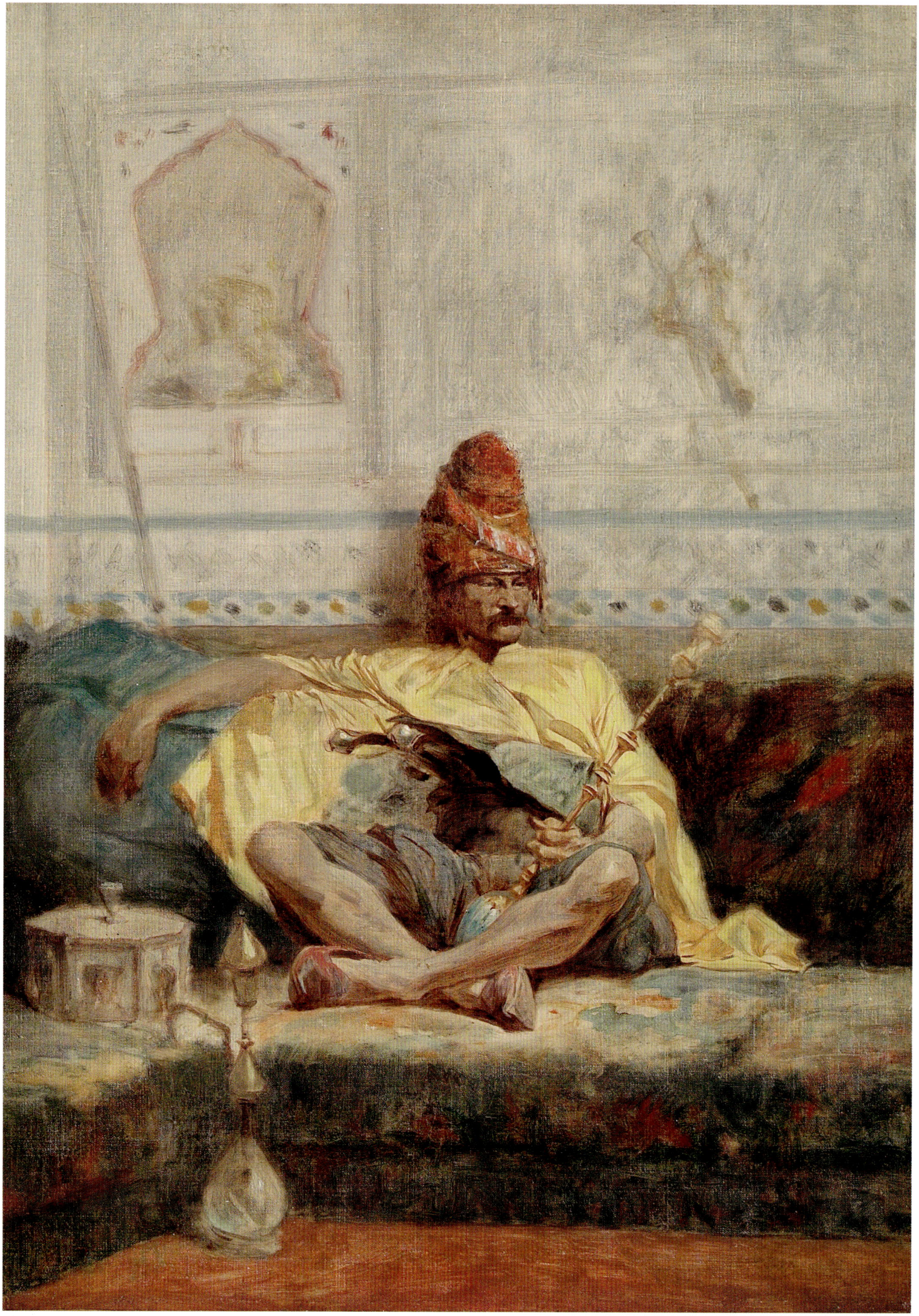

39

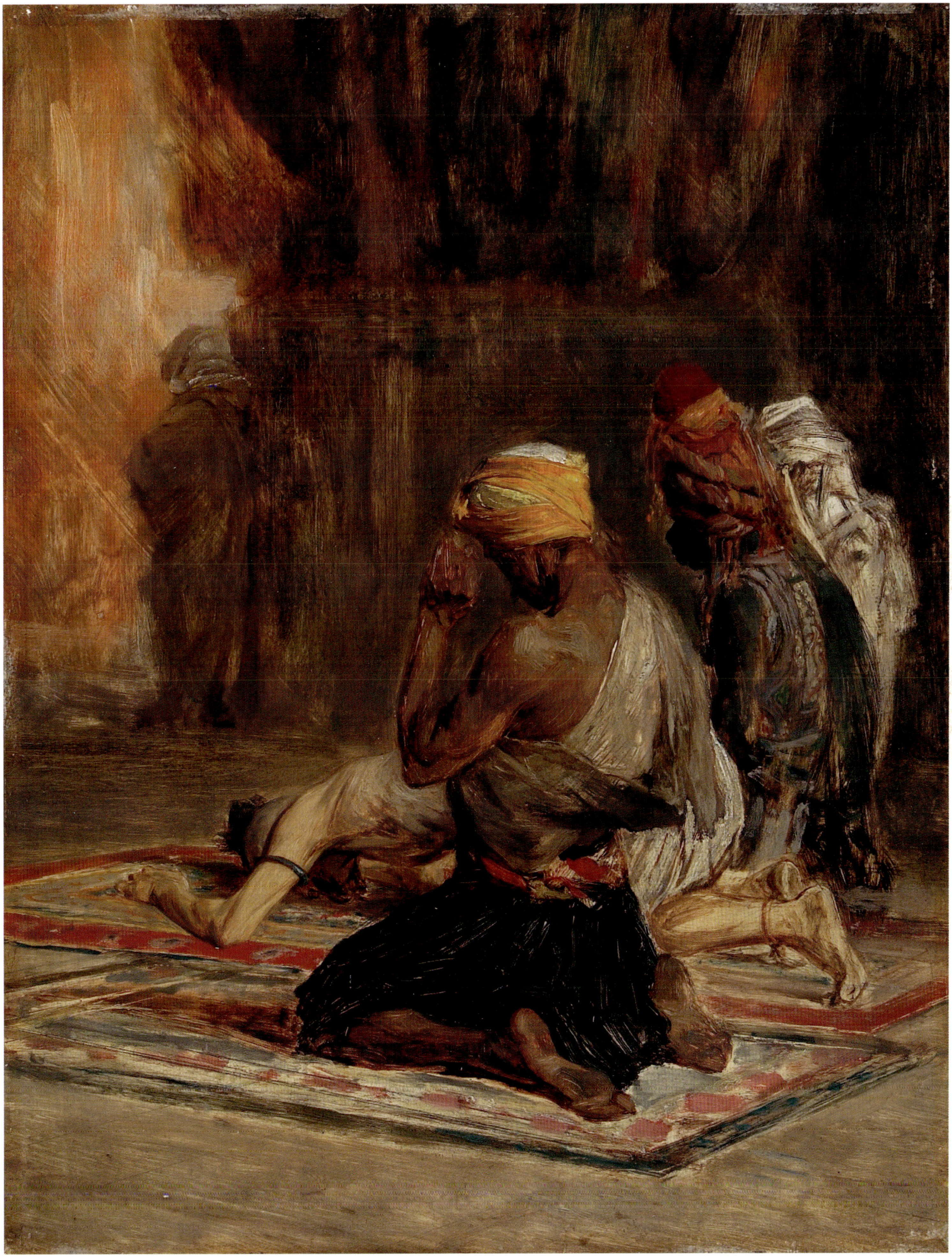

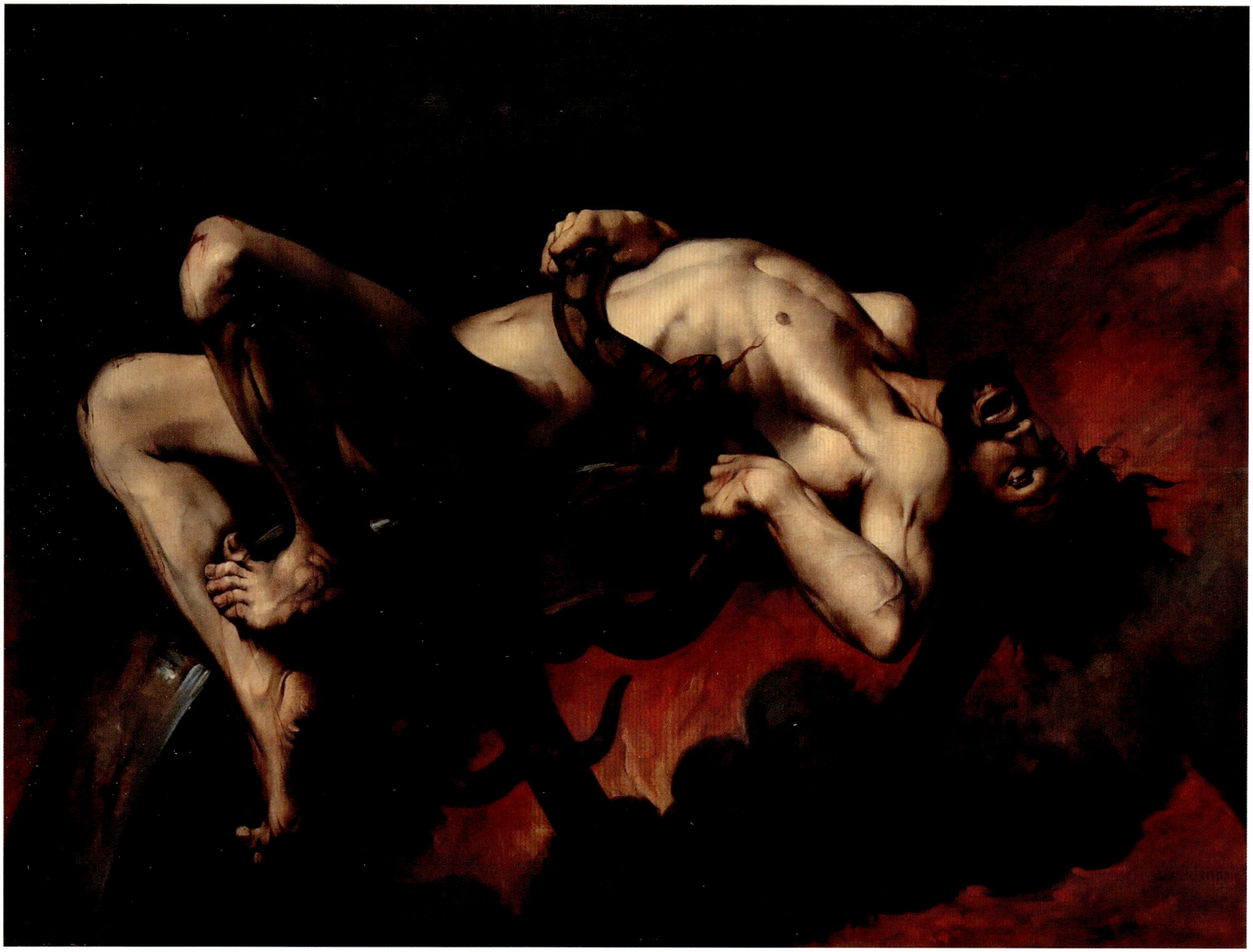

Jules-Élie Delaunay (French • 1828–1891)

40 — Ixion Plunged into Hades

c.1876–80 • oil on canvas • 115 × 150 cm • s.l.r. Elie Delaunay • Inv.2002.33.105

Two snakes encircle Ixion's torso and bind him to a large wooden wheel. As that wheel turns, Ixion's body will move into the fiery flames that await him in the underworld. In ancient Greek mythology, Ixion was king of Thessaly, a region also known as Aeolia. He committed a crime by killing his father-in-law, possibly to avoid making the payment expected for his bride. Ixion's crime against kin drove him mad; he was never cleansed of his misdeed and was consigned to a life wandering in exile. From Olympus, Zeus took pity on Ixion and invited him to join the realm of the gods. Before long, Ixion tried to seduce Zeus's wife Hera and infuriated his host. Zeus then had Hera appear to Ixion in the form of a cloud. Ixion was caught in the tryst and condemned to death. Ixion's story appears in numerous sources, and Delaunay took up the subject as he prepared to submit work to the Salon. Delaunay focused his canvas on the most dramatic moment in the narrative and presented Ixion's body already writhing in anticipation of the pain to come. Red and yellow flames fill much of the canvas and smoke billows in the foreground. To the viewer, Ixion's open mouth signals his fearful cries. The ancient sources Delaunay was likely drawing on indicate that Ixion was forced to call out repeatedly, "One should show gratitude to a benefactor."

Delaunay had been a successful history painter for two decades when he showed his painting of Ixion at the Salon of 1876 (no.248). He had won the Prix de Rome in 1856 and spent several years studying at the Académie de France in Rome, as did Houdon, Cabanel, and Chartran (see cats.1, 6, and 29). Even decades later, Delaunay still hoped to be recognized for his skill at painting the nude male body, and a mythological subject such as Ixion gave him a narrative context in which to display his talents. In 1880, Delaunay's first painting of *Ixion Plunged into Hades* was acquired for the Musée des Beaux-Arts in his hometown of Nantes.[1] The second version, depicted here, is nearly identical in scale to the first and was likely painted between 1876 and 1880. For many years this painting was also in Nantes, where it was acquired for a private collection. *Ixion Plunged into Hades* was considered such a strong example of Delaunay's abilities that it was loaned from the museum in Nantes for the world fairs held in Paris in both 1878 (no.248) and 1889 (no.277). Delaunay also made an etching of his work, which meant it could reach broader audiences and be reproduced in the contemporary press such as the *Gazette des Beaux-Arts*. These strategies meant Delaunay continued to reach the various markets that were interested in his work. He was also asked to paint portraits for numerous private patrons throughout his career, and he received many commissions for mural paintings both in Nantes and in Paris, among the most famous of which are his paintings for the Opéra and the staircase of the new Hôtel de Ville.

[1] Inv.918. The Musée des Beaux-Arts in Nantes also has five of Delaunay's preparatory drawings related to this subject: Inv.1357, 1402, 5443, 5444, 5445.

Provenance

Nantes, private collection

New York, Frederick J. Cummings, Inc., 1986

Toronto, Joey and Toby Tanenbaum, 1986–2002

Exhibition History

Hamilton, Art Gallery of Hamilton, 28 May 2005–28 May 2006; Victoria, Art Gallery of Greater Victoria, 25 January–11 May 2008, *Heaven and Earth Unveiled: European Treasures from the Tanenbaum Collection*, cat.32; 23–24, *84*

Hamilton, Art Gallery of Hamilton, 28 April–2 December 2007, *A Visual Bestiary*

Hamilton, Art Gallery of Hamilton, 21 May–5 September 2011, *The French Connection*

Bibliography

Benoist, Luc. *Élie Delaunay, 1828–1891: ses dessins, et son œuvre*. Nantes: Musée des Beaux-Arts, 1956.

Jouin, Henry. "Élie Delaunay," *L'Artiste* new series vol.2 (1891): 241–45.

Julia, Isabelle. *Jules-Élie Delaunay 1828–1891*. Paris: Réunion des musées nationaux, 1988, cat.92, *175*.

Toscano, Gennaro. "Paris-Venise 1857–1860: Delaunay, Moreau, Henner et les primitifs vénitiens," in Claire Barbillon and Gennaro Toscano, eds. *Venise en France: du romantisme au symbolisme*. Paris: École du Louvre, 2006, 183–211.

Léon Bonnat (French • 1833–1922)

41 — Portrait of Hermann (Jacques) Raffalovich

1877 • oil on canvas • 134.3 × 96 cm • s.d.l.l. Ln. Bonnat./1877. • Inv.2002.33.80

42 — Portrait of Dr. Adrien Doyon

1887 • oil on canvas • 70 × 54.5 cm • s.d.l.r. L[n] Bonnat -/1887; inscribed u.l. à mon ami/le Docteur Doyon • Inv.2002.33.5

These two works demonstrate why Bonnat was among the most expensive and most sought-after French portraitists of his period. Bonnat emphasized drawing, which gives his figures a strong physical presence, as well as descriptive details that appealed to patrons interested in capturing their likeness. Bonnat also knew how to compliment sitters. His practice combined working from photographs with in-person studio sittings and, at the height of his demand in the 1880s, he managed multiple studio visits on any given day. Bonnat's prodigious output resulted in criticisms that his works failed to convey a sitter's energy and liveliness. That was certainly not the case for Bonnat's *Portrait of Hermann (Jacques) Raffalovich* (cat.41). A smile begins to form: Bonnat modeled the cheeks, and defined the skin and lines around the eyes to capture a moment when expression builds and animates. Raffalovich's face and hands are bathed in light, he holds up a monocle and rests one hand on a red velvet chair, the only object in an otherwise undefined background space. Like Rembrandt, whose work Bonnat admired and collected, Bonnat uses lighting and expressive hands to evoke a sitter's inner life and personality. In Raffalovich's case, confidently posed hands and a contented face seem intimately connected to the summarily painted pin on his lapel, the characteristic red usually signifying the Legion of Honor, but here it may signify another award (or later addition) since Hermann was not then an officer of the order. Hermann and his wife Marie settled in Paris in 1863, emigrating from Odessa at a time when Jews were forced to convert to Christianity. Hermann (1823–1893) was a successful banker and Marie (1833–1921) a noted writer and translator proficient in eight languages. This portrait was likely commissioned to hang in their home at 19 avenue de la Reine Hortense (today avenue Hoche) near the Parc Monceau. Marie developed connections with numerous contemporary artists, and their collection included works by Gleyre, Henner, Gallé, and Moreau. Marie also held a regular salon that attracted actress Sarah Bernhardt and prominent writers including Anatole France, Jules Michelet, and Edgar Quinet. Seen by many in the context of these elite social and cultural gatherings, Bonnat's painting would have served its purpose well. Less than fifteen years after their move to Paris, Hermann appears as a confident and successful member of the haute bourgeoisie.

A decade later, when Bonnat painted the smaller-scale, bust-length *Portrait of Dr. Adrien Doyon* (cat.42), the circumstance and thus outcome was quite different. This work was likely a gesture of friendship rather than a commissioned portrait. Doyon (1827–1907) emerges from a background painted the same color as his flesh and, while Bonnat gives a good sense of Doyon's physiognomy, this is a portrait sketch and so paint suggests rather than describes hair and beard; the forms of the jacket are also loosely rendered. Yet Bonnat is again careful to include a flash of red paint to indicate the chevalier of the Legion of Honor Doyon received in 1871. Doyon's pince-nez glasses are also painted with much more descriptive detail, suggesting the importance Bonnat placed on what they signify: Doyon's ability to look, diagnose, and treat medical conditions (he founded the journal *Annales de dermatologie*). Indeed Bonnat's friendship with Doyon developed from the latter's expertise and his position as head of a medical clinic specializing in treatments for dermatology and rheumatology at Uriage-les-Bains (southeast of Grenoble) where Bonnat often sought treatment. Their rapport developed over the years such that Bonnat was asked to speak at the unveiling of a public monument to Doyon erected twenty-five years after he painted this portrait. Illness prevented Bonnat from presenting the speech in person, but his text was read and its emphasis on Doyon's "goodness of heart" meant their bonds of friendship came through as clearly as they do in this painting.

Bonnat's reputation grew significantly in the decade between his portraits of Raffalovich and Doyon. From 1865, Bonnat ran an independent studio that attracted students from Europe, Britain, America, and Scandinavia. Bonnat was himself made a chevalier of the Legion of Honor in 1867, and was promoted through the ranks to "grand officier." He likely identified with how much his sitters wanted their awards highlighted in their portraits.

Provenance

Portrait of Hermann (Jacques) Raffalovich
France, Countess J. de Sejorsac (great-great-granddaughter of sitter)
Toronto, Joey and Toby Tanenbaum, 1981–2002 (purchased through Jean-Pierre Selz, Paris)

Portrait of Dr. Adrien Doyon
Grenoble, Collection of Dr. Doyon
London, Norman Leitman, 1981
Toronto, Joey and Toby Tanenbaum, 1981–2002

Exhibition History

Portrait of Hermann (Jacques) Raffalovich
Hamilton, Art Gallery of Hamilton, 28 May 2005–28 May 2006, *Heaven and Earth Unveiled: European Treasures from the Tanenbaum Collection*, cat.12; 41–42, *103*
Hamilton, Art Gallery of Hamilton, 21 May–5 September 2011, *The French Connection*
Hamilton, Art Gallery of Hamilton, 9 February 2013–9 February 2014, *The Painter Pictured: French Nineteenth-Century Paintings and Portrait Photographs*

41

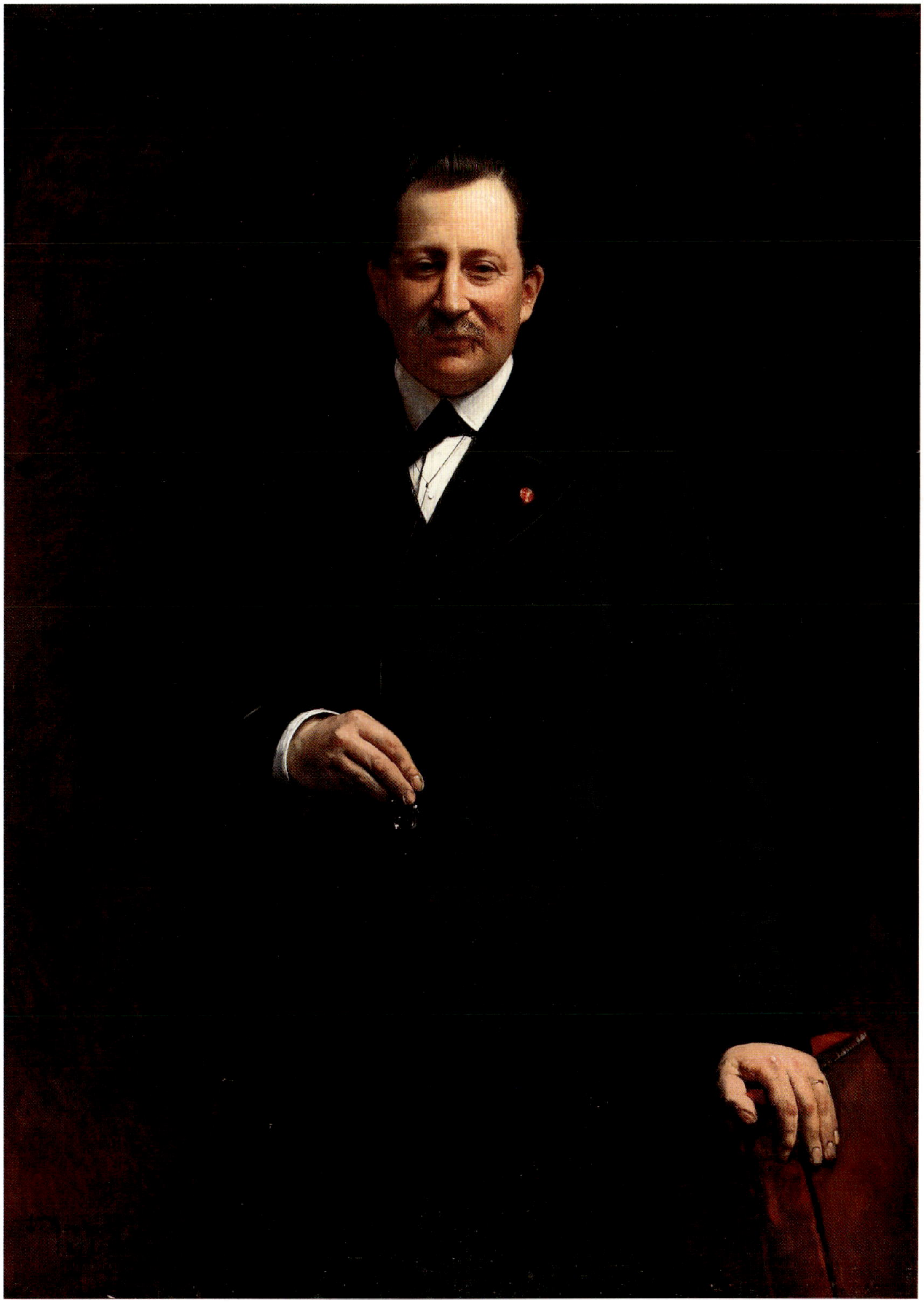

Portrait of Dr. Adrien Doyon

Hamilton, Art Gallery of Hamilton, 28 May 2005–28 May 2006, *Heaven and Earth Unveiled: European Treasures from the Tanenbaum Collection*, cat.11; 42, *105*

Hamilton, Art Gallery of Hamilton, 21 May–5 September 2011, *The French Connection*

Hamilton, Art Gallery of Hamilton, 9 February 2013–9 February 2014, *The Painter Pictured: French Nineteenth-Century Paintings and Portrait Photographs*

Bibliography

Bonnat, Léon. "Rembrandt," in Marcel Nicolle, *Rembrandt aux expositions d'Amsterdam et de Londres*. Paris: P. Ollendorff, 1899, i–vii.

Challons-Lipton, Siulolovan. *The Scandinavian Pupils of the Atelier Bonnat, 1867–1894*. Lewiston, NY: Edwin Mellen Press, 2001.

Ducourau, Vincent. *Léon Bonnat, 1833–1922: portraits d'apogée*. Bayonne: Musée Bonnat, 1998.

James, Anne Clark. "Léon Bonnat," in Gabriel P. Weisberg, *The Realist Tradition: French Painting and Drawing, 1830–1900*. Cleveland: Cleveland Museum of Art, 1980, 164–66, 177–80, 271–73.

Sloan, Rachel. "Gustave Moreau and the Raffalovich Family: New Documents for 'Sappho,'" *The Burlington Magazine* vol.148 no.1238 (May 2006): 327–31.

Usselman, H. "Léon Bonnat, d'après les témoignages de ses élèves nordiques," *Kunsthistorisk tidskrift* vol.55 no.2 (1986): 67–76.

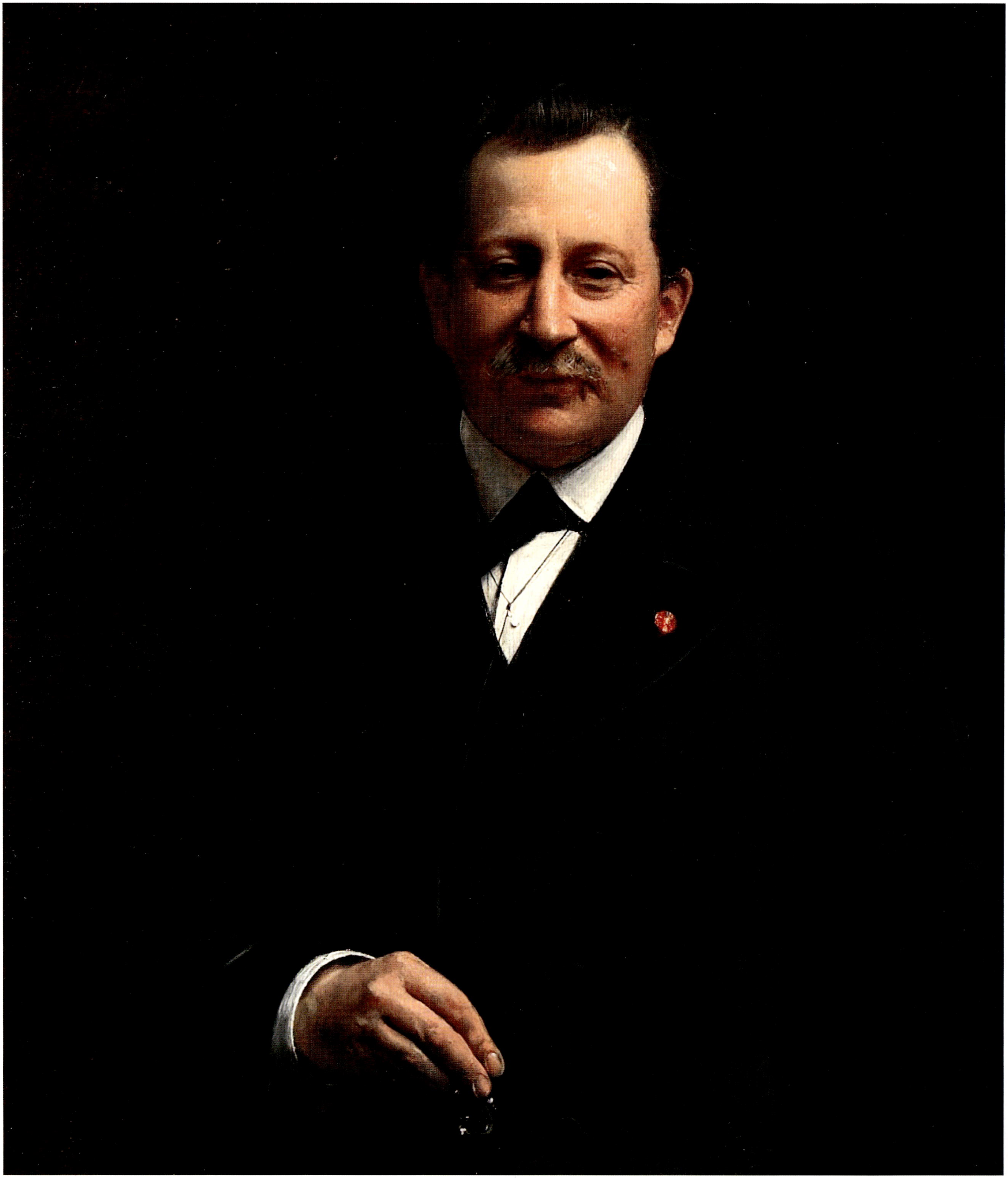

Edmund I

43 — Sapp

1879 • (

The ancient G
in the midst of
against the sho
ports herself by
blow away her
incidental figu

However,
how his own d
brooding skies,
matic lighting–
be understood
to educate him
of classical lanc
tradition devel
and he lived in
the date of Kar
or 1878—and h
1876, Kanoldt v
Germany, wher
he painted *Sapp*
successful that
suggests that th
the first of Kan

While Sapp
her figure repre
to the drama of
poets of antiqui
her attribute. B
some of the frag
autobiographica
accounts. The fo
believed to be t
boatman Phaon
Phaon rejected
the Ionian islan
herself into the
her passion or r
dramatic and de
her choices. A p
(43 BCE–17/18 C
on ancient heroi
women in variou
appears in anoth
In the years betv
protagonists of

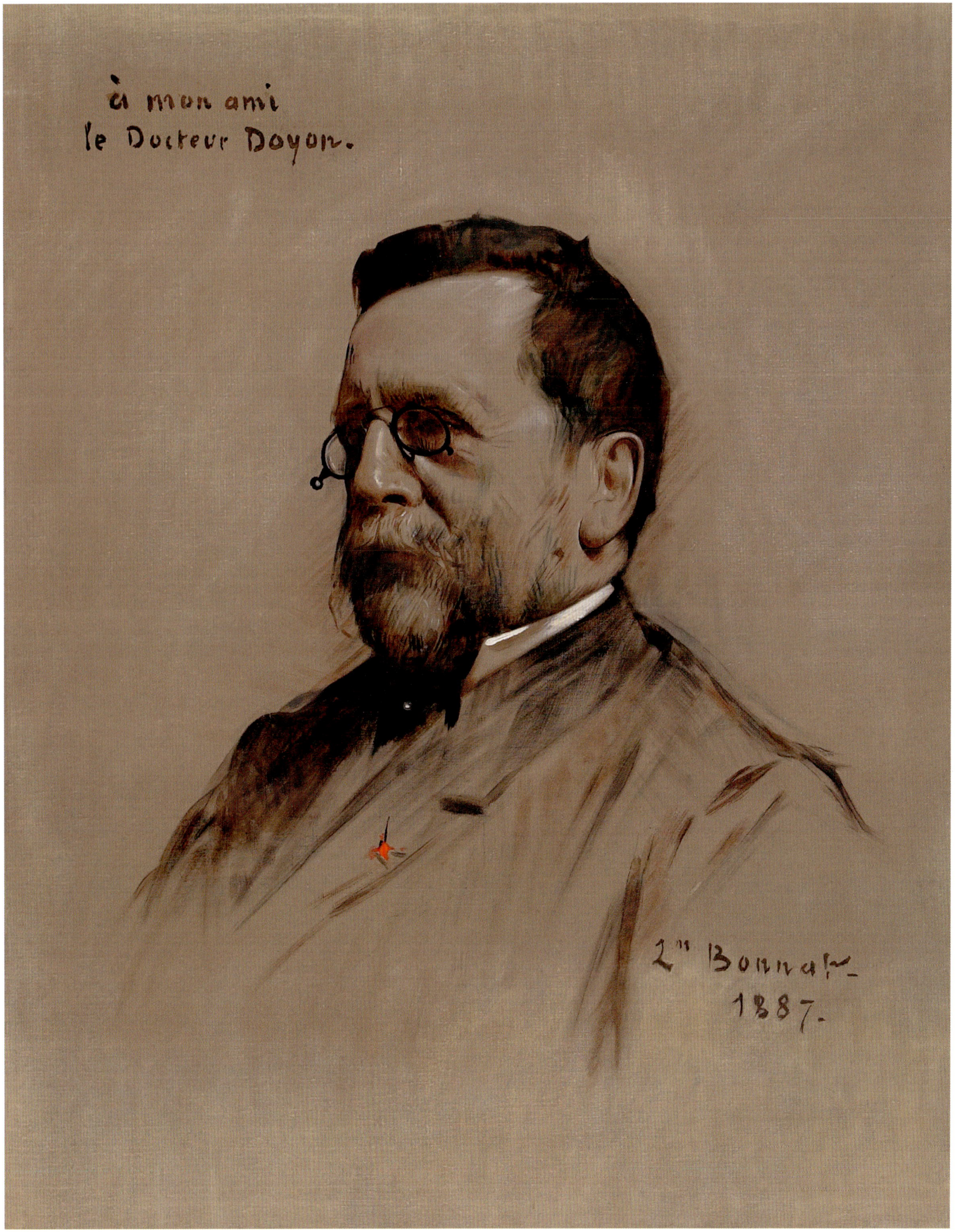

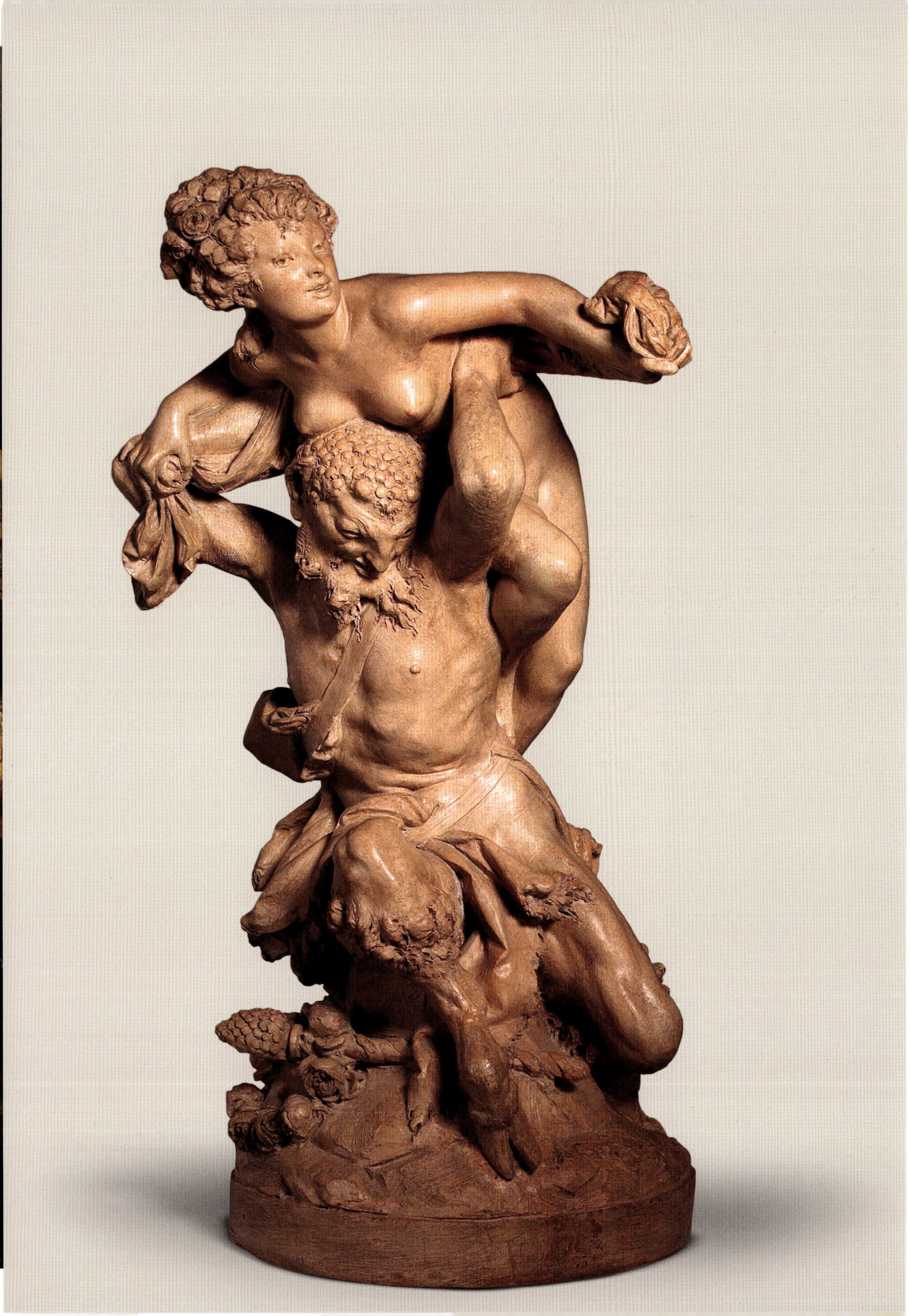

Albert-Ernest Carrier-Belleuse (French • 1824–1887)

46 — Nymph and Satyr

c.1880 • terracotta • 58.2 × 38 × 24 cm • s.base r. A. CARRIER BELLEUSE • Inv.2002.33.89

Carrier-Belleuse intended this statuette to appeal to contemporary collectors acquiring works for domestic spaces. He took inspiration from ancient mythology and focused on composition and modeling, offering viewers a scene of abduction as a vehicle for exploring visual pleasure. The satyr, a wood spirit and attendant of Bacchus, the Roman god of wine and fertility, is in the midst of picking up a nymph, a companion of Diana, the chaste goddess of the hunt. Carrier-Belleuse examined an aspect of the broader narrative of unsuspecting nymphs bathing with Diana, some of whom escape while one is captured by a satyr. The satyr's face registers his delight and, indeed, the nymph's body and facial expression hardly suggest resistance. Following a visual tradition from previous centuries, Carrier-Belleuse represents this distended moment as one of enjoyment, as the twisting bodies and intersecting forms provide a dynamic composition. He also combined realistic details, such as the folds of flesh at the satyr's waist, with an idealized representation of the female figure. The subject and playful forms of the terracotta *Nymph and Satyr* have strong connections with French Rococo art of the eighteenth century, a style that was again fashionable with many collectors in the period when Carrier-Belleuse produced this work.

Carrier-Belleuse was among the most entrepreneurial artists of his time. He exhibited at the Paris Salons beginning in 1857, and his works on mythological subjects drew increasing attention from 1863 when Napoleon III bought his marble *Bacchante Pouring a Libation over a Bacchic Term* for the Tuileries gardens. Carrier-Belleuse then began a practice of making terracotta reductions of his most popular compositions. He had the form cast and, while the work was still wet, added clay to certain areas to offer both descriptive details and surface interest. In *Nymph and Satyr*, these additions are evident in the bands of curls on the satyr's calves, the crown of roses below his knee, and the flowers in the nymph's hair. Carrier-Belleuse's skill at decorative ornamentation began with his early work for goldsmiths in Paris and the Minton china manufacturers in England (1850–55). His skill is evident in all of his works, from his terracotta statuettes to his numerous life-size portrait busts and the larger interior commissions such as his tall lamp *torchère* figures for the grand staircase of Garnier's new opera house (1873). To promote his career and ensure that his works reached a diverse market, Carrier-Belleuse also made his terracottas and other works available in four private sales he organized through Hôtel Drouot between 1868 and 1883. In an era when most sculptors relied on patrons to support the costs of their expensive materials and production processes, Carrier-Belleuse explored a wide range of possibilities. He was a pivotal figure in the intersecting spheres of art and industry, helped found the Union Centrale des Arts Décoratifs in 1863, and provided dynamic leadership as artistic director at the Sèvres porcelain factory from 1875 until his death.

Provenance

London, Thomas Agnew & Sons Ltd, 1984

Toronto, Joey and Toby Tanenbaum, 1984–2002 (purchased through Norman Leitman, London)

Exhibition History

Hamilton, Art Gallery of Hamilton, 28 May 2005–28 May 2006, *Heaven and Earth Unveiled: European Treasures from the Tanenbaum Collection*, cat. 152; 182–83, *162*

Hamilton, Art Gallery of Hamilton, 28 April–2 December 2007, *A Visual Bestiary*

Hamilton, Art Gallery of Hamilton, 5 March 2011–19 August 2012, *From Rude to Rodin*

Hamilton, Art Gallery of Hamilton, 9 February 2013–9 February 2014, *The Painter Pictured: French Nineteenth-Century Paintings and Portrait Photographs*

Bibliography

Carrier-Belleuse: œuvres, Paris, Hôtel Drouot, 26 December 1868; 21 December 1874; 25 April 1876; and 12 May 1883.

Carrier-Belleuse, Albert Ernest. *Application de la figure humaine à la décoration et à l'ornementation industrielles.* Paris: Goupil & Cie., 1884.

Draper, James. "French Terracottas," *Metropolitan Museum of Art Bulletin* vol.49 no.3 (Winter 1991/1992): 1–57.

Hargrove, June. *The Life and Work of Albert Carrier-Belleuse.* New York: Garland Publishing, 1977, 234–35, 250–51.

-----, et al. *Carrier-Belleuse: le maître de Rodin.* Paris: Réunion des musées nationaux, 2014, 125, *127.*

Segard, Achille. *Albert Carrier-Belleuse.* Paris: H. Champion, 1928.

Nicola Forcella (Italian • b. before 1868–d. after 1906)

47 — Portrait of an Arab

c.1880–90 • oil on wood panel • 32.5 × 24.3 cm • s.l.r. N. Forcella • Inv.2002.33.114

Unlike many European-born artists who were fascinated with orientalist subjects but who never traveled to North Africa or the Middle East, Forcella spent most of his career living and working in Egypt. In painting *Portrait of an Arab*, Forcella certainly appears to have worked from the live model, and he executed the sitter's face with meticulous attention to detail. He layered hues of paint and created a strong sense of three-dimensional form. Highlights draw attention to the man's lower lip, nose, and ear, as well as his beard. Forcella also sought to represent the sitter's age with the utmost authenticity: the facial hair includes much gray, the mature skin on the forehead and cheek reveal the shape of the man's skull, lines and shadows form around his right eye. Forcella also rendered the man's clothing in a highly descriptive manner. He created a strong sense of volume through the multiple, overlapping folds of the light-colored headscarf and he used quick brushstrokes to animate the frayed edge of the man's cloak. A markedly different technique is manifest in the impastoed surface of the cream-colored background. The strong line that forms around the sitter's profile suggests the background was added to enhance our attention to the man's face. The three-quarter pose and Forcella's choices around tonal harmonies clearly evoke the sitter's proud countenance. Forcella may have produced this painting as an individual portrait or in preparation for one of his multi-figure compositions, some of which can be found in private collections today. Forcella's paintings of everyday life in Egypt often focused on Islamic men gathering for prayer at mosques or on a mixture of Muslims and Europeans in open-air market scenes.[1]

Forcella was born in Castellaneta, in the Puglia region of southern Italy, and he immigrated to Egypt at an unknown date with his brother Paolo, who was also a visual artist and musician. Forcella often signed but rarely dated his paintings and, although the year 1877 has previously been assigned to this work, there is no conclusive evidence to support such an early date. Records of administrative and commercial businesses in late nineteenth-century Egypt document Forcella working as a professor of painting and drawing at a school for the applied arts in Cairo, the École Khédiviale d'Arts et Métiers. While much remains unknown, Forcella was certainly a well-respected artist and professor. He received the Order of the Medjidie, a knightly order of the Ottoman Empire, as well as the higher-ranked Order of Osmaniye.

[1] *Arrival at the Mosque* (private collection); *The Old Carpet Seller* (New York, Christie's, 27 May 1992, lot 111); and *In the Coppers' Souk* (Paris, Sotheby's, 24 October 1997, lot 26).

Provenance

Washington, D.C., Weschler's Galleries, 6 June 1976, lot 629

New York, Forbes Magazine Collection

New York, Christie's, 14 October 1993, lot 21

Toronto, Joey and Toby Tanenbaum, 1993–2002

Exhibition History

Hamilton, Art Gallery of Hamilton, 28 May 2005–28 May 2006, *Heaven and Earth Unveiled: European Treasures from the Tanenbaum Collection*, cat.45, *153* (dated 1877)

Hamilton, Art Gallery of Hamilton, 22 May–6 September 2010, *Europe's Exoticized East*

Bibliography

Balboni, Luigi Antonio. *Gl'Italiani nella civiltà egiziana del secolo XIX.* 3 vols. Alexandria: V. Penasson, 1906, vol.3, 339–40.

Juler, Caroline. *Les Orientalistes de l'école italienne.* Paris: ACR Édition, 1987, 135.

Poffandi, Stefano. *Indicateur égyptien administratif et commercial.* Alexandria: Imprimerie Générale, 1896, 28.

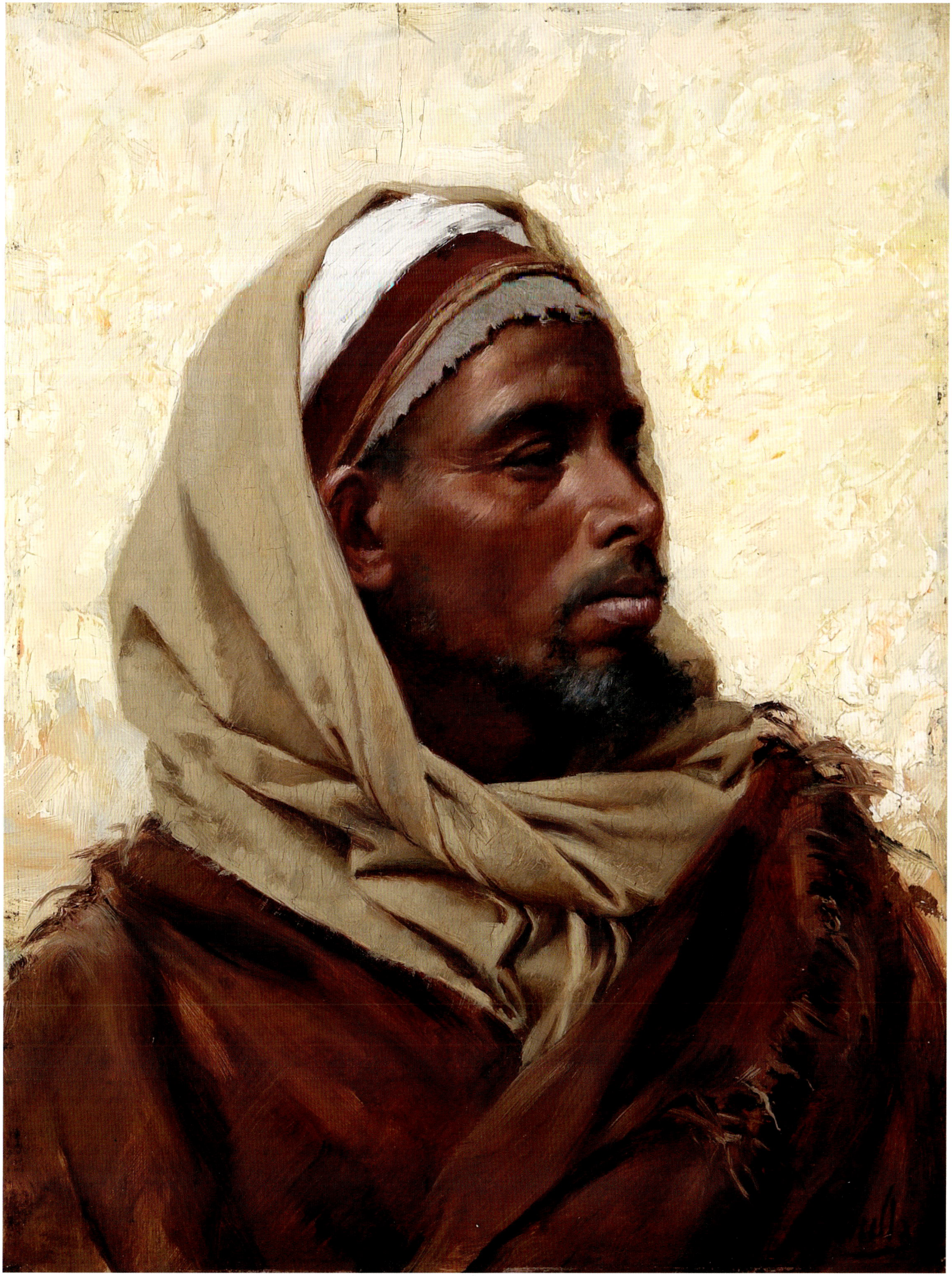

Albert Joseph Moore (English • 1841–1893)

48 — Seated Girl Reading

1880–93 • pastel on paper mounted on pasteboard • 80.5 × 60.5 cm • Inv.2002.33.39

Pastel was an important medium for Moore, and he often showed works at the pastel exhibitions that were mounted at the Grosvenor Gallery in London from 1888. Moore explored pastel both as a medium independent from his oil paintings and as an integral part of his preparatory work. The visual evidence suggests Moore created *Seated Girl Reading* as a study, and it was thus a vehicle to explore his well-defined aesthetic goals. The absence of a Greek anthemion, a motif of fan-shaped palm leaves that Moore first developed as his signature in 1866, suggests that he did not submit this pastel to an exhibition or perhaps even conceive of it as a work that would be seen by a broad public. A large number of Moore's preparatory works do however survive, many in the collection of the Victoria and Albert Museum, and they offer insight into both his working practices and his historical significance. According to recent scholarship, Moore's engagement with visual concerns—such as form, color, and beauty—positions him as one of the important figures of British aestheticism.

Moore advocated producing art for its own sake. In creating the highly idealized female forms that were the central focus of his production, Moore drew upon both his strong sense of chromatic harmony and his close observation of nature. Early in his career Moore began an intensive study of the Parthenon sculptures in the British Museum, and he had a sustained fascination with those "Elgin marbles" throughout his career. His interest in classical drapery is evident in this pastel, as it is with most of his works. Moore combined his fondness for Greek classicism with a studio practice centered around studies from the live model, and his careful rendering of the woman's face and forearms suggests this was the case for *Seated Girl Reading*. Moore created an impressive sense of three-dimensionality through his use of a strong contour line and his detailed attention to the woman's features. Beyond the immediate area of the woman's head, however, Moore took a quite different approach. He used black chalk to define the horizontal lines of a bench and to outline the form of the woman's upper body and lap. Moore's interest in descriptive detail then diminished as he moved further away from the figure's core. He used increasingly gestural and expressive strokes to add color to the dress and shawl that drapes behind the woman and across her lap. He enlivened the work by juxtaposing warm yellow and salmon with cool blue and green. Dense layers of white pastel, particularly in areas closest to the figure, make the background recede and contribute to our sense of the figure's volume. Moore also left portions of the paper's surface entirely untouched. He appreciated the immediacy of pastel, its textural qualities, and its ability to convey color. Moore also understood how to employ an economy of means to great effect. In removing overt allegorical or biblical narrative from his presentation of this figure, Moore encourages the viewer to focus on the visual aspects of *Seated Girl Reading*, and he transforms those into the principal subjects of the work.

Provenance

Sir Robert Abdy

New York, James Coats Gallery, 1965–68

Toronto, Joey and Toby Tanenbaum, 1968–2002

Exhibition History

Rochester, Memorial Art Gallery, University of Rochester, 8–31 October 1965, *The Pre-Raphaelite Movement & Its Influence on American Decorative Arts: Roycroft-Tiffany*, no.16 (no catalogue produced)

Toronto, Art Gallery of Ontario, *The Sacred and Profane in Symbolist Art*, 1–26 November 1969, unnumbered in catalogue

Hamilton, Art Gallery of Hamilton, 28 May 2005–28 May 2006, *Heaven and Earth Unveiled: European Treasures from the Tanenbaum Collection*, cat.80; *155*

Bibliography

Asleson, Robyn. *Albert Moore*. London: Phaidon Press, 2000.

-----. "Nature and Abstraction in the Aesthetic Development of Albert Moore," in Elizabeth Prettejohn, ed. *After the Pre-Raphaelites: Art and Aestheticism in Victorian England*. Manchester: Manchester University Press, 1999, 115–34.

Baldry, Alfred Lys. *Albert Moore: His Life and Works*. London: George Bell & Sons, 1894.

Benedetti, Maria Teresa. "Whistler, Moore e l'Art for Art's Sake,'" *Paragone* vol.32 no.375 (May 1981): 21–39.

Hedberg, Gregory, ed. *Victorian High Renaissance*. Minneapolis: Institute of Arts, 1987, 129–55.

Morgan, Hilary Jane. "Theory and Practice in the Work of Watts, Leighton, Burne-Jones and Moore," M.Phil. dissertation, Courtauld Institute of Art, University of London, 1982.

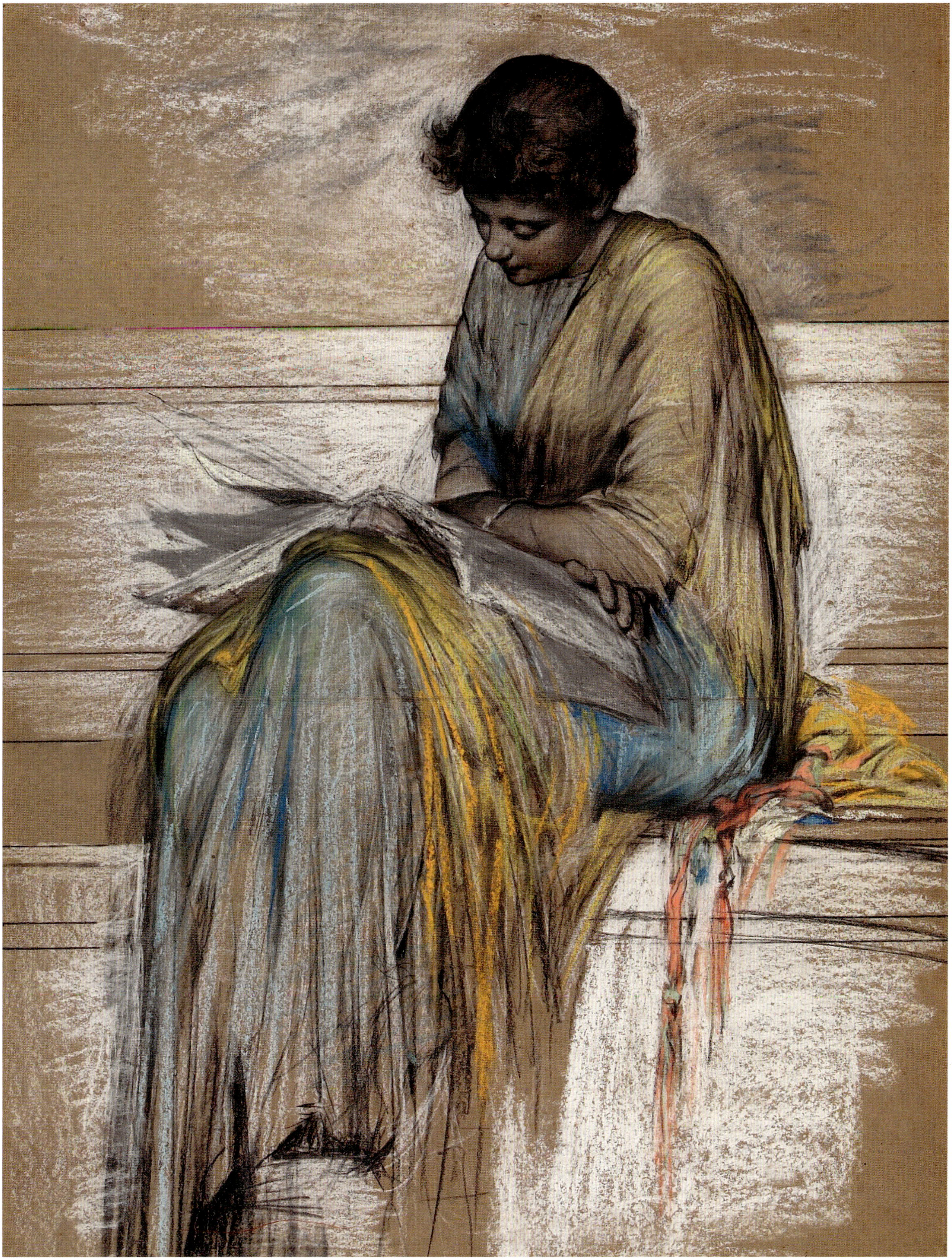

Mihály Munkácsy (Hungarian • 1844–1900)

49 — Christ before Pilate

1881 • oil on canvas • 417 × 636 cm • s.d.l.r. M. Munkacsy • Inv.2002.33.61 • Photograph by Michael Lalich

Few works of art have traveled more and been seen by larger crowds than Munkácsy's *Christ before Pilate*. People lined up to see it when it was first exhibited in Paris in 1881. From the early through later twentieth century the painting was displayed in a department store in Philadelphia for shoppers to enjoy during the Easter season. For much of the new millennium the work has hung at the Déri Múzeum in Debrecen, Hungary's second city, where it has been an object of great admiration. The appeal of this painting is manifold and has attracted people with interests ranging from religious devotion to commercial gain, and to national pride. The artist's motivations to produce this immense painting are equally complex, as is his compelling presentation of a decisive moment in Christ's life. Munkácsy pictorializes the trial of Christ, what various sources describe as the series of events between Christ's arrest and crucifixion. Of the dozens of figures who populate the canvas and demand our attention, with their expressive faces and gesturing hands, three are key to our understanding of the narrative. Dressed in a white gown, Christ stands as a prisoner, his wrists tied with rope and his gaze intent. Seated in an ornate niche, Pilate grimaces and casts his eyes downward. His arms are folded tightly below his chest and he opens one hand as he weighs his decision. Between Christ and Pilate stands Caiaphas, the high priest who declared it blasphemous for Christ to proclaim himself the Son of God. Caiaphas demands Pilate's verdict and his gestures unite all three protagonists. Behind Caiaphas sit members of the Sanhedrin, the senior Jewish council, who continue to debate their views. Only one woman is present in this otherwise all-male space. Standing with a young child in her arms, she evokes Marian imagery but she may in fact represent Pilate's wife, who sent a message imploring her husband to have nothing to do with the innocent man.

Munkácsy first attracted international attention in 1870 when his painting *The Last Day of a Condemned Man* was awarded a gold medal at the Paris Salon (no.2063). Munkácsy soon settled in Paris, and by 1878 he had secured a lucrative ten-year contract with art dealer Charles Sedelmeyer (1837–1925). That agreement afforded Munkácsy a regular income while it granted Sedelmeyer ownership of all works Munkácsy produced, as well as the rights to disseminate them in various forms. The art-going public expected to see *Christ before Pilate* at the Salon; however, either the combination of a small fire in Munkácsy's studio and an inflexible jury deadline, or simply a savvy marketing scheme meant the work was delayed and could only be seen at Sedelmeyer's private residence at 6 rue de La Rochefoucauld, a short distance from the busy Saint-Lazare train station. Whether contrived or not, that set of circumstances, and the perception of displaying a work that would otherwise be deprived to an expectant public, set the stage for how the work would consistently be received. From Paris, Sedelmeyer exhibited *Christ before Pilate* in nearly a dozen cities from Warsaw to Stockholm and London, and it was seen by hundreds of thousands of people. In 1886 Sedelmeyer took the painting on tour again, this time to the United States, where it was shown along with Munkácsy's *Christ on Golgotha* (1884). All of the money raised by the entrance fees in each venue, as well as the sales of reproductive prints, went to Sedelmeyer.[1] In New York, the paintings attracted the attention of John and Mary Wanamaker, whose wealth came from their famous family-run Philadelphia department store. They acquired both paintings for their private collection and paid more than $100,000 for each (accounts range as high as $170,000), the price said to be the most ever paid for a work by a living artist. Contemporary American press also referred to *Christ before Pilate* as the most inspiring painting of a sacred subject that had ever been made. The Wanamakers donated the proceeds from an additional six-month tour that allowed the painting to be seen by an estimated million more viewers. They then hung both of Munkácsy's works in an expressly designed gallery adjoining Lindenhurst, their private residence on the outskirts of Philadelphia. In 1907, a fire at Lindenhurst destroyed much of the collection, but both of Munkácsy's paintings were saved, restored, and transferred to the Philadelphia store in 1911. Even before that date, the paintings were regularly exhibited at Wanamaker's department store during the Easter season. The tradition continued well after the deaths of both Mary (1839–1920) and John (1838–1922), until the store changed owners in 1986.

Since 1995, *Christ before Pilate* has regularly been on long-term loan to the Déri Múzeum in Hungary.[2] There, it is presented as the first of three works Munkácsy completed on the life of Christ. Reunited with *Christ on Golgotha* and exhibited alongside *Ecce Homo* (1896), the paintings have come to form a trilogy that also commemorates the achievements of one of Hungary's most celebrated painters.

1 Charles Waltner's reproductive etching received the medal of honor at the Paris Salon in 1883.

2 At the time this book headed to press, negotiations over the prospective permanent transfer of *Christ before Pilate* to Debrecen were not conclusive. See also Nicole O'Reilly, "AGH considering selling painting valued at more than $5 million," *Hamilton Spectator* (30 July 2014); *The Budapest Times* (20 July 2014).

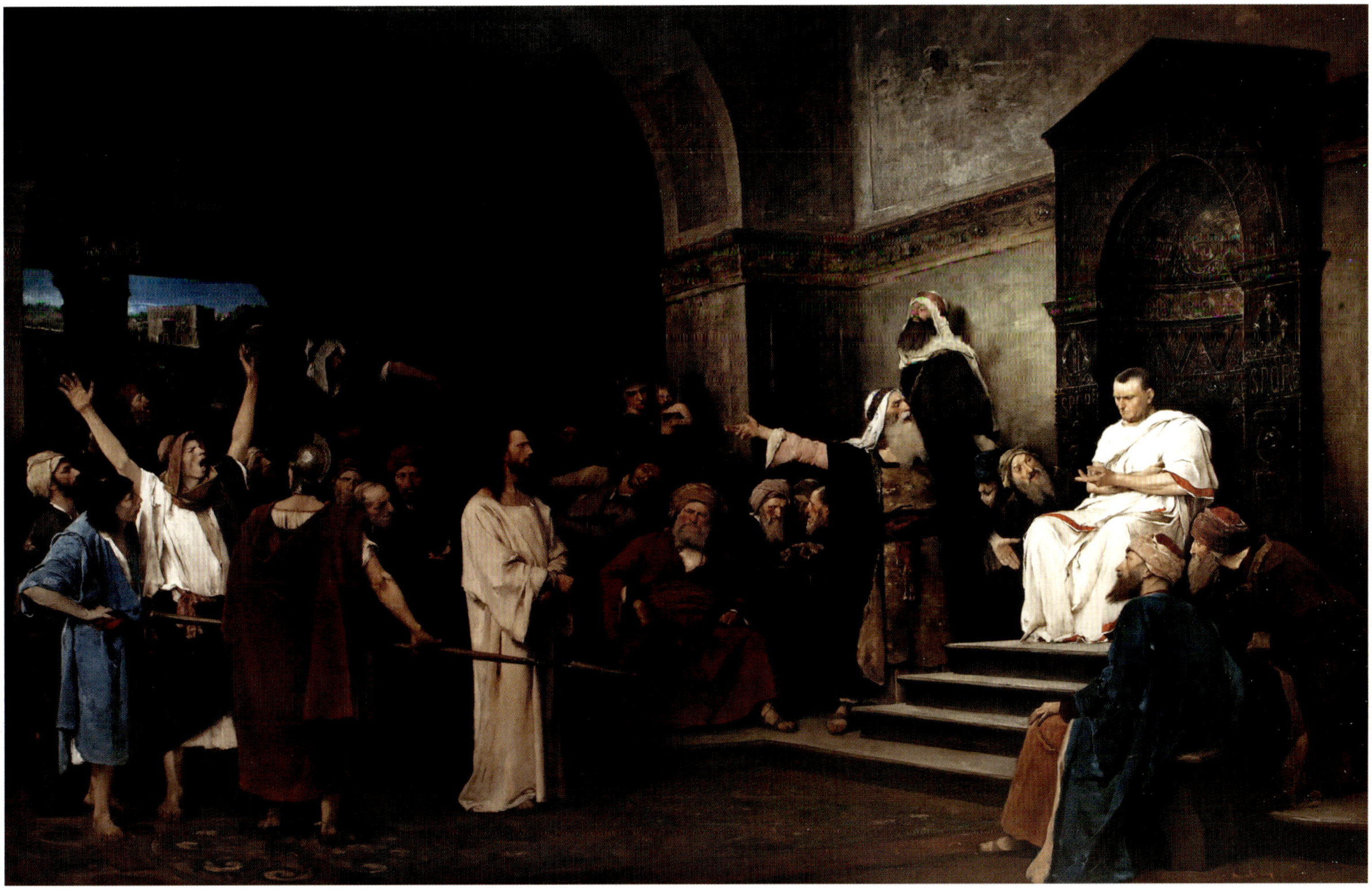

Provenance

Paris, Charles Sedelmeyer, 1881
Budapest, Adolf Wertheimer
Budapest, Képtár Fővárosi
Philadelphia, John and Mary Wanamaker, 1887–1928
Philadelphia, John Wanamaker Inc., 1928–88
New York, Sotheby's, 24 February 1988, lot 57
Toronto, Joey and Toby Tanenbaum, 1988–2002

Exhibition History

Paris, Galerie Sedelmeyer, 1881
International tour (including Vienna, Budapest, and twenty cities in Great Britain), 1881
United States tour, 1886
Paris, Exposition Universelle, 1889, no.76 (Austria-Hungary section)
Philadelphia, Central Department Store, 1911–88
Toronto, Canadian Opera Company, 1988–1992 (on long-term loan)
Debrecen, Déri Múzeum, August 1995–December 2000, December 2002–December 2007, July 2009–July 2014 (on long-term loan)

Bibliography

András, Edit. "Egy magyar Amerikában: A Munkácsy–trilógia és a Wanamaker Áruház," in *Angyalokra szükség van: tanulmányok Bernáth Mária tiszteletére.* Budapest: MTA Művészettörténeti Kutatóintézet, 2005, 21–34.
Bakó, Zsuzsanna. *Mihály Munkácsy.* Budapest: Kossuth Kiadó Rt., 2008, 37, 42, *50–51* (reduction).
-----, and Judit Boros. *Munkácsy a nagyvilában: Munkácsy Mihály müvei külfödi és Magyar magan és közgyüjteményekben.* Budapest: Szemmimpex Publishing, 2005, 61–86.
D'Argencourt, Louise, et al. *Heaven and Earth Unveiled: European Treasures from the Tanenbaum Collection.* Hamilton: Art Gallery of Hamilton, 2005, cat.81; *156* (not exhibited).
Gaál, Botond, Katalin Sz. Kürti, and József Hapák. *Mihály Munkácsy's Trilogy of Christ: Christ before Pilate, Ecce Homo, Golgotha.* Debrecen: Blende, 1995, 1–5.
Huemer, Christian. "Charles Sedelmeyer, 1837–1925: Kunst und Spekulation am Kunstmarkt in Paris," *Belvedere* no.2 (1999): 4–19 (10–11).
Kurtz, Charles M. *Christ before Pilate: The Painting by Munkacsy.* Rev. ed. Philadelphia: Kurtz, 1887.
Maas, John. "Munkácsy in America: New Light on *Christ before Pilate,*" *Müvészettörténeti Értesító* vol.3 nos.1–2 (1988): 33–44.
Michel, Natalie, et al. *Budapest, 1869–1914: modernité hongroise et peinture européenne.* Dijon: Musée des Beaux-Arts, 1995, 118–19.
Morowitz, Laura. "A Passion for Business: Wanamaker's, Munkácsy, and the Depiction of Christ," *The Art Bulletin* vol.91 no.2 (June 2009): 184–206.
Sandqvist, Tom. *The Sacred Cause, The Europe That Was Lost: Thoughts on Central European Modernism.* Frankfurt: Peter Lang, 2009, 400–403.
Sedelmeyer, Charles. *Michael von Munkácsy.* Paris: Sedelmeyer, 1914, 21–25, 28, 78–79.
Székely, András. *Mihály Munkácsy.* Saint Paul, MN, 1981, 12.
-----. *Munkácsy.* 2nd ed. Budapest: Corvina, 1979, 12–16, pl.63 (reduction).
Végvári, Lajos. *Mihály Munkácsy, 1844–1900.* Budapest: Képzőművészeti Kiadó, 1983, 70–74.

Medardo Rosso (Italian • 1858–1928)

50 — Head of a Laughing Boy

1881–82 • bronze with marble base • 46 × 32 × 22 cm • s.l. shoulder Rosso • Inv.2002.33.178

The title *Street Urchin* was previously assigned to this sculpture, but *Head of a Laughing Boy* is both a more accurate description and more nuanced title for this evocative work. A broad smile reveals the gaps of several missing teeth. The boy's cheeks rise and his pupils dance as he turns to look across his shoulder. He may be glancing to the source of his amusement, or perhaps he looks in the direction of a friend whom he invites to join in his escapades. Much of the success of this work comes from the remarkable way Rosso implies the moment of a narrative and yet leaves the viewer to fill in the specifics of the story. The spectator is immediately captivated by the child's energy, and our ears ring with the gleeful, infectious laughter we imagine pouring forth from his mouth. Rosso also skillfully contrasts surface texture. The most heavily worked areas are the collar of the boy's shirt and his cap, which hovers askew on his head. The flesh of the boy's nose, cheeks, and lower lip appear more taut. Rosso is not, however, simply contrasting flesh and fabric. The right side of the boy's face, and particularly his ear, is a pliable area where skin becomes an animated surface of indentations and protrusions that intersect with the network of lines around his eye. Surface variations absorb and reflect light, adding to the dynamic qualities of the sculpture.

This bronze relates to one of the earliest extant works that is documented in Rosso's oeuvre. He first exhibited a version of this sculpture in Milan in August 1882 at the Esposizione di Belle Arti di Brera, where it was entitled *After an Escapade* (*Dopo una scappata*, no.650). Rosso showed the work again, under the same title, at the Esposizione Internazionale di Belle Arti held in Rome the following year (no.19), and then in Paris in 1886 at the second exhibition of the Société des Artistes Indépendants (no.4493), where it was entitled *Gavroche*.[1] The French word, a synonym for *gamin*, refers to a child who spends their time playing in the street. As Rosso increasingly exhibited his works in international exhibitions, and was himself based in Paris from 1889 to around 1915, various titles became attached to this sculpture that imply meanings Rosso did not himself make explicit. In French and also in English, as the word "urchin" was increasingly identified with this sculpture, it became embedded in romanticized notions of waifs and vagabonds. In fact, nothing in the sculpture itself foregrounds urban life or homelessness as integral to its meaning, or any broader social context it might imply. The missing teeth might best be interpreted as an indicator of the innocence of the boy's mischievous actions: he is of an age where some of his adult teeth are merely starting to emerge. Recent scholarship proposes Rosso selected the subject for this work from a novel by one of the circle of "Scapigliatura" poets (*scapigliato* translates literally as unruly hair). Although the specific source remains unidentified, Rosso was part of the Milanese Scapigliatura group that was devoted to the union of painting, sculpture, architecture, music, and literature. Rosso produced numerous variations of the sculpture during the two decades following his original conception in bronze. This demonstrates both how the work was integral to Rosso's broader interest in creating expressive heads and suggests how the subject brought him considerable commercial success. In other versions, the head is an unmounted bronze or plaster, is fixed to an architectural fragment with a bracket, or is mounted on a marble base as in this example.[2] Extant photographs of the work in Rosso's studio (taken by him or made in collaboration with another artist) reveal how Rosso intended the head to be seen from a specific angle that conceals the bracket mount and foregrounds how narratives unfold across the surfaces of the sculpture.

[1] This sculpture has also been entitled *Lo scugnizzo, Il birichino, Garçon qui rit*, and *Il monello*. While Rosso often changed the titles of his works and was known to tailor titles to the context of specific exhibitions, many of the titles assigned to this head do not originate with the artist.

[2] A plaster is in the Museo Medardo Rosso, Barzio. A head mounted on an architectural fragment is in the Niigata City Art Museum, Niigata.

Provenance

Schaan, Regis Art Establishment

Toronto, Joey and Toby Tanenbaum, 1971–2002

Exhibition History

Hamilton, Art Gallery of Hamilton, 28 May 2005–28 May 2006, *Heaven and Earth Unveiled: European Treasures from the Tanenbaum Collection*, cat. 206; 186, *160* as *Street Urchin*

Hamilton, Art Gallery of Hamilton, 7 February 2009–14 February 2010, *Scultori Italiani*

Bibliography

Becker, Jane R. "Medardo Rosso: Photographing Sculpture and Sculpting Photography," in Dorothy Kosinski, ed. *The Artist and the Camera: Degas to Picasso.* Dallas: Dallas Museum of Art, 1999, 159–78.

Brunk, Birgit. "Sculpture for the Seeing: The 'punto di vista unico,' a Lifelong Search for the Truth," in Dieter Schwarz, ed. *Medardo Rosso.* Düsseldorf: Richter, 2004, 14–39 (15–16).

Caramel, Luciano. *Medardo Rosso: le origini della scultura moderna.* Milan: Skira, 2004, 70–71.

Hecker, Sharon. "Reflections on Repetition in Rosso's Art," in Harry Cooper et al. *Medardo Rosso: Second Impressions.* New Haven: Yale University Press, 2003, 22–67.

Mola, Paola. *Rosso: The Transient Form.* Milan: Skira, 2007.

-----, et al. *Medardo Rosso: catalogueo ragionato della scultura.* Milan: Skira, 2009, 227–33.

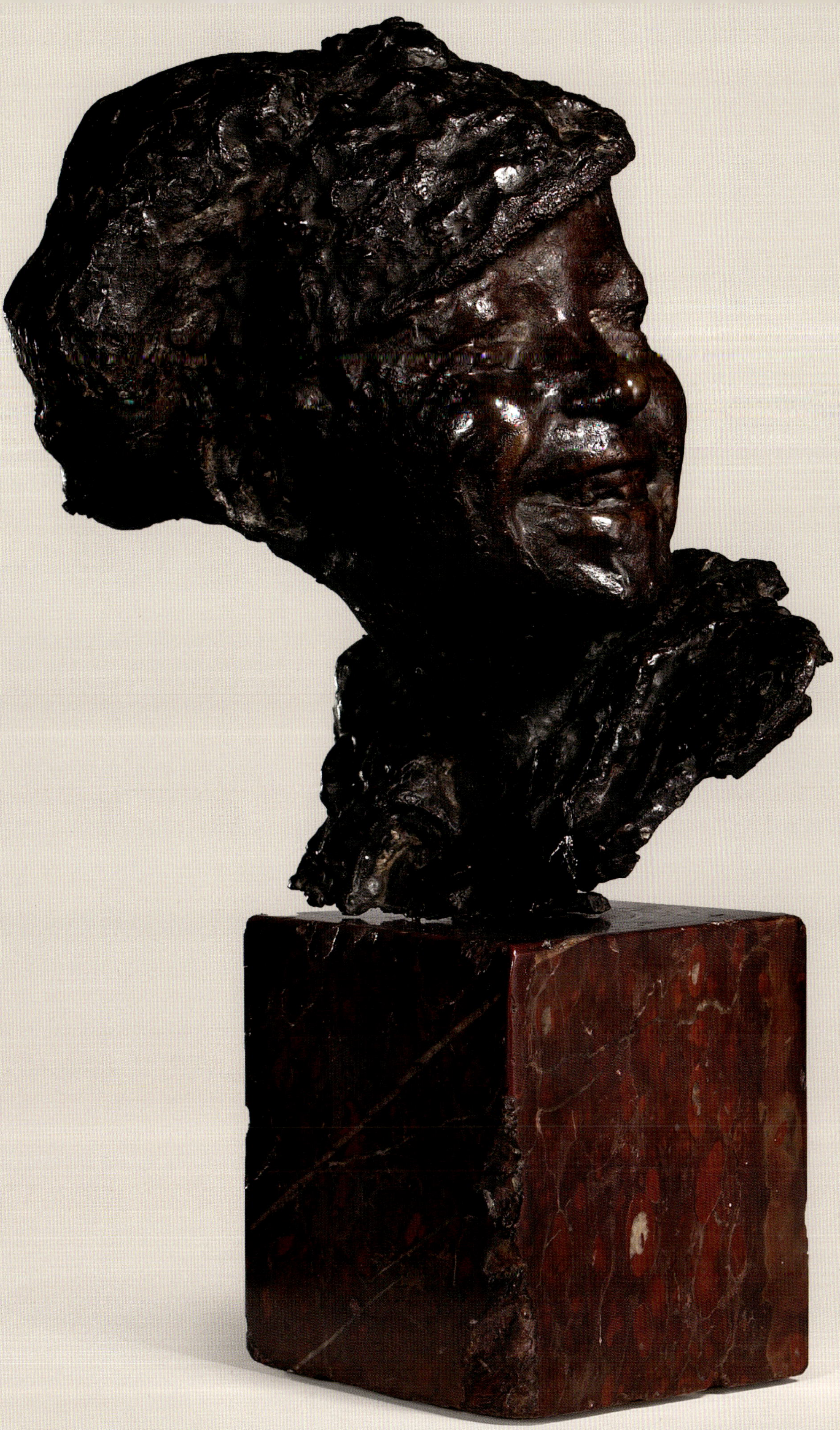

Mariya Bashkirtseva (Ukrainian • 1858–1884)

51 — Portrait of a Woman

1882 • oil on canvas • 55.5 × 46 cm • u.r. MB; s. verso, on stretcher, Marie Bashkirtseff and r. 1882 Paris • Inv.2002.33.78

Bashkirtseva's loose network of brushstrokes form the shape of her sitter's dress, suggest the seams of the sleeves, and define the ruffled neckline. Bashkirtseva juxtaposes this sketch-like lower section with the woman's clearly rendered face, with its modeled features, well-defined nose, eyes and lower lip glistening and moist. The black paint of the dress repeats in a more opaque, layered form in the woman's hair, a dark mass that becomes a fringe of wispy curls and feathery bangs. Dark gray areas of paint form a visual echo around the woman's head. The sitter's luminous skin glows in the center of the composition and suggests a light source outside the work. Positioned before this painting, the viewer looks on from the space of that external light, while the woman looks away, her attention drawn to her left. We are curious but we know none of the narrative around this moment, and Bashkirtseva evokes a momentary quality that successfully challenges the often-staged nature of portraiture. Bashkirtseva elected to use a restricted palette of colors that sets off the three-dimensionality of the woman's face. Her face is heightened by the line of shadow at her chin and is set against door paneling and the decorative fragment of a chair back that are only subtly suggested. We are captivated, just as the artist wanted us to be.

Bashkirtseva completed this work in 1882 in Paris, where she had been working for five years and where she was known as Marie Bashkirtseff. In the years both before and after *Portrait of a Woman*, Bashkirtseva exhibited works at the Salon under the name Marie-Constantin Russ (1880, no.3379), simply Andrey (1881, no.55), and also Mme Marie Bashkirseff (*sic*; 1883, no.2517), modifying her name on the latter occasion to appear both married and perhaps more French. Some female artists assumed male pseudonyms to hide their gender from the Salon jury. Others, like Bashkirtseva and Sophie de Boutellier, who exhibited as Henriette Browne, adopted female pseudonyms that masked their identity for reasons that are less easily explained. Born in a small town near Poltava, Ukraine, Bashkirtseva's pseudonyms seem at least in part to hide her position as a foreigner. However, many foreign artists exhibited at the Paris Salons of the nineteenth century, and Bashkirtseva appears to have felt quite at home in France, where she had lived since 1872. Further, she was always transparent in citing her birthplace as Russia in Salon catalogues. Alternate names may have offered some protection from direct judgment as Bashkirtseva exhibited and established her reputation before a new public audience. She was ambitious and, soon after arriving in Paris, she enrolled at the Académie Julian, which opened in 1880. At the time it offered the most progressive studio environment for female artists. The École des Beaux-Arts accepted female students only from 1897, whereas at the Académie Julian female art students had the possibility of studying from both the male and female nude.

Bashkirtseva was well respected by her contemporaries and, in 1885, just one year after her death, the Union des Femmes Peintres et Sculpteurs organized a retrospective of her work in Paris, and produced an illustrated exhibition catalogue. This large one-person show of 228 works captured the extent of her output and included 100 paintings, five sculptures, six pastels, and 117 drawings. It offered an impressive display of both her finished and preparatory work. The dimensions of *Portrait of a Woman* are close to those of three works in the retrospective, *Tête de Femme (étude), Étude*, and *Modèle* (nos.44, 45, and 80). These and other works indicate Bashkirtseva's extensive use of both sketch-like and more highly finished brushwork in one painting of an individual sitter, and how she regarded these objects as complete works of art. Bashkirtseva met with considerable critical acclaim while she was still alive, and the French state purchased one of her paintings, *The Meeting*, at the Salon of 1884 for the Musée du Luxembourg (Paris, Musée d'Orsay). Soon after, she died from tuberculosis at age twenty-five. Her personal diary was published in 1887 and in English translation first in 1888, with numerous republications to follow. As is too often the case for female artists, attention to biographical details has dominated the study of her work. The virtuosity of *Portrait of a Woman* demonstrates how, in order to understand the work of Bashkirtseva, it is less to her private journals and more to her accomplished and commanding paintings that we should direct our attention.

Provenance

New York, Schweitzer Gallery
Toronto, Joey and Toby Tanenbaum, 1980–2002 (purchased through Norman Leitman, London)

Exhibition History

Hamilton, Art Gallery of Hamilton, 28 May 2005–28 May 2006; Victoria, Art Gallery of Greater Victoria, 25 January–11 May 2008, *Heaven and Earth Unveiled: European Treasures from the Tanenbaum Collection*, cat.7, *153.*
Hamilton, Art Gallery of Hamilton, 10 February–13 May 2007, *Framed: The Art of the Portrait*
Hamilton, Art Gallery of Hamilton, 21 May–5 September 2011, *The French Connection*

Bibliography

Bashkirtseff, Marie. *Le Journal de Marie Bashkirtseff*. Pref. André Theuriet. 2 vols. Paris: G. Charpentier et Co., 1887.
-----. *Marie Bashkirtseff: The Journal of a Young Artist, 1860–1884*. Trans. Mary J. Serrano. New York: Cassell & Company, 1888.
-----. *The Journal of Marie Bashkirtseff*. Trans. Mathilde Blind, with a new introduction by Rozsika

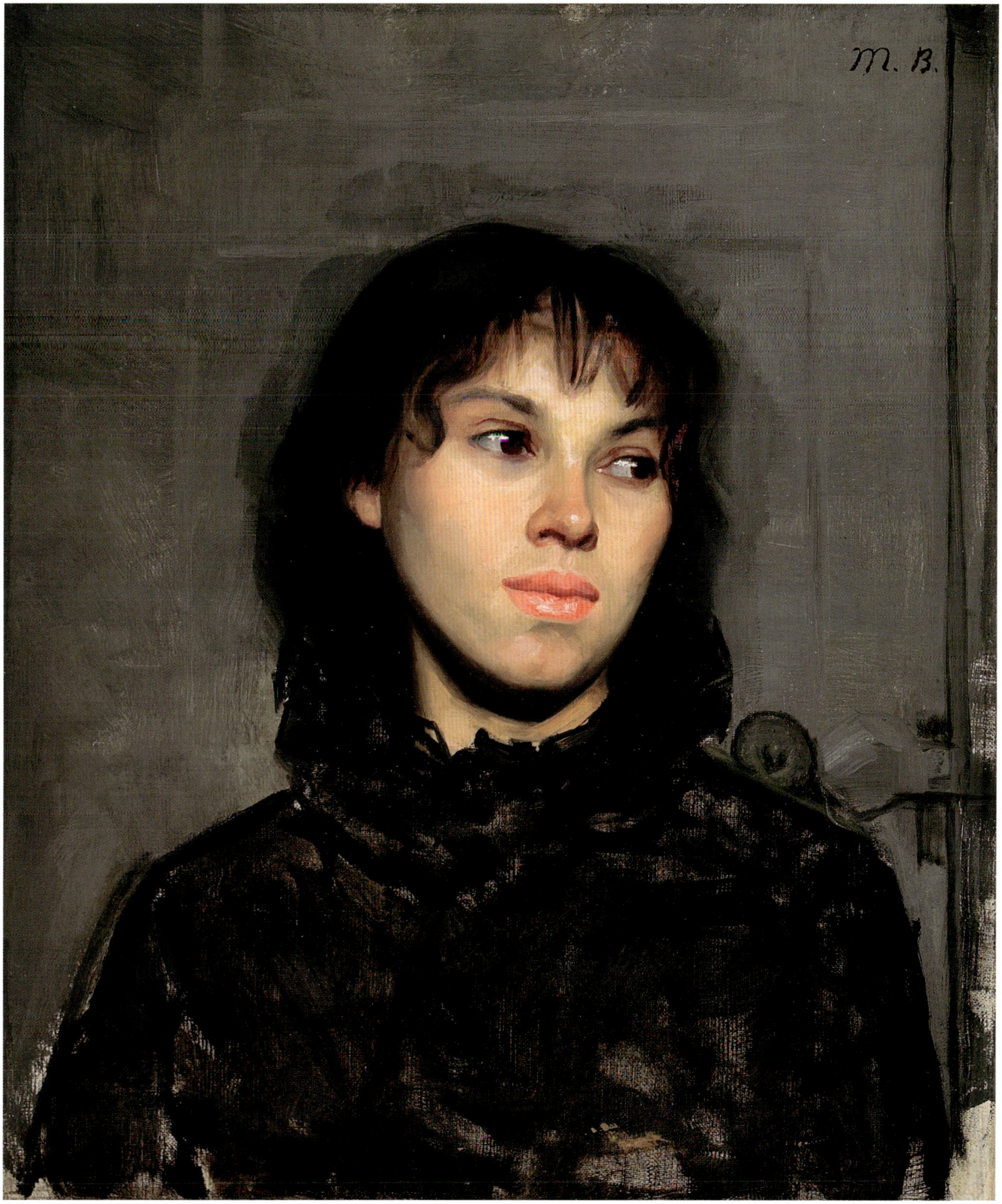

Parker and Griselda Pollock. London: Virago Press, 1985.
Becker, Jane R. "Nothing like a Rival to Spur One On—Marie Bashkirtseff and Louise Breslau," in Gabriel P. Weisberg and Jane R. Becker, eds. *Overcoming All Obstacles: The Women of the Académie Julian*. New Brunswick, NJ: Rutgers University Press, 1999, 69–113.
Catalogue des œuvres de Mlle Bashkirtseff. Intr. François Coppé. Paris: Ludovic Baschet, 1885.
Cosnier, Colette. *Marie Bashkirtseff: un portrait sans retouches*. Paris: Pierre Horay, 1985.
Garb, Tamar. *Sisters of the Brush: Women's Artistic Culture in Late Nineteenth-Century Paris*. New Haven: Yale University Press, 1994, 53–54, 81–82, 125.
Harris, Ann Sutherland, and Linda Nochlin. *Women Artists 1550–1950*. New York: Alfred A. Knopf, 1989, 255–57.
Rochay, Dominique, et al. *Marie Bashkirtseff: écrivain et témoin de son temps*. Nice: Musée des Beaux-Arts, 1995.
Slatkin, Wendy. *The Voices of Women Artists*. Englewood Cliffs, NJ: Prentice Hall, 1993, 66–78.

Jean-Paul Laurens (French • 1838–1921)

52 — The Vengeance of Urban VI

c.1884 • oil on canvas • 83.5 × 102.4 cm • s.l.r. Jean-Paul Laurens • Inv.2002.33.136

Power and revenge saturate this canvas, and light appears as an unlikely interloper in the shadowy interior of the prison cell. The meticulous details of the bee-hive architecture offer a convincing description of a historic space: the stone blocks are mottled and partially worn, and the pointing has flaked away in areas leaving crevices that form small, dark voids. The events that have taken place are as weighty as Urban VI's brocade robe. Four red hats form a border that punctuates and defines space around the prostrate bodies of the cardinals. Their four figures emerge from a concentrated mass: strong contour lines and tonal juxtapositions of red and burgundy create subtle contrasts in texture and form. While we see little of the cardinals' bodies—just two hands and portions of each head—it is more than enough to convey the horrors they have experienced. This highly theatrical scene refers to the historic schism when thirteen French cardinals left Rome for France and elected a second pope at Avignon in 1378. The four cardinals Laurens depicts had actually remained behind in Rome, but Pope Urban VI questioned their loyalty and had them executed. The careful arrangement of boots offers a poetic space in which we, like the pope, can more comfortably settle our gaze. When Laurens prepared to submit this work to the jury in 1884 (no.1422) he had been showing works at the Salon for over twenty years. He was a leading history painter who liked to mine the history of the Catholic Church and settle on a less well-known event. Laurens would translate his chosen historical moment into a crystallized scene that evoked a larger visual narrative. He often focused on macabre topics and was so fascinated with arcane subjects from Church history he was nicknamed "the Benedictine." Laurens's personal politics were republican and anticlerical, but he did admire some contemporary Church officials and certainly engaged with religious debates of his own time.

Parallel with his work on easel paintings, which did include more recent historical subjects, Laurens received numerous commissions for large-scale decorative projects. In Paris, he painted three scenes of the life of Saint Geneviève for the apse of the Panthéon (1877–80; installed 1882), the ceiling of the Théâtre de l'Odéon (1888), and panels for the Hôtel de Ville (1891–98) in a room later assigned his name. Demand for his work extended beyond Paris and included decorations for the Salle des Illustres, in the Capitole in Toulouse (1895–99), the Hôtel de Ville in Tours (1903), and the Orphan's Court in Baltimore, Maryland (1910). He was prolific as a painter, illustrator of books, and designer of tapestry cartoons for the Gobelins, in addition to a well-respected teacher. In 1886, just two years after completing *The Vengeance of Urban VI*, Laurens was appointed professor at the École des Beaux-Arts in Paris. He also became director of the École des Beaux-Arts in his native Toulouse as well as an instructor at the Académie Julian in Paris (see also cat.51).

Provenance

New York, Christie's, 21 May 1991, no.3

Toronto, Joey and Toby Tanenbaum, 1991–2002

Exhibition History

Hamilton, Art Gallery of Hamilton, 28 May 2005–28 May 2006; Victoria, Art Gallery of Greater Victoria, 25 January–11 May 2008, *Heaven and Earth Unveiled: European Treasures from the Tanenbaum Collection*, cat.70; 22, *80*

Toronto, Art Gallery of Toronto, *Drama and Desire: Artists and the Theatre*, 19 June–26 September 2010 (hors catalogue)

Hamilton, Art Gallery of Hamilton, 21 May–5 September 2011, *The French Connection*

Hamilton, Art Gallery of Hamilton, 9 February 2013–9 February 2014, *The Painter Pictured: French Nineteenth-Century Paintings and Portrait Photographs*

Bibliography

Beck, Sibylle. "Gemaltes Grauen: Jean Paul Laurens und die Historienmalerei der Pariser Salons," *Städel-Jahrbuch* vol.17 (1999): 361–78.

Des Cars, Laurence, et al. *Jean-Paul Laurens (1838–1921): peintre d'histoire*. Paris: Réunion des musées nationaux, 1997.

Driskell, Michael Paul. "To Be of One's Own Time: Modernization, Secularism, and the Art of Two Embattled Academicians," *Arts Magazine* vol.61 no.4 (December 1986): 80–89 (87).

Howell Jr, Samuel Harwell. "The Dilemma of the French History Painter, 1870–1914: Jean-Paul Laurens, Paul-Albert Besnard, Georges-Antoine Rochegrosse," Ph.D. dissertation, University of North Carolina at Chapel Hill, 1994.

Jones, Kimberly Ann. "Ressurecting History: Jean-Paul Laurens and the Politics of History Painting during the French Third Republic, 1871–1914," Ph.D. dissertation, University of Maryland at College Park, 1996.

Thomson, Richard. *Art of the Actual: Naturalism and Style in Early Third Republic France, 1880–1900*. New Haven: Yale University Press, 2012.

Valmy-Baysse, Jean. *Jean-Paul Laurens: sa vie, son œuvre*. Paris: Librairie Félix Juven, 1910.

Vergnette, François de. "Jean-Paul Laurens (1838–1921): peintre d'histoire," Ph.D. dissertation, Université de Lille III, 2000.

----- "Anticléricalisme et naturalisme au Panthéon: le décor de Jean-Paul Laurens," *Histoire de l'art* no.28 (1994): 51–56.

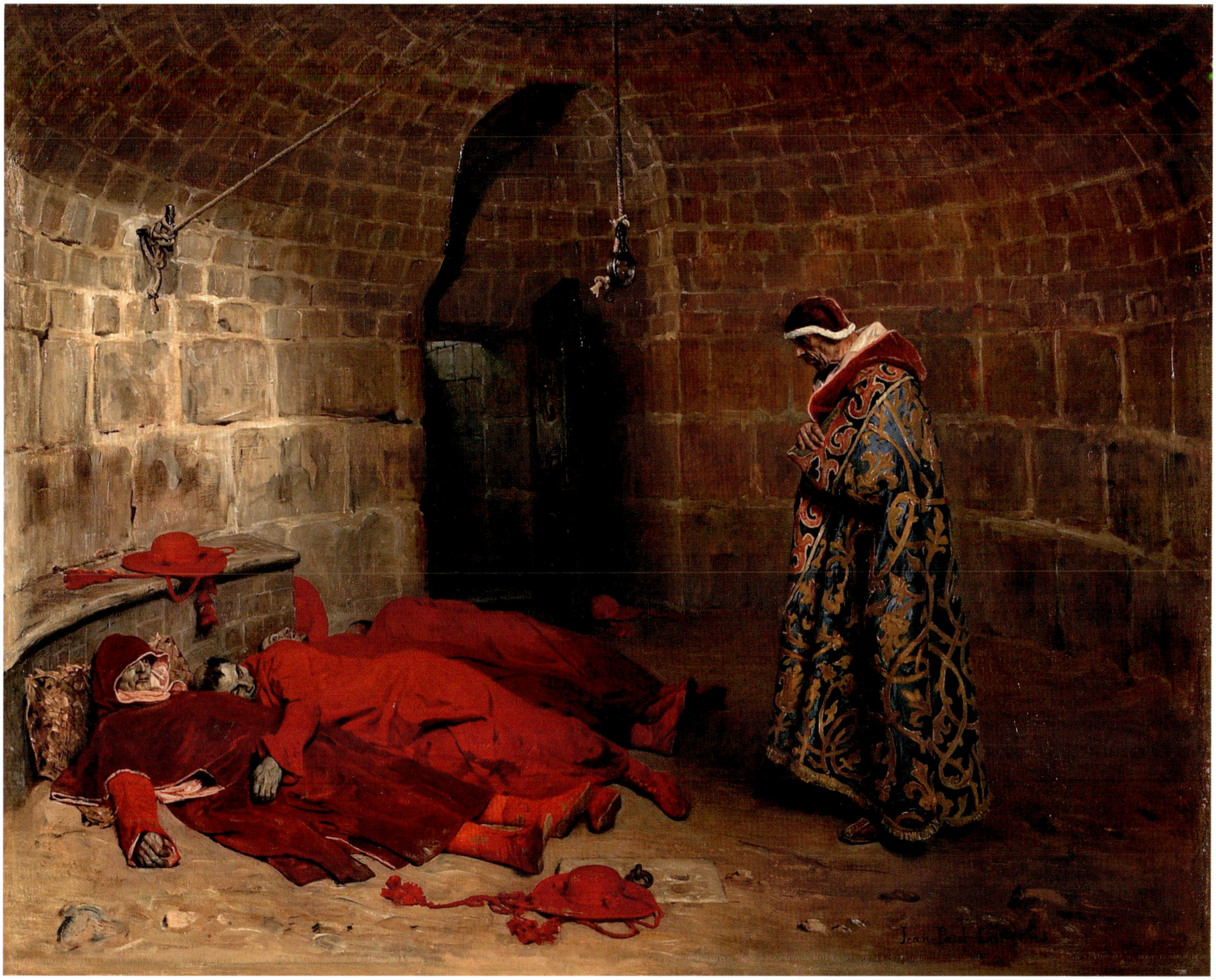

Constantin Meunier (Belgian • 1831–1905)

54 — The Dockhand

modeled 1885, cast after 1893? • bronze • 49.8 × 22 × 21 cm • s.r. back base "C. Meunier" (no foundry mark) • Inv.2002.33.142

55 — The Dockhand (half-length)

c.1890 • plaster with burlap painted to simulate bronze • 117 × 100 × 50 cm • Inv.2002.33.207

In the year before Meunier began sculpting *The Dockhand*, he was in Antwerp preparing studies for a large-scale painting of the port. He envisioned a painting with boats and dockworkers that would capture the bustling activity of the Belgian harbor. Meunier was then in his fifties and had a well-established career as a painter. He had also recently returned from a lengthy period of study in Spain, a trip supported by the Belgian government. According to Meunier's contemporary, writer Edmond-Louis de Taeye, the artist was struck one day by the "vigorous silhouette" of a dockworker. He decided then that only a statue could capture his impression of the man's figure, and so he returned to sculpture, a medium he had explored earlier in his career. Meunier did complete his painting *The Port* (1886; Brussels, Musées Royaux des Beaux-Arts de Belgique), but his first priority was to sculpt *The Dockhand* as a solitary wax figure. That standing figure of a dockworker and another sculpture, a seated figure of an iron worker (*The Puddler*), quickly became among Meunier's best-known works. He conceived of both as figures at rest but each captured markedly different responses to their respite from challenging physical labor. *The Puddler* was hunched over, with a bare torso and a look of complete exhaustion, whereas *The Dockhand* (cat.54) appeared fully dressed, calm, and stood upright with legs astride and one hand posed confidently on each hip. Meunier showed both sculptures for the first time in 1885 when he was invited to participate in the second exhibition of Les XX (Les Vingt). The Belgian group of twenty painters, sculptors, and designers had founded their own society two years earlier in order to mount independent exhibitions and thus circumvent the jury and institutionalized structure of the Antwerp Salon. Meunier was never a member of Les XX but, like many international figures (including Monet, Seurat, Cézanne, and van Gogh), he responded positively to their invitation to include his work.

Meunier's sculpture attracted considerable attention at the exhibition of Les XX, and art critic Max Waller remarked on the "superb pose" of *The Dockhand* in the review he published in *La Jeune Belgique* (10 March 1885). Waller also noted how Meunier explored new terrain by presenting the laborer in sculpture, a medium in which one was accustomed to seeing classical togas and bourgeois frocks but not "la blouse," a worker's tunic. Even before the exhibition closed, Belgian writer Georges Eekhoud had already commissioned Meunier to cast *The Dockhand* in bronze. Meunier went on to produce a large-scale plaster version, which he exhibited in Paris at the Salon de la Société Nationale des Beaux-Arts in 1889. The half-length plaster of *The Dockhand* illustrated here (cat.55) was originally keyed to fit into a lower half of the figure that has not survived.[1] Several bronze casts were commissioned of the full-length, large-scale figure, examples of which can be found today in six different countries.[2] Whether as a large-scale public sculpture or a small-scale statuette displayed in an interior space, *The Dockhand* is frequently interpreted as a symbol of the dignity of workers. From the late 1870s, Meunier turned his attention to representing physical labor, and sought out first-hand experiences with factory workers and industrial towns in southern Belgium. Later in his career, Meunier worked on a *Monument to Labor* for many years; however, that multi-figure sculpture remained unrealized at the time of his death. The half-length plaster and full-figure bronze statuette of *The Dockhand* are important examples of Meunier's commitment to representing everyday life, particularly the lives of workers, and to exploring aspects of the human condition throughout his career.

1 Another bronze half-length is in the Musée Cantonal des Beaux-Arts, Lausanne.

2 Full-length bronzes are in the following locations: Koninklijk Museum voor Schone Kunsten, Antwerp; Szépművészeti Múzeum, Budapest; Museum Folkwang, Essen; entrance to the Friedenbrücke, Frankfurt; Plaza Belgica, Lima; Folkets Hus, Stockholm; Österreichische Galerie Belvedere, Vienna. Full-length plasters are in: Staatliche Kunstsammlungen, Dresden; Ny Carlsberg Glyptotek, Copenhagen; Musée Constantin Meunier, Ixelles. Related bronze and plaster busts entitled *Antwerp* are in both the Musée Communal and Musée Constantin Meunier, Ixelles, as well as bronze busts in the Nationalgalerie, Berlin; Musées Royaux des Beaux-Arts, Brussels; Hessisches Landesmuseum, Darmstadt; Staatliche Kunstsammlungen, Dresden; Museum Folkwang, Essen; Museum der Bildenden Künste, Leipzig; Städtische Kunsthalle, Mannheim. Bronze statuettes are in: Musée Bonnat, Bayonne; Nationalgalerie, Berlin; Museum of Fine Arts, Boston; Albright-Knox Art Gallery, Buffalo; Art Institute, Chicago; Washington County Museum, Hagerstown; Kunstmuseum des Landes Sachsen-Anholt, Halle; M – Museum (formerly Museum Vander Kelen-Mertens), Leuven; Brooklyn Museum, New York; Musée d'Orsay, Paris; and Národní Galerie, Prague. The casts in Berlin, Boston, Chicago, and Hagerstown are also without foundry marks.

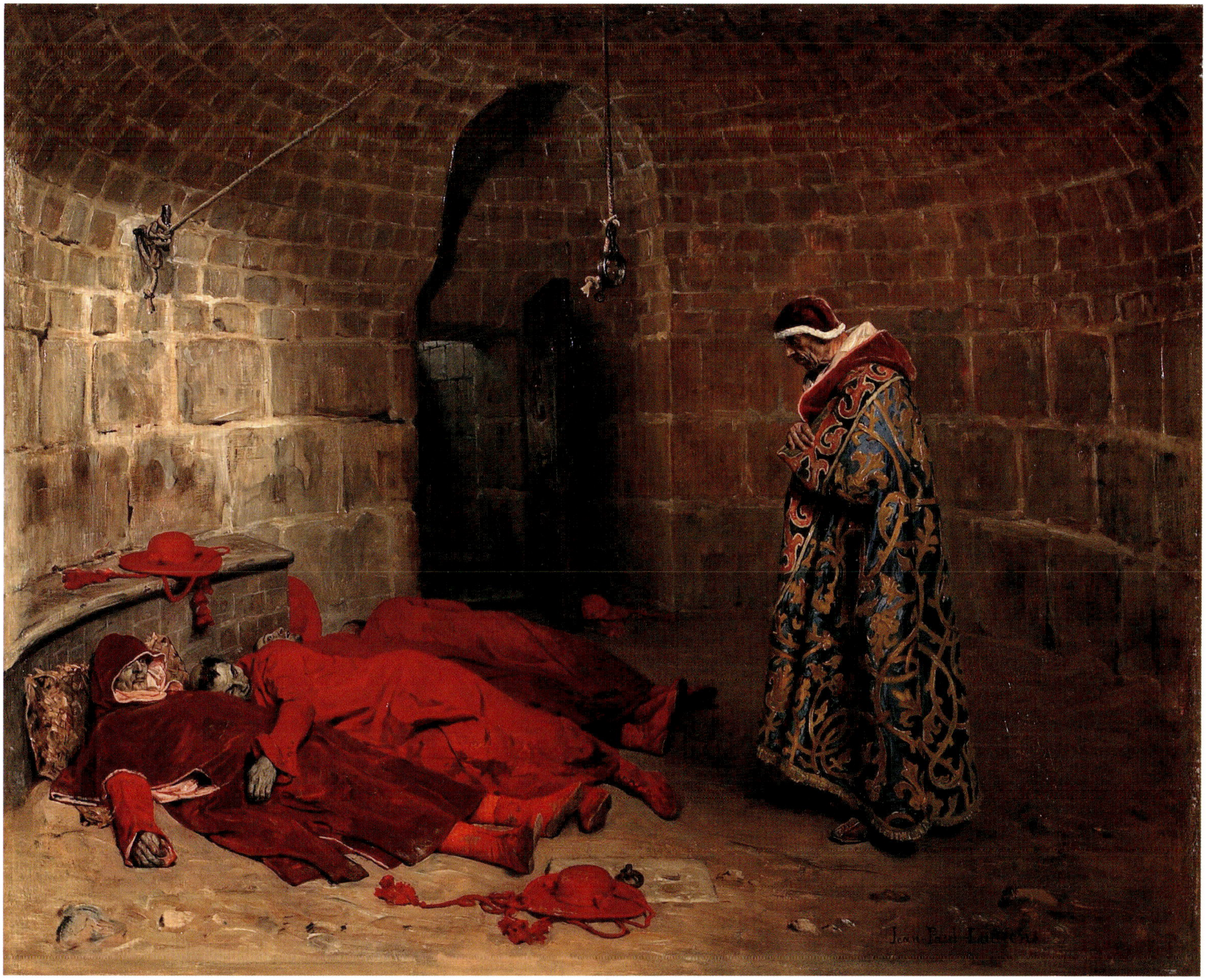

Edwin Lord Weeks (American • 1849–1903)

53 — The Last Voyage—Souvenir of the Ganges

1885 • oil on canvas • 192 × 289 cm • s.l.l. E.L. WEEKS • Inv. 2002.33.195

Edwin Weeks received a gold medal for this painting and four others he exhibited at the Exposition Universelle held in Paris in 1889. Each of the five works drew on his personal experiences traveling in what is today Pakistan and India. Weeks was an avid explorer, and his family's financial circumstances allowed him to travel extensively, including in South America and North Africa before he moved from his native Massachusetts and settled in Paris sometime between 1869 and 1871. During the following decade he led an itinerant lifestyle. Accompanied by his wife, Frances Rollins Hale, he traveled to Syria, Jerusalem, and Egypt, and lived for longer periods in Tangiers, Paris, and Boston, where he exhibited and established a temporary studio. From 1878 to 1900 Weeks showed his works at the Paris Salons, including *The Last Voyage—Souvenir of the Ganges*, which he presented for the first time at the Salon of 1885.[1] Weeks always identified himself as a student of Léon Bonnat (see cats.41 and 42), but he was also documented attending Gérôme's studio on one occasion in 1874 (see cats.11 and 12). He was thus an American expatriate artist connected with two of the principal painting instructors at the École des Beaux-Arts. But Weeks was never formally registered as a student at the school and likely received training and advice from Bonnat and Gérôme outside the parameters of that institutional context. By 1880, Weeks had his own studio in Paris, and it was there that he painted *The Last Voyage*. In preparing this large-scale canvas, he drew upon his sketches as well as photographs he took and developed himself during an extended trip in 1882 and 1883. Weeks returned to India from 1886 to 1887 and again from 1892 to 1893. He recorded his experiences in travel accounts that he published in *Harper's New Monthly Magazine* (October 1893–November 1895), accompanied by his own illustrations, and again in expanded form in a book he produced in 1896.

Weeks's painting technique, replete with the descriptive details we see in *The Last Voyage*, was designed to make viewers believe they were looking at an authentic presentation of Indian social customs and religious practices in their actual architectural context. Weeks had established a reputation in Paris as an intrepid "painter explorer" by the fall of 1881 when he exhibited thirty sketches in the office of the newspaper *La Gauloise*. The following year, prominent art dealer Paul Durand-Ruel arranged to buy many of his works. Viewers at the Salon of 1885, the Exposition Universelle of 1889, and the numerous other international venues where Weeks exhibited *The Last Voyage*, responded to his work as a truthful record of lived experiences. Weeks's writings afford considerable insight into his perspectives during his travels. The section of his book *From the Black Sea through Persia and India* in which he recounts the days he spent at Vārānasī (known to him as Benares) suggests his outlook as he painted the canvas. Weeks was fascinated by all the Hindu practices he witnessed, including reverence for the sacred waters of the Ganges river, and in this painting he appears to document a dying man transported to India's holiest of cities. In Weeks's writing, however, he also reveals his sense of his own superiority. He seems to write admiringly of the "holy men" gathered on the stone steps who "sit in rapt meditation and silent ecstasy," but he also describes Vārānasī as "the principal gathering place of this motley tribe of zealots and ascetics." Weeks's comments make clear he was both intrigued and judgmental. His perspective remained one of a financially and socially empowered foreigner traveling in India during the British Raj. His works are now understood as implicated in the politics of empire and capitalism that informed orientalist painting practices for American and European artists. When Weeks shipped the painting to the United States and exhibited it at a gallery in Boston in spring of 1886, a newspaper quoted him recounting in a letter how bodies floated in the water and had to be pushed out of the way as he sketched the scene from a boat, "[t]he background is absolutely as I found it, and I saw the incident of the dying man being carried across…"[2] The actual source of this anecdote, and its validity, remains unclear. While Weeks sought to present the architectural setting with meticulous accuracy, he structured the composition to elicit particular responses. Exhibited in four countries on two continents during the artist's lifetime, *The Last Voyage—Souvenir of the Ganges* did much to promote both Weeks's reputation and the colonialist-informed framework of such exoticized scenes.

[1] *Le dernier voyage—Souvenir du Gange* illustrated in E. Francfort, *Album artistique et biographique, Salon 1885*. Paris: Lemercier & Cie., 1885, vol.2.

[2] *Boston Evening Transcript*, Saturday 24 April 1886, page 11.

Provenance

Frances Rollins Hale Weeks (artist's estate)
New York, Metropolitan Museum of Art, 1905–56 (donated by Frances Weeks)
New York, Sotheby Parke-Bernet, 28 March 1956
New York, Solow Galleries, 1956
New York, Ira Spanierman Gallery, 1977–81
New York, Stuart Pivar, 1981–95 (partially on extended loan to Bayly Art Museum, University of Virginia)
New York, Sotheby's, 24 May 1995, lot 91
Toronto, Joey and Toby Tanenbaum, 1995–2002

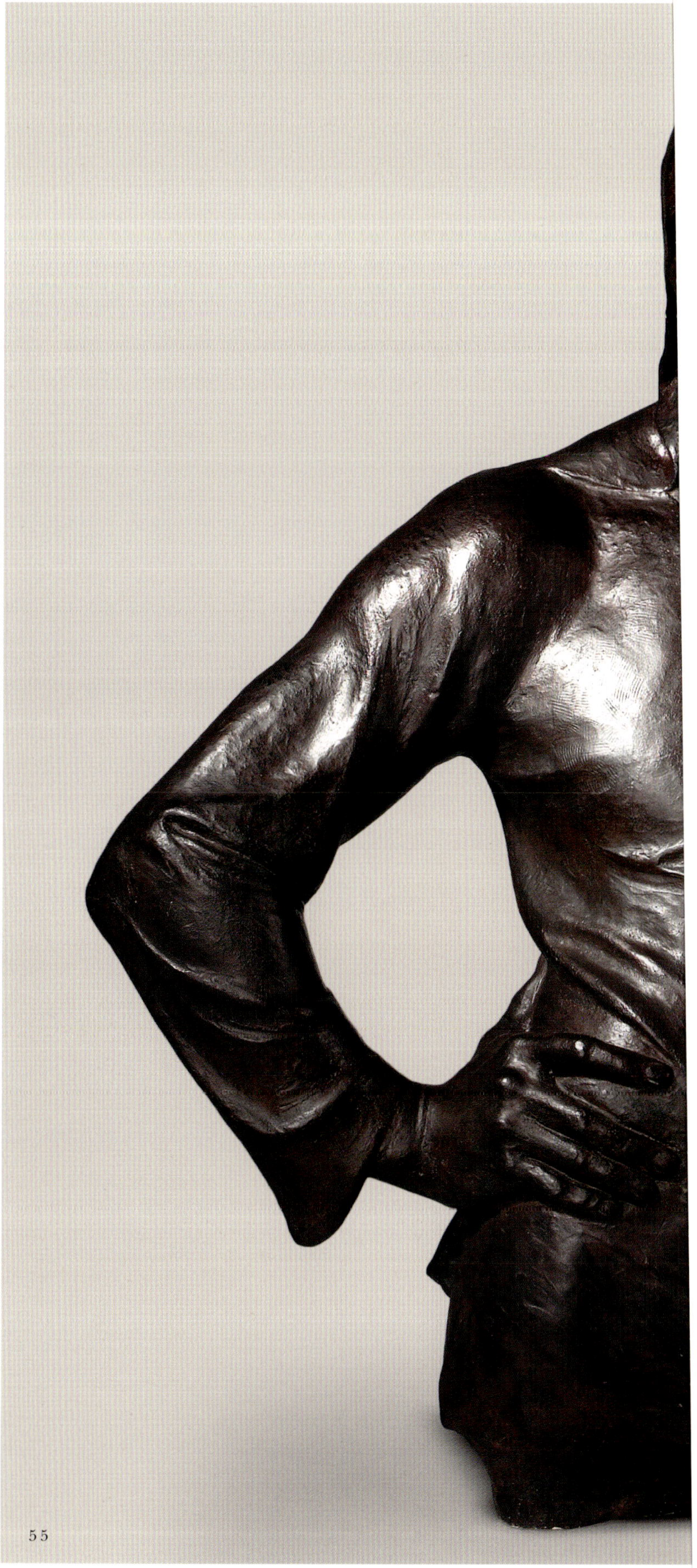

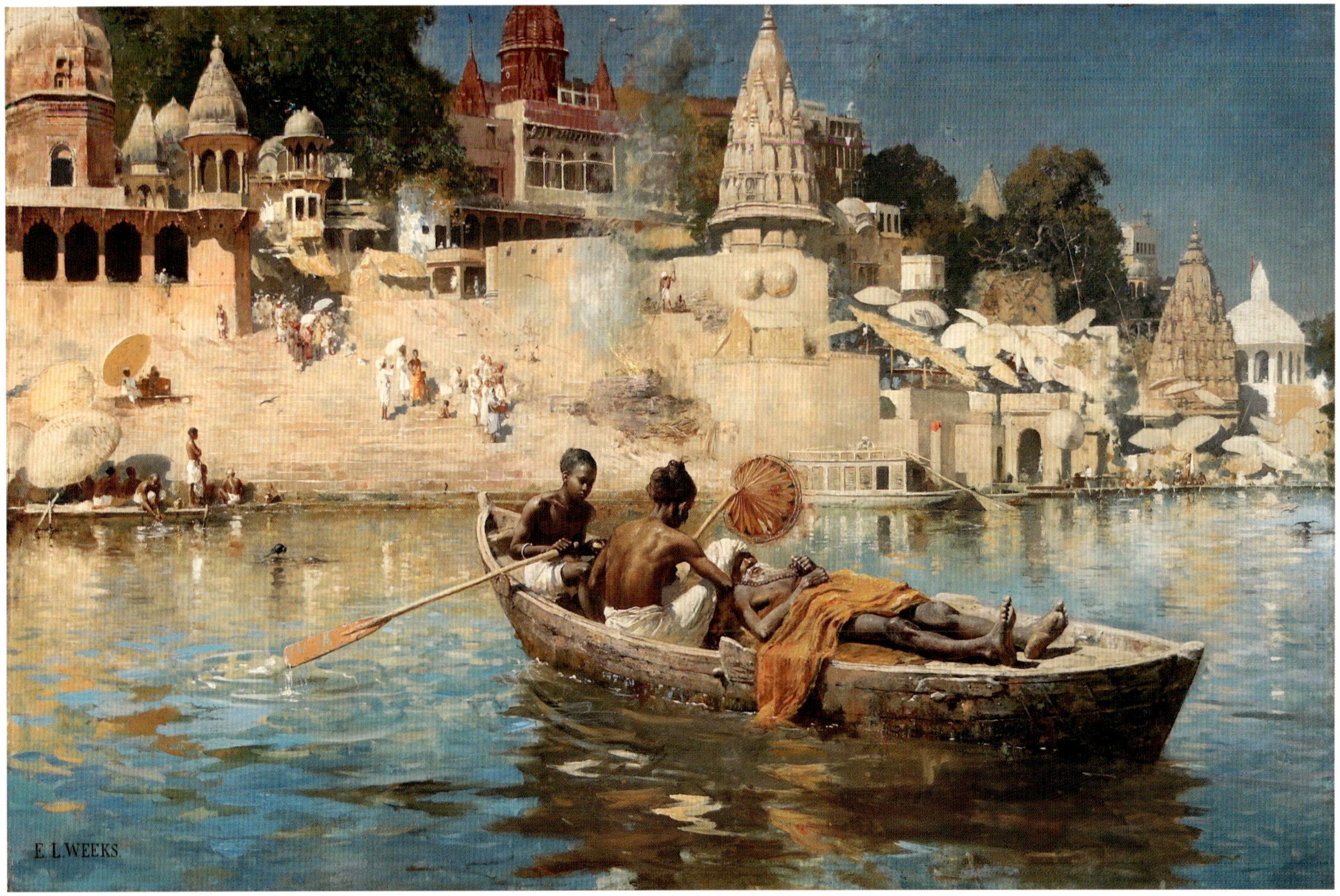

Exhibition History

Paris, Salon, 1885, no.2449

Boston, Noyes and Blakeslee Gallery, April 1886

Munich, Internationale Kunstausstellung, 1888

Paris, Exposition Universelle, 1889, no.319

Chicago, World's Columbian Exhibition, 1893, no.410

Antwerp, Exposition Internationale, 1894

Detroit, Detroit Institute of Arts, 22 August–30 October 1983, *The Quest for Unity: American Art between World's Fairs 1876–1893*, cat.66, *140*

Norfolk, Chrysler Museum of Art, 29 September–17 December 1989; Philadelphia, Pennsylvania Academy of the Fine Arts, 1 February–15 April 1990; Memphis, Memphis Brooks Museum of Art, 6 May–15 July 1990, *Paris 1889: American Artists at the Universal Exposition*, cat.319, *224*

Hamilton, Art Gallery of Hamilton, 28 May 2005–28 May 2006, *Heaven and Earth Unveiled: European Treasures from the Tanenbaum Collection*, cat.136; 56–57, *134–35*

Hamilton, Art Gallery of Hamilton, 22 May–6 September 2010, *Europe's Exoticized East*

Bibliography

Ackerman, Gerald. *American Orientalists.* Paris: ACR Édition, 1994, 234–44 (240), *256.*

Burke, Doreen Bolgur. "Edwin Weeks," in Kathleen Luhrs, ed. *American Paintings in the Metropolitan Museum of Art.* Vol.3. New York: Metropolitan Museum of Art, 1980, 77–79.

Davies, Kristian. *The Orientalists: Western Artists in Arabia, the Sahara, Persia and India.* New York: Laynfaroh, 2005, 280, *280–81.*

Dodge, Thomas D. "Edwin Lord Weeks, American Painter of India," *Magazine Antiques* vol.128 (August 1985): 246–58 (*254*).

Edwards, Holly. *Noble Dreams, Wicked Pleasures: Orientalism in America 1870–1930.* Princeton: Princeton University Press, 2000, 67–70, 137–38.

Hiesinger, Ulrich W. "Edwin Lord Weeks, Painter and Explorer," *Magazine Antiques* vol.162 (November 2002): 164–75.

T.C. "The Paris Salon," *The Art Amateur* vol.13 no.2 (July 1885): 23–24, 32.

Weeks, Edwin Lord. *From the Black Sea through Persia and India.* New York: Harper & Bros., 1896, 376–85.

Weinberg, Barbara H. *The American Pupils of Jean-Léon Gérôme.* Fort Worth: Amon Carter Museum, 1984, 51–55, *54.*

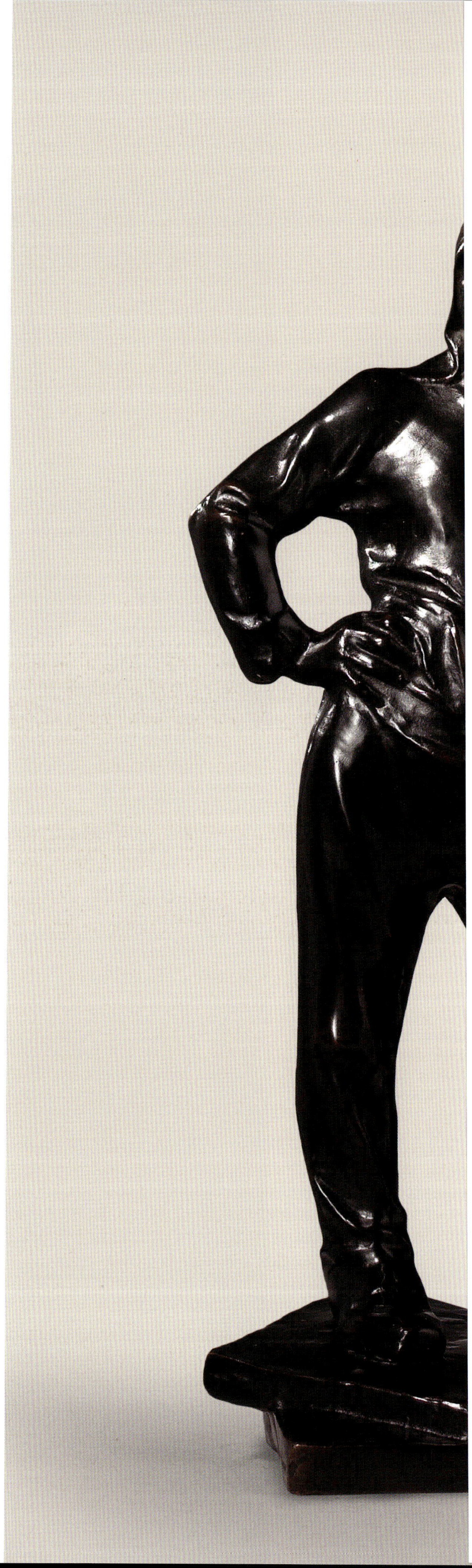

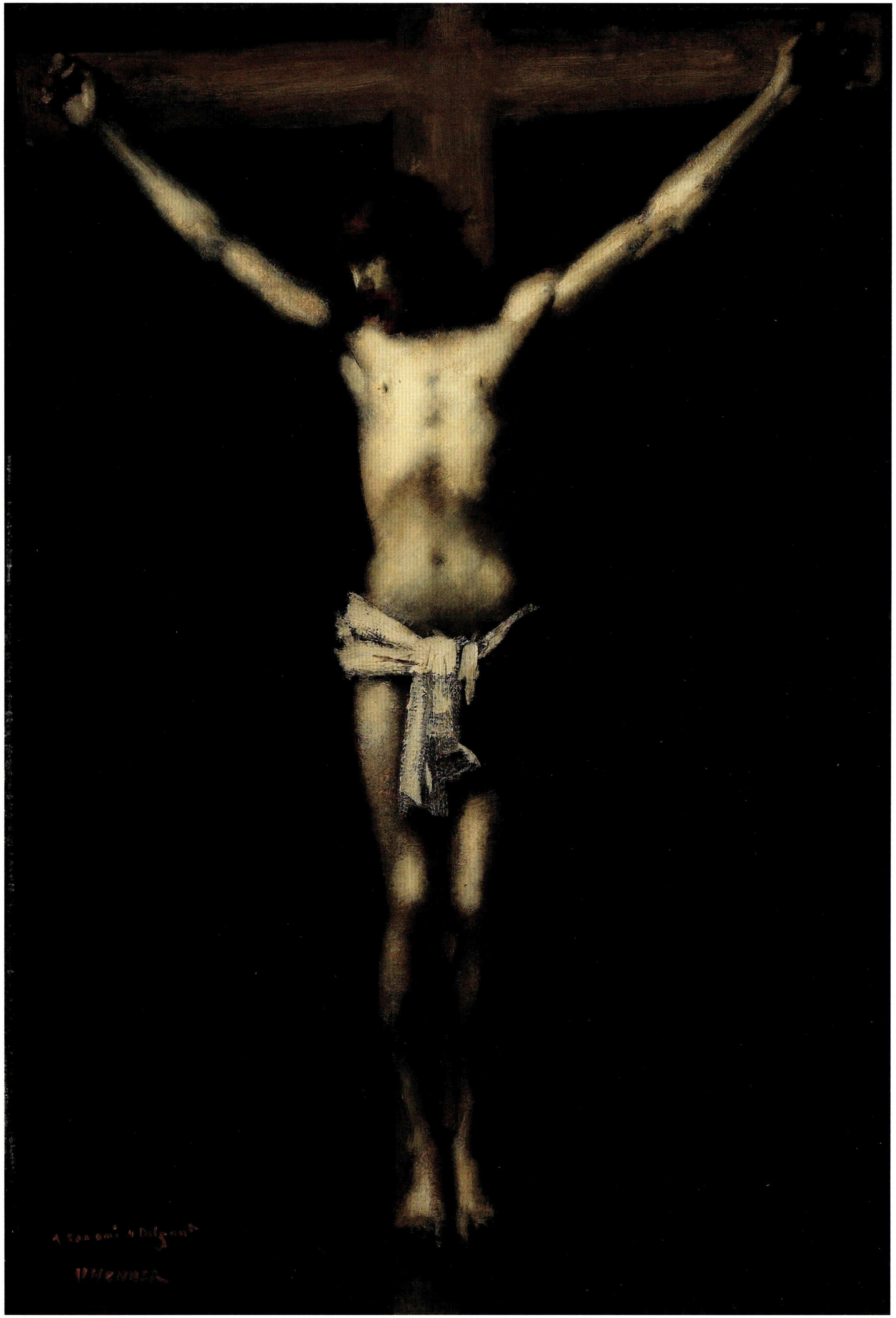
JJHENNER

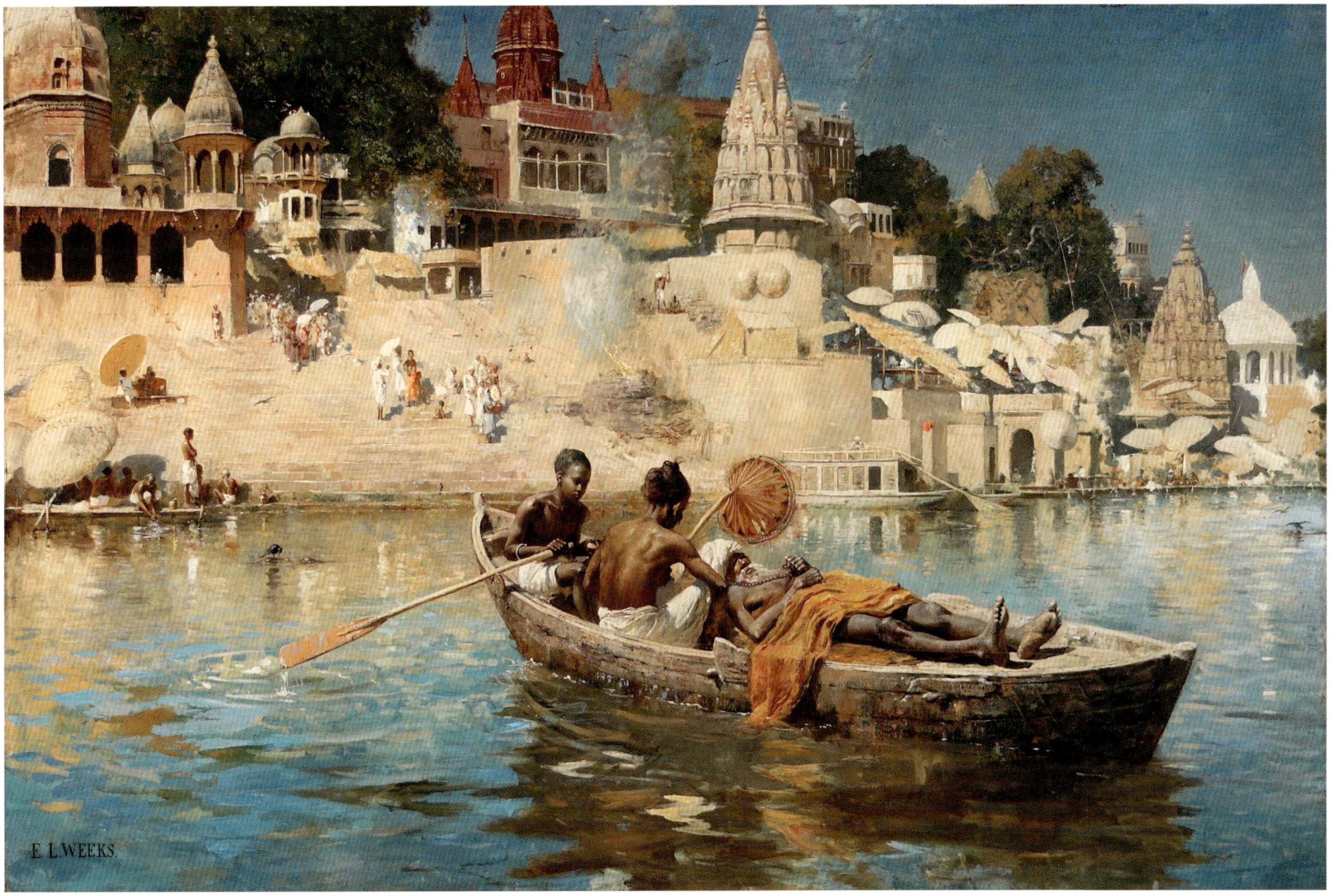

Exhibition History

Paris, Salon, 1885, no.2449

Boston, Noyes and Blakeslee Gallery, April 1886

Munich, Internationale Kunstausstellung, 1888

Paris, Exposition Universelle, 1889, no.319

Chicago, World's Columbian Exhibition, 1893, no.410

Antwerp, Exposition Internationale, 1894

Detroit, Detroit Institute of Arts, 22 August–30 October 1983, *The Quest for Unity: American Art between World's Fairs 1876–1893*, cat.66, *140*

Norfolk, Chrysler Museum of Art, 29 September–17 December 1989; Philadelphia, Pennsylvania Academy of the Fine Arts, 1 February–15 April 1990; Memphis, Memphis Brooks Museum of Art, 6 May–15 July 1990, *Paris 1889: American Artists at the Universal Exposition*, cat.319, *224*

Hamilton, Art Gallery of Hamilton, 28 May 2005–28 May 2006, *Heaven and Earth Unveiled: European Treasures from the Tanenbaum Collection*, cat.136; 56–57, *134–35*

Hamilton, Art Gallery of Hamilton, 22 May–6 September 2010, *Europe's Exoticized East*

Bibliography

Ackerman, Gerald. *American Orientalists*. Paris: ACR Édition, 1994, 234–44 (240), *256*.

Burke, Doreen Bolgur. "Edwin Weeks," in Kathleen Luhrs, ed. *American Paintings in the Metropolitan Museum of Art*. Vol.3. New York: Metropolitan Museum of Art, 1980, 77–79.

Davies, Kristian. *The Orientalists: Western Artists in Arabia, the Sahara, Persia and India*. New York: Laynfaroh, 2005, 280, *280–81*.

Dodge, Thomas D. "Edwin Lord Weeks, American Painter of India," *Magazine Antiques* vol.128 (August 1985): 246–58 (*254*).

Edwards, Holly. *Noble Dreams, Wicked Pleasures: Orientalism in America 1870–1930*. Princeton: Princeton University Press, 2000, 67–70, 137–38.

Hiesinger, Ulrich W. "Edwin Lord Weeks, Painter and Explorer," *Magazine Antiques* vol.162 (November 2002): 164–75.

T.C. "The Paris Salon," *The Art Amateur* vol.13 no.2 (July 1885): 23–24, 32.

Weeks, Edwin Lord. *From the Black Sea through Persia and India*. New York: Harper & Bros., 1896, 376–85.

Weinberg, Barbara H. *The American Pupils of Jean-Léon Gérôme*. Fort Worth: Amon Carter Museum, 1984, 51–55, *54*.

Constantin Meunier (Belgian • 1831–1905)

54 — The Dockhand

modeled 1885, cast after 1893? • bronze • 49.8 × 22 × 21 cm • s.r. back base "C. Meunier" (no foundry mark) • Inv.2002.33.142

55 — The Dockhand (half-length)

c.1890 • plaster with burlap painted to simulate bronze • 117 × 100 × 50 cm • Inv.2002.33.207

In the year before Meunier began sculpting *The Dockhand*, he was in Antwerp preparing studies for a large-scale painting of the port. He envisioned a painting with boats and dockworkers that would capture the bustling activity of the Belgian harbor. Meunier was then in his fifties and had a well-established career as a painter. He had also recently returned from a lengthy period of study in Spain, a trip supported by the Belgian government. According to Meunier's contemporary, writer Edmond-Louis de Taeye, the artist was struck one day by the "vigorous silhouette" of a dockworker. He decided then that only a statue could capture his impression of the man's figure, and so he returned to sculpture, a medium he had explored earlier in his career. Meunier did complete his painting *The Port* (1886; Brussels, Musées Royaux des Beaux-Arts de Belgique), but his first priority was to sculpt *The Dockhand* as a solitary wax figure. That standing figure of a dockworker and another sculpture, a seated figure of an iron worker (*The Puddler*), quickly became among Meunier's best-known works. He conceived of both as figures at rest but each captured markedly different responses to their respite from challenging physical labor. *The Puddler* was hunched over, with a bare torso and a look of complete exhaustion, whereas *The Dockhand* (cat.54) appeared fully dressed, calm, and stood upright with legs astride and one hand posed confidently on each hip. Meunier showed both sculptures for the first time in 1885 when he was invited to participate in the second exhibition of Les XX (Les Vingt). The Belgian group of twenty painters, sculptors, and designers had founded their own society two years earlier in order to mount independent exhibitions and thus circumvent the jury and institutionalized structure of the Antwerp Salon. Meunier was never a member of Les XX but, like many international figures (including Monet, Seurat, Cézanne, and van Gogh), he responded positively to their invitation to include his work.

Meunier's sculpture attracted considerable attention at the exhibition of Les XX, and art critic Max Waller remarked on the "superb pose" of *The Dockhand* in the review he published in *La Jeune Belgique* (10 March 1885). Waller also noted how Meunier explored new terrain by presenting the laborer in sculpture, a medium in which one was accustomed to seeing classical togas and bourgeois frocks but not "la blouse," a worker's tunic. Even before the exhibition closed, Belgian writer Georges Eekhoud had already commissioned Meunier to cast *The Dockhand* in bronze. Meunier went on to produce a large-scale plaster version, which he exhibited in Paris at the Salon de la Société Nationale des Beaux-Arts in 1889. The half-length plaster of *The Dockhand* illustrated here (cat.55) was originally keyed to fit into a lower half of the figure that has not survived.[1] Several bronze casts were commissioned of the full-length, large-scale figure, examples of which can be found today in six different countries.[2] Whether as a large-scale public sculpture or a small-scale statuette displayed in an interior space, *The Dockhand* is frequently interpreted as a symbol of the dignity of workers. From the late 1870s, Meunier turned his attention to representing physical labor, and sought out first-hand experiences with factory workers and industrial towns in southern Belgium. Later in his career, Meunier worked on a *Monument to Labor* for many years; however, that multi-figure sculpture remained unrealized at the time of his death. The half-length plaster and full-figure bronze statuette of *The Dockhand* are important examples of Meunier's commitment to representing everyday life, particularly the lives of workers, and to exploring aspects of the human condition throughout his career.

1 Another bronze half-length is in the Musée Cantonal des Beaux-Arts, Lausanne.

2 Full-length bronzes are in the following locations: Koninklijk Museum voor Schone Kunsten, Antwerp; Szépművészeti Múzeum, Budapest; Museum Folkwang, Essen; entrance to the Friedenbrücke, Frankfurt; Plaza Belgica, Lima; Folkets Hus, Stockholm; Österreichische Galerie Belvedere, Vienna. Full-length plasters are in: Staatliche Kunstsammlungen, Dresden; Ny Carlsberg Glyptotek, Copenhagen; Musée Constantin Meunier, Ixelles. Related bronze and plaster busts entitled *Antwerp* are in both the Musée Communal and Musée Constantin Meunier, Ixelles, as well as bronze busts in the Nationalgalerie, Berlin; Musées Royaux des Beaux-Arts, Brussels; Hessisches Landesmuseum, Darmstadt; Staatliche Kunstsammlungen, Dresden; Museum Folkwang, Essen; Museum der Bildenden Künste, Leipzig; Städtische Kunsthalle, Mannheim. Bronze statuettes are in: Musée Bonnat, Bayonne; Nationalgalerie, Berlin; Museum of Fine Arts, Boston; Albright-Knox Art Gallery, Buffalo; Art Institute, Chicago; Washington County Museum, Hagerstown; Kunstmuseum des Landes Sachsen-Anholt, Halle; M – Museum (formerly Museum Vander Kelen-Mertens), Leuven; Brooklyn Museum, New York; Musée d'Orsay, Paris; and Národní Galerie, Prague. The casts in Berlin, Boston, Chicago, and Hagerstown are also without foundry marks.

Provenance

The Dockhand

New York, Galerie Osten-Kaschey, Ltd.

Toronto, Joey and Toby Tanenbaum, 1971–2001

The Dockhand (half-length)

New York, Shepherd Gallery

Toronto, Joey and Toby Tanenbaum, 1991–2002

Exhibition History

The Dockhand

Hamilton, Art Gallery of Hamilton, 28 May 2005–28 May 2006, *Heaven and Earth Unveiled: European Treasures from the Tanenbaum Collection*, cat.186; 185 (as *Longshoreman*, 1885)

Hamilton, Art Gallery of Hamilton, 13 September 2008–4 January 2009, *Blood, Sweat and Tears: Labour in Art*

The Dockhand (half-length)

New York, Shepherd Gallery, 25 November 1987–10 January 1988, *Füssli through Tiffany: 19th and Early 20th Century Paintings, Drawings and Sculpture*, cat.VI (reproduced)

Hamilton, Art Gallery of Hamilton, 28 May 2005–28 May 2006, *Heaven and Earth Unveiled: European Treasures from the Tanenbaum Collection*, cat.187; 185, *171* (as *Longshoreman, half-length*, 1885)

Hamilton, Art Gallery of Hamilton, 13 September 2008–4 January 2009, *Blood, Sweat and Tears: Labour in Art*

Bibliography

Baudson, Pierre. "Constantin Meunier au delà du réalisme," *Bulletin des Musées Royaux des Beaux-Arts de Belgique* vol.38–40 (1989–91): 423–32.

-----. *Les Trois Vies de Constantin Meunier*. Brussels: Banque nationale de Belgique, 1979, 10.

Bouchard, Marie. "'Un Monument au travail': The Projects of Meunier, Dalou, Rodin and Bouchard," *Oxford Art Journal* vol.4 no.2 (November 1981): 28–35 (29, 35).

Facos, Michelle. "New Documents Regarding a Meunier Sculpture in Stockholm," *Konsthistorisk Tidskrift* vol.65 no.1 (1996): 27–32.

Hanotelle, Micheline. *Paris/Bruxelles, Rodin et Meunier: relations des sculpteurs français et belges à la fin du XIXe siècle*. Pref. Cécile Goldscheider. Paris: Le Temps, 1982, 148–49.

Jerome-Schotsmans, Michelle. *Constantin Meunier: sa vie, son œuvre*. Brussels: Olivier Bertrand, 2012, 145–48, 166–67, 353–79.

Lemonnier, Camille. *Constantin Meunier, sculpteur et peintre*. Paris: H. Floury, 1904, *74a*.

Levine, Sura, and Françoise Urban. *Hommage à Constantin Meunier, 1831–1905*. Antwerp: Galerie Maurice Tzwern-Pandora, 1998.

Maus, Octave. *Catalogue des dix expositions annuelles*. Brussels: Centre International pour l'étude du XIXe siècle, 1981, 55.

Pauseback, Wolf Michael. "Constantin Meunier (1830–1906). Genese und Analyse früher Arbeiterplastik Teil I," *Giessener Beiträge zur Kunstgeschichte* vol.4 (1979): 81–164.

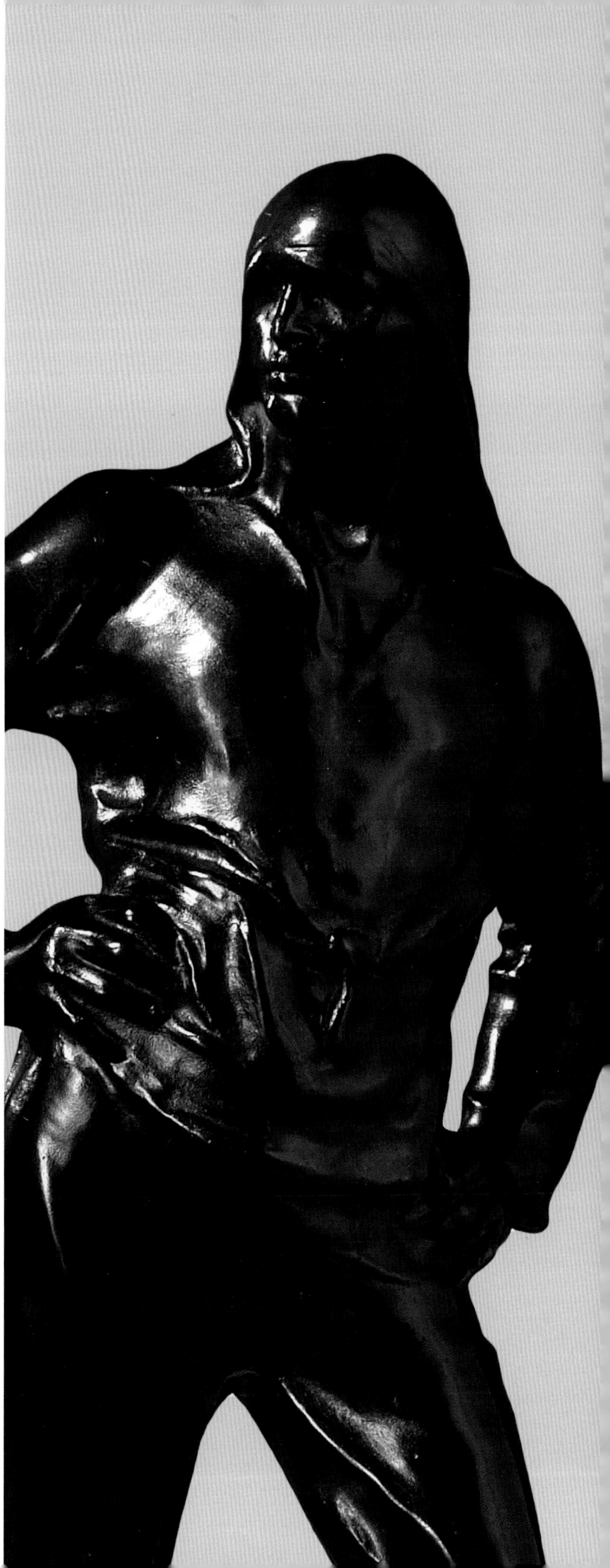

54

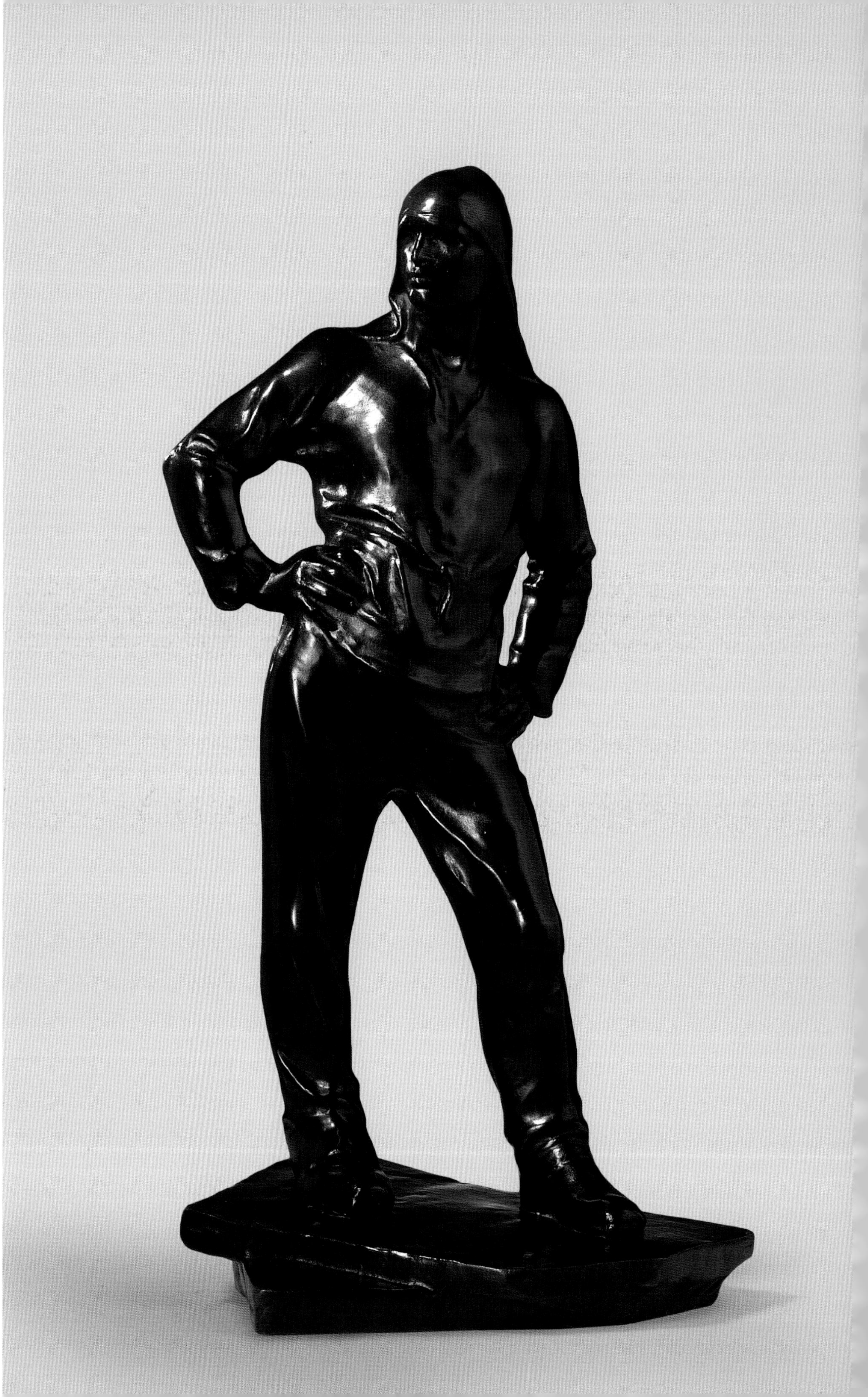

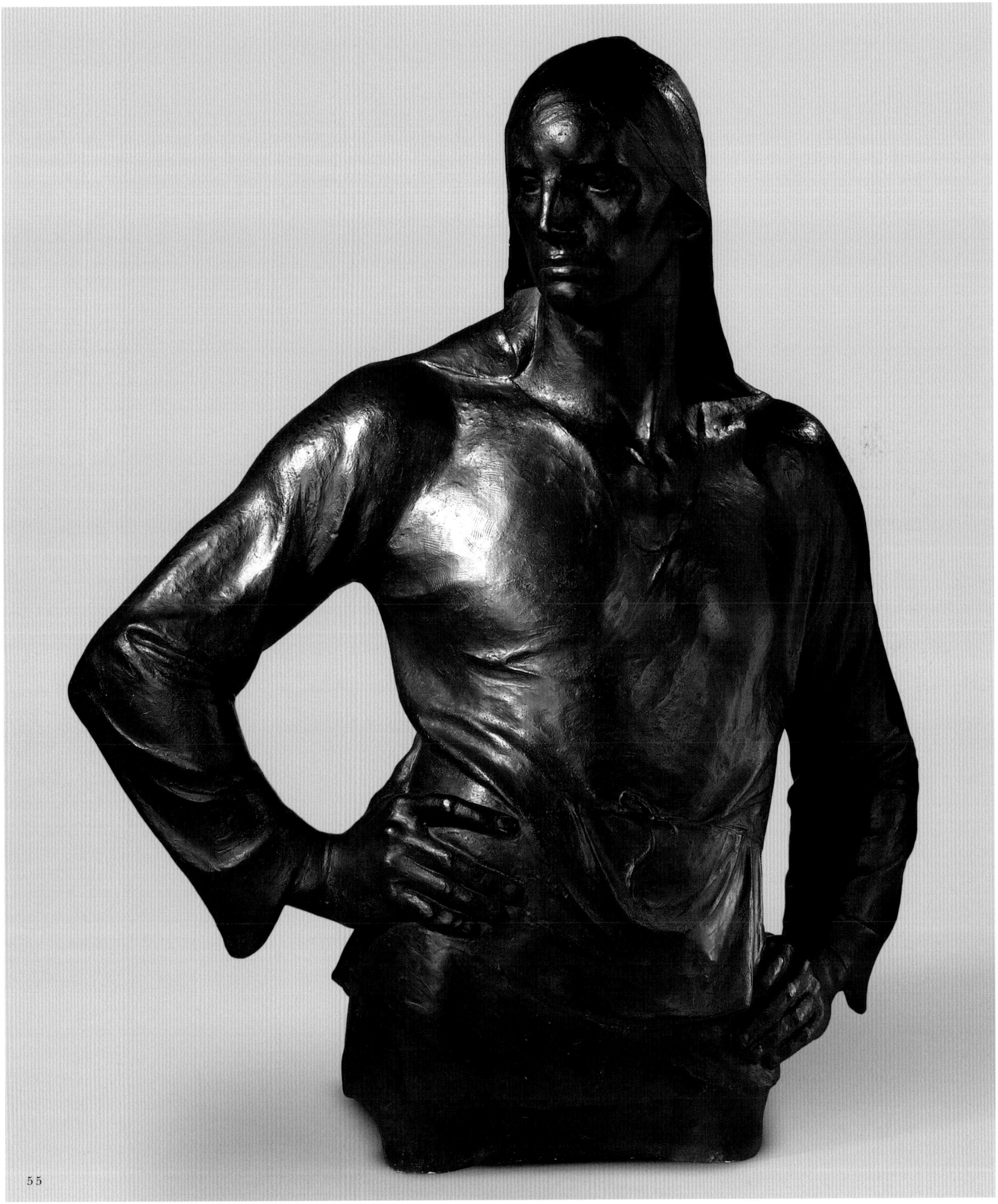

55

remain entirely unknown. Indeed the narrative aspect was so ambiguous that a critic who saw the work at the Salon of 1898, but who did not know the title, thought the painting depicted Christ crying over the Magdalene's body. Efforts to interpret Henner's repeated presentation of bodies that were either dead or dying have, at times, turned to his personal experiences with the death of siblings and fellow artists, including a sculptor friend whom Henner described as "[d]ead, he was beautiful as he had never been."[5]

1 AN F/21/4859. The large *Crucified Christ* (207 × 142 cm) hung in the court until 1904 and is now on deposit at the Musée d'Art Moderne et Contemporain in Strasbourg (LUX596). A nearly full-scale replica is in the Musée du Petit Palais, Paris (PPP00188). Two preparatory works are in the collection of the Musée National Jean-Jacques Henner (JJHP 220 and JJHP 1936-3).

2 Musée des Beaux-Arts, Mulhouse (Inv.D.58.1.36)

3 *Christ in the Tomb*, 1879, Musée d'Orsay (Inv.20547) and 1884, Musée des Beaux-Arts, Lille (Inv.P.514). Four related replicas painted on canvas and wood of various scales are in the collection of the Musée Henner (JJHP 202, 203, 208, 212).

4 Four related studies are in the collection of the Musée Henner (JJHP 338-341). A smaller-scale replica is in the Princeton University Art Museum (c.1898; Inv.1986-80)

5 Jean Coirat, "Rendre l'âme: Jean-Jacques Henner et le spiritualisme," in *Sensualité et spiritualité: à la recherche de l'absolu*, Marie-Hélène Lavallée et al., eds. (Paris: Gourcuff Gradenigo, 2012), 27–41 (39).

Provenance

Christ on the Cross
New York, Galerie Osten-Kashey Ltd.
Toronto, Joey and Toby Tanenbaum, 1971–2002

The Dead Christ
New York, Shepherd Gallery
Toronto, Joey and Toby Tanenbaum, 1984–2002

The Levite of Ephraim and His Dead Wife
Alfred Engel (purchased at the Salon of 1898 for 16,000 francs)
London, Charles Jerdein
Toronto, Joey and Toby Tanenbaum, 1970–2002

Exhibition History

Christ on the Cross
New York, Shepherd Gallery, 20 May–28 June 1975, *Ingres and Delacroix through Degas and Puvis de Chavannes: The Figure in French Art, 1800–1870*, cat.126, *298*
Toronto, York University, 12 January–1 February 1976, *Another World: Salon and Academy Painting, 1805–1925*, cat.15
New York, Shepherd Gallery, 20 May–26 July 1980, *Christian Imagery in French Nineteenth Century Art 1789–1906*, cat.128, *333*
Hamilton, Art Gallery of Hamilton, 28 May 2005–28 May 2006, *Heaven and Earth Unveiled: European Treasures from the Tanenbaum Collection*, cat.53; 26–27, *86*
Hamilton, Art Gallery of Hamilton, 15 December 2007–21 September 2008, *The Word Made Flesh: Images of Devotion*
Hamilton, Art Gallery of Hamilton, 9 February 2013–9 February 2014, *The Painter Pictured: French Nineteenth-Century Paintings and Portrait Photographs*

The Dead Christ
New York, Shepherd Gallery, 20 May–26 July 1980, *Christian Imagery in French Nineteenth Century Art 1789–1906*, cat.127, *331*
New York, Shepherd Gallery, 1984, *The French Neo-Classical and Academic Tradition, 1800–1900: Figurative and Compositional Painting, Oil Sketches and Works on Paper*, cat.71
Memphis, Dixon Gallery and Gardens, 24 September–17 December 1995; Palm Beach, Society of the Four Arts, 5 January–4 February 1996; Santa Barbara, Santa Barbara Museum of Art, 24 February–21 April 1996; Washington, D.C., Meridian International Center, 15 May–1 July 1996, *Redefining Genre: French and American Painting, 1850–1900*, cat.45, *81*
Hamilton, Art Gallery of Hamilton, 28 May 2005–28 May 2006, *Heaven and Earth Unveiled: European Treasures from the Tanenbaum Collection*, cat.54; 27, *87*
Hamilton, Art Gallery of Hamilton, 15 December 2007–21 September 2008, *The Word Made Flesh: Images of Devotion*

The Levite of Ephraim and His Dead Wife
Paris, Salon, 1898, no.1012
Ottawa, National Gallery of Canada, 26 May–10 September 1978; Victoria, Art Gallery of Greater Victoria, 19 October–3 December 1978; Edmonton, Edmonton Art Gallery, 15 December 1978–14 January 1979; Calgary, Glenbow-Alberta Institute, 3 February–22 March 1979; Montreal, Montreal Museum of Fine Arts, 5 April–13 May 1979; Toronto, Art Gallery of Ontario, 15 June–29 July 1979, *The Other Nineteenth Century: Paintings and Sculpture in the Collection of Mr. and Mrs. Joseph M. Tanenbaum*, cat.40, *125*
London, Royal Academy of Arts, 16 January–3 April 2000; New York, Solomon R. Guggenheim Museum, 18 May–13 September 2000, *1900: Art at the Crossroads*, cat.21, *92*
Hamilton, Art Gallery of Hamilton, 28 May 2005–28 May 2006, *Heaven and Earth Unveiled: European Treasures from the Tanenbaum Collection*, cat.56; 19–21, *79*
Hamilton, Art Gallery of Hamilton, 15 December 2007–21 September 2008, *The Word Made Flesh: Images of Devotion*
Hamilton, Art Gallery of Hamilton, 21 May–5 September 2011, *The French Connection*
Hamilton, Art Gallery of Hamilton, 9 February 2013–9 February 2014, *The Painter Pictured: French Nineteenth-Century Paintings and Portrait Photographs*

Bibliography

Lannoy, Isabelle de. *Jean-Jacques Henner: catalogue raisonné*. Paris: Musée National Jean-Jacques Henner, 2008.
-----. *Musée national Jean-Jacques Henner: catalogue des peintures*. 2nd ed. Paris: Réunion des musées nationaux, 2003, 180–81, 191, 198–99.
Lavallée, Marie-Hélène, et al. *Sensualité et spiritualité: à la recherche de l'absolu*. Paris: Gourcuff Gradenigo, 2012.
Lorenzi, Giovanna de. *Jean-Jacques Henner e lo spiritualismo*. Florence: S.P.E.S., 1982, 42–44.

57

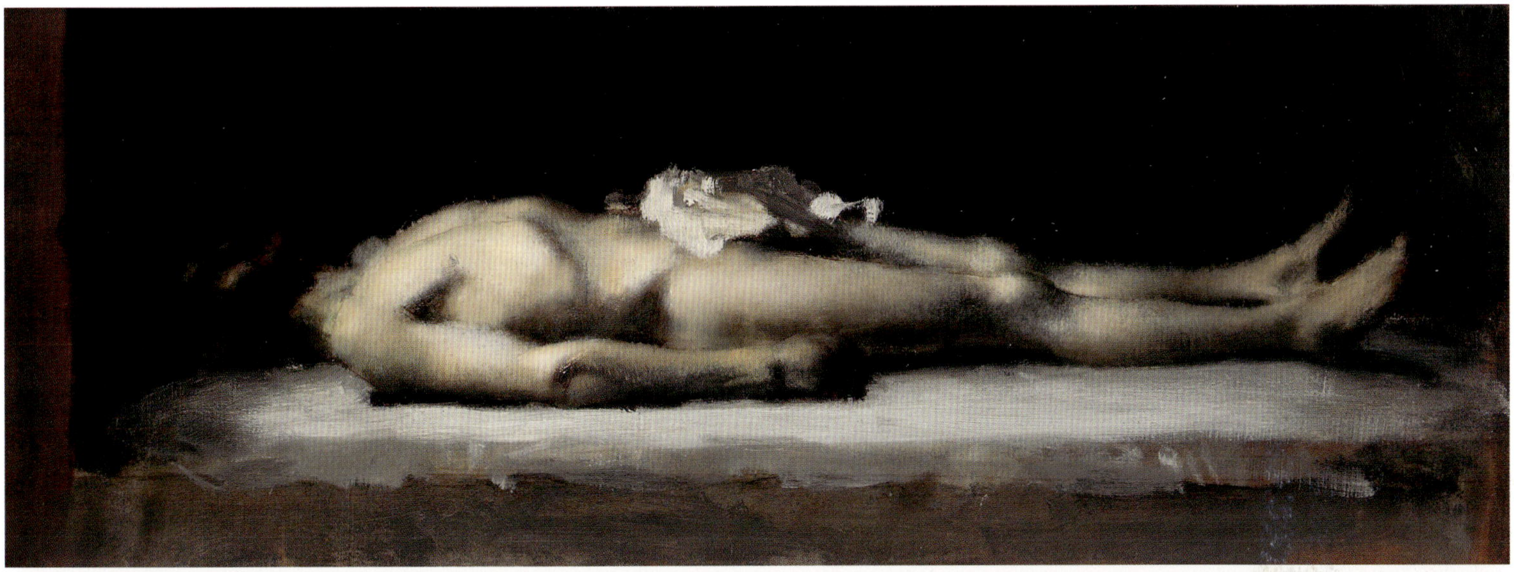

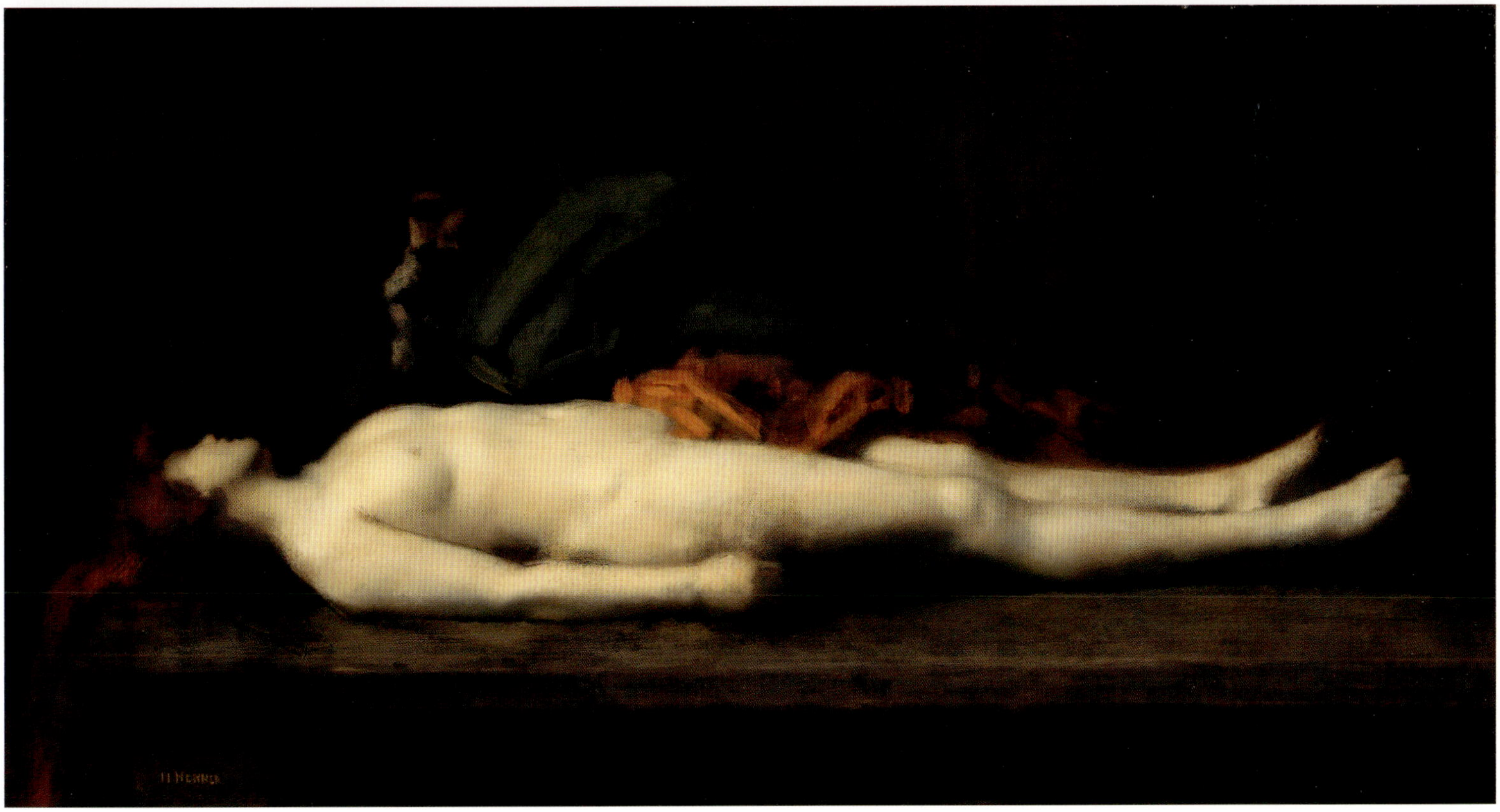

58

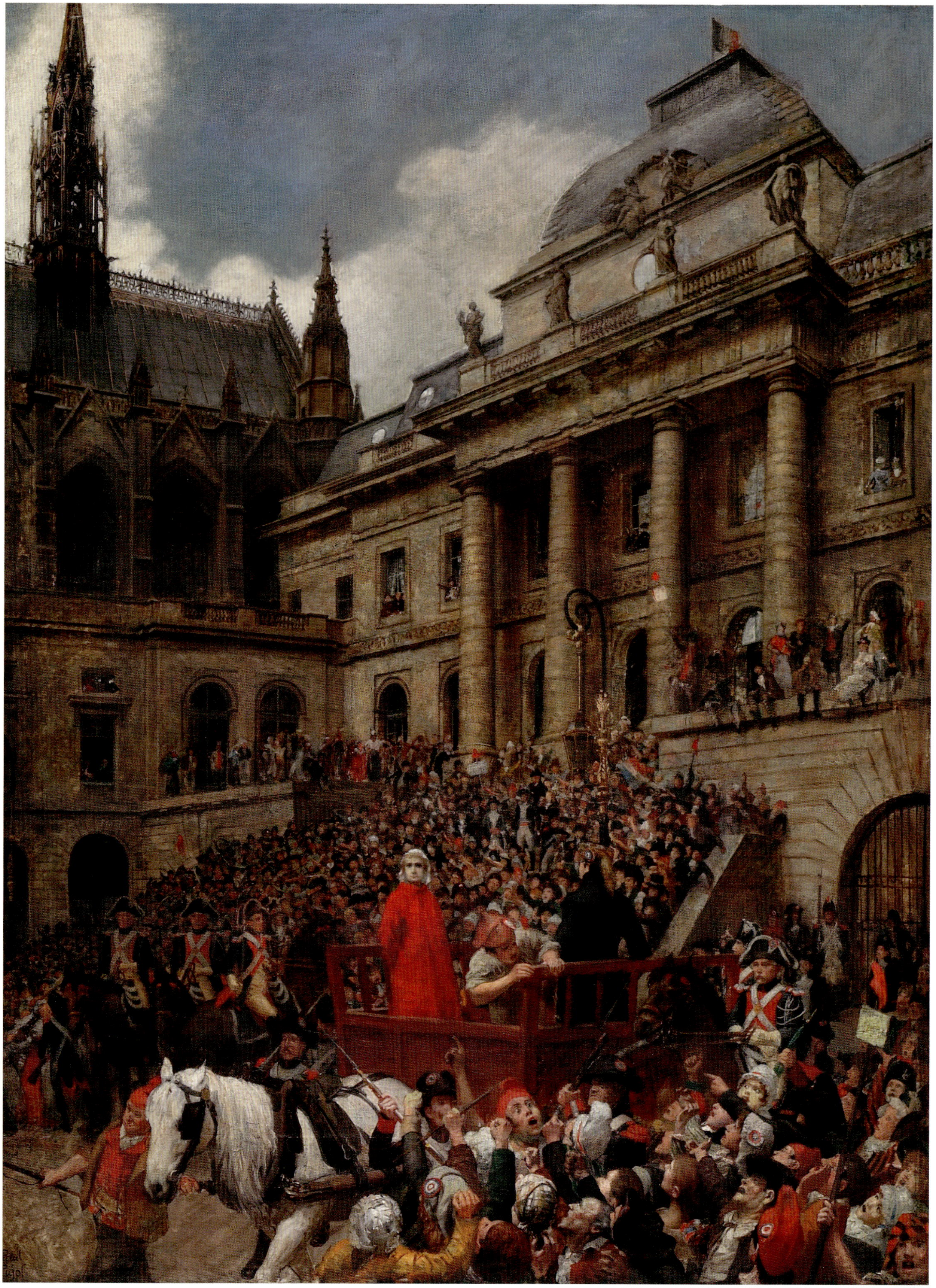

Paul Pujol (French • 1848–after 1902)

59 — The Palais de Justice during the Time of the Revolution

c.1889–92 • oil on canvas • 188 × 139 cm • s.l.l. Paul/Pujol • Inv.2002.33.156

Pujol focuses our attention on the condemned prisoner, who is dressed in a long, ominously colored red cloak and looks directly out at the viewer. The prisoner's face is pale, his eyes darkened, and his hair washed out. His head floats awkwardly above an ill-defined body and he appears to be set apart, both literally and metaphorically, from the surrounding masses of people. This prisoner does, though, stand upright, fearless and resolute as he travels to face his sentence. He is likely headed to the Place de la Révolution, now the Place de la Concorde in Paris, where tens of thousands of people were executed by guillotine during the Reign of Terror (1793–94). The prison cart moves slowly through the Cour du Mai, the large courtyard space that connects with the archway on the right, with its wrought-iron fence and guards. This was the main entrance to the Conciergerie, which served from 1789 as the principal prison for those awaiting trial before the Revolutionary Tribunal. An active crowd scene unfolds around the prisoner. In the foreground, men and women of all ages clamor to get closer to the cart. While Pujol depicts gestures that express a range of emotional responses, the yelling, raised fists and pointing fingers convey a general sense of animosity and show the public's support for the sentence. Hundreds of people also fill the grand staircase and stand along the ledge of the Galerie Mercière. This gallery, with its two-storey Doric portico, was the principal entrance to the Palais de la Cité, known today as the Palais de Justice. Flying above the rooftop is the tricolor that was adopted as France's national flag in 1790. And prominent on numerous hats is the cockade, a knot of blue, red, and white ribbon that was first worn by those who stormed the Bastille.

The charged narrative that unfolds in this work appears as something of a pretext for Pujol's real interest and strength as an artist, which was his ability to depict architecture. Pujol captures the details of the building and the sculpture decorating the Palais de la Cité with great precision. Behind the Palais, Pujol renders the Gothic architecture of the Sainte-Chapelle with equal skill, all of which suggests he had extensive training in architectural drawing. While there is little surviving documentation on Pujol as a painter, there is a strong correlation between the buildings in *The Palais de Justice during the Time of the Revolution* and three other extant works signed by "Pujol" that depict other architectural monuments in Paris: *The Pont de la Concorde* (1892), *View of Val de Grâce* (1892), and *At the Studio Exit, Rue de la Paix* (1889).[1] Stylistic similarities suggest these works may be by the hand of the architect often identified as Casimir Paul Pujol, who trained in Paris in the architecture section of the École des Beaux-Arts. Pujol was architect of the Capitole in his hometown of Toulouse, where he also designed much of the decorative scheme of the Salle des Illustres. Paintings in this hall were assigned in large part to Laurens (see cat.52), and Pujol himself completed some of the smaller scenes along the walls and ceiling.

[1] *The Pont de la Concorde* was sold by Osenat, 6 April 2014, lot 3.

Provenance

New York, Sotheby's, 22 January 1992, no.378

Toronto, Joey and Toby Tanenbaum, 1992–2002

Exhibition History

Hamilton, Art Gallery of Hamilton, 28 May 2005–28 May 2006, *Heaven and Earth Unveiled: European Treasures from the Tanenbaum Collection*, cat.84, 157 (as *The Palais de Justice*)

Bibliography

Ayers, Andrew. *The Architecture of Paris: An Architectural Guide.* London: Edition Axel Menges, 2004, 19–23.

Jones, Kimberley A. "Art and Regional Identity: Jean-Paul Laurens and the Murals of the Capitole de Toulouse, 1892–1915," *Studies in the Decorative Arts* vol.12 no.2 (Spring/Summer 2005): 96–128 (103).

"Nouvelles," *Gazette des architectes et du bâtiment* no.12 (1878): 73.

Jacques-Émile Blanche (French • 1861–1942)

60 — Portrait of Maximiano Errázuriz

1890 • pastel on linen • 129.5 × 78.8 cm • s.d.l.r. J.E. Blanche/90 • Inv.2002.33.4

When Blanche completed the commission for this pastel in 1890, he was emerging as one of the leading portraitists in Paris. The previous year he had exhibited pastels in two important shows, including the annual display of the Salon des Pastellistes at the prominent Galerie Georges Petit. Blanche was also honored with an entire room dedicated exclusively to his works—eighteen in total—in the pavilion of the Société des Pastellistes at the Exposition Universelle held in Paris in 1889. If his work had not already caught the attention of the Chilean expatriate couple Eugenia Huici Arguedas de Errázuriz (1860–1951) and José Tomás Errázuriz (1856–1927), those exhibitions certainly promoted Blanche's talents in their elite social circles. Blanche may well have known the Errázurizes for some time as they were all regular attendees at the social gatherings of the Princesse de Polignac's salons in Paris. The Errázurizes, like Blanche, were later based for a time in London but this pastel was likely executed in Paris.

The couple commissioned this charming portrait of their son, as well as a large-scale full-length pastel portrait of his mother.[1] José, the boy's father, was himself an amateur landscape painter and his mother, Eugenia, was becoming an important patron of the arts. She went on to support Diaghilev's Ballets Russes and she was also the subject of portraits by Sargent, Boldini, and Picasso. The Errázurizes had four children—two daughters, Carmen and María, and one son, Maximiano—all of whom were born in Paris in the 1880s, as well as a son born in Santiago who did not survive infancy. Blanche may have undertaken portraits of the three surviving children; however, the only one known today is this portrait of Maximiano, who was known to his family as Max. Blanche certainly knew how to compliment his sitters, and that was part of his appeal. His portraits also offer considerable psychological depth, not just in the depiction of facial expressions but in how Blanche presents a figure such as Max engulfed in an ambiguous space. Max stands quite poised with a large, frothy white bow tied close to his neck. He relaxes his stance, and plays with the belt that hangs below his jutting-out stomach. His large brown eyes look off plaintively. Whether Max has just thrown down the segments of orange that lay at his feet is unclear, but he certainly looks impatient, as if he would rather run off and play. The materiality of this work contributes to the sense of urgency. The linen support emerges in sections to the left and at the top in the area of the doorway. Blanche also suggests movement by loosely defining the lower left edge of Max's diagonally checkered dress. A few dark lines indicate a floor pattern, likely in the family's domestic space, but Blanche has intentionally left off descriptive details in this part of the work. He contrasts that ambiguity with a more dense layering of pastel in the space to Max's right, and in the area of shadows cast by his legs below. Blanche extends the pastel marks that flow from Max's auburn hair into the gestural lines that define the volume of his face. In the seeming simplicity of this portrait of a young boy Blanche reveals many of his most sophisticated techniques as a pastellist.

[1] *Señora Eugenia Huici de Errázuriz*, pastel, 163.8 × 97.8 cm, now in the Dixon Gallery and Gardens, Memphis (2012.1).

Provenance

Rafael Errazuriz Edwards

New York, Sotheby's, 24 May 1995, no.313 (as *Portrait of Master Errazuriz*)

Toronto, Joey and Toby Tanenbaum, 1995–2002

Exhibition History

Hamilton, Art Gallery of Hamilton, 28 May 2005–28 May 2006, *Heaven and Earth Unveiled: European Treasures from the Tanenbaum Collection*, cat.10, *138* (as *Portrait of Master Errazuriz*)

Bibliography

Albert, Katharine J. "Jacques-Émile Blanche," in Sarah Lees, ed. *Nineteenth-Century European Paintings at the Sterling and Francine Clark Art Institute*. Vol.1. New Haven: Yale University Press, 2012, 36–38.

McPherson, Heather. *The Modern Portrait in Nineteenth-Century France*. New York: Cambridge University Press, 2001, 145–69.

Neutres, Jérôme. *Du côté de chez Jacques-Émile Blanche: un salon à la Belle Époque*. Paris: Flammarion, 2012.

Petry, Claude, et al. *Jacques-Émile Blanche, peintre: 1861–1942*. Paris: Seuil, 1997, 98, 259.

Richardson, John. "Eugenia Errazuriz," *House and Garden* (April 1987): 76–84.

Roberts, Jane. *Jacques-Émile Blanche*. Montreuil: Gourcuff Gradenigo, 2012, 50.

Subercaseaux, Pedro. *Memorias*. Santiago: Editorial del Pacífico, 1962.

Weisberg, Gabriel P. "Jacques-Émile Blanche and the Stylish Portrait," *Arts Magazine* vol.59 no.10 (Summer 1985): 97–101.

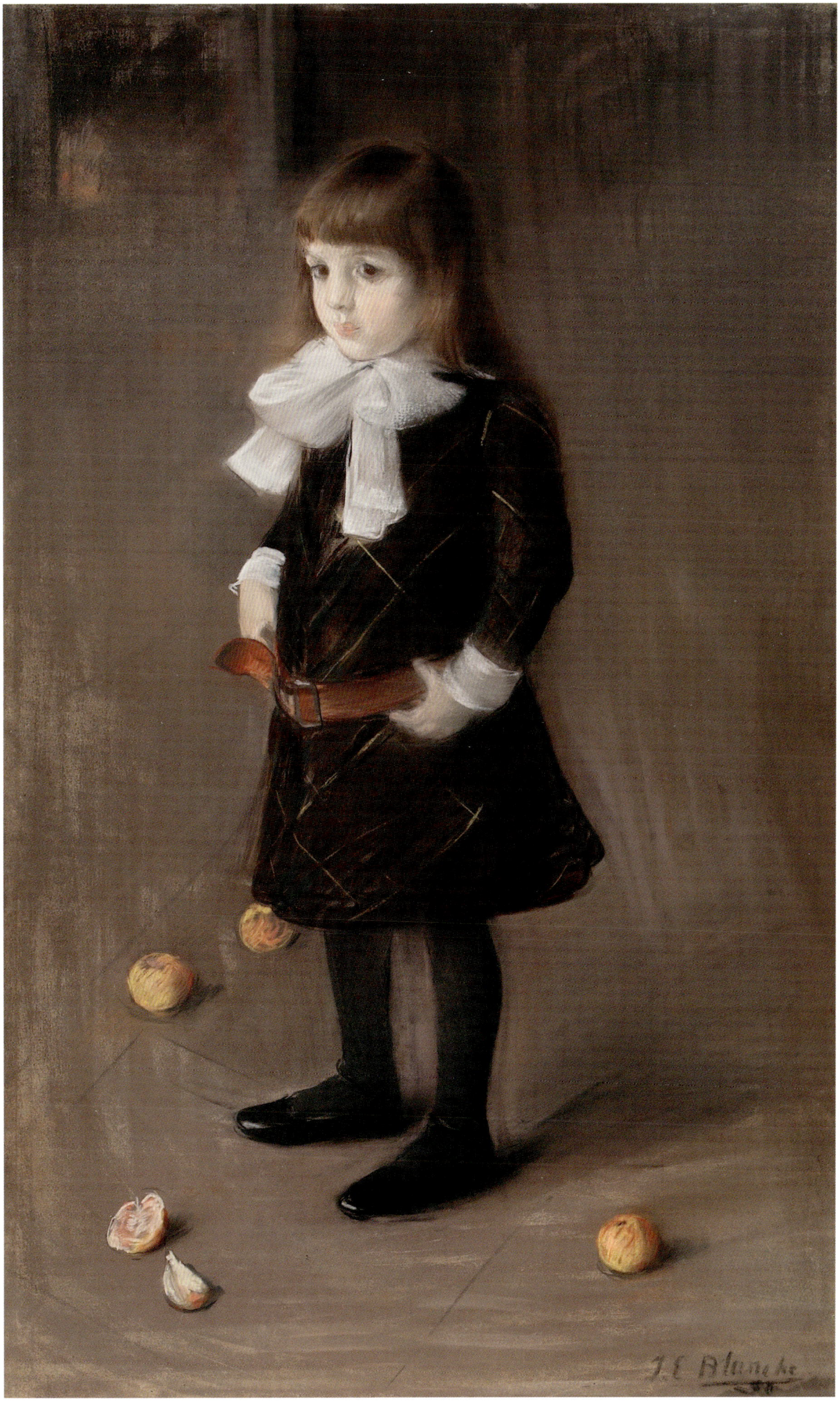
J. E. Blanche

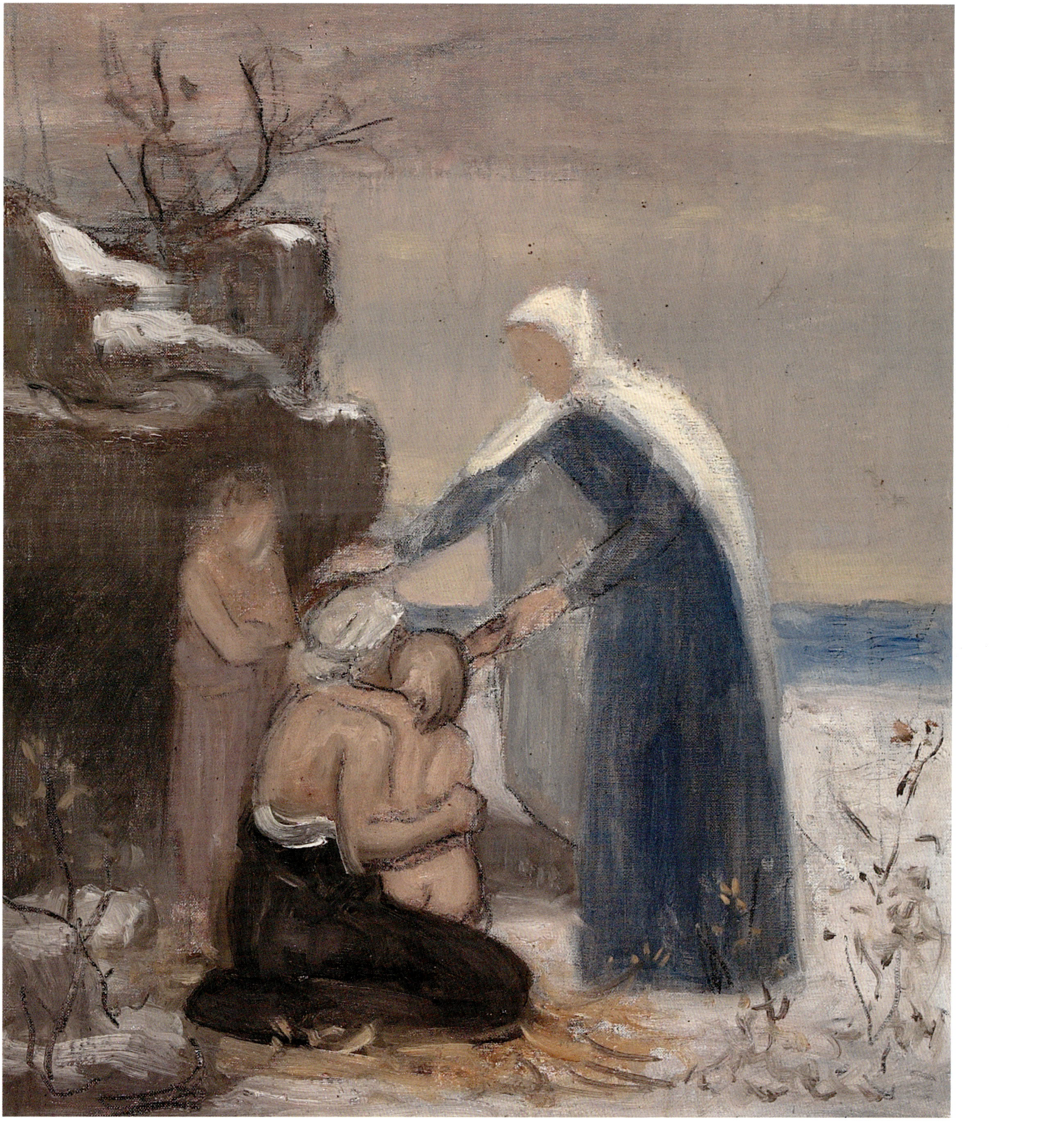

Pierre Puvis de Chavannes (French • 1824–1898)

61 — Study for "Charity"

c.1893–94 • oil with traces of black chalk on canvas • 49.2 × 42.3 cm • red wax studio stamp on stretcher P. Puvis de Chavannes • Inv.2002.33.41

A rocky crag on a desolate coastline sets the stage for this scene of human exchange. A standing woman, dressed in a hooded white cloak over a long blue robe, extends both hands towards a family clustered together for protection against the elements. One hand holds tight, and connects the bodies of the adult women, while the other hovers above the crouching woman's head in a rhetorical gesture of benevolence. This painting was part of the preparatory work for one of the most important mural commissions of Puvis de Chavannes's career. The austere beauty of this small-scale study, with its simplicity of form and harmony of tonalities, is also characteristic of Puvis's highly original pictorial style. Puvis selected charity as one of the principal virtues of civic life and worked through his ideas as he prepared a complex ceiling painting for the new Hôtel de Ville in Paris. The original city hall was among the many buildings set ablaze in spring 1871 during the Paris Commune. During the lengthy period of reconstruction that was finally completed in 1894, artists were able to compete for commissions to decorate the interior spaces of the new city hall. Puvis ultimately received two large commissions, the first a set of wall paintings representing the seasons for the large Zodiac Salon (1889–92).

Study for "Charity" relates to Puvis's second commission for the Hôtel de Ville, a ceiling painting for the grand stairway (*escalier d'honneur*) known as the Prefects' Staircase that led to the principal chambers of the municipal government. Puvis was given complete freedom to design the iconographic program, and he successfully wove together general themes of civic virtue with subjects specific to the nation's capital. He worked in his studio and executed a total of sixteen canvases that were then permanently mounted on the ceiling through *marouflage*, a technique using white lead and oil to adhere canvas to a solid surface. For the large central scene Puvis chose as his subject *Victor Hugo Offering his Lyre to the City of Paris*. With the recently deceased and much revered poet and politician Hugo (1802–1885) as the main protagonist, Puvis focused on the importance of freedom of artistic expression in modern, republican Paris (Hugo lived in exile 1851–70). Framing the large central scene, Puvis had to work with a challenging framework of varying sizes and shapes: seven tympana (arched semicircles), two small triangles, two large curve-topped rectangles, and four sizeable trapezoids. *Charity* was one of the large trapezoid-shaped vaults, positioned as a pendant to *Patriotism*, which were flanked by *Home of Intellect*, and *Artistic Ardour*. Puvis painted *Modern Paris* and *Medieval Paris* for the triangles, and the tympana conveyed traits he deemed central to the spirit of the capital: *Industry*, *Fame*, *Spirit*, *Elegance*, *Urbanity*, *Fantasy*, *Nostalgia*, *Intrepidness*, and *Generosity*. Of the two principal forms of ceiling painting established in previous centuries, Puvis preferred *quadro riportato*, the technique that presented "transferred pictures" to the spectator below rather than illusionistic compositions. Puvis ultimately developed the frame-like edge of *Study for "Charity"* into a floral border that defined the limits of the scene. He added tree trunks around the figures and foliage to the broad sky in his final version of *Charity* and exhibited it and all but four elements of the finished work at the exhibitions of the Société Nationale des Beaux-Arts in 1893 and 1894. Puvis thus ensured the work he achieved for the grand stairway could be seen by a large and appreciative public audience.

Provenance

Studio and estate of Puvis de Chavannes (Delapalme Inventory)
Saint-Sever, Grandin de l'Eprevier
Saint-Sever, Mme de Bary
Paris, Galerie Fischer-Kiener
Toronto, Joey and Toby Tanenbaum, 1985–2002

Exhibition History

Paris, Musée Galliera, 18 April–12 May 1952, *Exposition: "Dessins" et petits tableaux de Pierre Puvis de Chavannes*, cat.34 (? "esquisse ... camaieu bleuté", 50 × 40.5 cm)
Hamilton, Art Gallery of Hamilton, 28 May 2005–28 May 2006, *Heaven and Earth Unveiled: European Treasures from the Tanenbaum Collection*, cat.85; 33, *95*
Hamilton, Art Gallery of Hamilton, 15 December 2007–21 September 2008, *The Word Made Flesh: Images of Devotion*
Hamilton, Art Gallery of Hamilton, 9 February 2013–9 February 2014, *The Painter Pictured: French Nineteenth-Century Paintings and Portrait Photographs*

Bibliography

Boucher, Marie-Christine. "Decoration of the Staircase of Honour in the Paris City Hall," in Louise d'Argencourt et al. *Puvis de Chavannes, 1824–1898*. Ottawa: National Gallery of Canada, 1977, 220–27.
Petrie, Brian. *Puvis de Chavannes*. Pref. Simon Lee. Aldershot: Ashgate, 1997, 140–44.
Pinette, Matthew. *Puvis de Chavannes: une voie singulière au siècle de l'impressionisme*. Amiens: Musée de Picardie, 2005, 210.
Price, Aimée Brown. *Pierre Puvis de Chavannes: A Critical Study of His Life and Art*. 2 vols. New Haven: Yale University Press, 2010, vol.1 143–47, vol.2 334–68.
-----, Jon Whiteley, and Geneviève Lacambre. *Pierre Puvis de Chavannes*. New York: Rizzoli, 1994, 225–28.
Shaw, Jennifer Laurie. "Imagining the Motherland: Modernism and Fantasy in the Hôtel de Ville," in *Dream States: Puvis de Chavannes, Modernism, and the Fantasy of France*. New Haven: Yale University Press, 2002, 143–84.

Adrien Karbowsky (French • 1855–1945)

62 — Rest

1894 • oil on canvas • 91 × 200 cm • s.d.l.r. A. Karbowsky.94 • Inv.2002.33.134

Karbowsky assigned the simple title *Rest* to this placid scene of everyday life. In this image of early spring, only some leaves have opened on the trees. That allows the viewer to see through to the large building in the background. Arched windows and buttresses emerge and denote the building as a church or cathedral. Women of all ages appear across the canvas. Three adult women sit in the foreground with a reclining child. They gather and form a group, although each appears emotionally detached and caught in her own thoughts. On the far right, in the distance, several women walk in a processional manner. They wear a range of types of dress, from an apron to a long, sheath-like gown and they head away from the door of the transept, which is surmounted by a sculpted cross. In the middle ground of the composition, a woman and two children cross the grass in the direction of that same door. The title of this painting and the calm events it presents, the comings and goings from the church, suggest women and children from various social groups who participate in Catholic rites that are integral to the structure of their daily lives. Karbowsky's regular placement of trees creates a pattern across the canvas that structures the composition and supports the viewer's response to the serenity of the work. The muted tones of the soft, pastel colors also inform how we perceive this everyday scene. When Karbowsky exhibited this painting at the Salon in 1894, he was quoting from parts of his own recent wall paintings that not all of his audience would have had an opportunity to see in situ. Such references made it possible for him to promote his abilities as a mural painter to a broader audience, and he did so with success.

The two groups of women and children in the fore- and middle-ground quote directly from the large wall painting *Rest and Navigation* that Karbowsky completed for the town hall of Nogent-sur-Marne, a town east of Paris, just beyond the Bois de Vincennes. When Karbowsky submitted his proposal to the competition, he had considerable freedom, and his only guidelines were to evoke "the picturesque aspects or the scenes of modern life that characterize the specificity of the location." The jury included Bonnat, Laurens, and his former teacher Puvis de Chavannes (see cats.41, 42, 52, and 61). They selected Karbowsky's proposal from among the forty-eight submissions. Karbowsky modified the more standard approach of depicting the seasons and a cycle of life. His subjects included allegorical allusions to important life events that brought citizens to the town hall—birth, marriage, and death. However, Karbowsky also focused on the landscape around the town: the Marne river and the viaduct that separated Nogent from neighboring Perreux. His cycle included six scenes: *A Stay in the Country*, *Ploughing*, *Youth*, *Navigation*, *Rest*, and *Funeral Ceremonies*.[1] Before he mounted his works on the walls of the town hall, Karbowsky exhibited two of the murals at the exhibition of the Société Nationale des Beaux-Arts in 1891 (no.527). He then reworked some of his ideas from *Rest*. He changed the context of the women from a riverside repose to daily, communal experiences on the lawn and pathway outside a church. Karbowsky's commission was part of a broader trend to decorate town and city halls and particularly the *salles de mariage* (wedding halls) of French communes during the early decades of the Third Republic. Karbowsky was adept both at translating his work to a scale that could be acquired by a private collector, and to using a painting such as *Rest* to remind patrons of his abilities as a painter of monumental wall decorations. The presence of such works at important exhibitions helped garner further private commissions such as the one he went on to receive for murals at the Villa Kerylos at Beaulieu-sur-Mer (1902–8).

[1] Preparatory sketches *Small Boat, Navigation, Ages of Life,* and *Cemetery* are in the collection of the Petit Palais, Paris (PPP04058, PPP04057, PPP04059, PPP04060).

Provenance

New York, Christie's, 6 December 1995, lot 101 (as *Le Jardin du prieuré*)

Toronto, Joey and Toby Tanenbaum, 1995–2002

Exhibition History

Paris, Salon de la Société Nationale des Beaux-Arts, 1894, no.657

Hamilton, Art Gallery of Hamilton, 28 May 2005–28 May 2006; Victoria, Art Gallery of Greater Victoria, 25 January–11 May 2008, *Heaven and Earth Unveiled: European Treasures from the Tanenbaum Collection,* cat.68; 19, *77*

Bibliography

Burollet, Thérèse, et al. "Grand décors républicains à Paris, 1870–1914," in *Le Triomphe des mairies.* Paris: Petit Palais, 1986, 220–25.

Noël, Benoît. *Adrien Karbowsky, 1855–1945.* Chatou: Musée Fournaise, 1996.

Vaisse, Pierre. *La Troisième République et les peintres.* Paris: Flammarion, 1995.

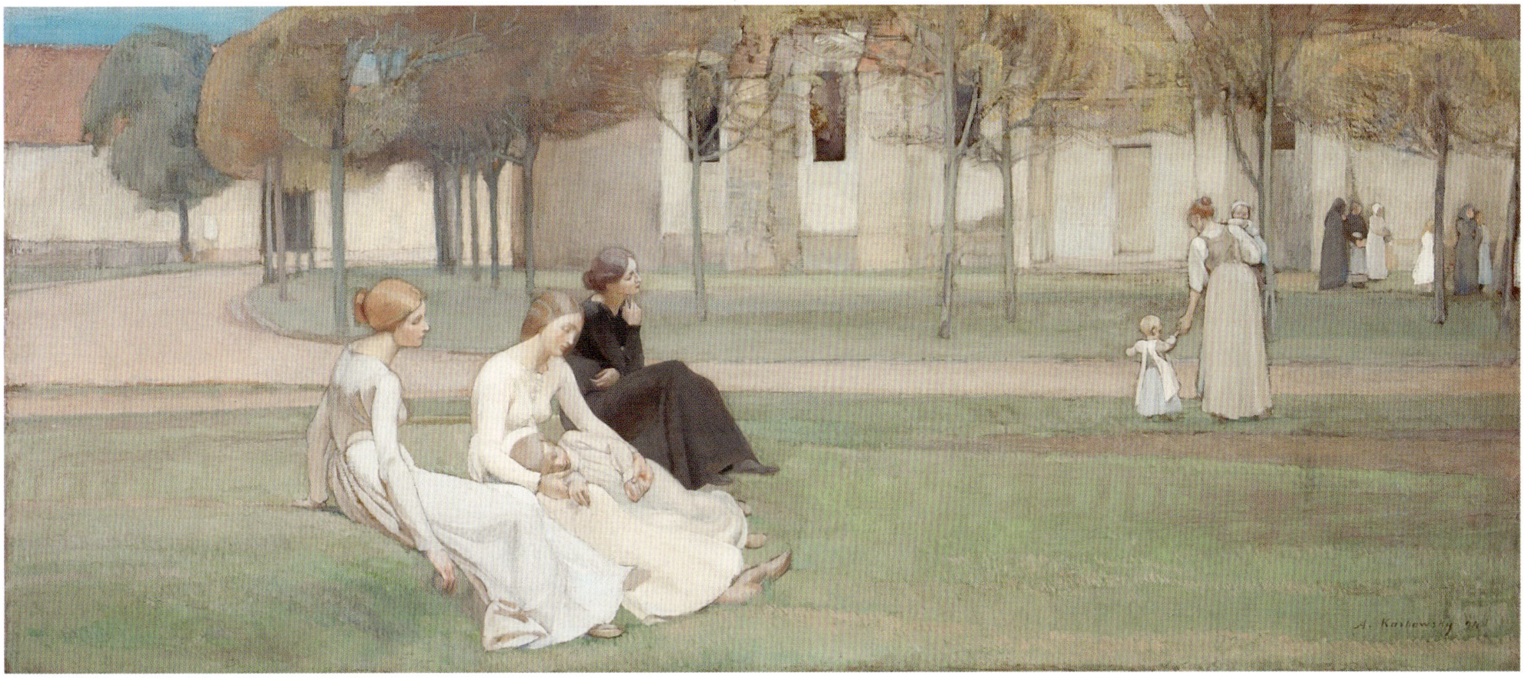

Paul Chabas (French • 1869–1937)

63 — In the Garden of Alphonse Lemerre at Ville d'Avray

1895 • oil on canvas • 278.4 × 339.2 cm • s.d.l.r. Paul-Chabas/1895 • Inv.2002.33.8

Prominent French publisher Alphonse Lemerre (1838–1912) stands in a relaxed pose, the third figure from the right of the composition. He looks neither out to the viewer, nor in the direction of the large social gathering, but off into the distance. Although a substantial form in this large, multi-figure composition, Lemerre remains close to the periphery of the group. People appear to have gathered and then formed discrete units in the secluded space of Lemerre's property southwest of Paris. Chabas created pictorial interest in this work by contrasting his painting techniques. The sketch-like strokes of the pond water and umbrella of trees serve as a frame for the more highly detailed, descriptive painting method Chabas reserved for the principal figures. When Lemerre commissioned this painting he certainly wanted it to focus on the French writers and poets whose work he published and promoted. He took pride in the success of these authors, who were known as the Parnassian school. The literary movement derived its name from Mount Parnassus, home of the Greek Muses, and Lemerre published three collections of the poetry journal *Le Parnasse contemporain* in 1866, 1871, and 1876. At a time when many publishers were cutting their costs, Lemerre remained committed to high-quality editions that often included illustrations. Chabas had worked on illustrations for Lemerre's publishing house for several years when he received the commission for this group portrait. Chabas was then a young, emerging artist, and in 1895 he was only twenty-six when the painting received a third-class medal at the Salon de la Société des Artistes Français.

The literary figures of the Parnassian school appear to enjoy a high level of sociability, and Chabas suggests their success both through the substantial number of figures and their bourgeois attire. Aspects of the composition also raise interesting questions about the cohesiveness of this avant-garde group. Such questions emerged over two decades earlier when Fantin-Latour painted a group portrait of Parnassian poets in *Corner of a Table*, a work he exhibited at the Salon of 1872. Chabas's painting indicates the related challenges he faced as he sought to capture a large number of individuals, many of whom had strong personalities and, at times, tense relations and divergent views. Chabas responded to the complex dynamics of the group specifically following the recent death of Leconte de Lisle (1818–1894). De Lisle was an acknowledged leader within the group, and he stands in profile with cigarette in hand. Although positioned at a slight remove, de Lisle still appears literally and symbolically at the head of the long rectangular table. His dominant position remains clear even as Lemerre stands at the other end. Cuban-born poet José-Maria de Heredia (1842–1905) also stands to speak from the long side of the table. Of the men closest to Heredia, at least some seem to engage with his views. Others, like poet and essayist Sully Prudhomme (1839–1907), seated to his left, and Alphonse Daudet to his right, appear entirely lost in their own thoughts. Wearing glasses and seated on the far left of the work, Jules Breton is the lone visual artist included in this social circle. Behind him stands poet and historical novelist Judith Gautier (1845–1917), the one identifiable female figure within this otherwise exclusively male network. The woman looking out on the far right is believed to be Lemerre's wife, and she may be presented with other family members. Chabas undertook extensive preparatory work and completed separate bust-length studies of the principal male literary figures.[1] Others proved elusive and, according to a contemporary account, either rebelled against the idea of posing or simply refused to set aside the necessary time. In his final work Chabas successfully evokes the palpable tensions of this avant-garde literary group. Many figures appear in fragmented compositional planes as if they embody disparate psychological spaces. Chabas seems not to have intended his group portrait to serve simply as a photograph-like documentation of a genteel afternoon gathering. Rather, his composition suggests that, while the personalities involved may have enjoyed the benefits of their collective identity, each valued and always maintained a strong sense of their own individuality.

[1] There are extant studies for ten of the portraits. The following nine are now in the collection of the Châteaux de Versailles et de Trianon, and Chabas donated the first seven of these to the state in 1931: José-Maria de Heredia (MV6092, RF3154), Auguste Dorchain (MV6095, RF3155), Sully Prudhomme (MV6094, RF3156), Jules Breton (MV6093, RF3157), Paul Bourget (MV6096, RF3158), Paul Hervieu (MV6097, RF3159), François Coppée (MV6098, RF3160), André Theuriet (MV6267), and Marcel Prevost (MV6268). A study for the portrait of Paul Arène is in the collection of the Musée d'Orsay (INV20398).

Provenance

Paris, Alphonse Lemerre
France, private collection
Paris, Casa-Bella Antiquities, 1985
Toronto, Joey and Toby Tanenbaum, 1985–2002

Exhibition History

Paris, Salon de la Société des Artistes Français, 1895, no.396
Toronto, Art Gallery of Ontario, March 1986–April 1991 (on long-term loan)
Hamilton, Art Gallery of Hamilton, 28 May 2005–28 May 2006, *Heaven and Earth Unveiled: European Treasures from the Tanenbaum Collection*, cat.22; 35–36, *97*
Hamilton, Art Gallery of Hamilton, 10 February–13 May 2007, *Framed: The Art of the Portrait*

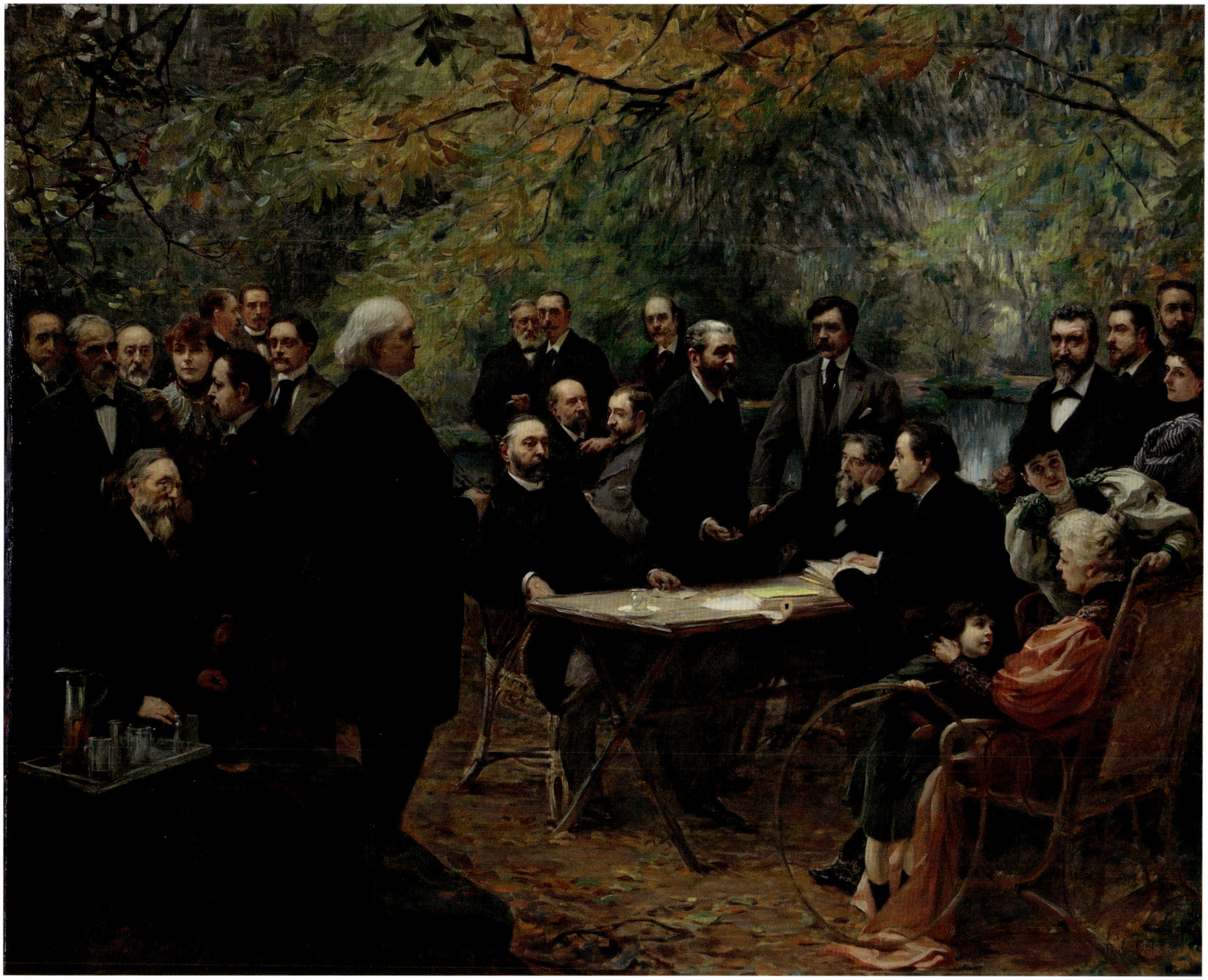

See also detail on pages 158-159

Bibliography

Alsdorf, Bridget. *Fellow Men: Fantin-Latour and the Problem of the Group in Nineteenth-Century French Painting*. Princeton: Princeton University Press, 2013, 156–202.

Carrère, Christophe. *Leconte de Lisle, ou, La passion du beau*. Paris: Fayard, 2009, 426–27.

Constans, Claire. *Musée national du château de Versailles: Les peintures*. Vol.1. Paris: Reunion des musées nationaux, 1995, nos.819–27.

Geffroy, Gustave. *Vie artistique*. Vol.4. Paris: E. Dentu, 1895, 295.

Mortelette, Yann. *Histoire du Parnasse*. Paris: Fayard, 2005, 386.

Valmy-Baysse, Jean. *Paul Chabas: sa vie, son œuvre*. Paris: Félix Juven, 1910, 5–8.

Eugène Carrière (1849–1906)

64 — Head of a Woman (Madame Carrière)

c.1896–1900 • oil on canvas • 54.7 × 46 cm • s.l.l. Eugène Carrière • Inv.2002.33.86

65 — Painting

c.1899 • oil on canvas • 112.7 × 135.8 cm • s.l.l. Eugène Carrière • Inv.2002.33.7

Produced during the final decade of his life, *Head of a Woman* and *Painting* both exemplify the atmospheric nature of Carrière's later work. He achieved an ethereal quality in each painting, and did so through the monochromatic palette he preferred during these years. The works also manifest Carrière's markedly different approaches to handling paint. In *Painting* (cat.65), we witness how Carrière diluted his oils and created a wash-like medium that allowed him to paint more freely. His practice served as a metaphor for his subject. Carrière presented a female painter whose body partially emerges from the background. With palette and brushes to one side, the woman takes the hand with which she paints and lightly tilts her model's head. As spectators to this contemplative scene we study the painter's profile at the same time as she examines the profile of her model. Carrière also reminds us of the importance of physical contact. The painter touches her model and the young woman fingers the neckline of her dress. The very surface of this painting emphasizes how Carrière used his paintbrushes to gently touch the canvas. Every element of the work suggests the painter's craft. Touch and the application of paint play equally important roles in *Head of a Woman* (cat.64), but with quite different results. Areas of bare canvas emerge at the lower edges of the work, but Carrière used thicker, yet still wash-like layers as he defined the figure's upper body and background with utmost subtlety. Dense, impastoed areas of paint highlight and model the forms of the head and hand joined at rest. While touch appears again in this work as a physical gesture, it is primarily a sign of the woman's withdrawal into a calm, internal sphere. These two works convey Carrière's success as a highly tactile and sensual painter.

There are notable similarities in the facial features of the adult female figures in *Head of a Woman* and *Painting*. Carrière regularly used his family members as his models, but he does not present them here as traditional portraits. Carrière's wife was the model for *Head of a Woman*, and their daughters Marguerite and Élise assumed the roles of artist and model in *Painting*. Earlier in his career, Carrière was often connected with realist practices. As he developed his own style, Carrière remained committed to figurative traditions and continued to pursue subjects from intimate family life. Over time, he also transformed the roles of observation and description within his work, and his later compositions, such as these, have important connections with the emerging symbolist movement. While symbolism was first identified as a trend in literature, it was connected with the visual arts by the mid-1880s. Symbolist interests in imagination and fantasy are evident in Carrière's work, and offer a meaningful context in which we can understand his poetic compositions. Tonal harmonies of predominantly earth-colored paint coalesce and convey evocative dream-like spaces. Maurice Denis, a contemporary symbolist painter in the Nabis group, acquired *Painting* from Carrière, and a second version of this subject was once in the collection of artist Henry Lerolle.[1] Carrière enjoyed considerable support from critics and artists and was recognized as a leader among his peers. In Paris, he was one of the founding members of both the Société Nationale des Beaux-Arts and the Salon d'Automne. He was also actively involved in vanguard artistic circles in Munich and Brussels.

[1] The second version is now in the Museum of Modern Art in Ibaraki.

Provenance

Head of a Woman (Madame Carrière)

Paris, Max Robin (until c.1967)
New York, Schweitzer Gallery
New York, Berry Hill Galleries
Toronto, Joey and Toby Tanenbaum, 1969–2002

Painting

Saint-Germain-en-Laye, Maurice Denis
Rouen, Jean-Baptiste Denis (by 1943)
Paris, Georges Martin-du-Nord
Paris, Hôtel George V sale, 25 June 1975, no.99
New York, Shepherd Gallery
Toronto, Joey and Toby Tanenbaum, 1977–2002

Exhibition History

Head of a Woman (Madame Carrière)

Paris, Galerie Manzi, Joyant et Cie, 2–3 February 1920, *Catalogue des tableaux, dessins, lithographies, provenant de l'atelier d'Eugène Carrière*, cat.85
Allentown, Allentown Art Musem, 2 November 1968–26 January 1969; Atlanta, High Museum, 16 February–16 March 1969; Akron, Akron Art Institute, 20 May–3 August 1969; San Francisco, California Palace of the Legion of Honor, 15 November 1969–11 January 1970; Minneapolis, Minneapolis Institute of Arts, 22 February–5 April 1970, *Eugène Carrière 1849–1906: Seer of the Real*, cat.45, *61*
Toronto, Art Gallery of Ontario, 1–26 November 1969, *The Sacred and Profane in Symbolist Art*, cat.169, *151* (as *Portrait of M.me Carrière*)
Ottawa, National Gallery of Canada, 26 May–10 September 1978; Victoria, Art Gallery of Greater Victoria, 19 October–3 December 1978; Edmonton, Edmonton Art Gallery, 15 December 1978–14 January 1979; Calgary, Glenbow-Alberta Institute, 3 February–22 March 1979; Montreal, Montreal Museum of Fine Arts, 5 April–13 May 1979; Toronto, Art Gallery of Ontario, 15 June–29 July 1979, *The Other Nineteenth Century: Paintings and Sculpture in the Collection of Mr. and Mrs. Joseph M. Tanenbaum*, cat.15, *65*
Hamilton, Art Gallery of Hamilton, 28 May 2005–28 May 2006, *Heaven and Earth Unveiled: European Treasures from the Tanenbaum Collection*, cat.20; 42–43, *105*
Hamilton, Art Gallery of Hamilton, 10 February–13 May 2007, *Framed: The Art of the Portrait*
Hamilton, Art Gallery of Hamilton, 22 January–8 May 2011, *Eugène Carrière: Shadow and Substance* (hors catalogue)

Painting
Paris, Musée de l'Orangerie, 1970, *Eugène Carrière 1849–1906*, cat.D (as *Le Peintre et son modèle*)
Ottawa, National Gallery of Canada, 26 May–10 September 1978; Victoria, Art Gallery of Greater Victoria, 19 October–3 December 1978; Edmonton, Edmonton Art Gallery, 15 December 1978–14 January 1979; Calgary, Glenbow-Alberta Institute, 3 February–22 March 1979; Montreal, Montreal Museum of Fine Arts, 5 April–13 May 1979; Toronto, Art Gallery of Ontario, 15 June–29 July 1979, *The Other Nineteenth Century: Paintings and Sculpture in the Collection of Mr. and Mrs. Joseph M. Tanenbaum*, cat.16, *67*
Hamilton, Art Gallery of Hamilton, 28 May 2005–28 May 2006 [March 2006], *Heaven and Earth Unveiled: European Treasures from the Tanenbaum Collection*, cat.21; 32, *95*
Tokyo, National Museum of Western Art, 6 March–4 June 2006; Paris, Musée d'Orsay, 11 July–1 October 2006, *Auguste Rodin—Eugène Carrière*, cat.21, *101*
Hamilton, Art Gallery of Hamilton, 22 January–8 May 2011, *Eugène Carrière: Shadow and Substance* (hors catalogue)

Bibliography
Bajou-Charpentreau, Valérie. *Eugène Carrière: portrait intimiste*, 1849–1906. Lausanne: Acatos, 1998.
Bantens, Robert James. *Eugène Carrière: The Symbol of Creation.* New York: Kent Fine Art, 1990.
-----. *Eugène Carrière: His Work and Influence*. Ann Arbor: UMI Research Press, 1983.
Nora-Milin, Véronique, and Alice Lamarre. *Eugène Carrière, 1849–1906: catalogue raisonné de l'œuvre peint*. Paris: Gallimard, 2008, cat.900, *277* (as study for *Painting*).
Séailles, Gabriel. *Eugène Carrière: essai de biographie psychologique.* Paris: A. Colin, 1911, 267.

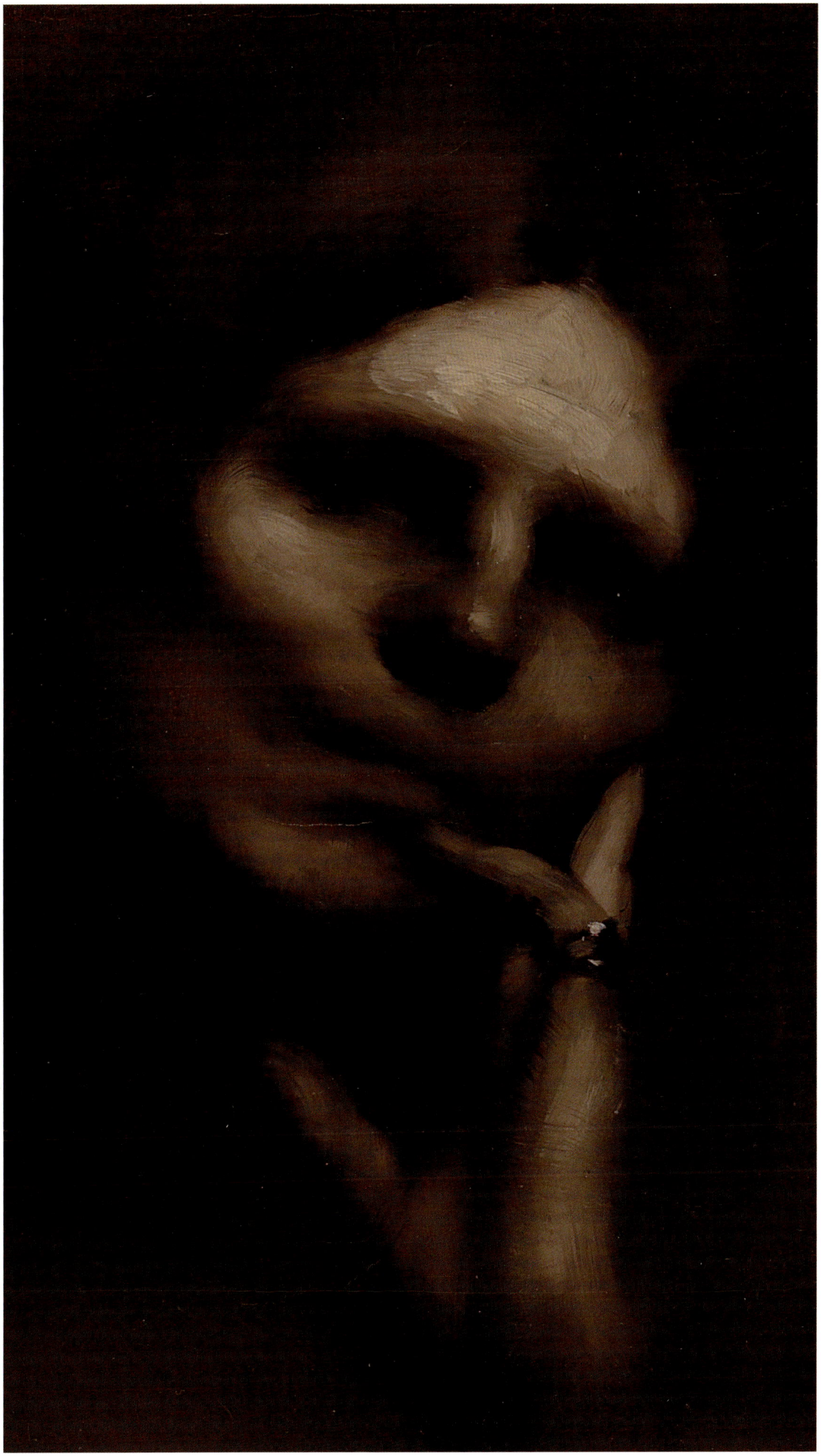

64 (Detail)

64

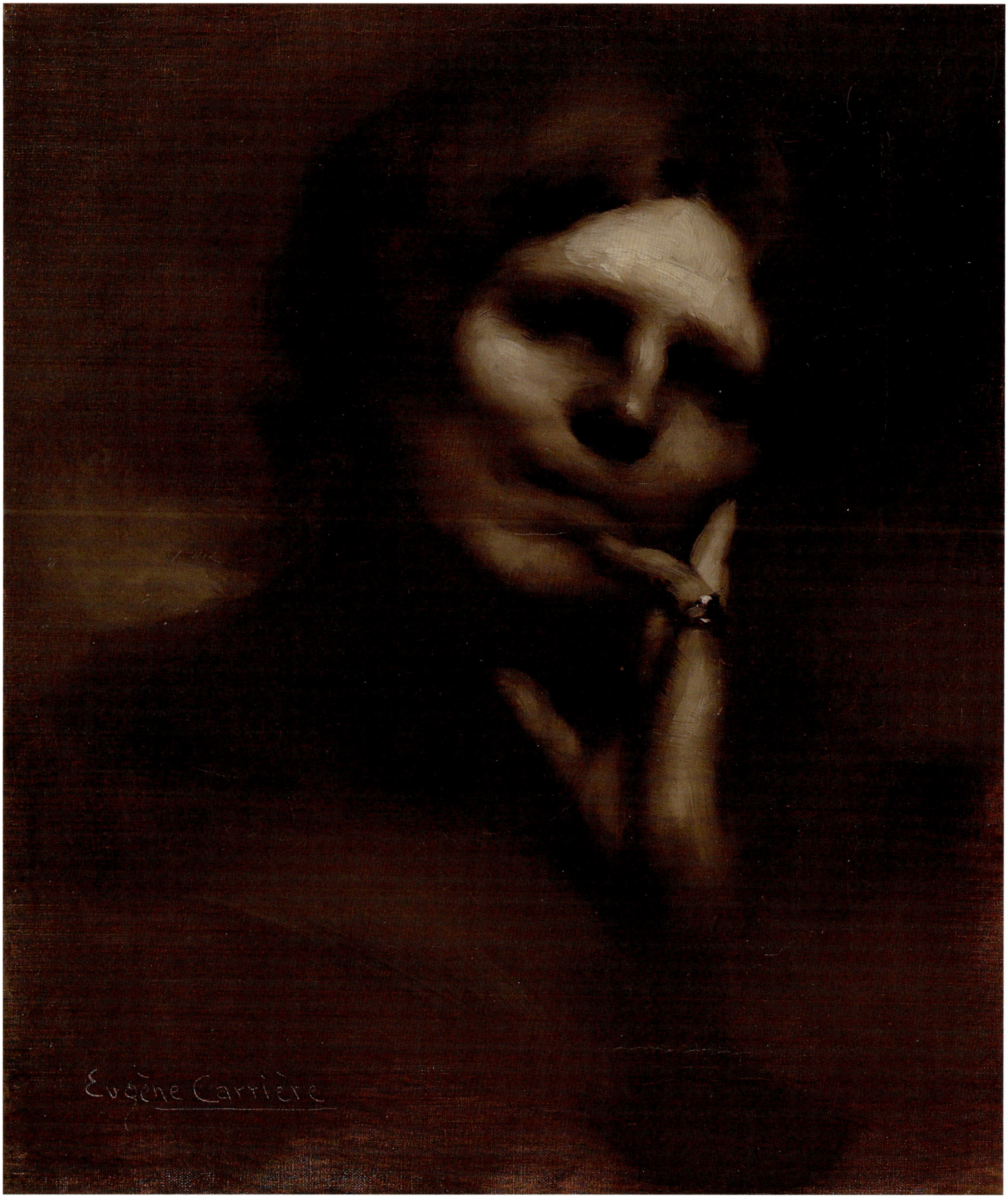

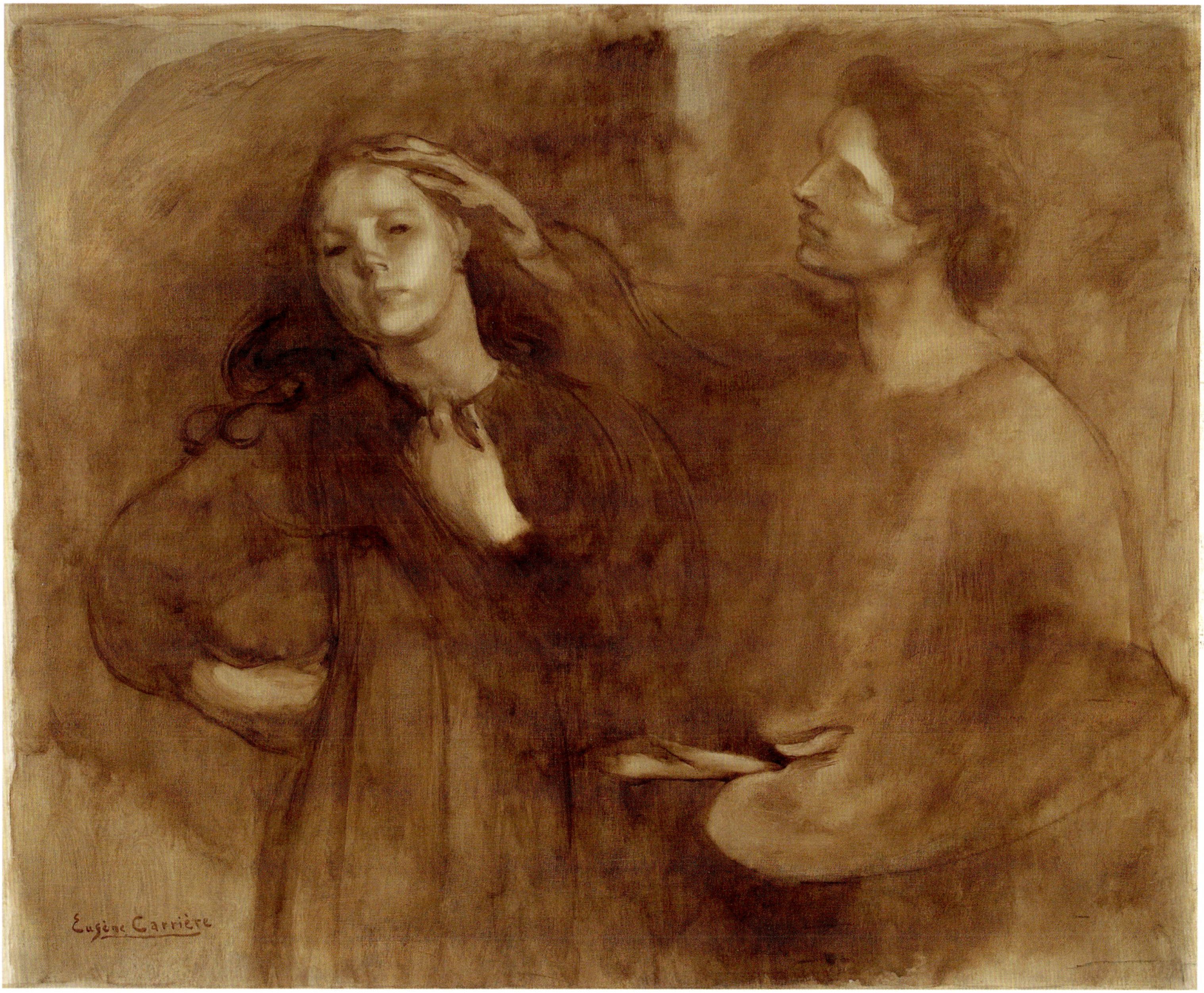

65

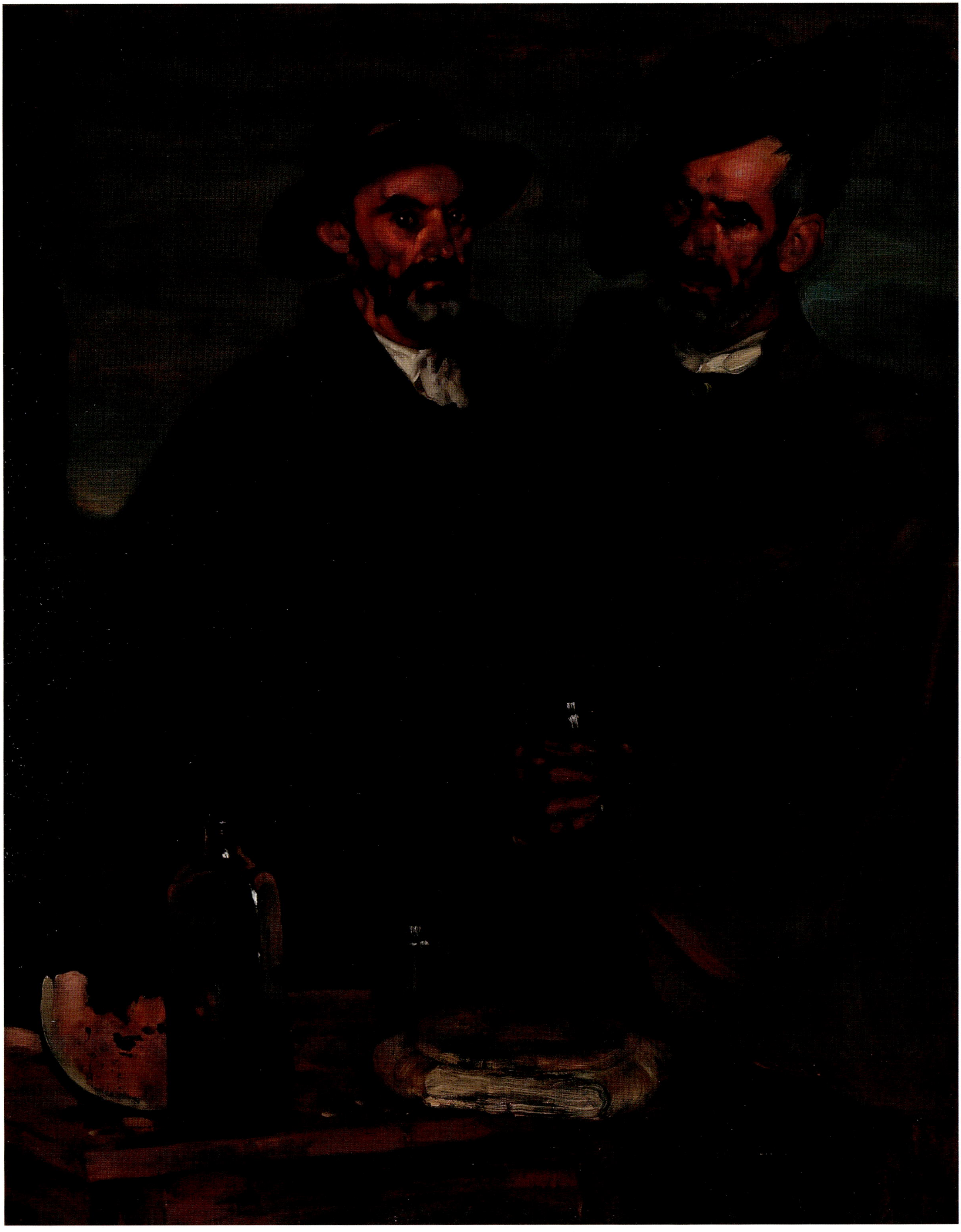

Ignacio Zuloaga (Spanish • 1870–1945)

66 — Two Drinkers, Segovia

1902–3 • oil on canvas • 118.2 × 92.8 cm • Inv.2002.33.199

Zuloaga's painting *Two Drinkers, Segovia* celebrates Spanish peasants as an embodiment of the nation's authentic identity. Although he was born in the northern, Basque region, Zuloaga focused primarily on representing the landscape and inhabitants of cities in Castile, the most central province of Spain. Zuloaga's personal interest in the Castilian region related to a larger nationalist movement that developed following defeat in the Spanish-American War of 1898 and the loss of Cuba and the Philippines, the last of Spain's colonies. Historically, the Castilian region had not been touched by foreign invasion. Zuloaga was among those who regarded the desolate and mountainous Castilian landscape, and its local population, as not only the geographical but also the symbolic core of the nation. Zuloaga traveled to the Castilian town of Segovia in 1898 when he visited his uncle, a well-known ceramicist. From then on he returned to Segovia every fall for the next fifteen years. It was there that he produced *Two Drinkers, Segovia*, a painting that in both technique and subject matter exemplifies the work for which Zuloaga is best known today.

Zuloaga identified himself as "the painter of Spain" of his time. He also defined himself as a descendant of El Greco, Velázquez, and Goya, painters who had been based in Madrid and Toledo and who had focused on portraits, religious subjects, and scenes of everyday life. In reality, Zuloaga divided his time between a studio he shared with his uncle in Spain and another that he rented in Montmartre. Zuloaga went to Paris first in 1890 and maintained a studio there consistently from 1898. He enjoyed strong connections with artistic circles in France, including friendships with painters Blanche and Carrière (see cats.60, 64, and 65), among others. Zuloaga often supported himself with portrait commissions, but it was his paintings of Castilian subjects that brought him critical acclaim across Europe from as early as 1903. He exhibited works in numerous venues including Paris, Venice, Düsseldorf, and Barcelona. Even when based in France, Zuloaga spent a portion of his time thinking about the work he would undertake on his next trip to Spain. It was from Paris in both 1902 and 1903 that Zuloaga wrote his uncle and asked him to prepare for the trips that they would take by car to several Castilian cities each of those years. These were busy trips in which Zuloaga was focused on gathering materials. He often took photographs and called upon his uncle's contacts to organize sittings with local models. Zuloaga had a specific idea of how his models should look, and wrote to his uncle that he wanted people wearing "capes, hats and rope-soled country shoes, and that the clothing be faded, because I have an idea of what I would like to do." He drew upon such travels for *Two Drinkers*, presenting the two heavily cloaked men in a compressed space and staging them before a dark, mountainous landscape setting.

While Zuloaga had many contemporary supporters, his detractors claimed his work advanced a view of Spain as a backward nation, one on the periphery of the modernizations of surrounding European nations. Zuloaga later aligned himself with the Generación del 98, a group of writers and poets who promoted a regeneration of the Spanish nation after the 1898 defeat and who argued that by valuing Spain's past the nation would emerge triumphant in the modernist age. Recent scholarship suggests that works like Zuloaga's *Two Drinkers, Segovia* straddle both tradition and modernity, and offer important insight into regional-based concepts of nationalism that are central to understanding the cultural history of early twentieth-century Spain.

Provenance

Groß-Lichterfelde, Collection of C. Steinbart, by 1904

Toronto, Joey and Toby Tanenbaum, 1971–2002

Exhibition History

Venice, 1903, Esposizione Internazionale d'Arte, no.7

Düsseldorf, 1 May–23 October 1904, Internationale Kunstausstellung, cat.136

Barcelona, April 1907, V Exposición Internacional de Arte, no.18 (Salas V and VI, as *Bebedores*)

Hamilton, Art Gallery of Hamilton, 28 May 2005–28 May 2006, *Heaven and Earth Unveiled: European Treasures from the Tanenbaum Collection*, cat.140; 61, *139*

Bibliography

Crosson, Dena. "Ignacio Zuloaga and the Problem of Spain," Ph.D. dissertation, University of Maryland, 2009, 18–87 (65, fn.126).

Gallego, Julian, et al. *Ignacio Zuloaga, 1870–1945*. Vitoria: Eusko Jaurlaritza, 1990, 60–77.

Lafuente Ferrari, Enrique. *La vida y el arte de Zuloaga*. 2nd ed. Madrid: Revista de Occidente, 1972, 79–94.

Lorandi, Marco. *Dalla tradizione alla tradizione: Rusiñol, Sorolla, Zuloaga, Anglada e la pittura della reiberizzazione in Spagna 1874–1945*. Viareggio: M. Baroni, 2000, 106–45.

Pena Lopez, Carmen. "Las ciudades de Ignacio Zuloaga," in *Homenaje al profesor Hernández Perera*. Madrid: Universidad Complutense de Madrid, 1992, 395–97.

Plessier, Ghislaine. *Ignacio Zuloaga et ses amis français*. Paris: L'Harmatta, 1995.

Tomás Ferré, Facundo. *Zuloaga y Sorolla: artistas en una edad de plata*. Valencia: Consorci de Museus de la Comunitat Valenciana, 2012, 127–56.

Henry de Groux (Belgian • 1866–1930)

67 — The Death of Savonarola

1903–4 • oil on wood panel • 129 × 91 cm • s.l.l. HENRY DE GROUX • Inv.2002.33.15

Charged emotions swirl through this composition. Energy surges, following an arc that runs counterclockwise and gains momentum as it ascends on the right-hand side of the painting. A dense crowd has gathered to witness an execution and surrounds a large pyre. Flames threaten to engulf even the spectators. Given that this execution scene represents three figures tied to a cross, it is not surprising that the subject was at one time believed to be a scene of the Crucifixion, with Christ flanked by two thieves. The subject has also been identified as *Autodafé*, a scene of heretics burned at the stake during the time of the Inquisition. The most recent research into de Groux's journals reveals, however, that this is in fact a scene of the death of Girolamo Savonarola (1452–1498), a famous Dominican monk from the Italian Renaissance. For a period of time, Savonarola enjoyed considerable power and was regarded as a prophet. He attacked all who abused power and promoted social and religious reform. Savonarola is often associated with the infamous Bonfires of the Vanities, public burnings of objects that represented sin, although he was later declared a heretic and excommunicated. Savonarola and two other monks were burned at the stake in Florence on 23 May 1498.

In May 1903, de Groux wrote in his journal that he was starting a series of works on the "punishment of Savonarola." De Groux had been interested in crowd scenes for well over a decade. He had exhibited his most famous work, *Christ aux outrages* (The Mocking of Christ), in Brussels in 1890, and his presentation of Christ surrounded and insulted by a large mass of people was so well received that the Belgian queen Marie Henriette paid for the painting to be shipped to Paris so it could be seen by a larger audience.[1] Throughout his career, de Groux was intrigued by figures he regarded as victims of circumstances, particularly individuals who experienced attacks by large crowds. He explored this interest through various compositions, including representations of Christ, Napoleon Bonaparte, Emperor Andronicus, Siegfried from Wagner's *Ring*, and his contemporary Émile Zola. Based in Paris beginning in 1891, de Groux followed with great interest Zola's trial following his defense of the Jewish captain Alfred Dreyfus who was falsely accused of treason and later exonerated. In his *Zola aux outrages* of 1898[2] and this later scene of *The Death of Savonarola*, de Groux consistently examines the position of a lone individual who is physically engulfed and also psychologically attacked by an unrelenting throng of humanity. It is from this context that scholarship on de Groux aligns his works with both the symbolist movement and theories of crowd behavior that were emerging in the field of sociology in the fin-de-siècle period.

1 *Christ aux outrages* (1888–89) is now in the Palais du Roure, Avignon, and a smaller version dated c.1925 is in the Musées Royaux des Beaux-Arts de Belgique, Brussels.

2 Musée Émile Zola, Medan.

Provenance

Paris, Galerie Fischer-Kiener, 1985

Toronto, Joey and Toby Tanenbaum, 1985–2002

Exhibition History

Montreal, Montreal Museum of Fine Arts, 8 June–15 October 1995, *Lost Paradise: Symbolist Europe*, cat.74, *99* (as *The Auto-da-fé*)

Hamilton, Art Gallery of Hamilton, 28 May 2005–28 May 2006, *Heaven and Earth Unveiled: European Treasures from the Tanenbaum Collection*, cat.30; 23, *81* (as *Autodafé*)

Hamilton, Art Gallery of Hamilton, 15 December 2007–21 September 2008, *The Word Made Flesh: Images of Devotion*

Bibliography

Davenport, Nancy. "'Christ aux Outrages' by Henry de Groux: Fin de Siècle Religion, Art Criticism, and the Sociology of the Crowd," *Religion and the Arts* vol.7 no.3 (2003): 275–98.

-----. "Henry De Groux, the Great War and the Apocalypse," *Print Quarterly* vol.19 no.2 (June 2002): 147–69.

Derrey-Capon, Danielle. "Henry de Groux," in *Académie Royale des Beaux-Arts de Bruxelles: 275 ans d'enseignement*. Brussels: Crédit Communal, 1987, 153–55.

Rappetti, Rodolphe. "Un chef-d'œuvre pour ces temps d'incertitude: 'Le Christ aux outrages' d'Henry de Groux," *Revue de l'art* no.96 (1992): 40–50.

-----, et al. *Henry de Groux, 1866–1930, journal*. Paris: Institut National d'Histoire de l'Art, 2007, 92, 97, 154, 208, 268, *304*.

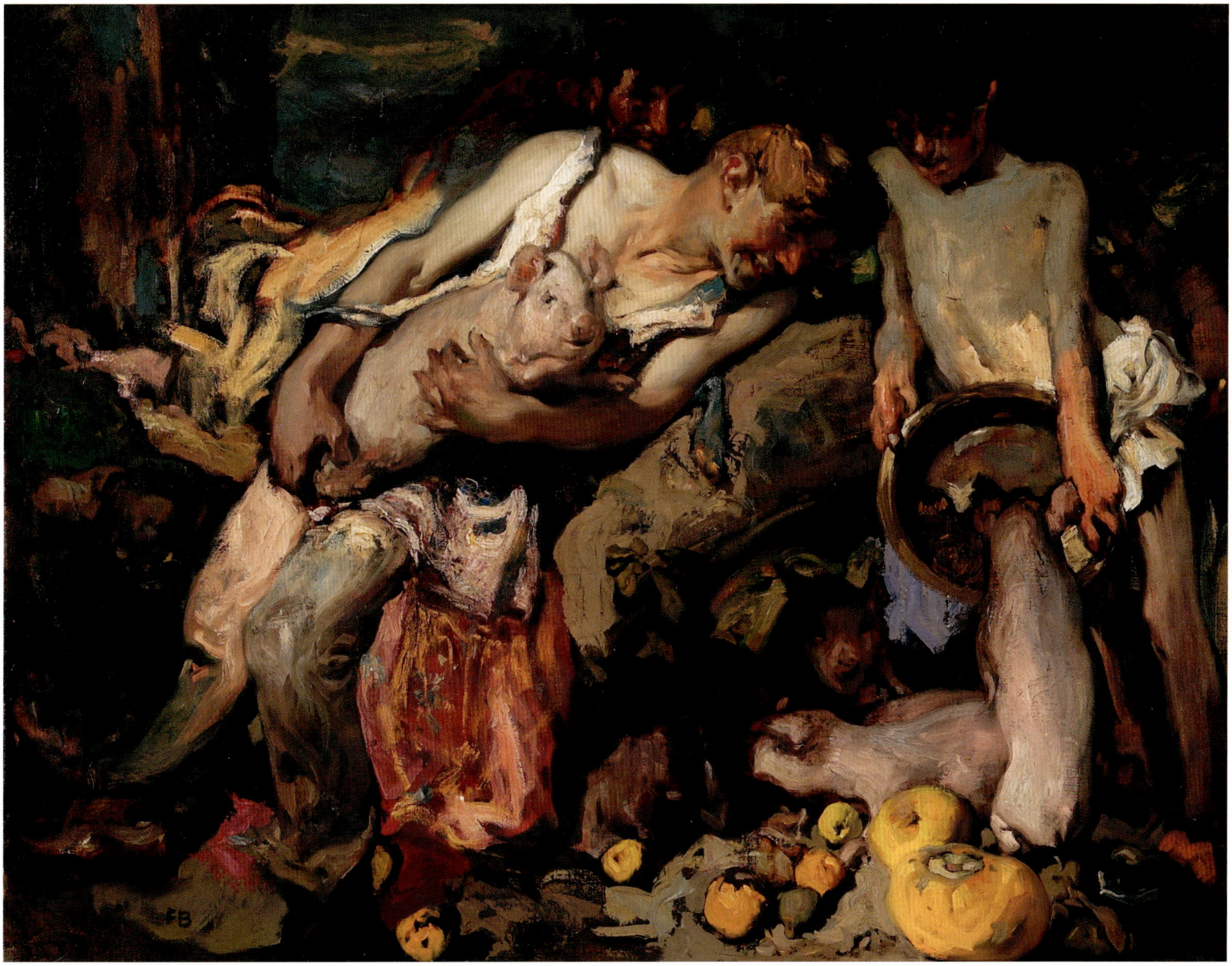

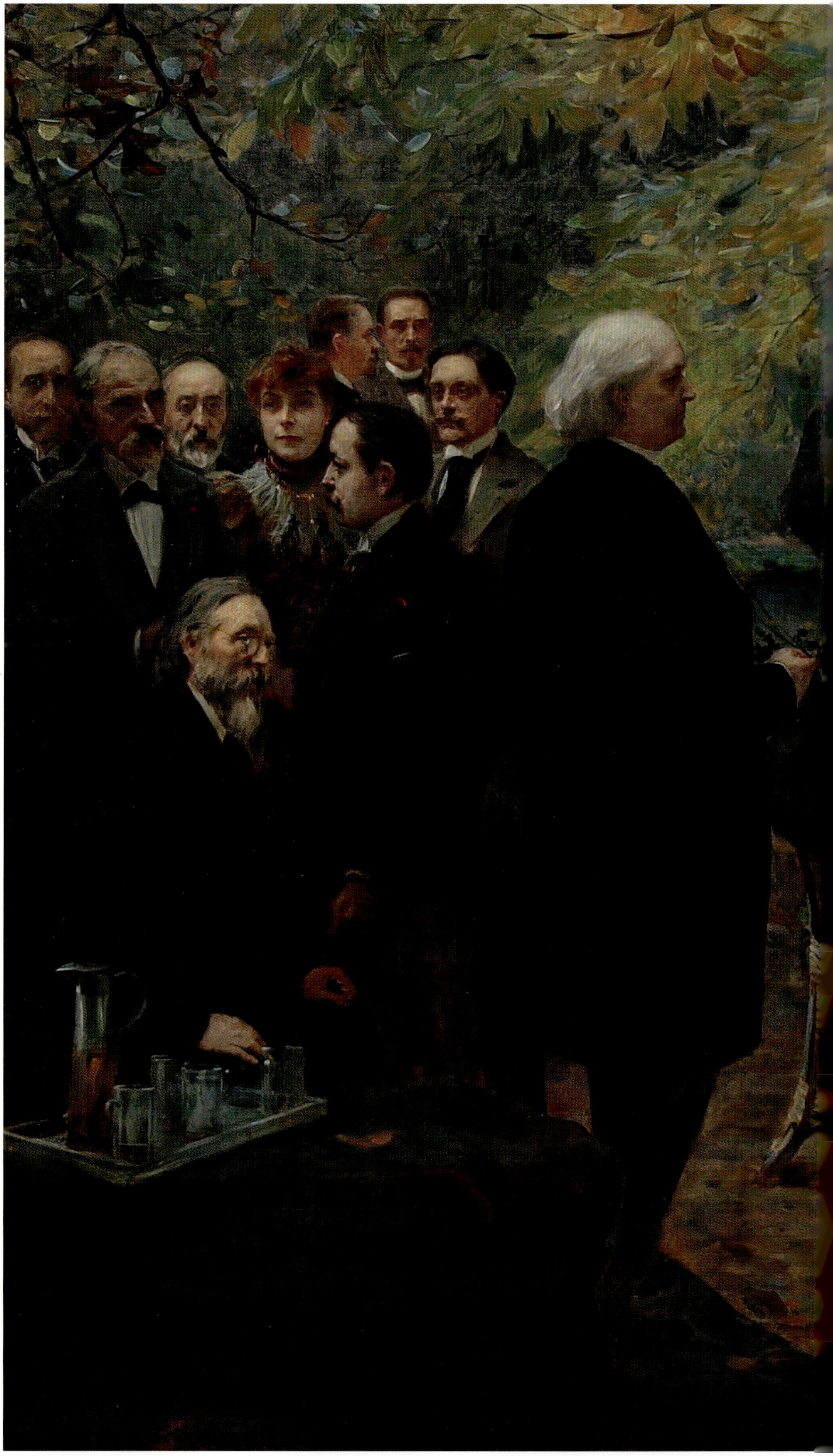

Cat. 63 (Detail)

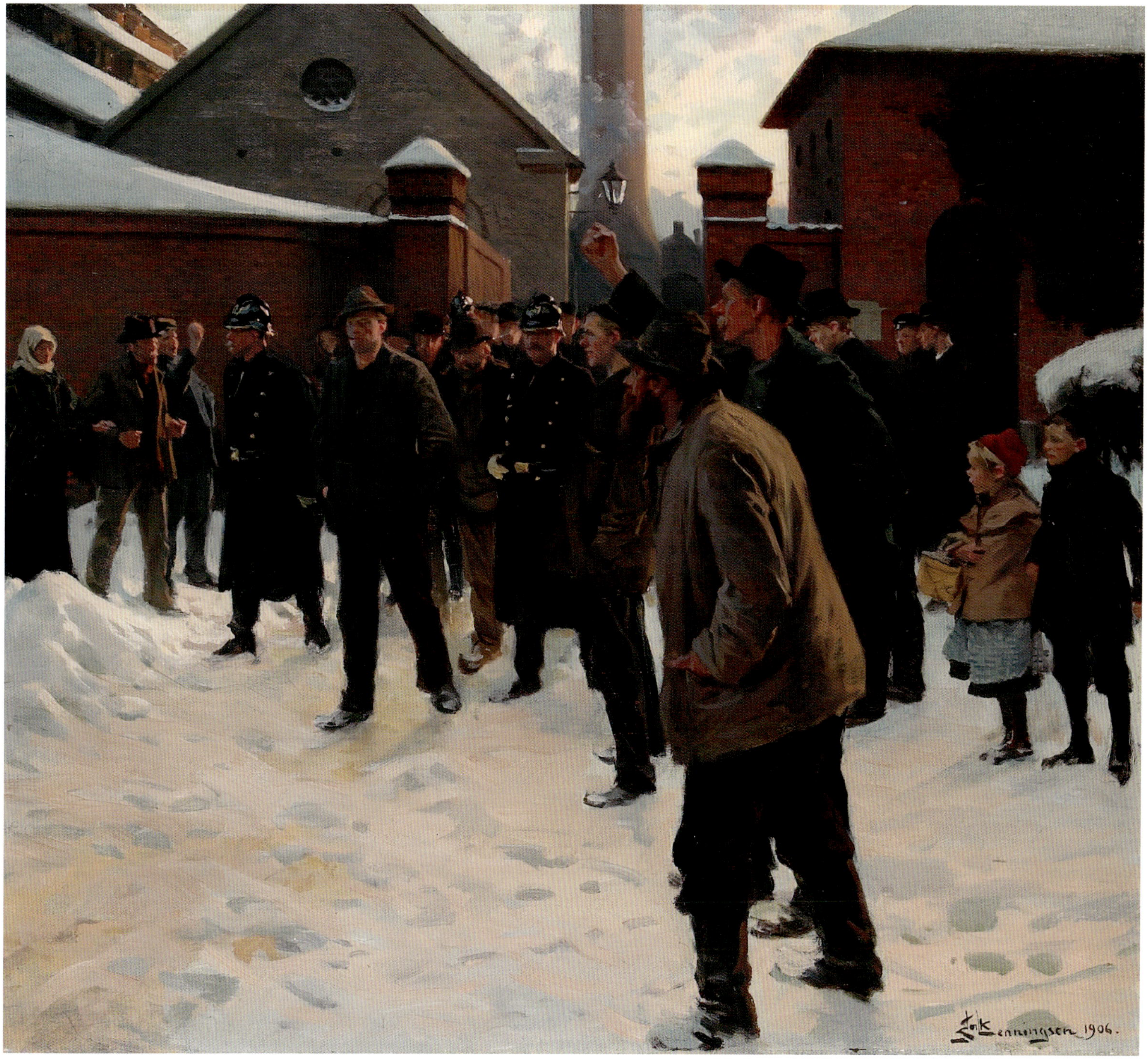
Henningsen 1906.

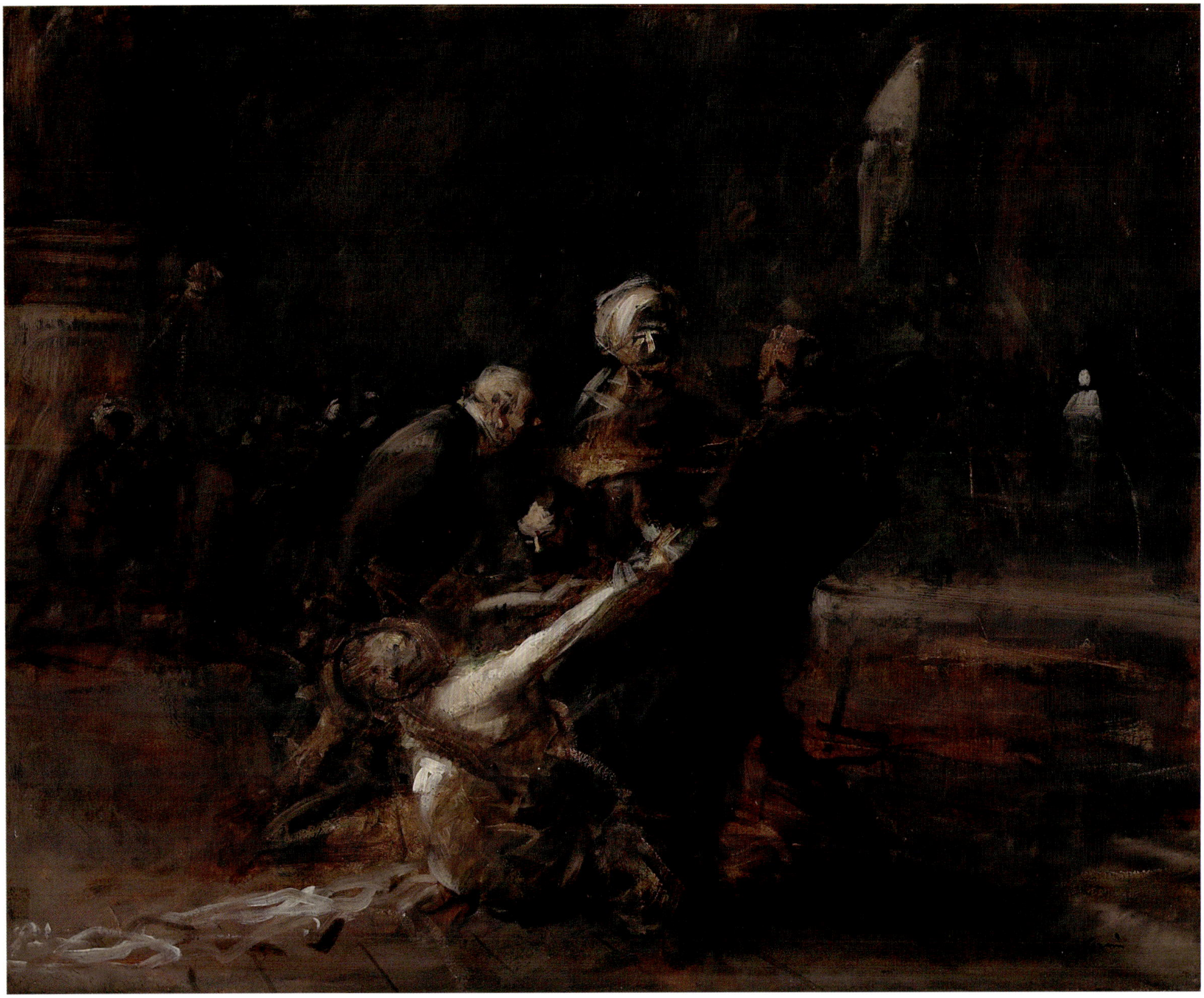

Jean-Louis Forain (French • 1852–1931)

71 — The Adulteress

c.1906–7 • oil on canvas • 60.2 × 73.5 cm • s.l.r. forain • Inv.2002.33.112

In this work Forain takes up the New Testament subject of the Woman taken in Adultery (John 8:2–11). According to the biblical story, Christ was teaching in the Temple of Jerusalem when a woman was brought before him. She had been accused of adultery, and the Pharisees, historically an influential group of Jewish men who were separatists and opponents of Christ, wanted to punish her. However, contemporary law prevented them from employing the death penalty. When they sought Christ's advice he replied, "He who is without sin among you, let him cast the first stone."

Forain's painting presents the interior of the temple with figures gathered around a pulpit, and a few architectural details such as a column and archway emerge in the background. Light enters through a large doorway and descends on an isolated figure standing on the far right of the composition. That figure, painted with just a few brushstrokes and no descriptive detail, is consistently interpreted as Christ. Throughout the composition, Forain uses a restricted palette including gray, white, and umber tones. With his gestural strokes, he successfully evokes how the woman is dragged across the floor—fluid white lines suggest the space she has crossed—and the lack of detail in her figure and face suggests she is still moving. Forain conveys most clearly the bodies and faces of a few of her captors. The features of the men closest to her, as well as the round top hat of the man on the far right of the group, each appear as figures of the early twentieth century rather than the distant era of Christ. Forain focused on the dramatic, distended period of resistance and mounting tensions, the moments before the woman is presented and prior to Christ's declaration that each person must first judge him or herself.

Biographical information suggests Forain was always a religious person and that he likely became more invested in religious subjects in the early twentieth century, particularly through his friendship with writer Joris-Karl Huysmans (1848–1907), whose novels often examined Catholic subjects and aspects of conversion. Whether Forain was attracted to this narrative simply for personal reasons is unclear, but he did explore the same story in three etchings and one lithograph.[1] In each of his prints Forain presented a prostrate woman whose clothing rises above her waistline as she is pulled by two or three men. In the painting *The Adulteress*, the woman's body appears as a stronger force of resistance against her perpetrators. Scholars have long suggested that a larger social context likely informed Forain's interest in this religious story. He focused on the inappropriate treatment of a woman who has been granted neither the right to defend herself nor to be presumed innocent. Forain may, in part, have used this subject as a means to explore his frustrations with contemporary events, as religious orders were suppressed in France by 1903, and Church and State were legally divided in 1905. For decades, Forain had been well recognized as an artist who addressed contemporary subjects including scenes in cafés, at law courts, racetracks, and on stage. In the first decade of the twentieth century he brought that close scrutiny of contemporary concerns together with his personal investment in religious subjects.

1 Guérin 1912, 121, 122; Faxon 1982, 131, 132, 133, 277. Faxon dates all the prints to 1910–12.

Provenance

Collection of Dr. Funck-Brentano

New York, H. Shickman Gallery, 1970

Toronto, Joey and Toby Tanenbaum, 1970–2002

Exhibition History

Ottawa, National Gallery of Canada, 26 May–10 September 1978; Victoria, Art Gallery of Greater Victoria, 19 October–3 December 1978; Edmonton, Edmonton Art Gallery, 15 December 1978–14 January 1979; Calgary, Glenbow-Alberta Institute, 3 February–22 March 1979; Montreal, Montreal Museum of Fine Arts, 5 April–13 May 1979; Toronto, Art Gallery of Ontario, 15 June–29 July 1979, *The Other Nineteenth Century: Paintings and Sculpture in the Collection of Mr. and Mrs. Joseph M. Tanenbaum*, cat.28, *99*

New York, H. Shickman Gallery, February 1970, *The Neglected 19th Century: An Exhibition of French Paintings*, cat.15 (reproduced)

West Palm Beach, Norton Gallery of Art, 9 October–14 November; Nashville, Cheekwood Museum of Art, 4 December 1982–16 January 1983; San Antonio, The McNay Art Institute, 5 February–20 March 1983; Cedar Rapids, Cedar Rapids Museum of Art, 9 April–22 May 1983; Ann Arbor, University of Michigan Art Museum, 11 June–24 July 1983; Kansas, Edwin A. Ulrich Museum of Art, Wichita State University, 13 August–25 September 1983; Springfield, Museum of Fine Arts, 15 October–30 November 1983, *Jean-Louis Forain: Artist, Realist, Humanist*, cat.12, *39*

Hamilton, Art Gallery of Hamilton, 28 May 2005–28 May 2006, *Heaven and Earth Unveiled: European Treasures from the Tanenbaum Collection*, cat.39; 29–30, *91*

Bibliography

Brayer, Yves. *Jean-Louis Forain, 1852–1931*. Paris: Musée Marmottan, 1978.

Browse, Lillian. *Forain the Painter*. London: P. Elek, 1978.

Faxon, Alicia Craig. *Jean-Louis Forain: A Catalogue Raisonné of His Prints*. New York: Garland, 1982, 132–33, 196–97.

Guérin, Marcel. *J.L. Forain, aquafortiste: catalogue raisonné de l'œuvre gravé de l'artiste*. 2 vols. Paris: H. Floury, 1912.

Kunstler, Charles. *Forain*. Paris: Rieder, 1931, pl.46.

Sloane, John C. Jr. "Religious Influences on the Art of Jean-Louis Forain," *The Art Bulletin* vol.23 no.3 (September 1941): 199–207.

Valdès-Forain, Florence. *Jean-Louis Forain*. Avignon: Musée Angladon, 2003.

-----, et al. *Jean-Louis Forain: La Comédie Parisienne*. Memphis: Dixon Gallery and Gardens, 2011, 154–59.

Émile Friant (French • 1863–1932)

72 — Capital Punishment

1908 • oil on canvas • 166 × 176.6 cm • s.d.l.l. E. Friant. 1908 • Inv.2002.33.25

Friant promoted his talents as a contemporary history painter when he submitted this work to the Salon de la Société Nationale des Beaux-Arts in 1908. The large-scale canvas, with its unusual, nearly square format, attracted considerable attention and was among the works chosen to illustrate the exhibition catalogue that year. Friant had been appointed a professor of drawing at the École des Beaux-Arts two years earlier, in 1906. He then invested considerable energy into the preparatory work and the final canvas of *Capital Punishment.*[1] This painting is significant within Friant's oeuvre in part because it made a strong declaration of his abilities as a draftsman at a time when attracting students and public recognition for his drawing skills was particularly important for advancing his career. Friant set himself a challenging composition and drew the viewer's attention to the convict by positioning him as a repoussoir: standing closest to the picture plane, draped in a dramatic red cloak, and turning in to the scene, the condemned man's body leads the viewer's eye into the composition and beyond the dense arrangement of figures in the foreground. Implied lines extend from the prisoner's eyes, through the crucifixion held high in the priest's well-formed hand, and direct our attention to the looming blade of the guillotine.

As a spectator we may resist looking at this unsettling scene, but Friant uses various strategies to help ease that challenge. He clarifies all the necessary details of the shallow, stage-like middle ground and animates that space with a play of lines. The form of the guillotine's wood frame runs parallel to that of the board which, while smaller in size, commands interest: the clearly defined semicircular indentation suggests the next moment of the narrative. As events unfold, the prisoner will place his head in that notch. Angled lines of military armaments frame the scaffolding and the receding lines of the coffin which, with its lid open in anticipation, denotes the spaces that first the prostrate body and then corpse will inhabit. All these details declare Friant's abilities within the academic tradition and he had, in fact, trained briefly with Cabanel (see cat.6) earlier in his career. However, Friant contrasted his clarity of form, space, and detail—particularly of facial features in the foreground and middle ground—with how he defined the background setting. Gas lighting punctuates and helps delimit the border between those closest to the execution and the crowds that gather on surrounding rooftops despite the rain. Architecture and distant spectators are blurred, both metaphorically and actually. Friant's techniques connect his work with the then dominant aesthetic of naturalism. Naturalist artists such as Friant addressed a range of artifices in their work, including experimentation with photography. Recent scholarship argues that naturalist works also deployed surface description as a means for artists to interrogate contemporary republican values such as rationality and collective identity.

Friant exhibited a total of six works—three paintings and three prints—at the Société Nationale show in 1908. Those who looked closely would have likely noticed similarities between the build and facial features of the condemned man and those of the artist himself from his *Self-Portrait* on display in the print section (no.2201). It is unlikely Friant intended to infer any specific meaning by positioning himself as the condemned man. He was highly regarded as an artist, particularly after 1889 when he won the Grand Prix at the Salon for his painting *All Saints' Day.*[2] Also in 1889, he was awarded a gold medal at the Exposition Universelle and made a chevalier of the Legion of Honor. It has been suggested that Friant was inspired to paint this specific scene after he witnessed the death of a customs officer who was accused of a triple murder and executed in Nancy in 1891. Friant used himself as a model on numerous occasions, and it seems particularly appropriate that he did so with this painting because his choice of subject matter placed the work within a larger social debate. Capital punishment was still legal in France when Armand Fallières was elected president of the French Republic in 1906. But Fallières supported abolishing the practice and, until the end of his term in 1913, he pardoned nearly all who were condemned to death. The Chamber of Deputies also debated the allocation of funds for the guillotine, and a law to abolish capital punishment was drafted in 1906 and submitted to a vote in the summer of 1908. When Friant showed his *Capital Punishment* at the Salon in spring 1908 he was, thus, bravely presenting himself as a painter who would dare to address the most challenging social issues of his day. Later that same year, in November 1908, the Chamber rejected the law by a sixty-two percent vote and capital punishment remained legal in France through 1981, although the last execution took place in 1977.

1 A small-scale (24.5 × 35.2 cm) preparatory study painted in oil on wood is in the collection of the Musée des Beaux-Arts in Nancy.

2 Musée des Beaux-Arts, Nancy.

Provenance

Paris, Galerie Félix Marcilhac

Toronto, Joey and Toby Tanenbaum, 1985–2002

Exhibition History

Paris, Salon de la Société Nationale des Beaux-Arts, 1908, no.437

Hamilton, Art Gallery of Hamilton, 28 May 2005–28 May 2006, *Heaven and Earth Unveiled: European*

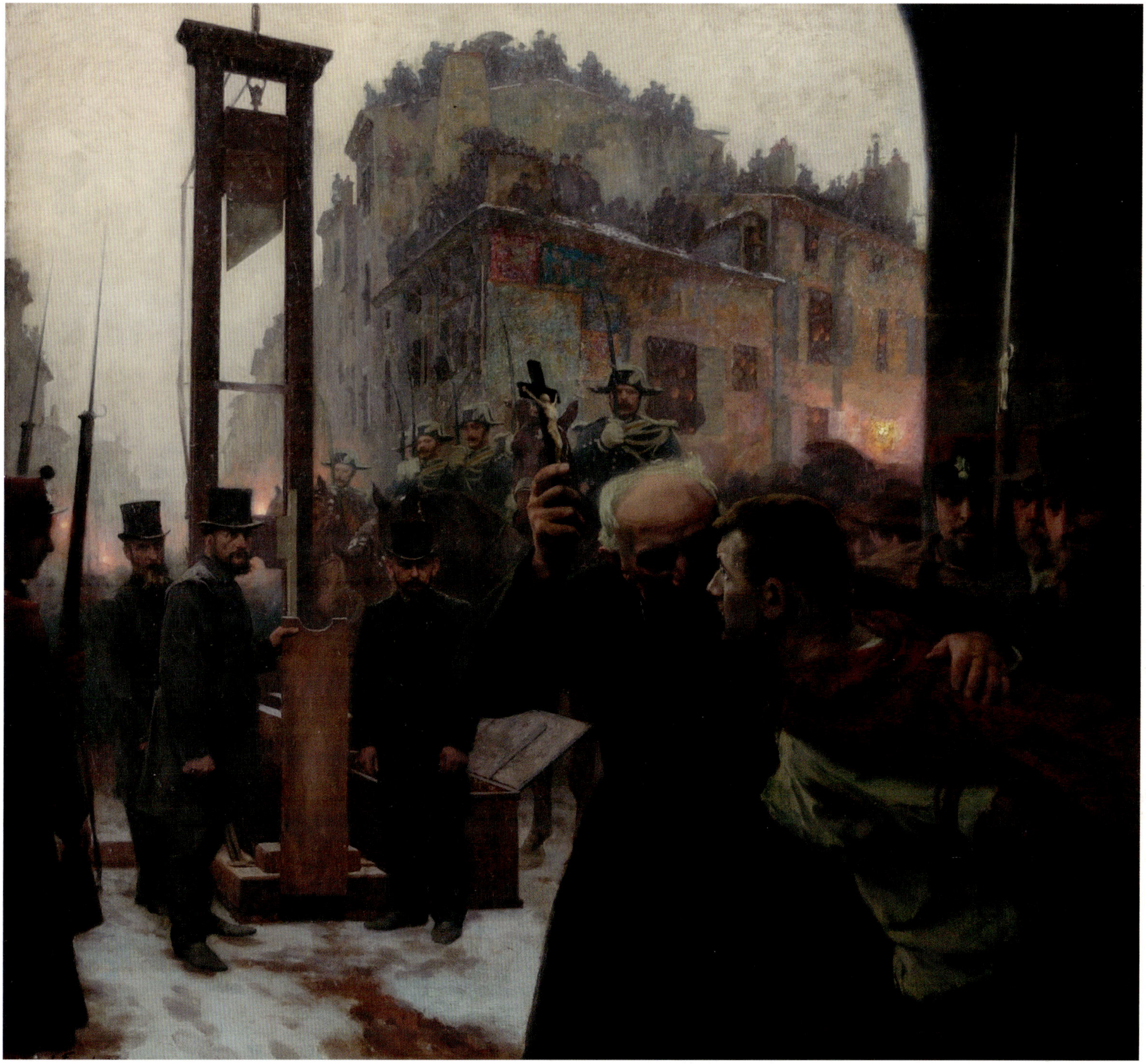

Treasures from the Tanenbaum Collection, cat.46; 53, *125*
Hamilton, Art Gallery of Hamilton, 15 December 2007–21 September 2008, *The Word Made Flesh: Images of Devotion*
Paris, Musée d'Orsay, 15 March–27 June 2010, *Crime et châtiment*, cat.213, *207*

Bibliography

Alexandre, Arsène. *Émile Friant et son œuvre*. Mulhouse: Braun, 1930.
Baschet, Ludovic. *Catalogue illustré du Salon de 1908*. Paris: Bibliothèque des annales, 1908, xii, xlix, *20*.
Claude, Henri. *Friant*. Pref. Philippe Claudel. Metz: Serge Domini, 2005, 150, *151*.
Kisiel, Marine. "La gravure: un pan méconnu de l'œuvre d'Émile Friant," *Nouvelles de l'estampe* vol.235 (2011): 15–23.
Lacassagne, A. *Peine de mort et criminalité: l'accroissement de la criminalité et l'application de la peine capitale*. Paris: A. Maloine, 1908.
McIntosh, Decourcy E. "Émile Friant: A Forgotten Realist of the Gilded Age," *The Magazine Antiques* vol.151 (April 1997): 582–91.
Peltre, Christine, and Claude Pétry. *Émile Friant (1863–1932): regard sur l'homme et l'œuvre*. Nancy: Musée des Beaux-Arts, 1988.
Thomson, Richard. *Art of the Actual: Naturalism and Style in Early Third Republic France, 1880–1900*. New Haven: Yale University Press, 2012.
Weisberg, Gabriel P. *Beyond Impressionism: The Naturalist Impulse*. New York: Harry N. Abrams, 1992, 82–87.

Anders Zorn (Swedish • 1860–1920)

73 — Portrait of David Jayne Hill

1910 • oil on canvas • 125.5 x 91 cm • s.d.l.l. Zorn/Stockholm 1910 • Inv.2002.33.198

This was the first of two portraits Zorn executed of David Jayne Hill (1850–1932), who commissioned the works while he was American ambassador to Germany from 1908 to 1911. Zorn presented a three-quarter-length view of Hill caught in a moment of introspection. Hill directs his gaze down and within the imaginary, ill-defined space he inhabits. One hand rests in a pocket and the other is poised so that thumb and first finger connect. While Hill concentrates and his face appears impassive, his hand gesture expresses his lively internal thoughts in a concrete form. The strong three-dimensionality of Hill's body, and particularly the layers of his formal black dress, emerges with impressive clarity against the dark, loosely painted background. Zorn painted this canvas with the fluid brushstroke and characteristic confidence that was the basis of his international reputation as a portraitist. Zorn first established his reputation with American patrons in 1893 when he served as commissioner of the Swedish exhibition at the World's Columbian Exposition and spent nearly a year in Chicago. It was the first of seven extended visits to the United States, that continued through 1911. During these years Zorn was much sought after, and he completed nearly a hundred commissioned portraits of American politicians, industrialists, financiers, art collectors, and philanthropists. His American sitters included Isabella Stewart Gardner (1894), Bertha Potter Palmer (1893), Andrew Carnegie (1911), and Presidents Grover Cleveland (1899) and William Howard Taft (1911).

It remains unclear how Hill and Zorn met, but Hill likely knew of Zorn's reputation before he left the United States and took up his first foreign post in 1903. Hill began his career in university administration and had served as president of the Universities of Lewisburg (now Bucknell) and Rochester. Over the course of his lifetime he also wrote twenty-one books including several studies on the history of foreign affairs. From 1896 Hill's career focused on international diplomacy, and prior to his appointment in Germany he was assistant secretary of state and he also held posts in Switzerland, the Netherlands, and Luxembourg. Zorn maintained a studio in Stockholm from 1902, and it was there that he completed this portrait. Zorn made the location clear by including it as part of his signature in the lower left-hand corner of the canvas. Hill was so satisfied with this work that he commissioned a second portrait, which Zorn painted during a visit to Berlin in 1911. In the later portrait Zorn followed an approach he often used for male sitters and presented Hill in his study, seated at a writing desk before shelves of books. Zorn captured Hill's intellectual life in an evocative way in the first portrait and then turned to a more well-established trope of interior masculine space in his second work. During the final decade of Hill's life, when he had returned from his foreign posts, it was this first portrait that was the highlight of the large art collection he and his wife Juliet Lewis Packer Hill (1853–1923) displayed at their home near Washington, D.C. When asked about the portrait Hill replied: "[It] is the conception of a great Swedish painter who portrays me as emerging from the shadow of doubts and indecision into the light of determined aim. It was painted during the middle of my diplomatic career."[1] At Hill's death in 1932, he fulfilled his wife's wish and bequeathed both portraits to the Corcoran Gallery of Art in Washington, D.C. In a decision likely informed by financial challenges that strained the institution over the course of several decades, the Corcoran Gallery parted with both works in 1979.[2]

[1] N. Reynolds Packard, "David Jayne Hill," *Bucknell Alumni Monthly* vol.8 no.7 (April 1924): 17–18.

[2] The first portrait has a plaque on the back of the stretcher that reads: "PORTRAIT OF DR. DAVID JAYNE HILL/BY/ANDERS ZORN/PRESENTED BY/DAVID JAYNE HILL/IN COMPLIANCE WITH A WISH OF HIS BELOVED WIFE/JULIET LEWIS PACKER HILL." The second portrait was sold at auction: New York, Sotheby Parke Bernet, 3 May 1979, lot 27; London, Sotheby's, 19 June 1985, lot 304; London, Sotheby's, 27 June 2007, lot 425.

Provenance

Collection of David Jayne Hill and Juliet Lewis Packer Hill, 1910–32
Washington, D.C., Corcoran Gallery of Art, 1932–79
New York, Sotheby Parke Bernet, 3 May 1979, lot 28
Toronto, Joey and Toby Tanenbaum, 1979–2002

Exhibition History

Hamilton, Art Gallery of Hamilton, 28 May 2005–28 May 2006; Victoria, Art Gallery of Greater Victoria, 25 January–11 May 2008, *Heaven and Earth Unveiled: European Treasures from the Tanenbaum Collection*, cat.139; 44–45, *107*

Bibliography

Brummer, Hans Henrik. "Anders Zorn in America," in Johan Cederlund et al. *Anders Zorn: Sweden's Master Painter*. New York: Skira Rizzoli, 2013, 29–57.
Clayson, S. Hollis. "Anders Zorn's Etched Portraits of American Men, or the Trouble with French Masculinity," in Tema Balducci, Heather Belnap Jensen, and Pamela J. Warner, eds. *Interior Portraiture and Masculine Identity in France, 1789–1914*. Farnham: Ashgate Press, 2011, 177–95.
Sandström, Birgitta. *The Artist Anders Zorn, 1860–1920*. Rev. ed. Mora: Zornmuseet, 2009, 31, 44.
-----. *Porträtt av Anders Zorn*. Mora: Zornsamlingarna, 1990.
Shaw, Carrell, "Anders Zorn: American Patronage," in Jane K. Bledsoe, ed. *Anders Zorn Rediscovered*. Longbeach: The University Art Museum, California State University, 1984, 18–23.
Tostmann, Oliver, et al. *Anders Zorn: A European Artist Seduces America*. Boston: Isabella Stewart Gardner Museum, 2013, 13–26, 66–77.

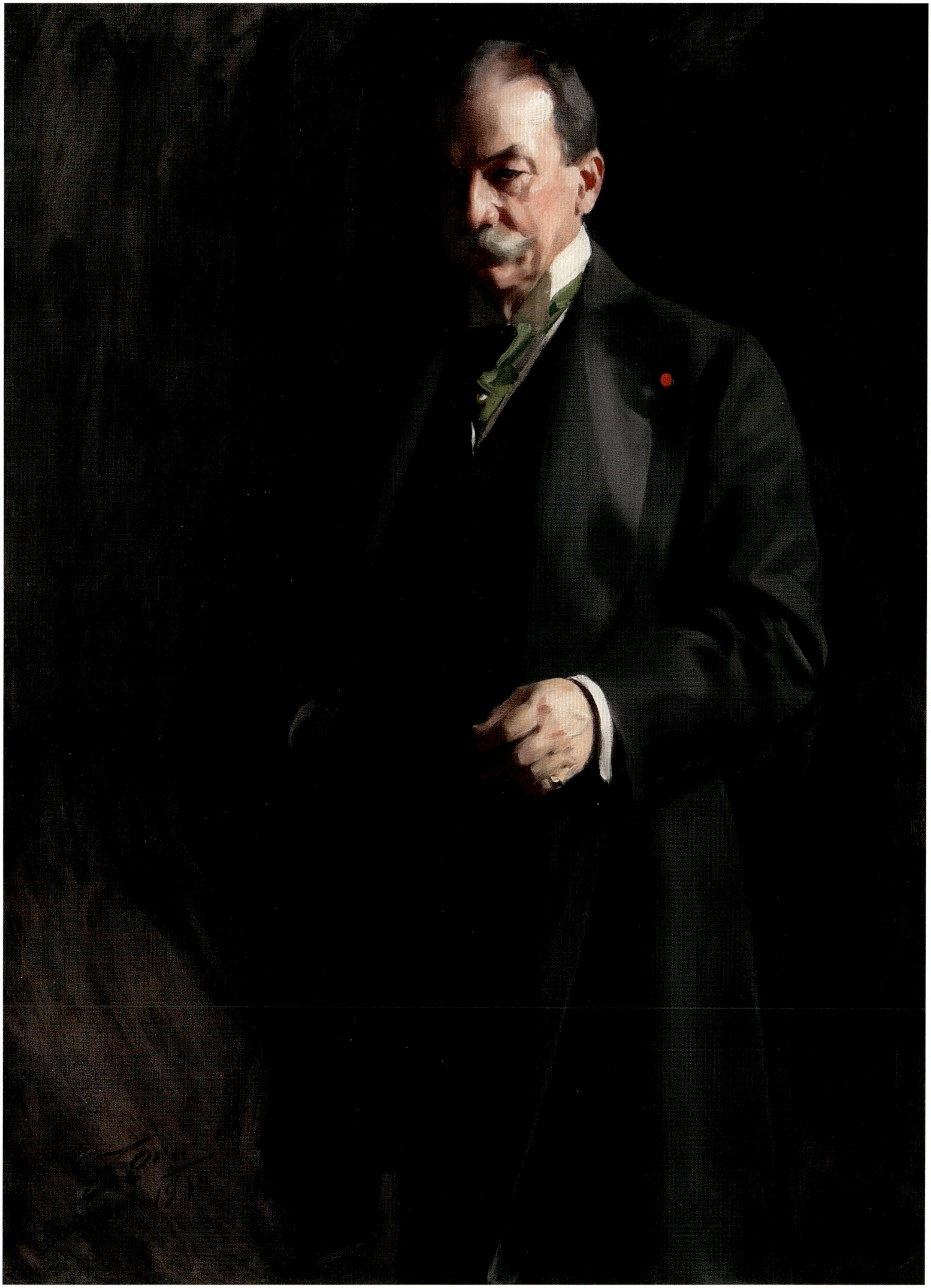

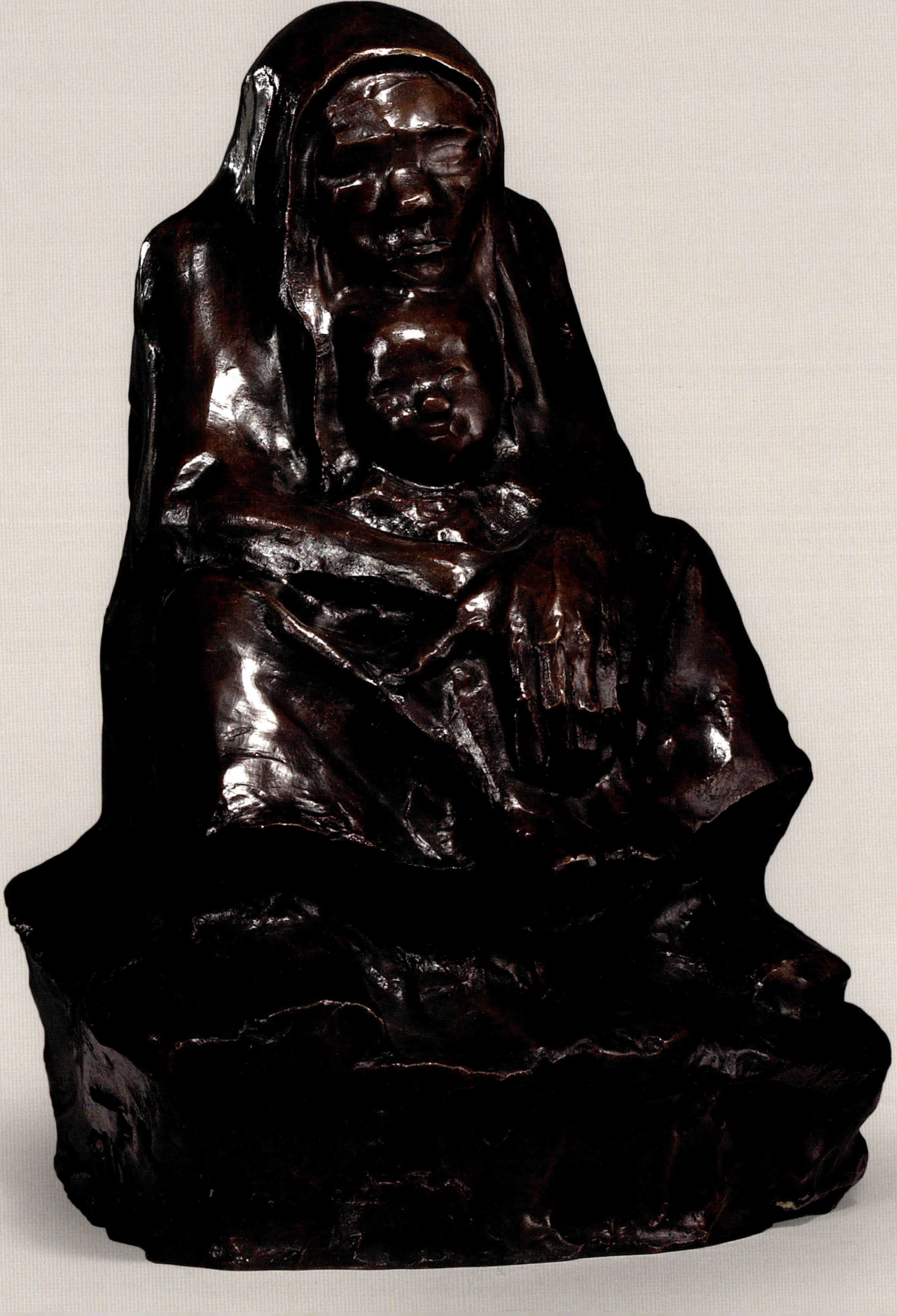

Käthe Kollwitz (German • 1867–1945)

74 — Woman with Child in Her Lap

1911–15 • bronze • 40 × 28 × 28 cm • s. back base Kollwitz, stamp H. NOACK BERLIN • Inv.2002.33.204

Women protecting children constitutes one of the most important themes in Kollwitz's work. For Kollwitz (née Schmidt), a woman's body, and particularly her arms and hands, are the principal way for a female figure to shield a child from negative external forces. In this sculpture, Kollwitz depicted a woman with angular facial features and hollowed-out eyes. The woman purses her lips as she rests her chin on the child's head. Kollwitz presents this adult female figure with a face that is quite noticeably not the face of a young woman. Instead, the artist intentionally portrayed a woman whose life circumstances and experiences have left their mark on her physiognomy. Kollwitz also portrayed the woman with particularly large hands that have pronounced knuckles and prominent tendons that are taut and suggest tension coursing through her body. As with many of Kollwitz's sculptures, the viewer must rely on hands and faces as important vehicles for the work's meaning. Bodies are largely shrouded and concealed by cloth that envelops the figures and forms a defensive layer against the outside world. Physical forms merge, and it becomes difficult to distinguish the child's feet from the hem of the woman's skirt. Woman and child remain still but they are not passive. They are physically united in their resolve. The adult woman may be the child's mother, as English versions of the title often suggest; in German, however, she is identified as a more general *Frau* (woman) rather than a specific *Mutter* (mother). The meaning of this sculpture need not be confined to a specific familial relationship; it invites a larger metaphorical interpretation of intergenerational kinship.

Despite the open and suggestive nature of Kollwitz's sculpted forms, scholars have often interpreted her work primarily in terms of her own personal experiences. Certainly the traumatic events that she experienced during the period that coincides with Kollwitz's work on this particular sculpture, dated between 1911 and 1915, have helped foster the tendency to analyze her works as unmediated manifestations of her biography. Kollwitz's diary survives and has been readily available in published form, and this has supported interpretations of her work through a biographical lens. During World War I, Kollwitz's sons volunteered for service and her second son, Peter, died in Belgium in October 1914. Many entries in her diary record her grief, and she later wrote of a dream in which she had a baby, a child of one or two years of age whom, she wrote, "I could go on always holding it in my arms … and I would not have to give it away" (18 April 1916). Kollwitz may have intended the middle-aged woman in this sculpture as a specific evocation of herself, just as she appeared in the dream with a young child whom she refused to relinquish. However, central to the enduring power of Kollwitz's expressive forms, her work remains open to multiple interpretations. In the period when Kollwitz produced this sculpture she was an active member and part of the executive of the secession in Berlin, one of a number of German-speaking cities in which artists formed associations that organized juried exhibitions and offered opportunities for alliances outside academic institutions.

Provenance

New York, Shickman Gallery
Toronto, Joey and Toby Tanenbaum, 1971–2002

Exhibition History

Hamilton, Art Gallery of Hamilton, 28 May 2005–28 May 2006, *Heaven and Earth Unveiled: European Treasures from the Tanenbaum Collection*, cat.176; 187, *301* (as *Mother with Child in Her Lap*)

Bibliography

Apel, Dora. "'Heros' and 'Whores': The Politics of Gender in Weimar Antiwar Imagery," *The Art Bulletin* vol.79 no.3 (September 1997): 366–84 (380–84).
Die Bronze-Skulpturen von Käthe Kollwitz. Düsseldorf: Galerie Vömel, 1973, 14.
Draper, Tom. "Käthe Kollwitz Revealed in Sculpture," *Sculpture Review* vol.41 no.4 (Fall 1992): 10–13.
Guratzsch, Herwig. *Käthe Kollwitz—Druckgraphik—Handzeichnungen.* Stuttgart: G. Hatje, 1990, 65, fig.8.
Kollwitz, Hans, ed. *The Diary and Letters of Käthe Kollwitz.* Trans. Richard and Clara Winston. Chicago: Henry Regnery Company, 1955, 69, fig.40 (related lithograph).
Nagel, Otto, and Sibylle Schallenberg-Nagel. *Käthe Kollwitz: die Handzeichnungen.* Stuttgart: Verlag W. Kohlhammer, 1980, 374–75, no.925.
Prelinger, Elizabeth, et al. *Käthe Kollwitz.* Washington, D.C.: National Gallery of Art, 1992.
Skrapits, Joseph C. "Mother Courage: The Drawings of Käthe Kollwitz," *American Artist: Drawing* vol.5 no.17 (Spring 2008): 48–65.

Frank Brangwyn (English • 1867–1956)

75 — The Swineherd

before 1914 • oil on canvas • 137.8 × 175.6 cm • s.l.l. FB • Inv.2002.33.82

Brangwyn enjoyed a prominent international profile in 1914 when he sent *The Swineherd* to Venice as one of the paintings he showed at the exhibition known today as the Venice Biennale. Brangwyn had already designed works that filled the British rooms at two previous Venice Biennales, in 1905 and 1907. In the 1890s he was a member of the secession groups in Munich and Vienna, and in 1895 he received an important commission to paint two exterior murals for the Maison de l'Art Nouveau, the Paris gallery of leading art dealer Siegfried Bing. Brangwyn was well known as a visual artist who successfully unified the arts into a decorative whole. *The Swineherd* is a vigorously executed and highly expressive canvas that demonstrates his technical virtuosity.[1] Three figures tend to a herd of pigs, some gather around to eat, while others wander in the landscape to the left. Figures merge with the background setting, as does the gleeful woman in the foreground, her legs forming branch-like extensions of the tree trunk on which she leans. Brangwyn intends the two adults and young man to be understood as laborers, and yet he presents them working with such sensual abandon. Pleasure permeates Brangwyn's canvas: the pigs relish their meal, the humans delight in their care-taking and physical contact, and the artist clearly derives considerable enjoyment from his painting practice. In some areas, such as the food dish or the vegetables in the foreground, Brangwyn's brushstrokes offer a visual description of the three-dimensional form of an object. In other areas, such as the passage of violet below the food dish or the section of pink and orange below the woman, Brangwyn allows the paint to represent itself. In those and other sections of this canvas, paint does not appear to stand in for anything beyond its own material form.

In 1914, when Brangwyn exhibited *The Swineherd* in Venice, he also showed *The Cider Press*, a painting that focused on a moment of rest during an apple harvest (1902; private collection). Both paintingss were acquired by George Harold Winterbottom (1861–1934) and Georgina MacLeod Winterbottom (1881–1973) and hung at Horton House, their eighteenth-century mansion near Northampton, southeast of Birmingham.[2] The estate at Horton House was roughly midway between London and Manchester, then the two urban bases of the Winterbottom Book Cloth Company that sold bookbinding materials and was the basis of their increasingly substantial fortune. In 1915 the Winterbottoms also commissioned Brangwyn to design the lighting and to paint a cycle of mural paintings for their billiard room at Horton House. Brangwyn was inspired by Venetian subjects for many of the ten scenes he completed for that billiard room. The ten murals, Brangwyn's *The Swineherd*, and at least two other easel paintings by him hung at Horton House until George Winterbottom's death in 1934. Significant levels of estate taxes then brought about the sale of the property and the dispersal of the works the Winterbottoms had bought and commissioned from Brangwyn.

1 A possible related drawing in sanguine, charcoal, and white heightening is cited in the catalogue of the William Morris Gallery exhibition in 1974 (D 255).

2 They also acquired *The Market, Bagdad* (private collection).

Provenance

Horton House, near Northampton, George Harold Winterbottom and Georgina MacLeod Winterbottom, to 1934
Mr. and Mrs. Fred O. Thomson
Des Moines, IA, Des Moines Art Center, 1948–91
New York, Sotheby's, 27 February 1991, lot 269
London, Fine Art Society, 1991
Toronto, Joey and Toby Tanenbaum, 1991–2002

Exhibition History

Venice, 1914, XI Esposizione Internazionale d'Arte della Città di Venezia, no.1402
London, Queen's Gate, May–July 1924, *Exhibition of Paintings, Drawings and Etchings by Frank Brangwyn, RA*, no.39
London, Barbizon House, 1931, no.11
Chicago, Caron Pirie Scott & Company, 1931, *Frank Brangwyn R.A.*, no.2
Des Moines, Des Moines Public Art Galleries, 1931, *Paintings and Watercolours by Frank Brangwyn*
Hamilton, Art Gallery of Hamilton, 28 May 2005–28 May 2006, *Heaven and Earth Unveiled: European Treasures from the Tanenbaum Collection*, cat. 14; 64, *142*
Hamilton, Art Gallery of Hamilton, 28 April–2 December 2007, *A Visual Bestiary*
Hamilton, Art Gallery of Hamilton, 13 September 2008–4 January 2009, *Blood, Sweat and Tears: Labour in Art*

Bibliography

Catalogue of the Works of Sir Frank Brangwyn, RA, 1867–1956. Walthamstow: William Morris Gallery, 1974, 14–15.
Galloway, Vincent. *The Oils and Murals of Frank Brangwyn, 1867–1956*. Leigh-on-Sea: F. Lewis, 1962, no.677, pl.23.
Horner, Libby. *Frank Brangwyn: A Mission to Decorate Life*. London: Fine Art Society, 2006.
-----. "Brangwyn and the Horton House Mystery," *British Art Journal* vol.6 no.2 (Autumn 2005): 40–51.
-----, and Gillian Naylor, eds. *Frank Brangwyn 1867–1956*. Leeds: Leeds Museum and Galleries, 2006, 165, 176.
Weisberg, Gabriel, et al. *The Origins of Art Nouveau: The Bing Empire*. Amsterdam: Van Gogh Museum, 2005.

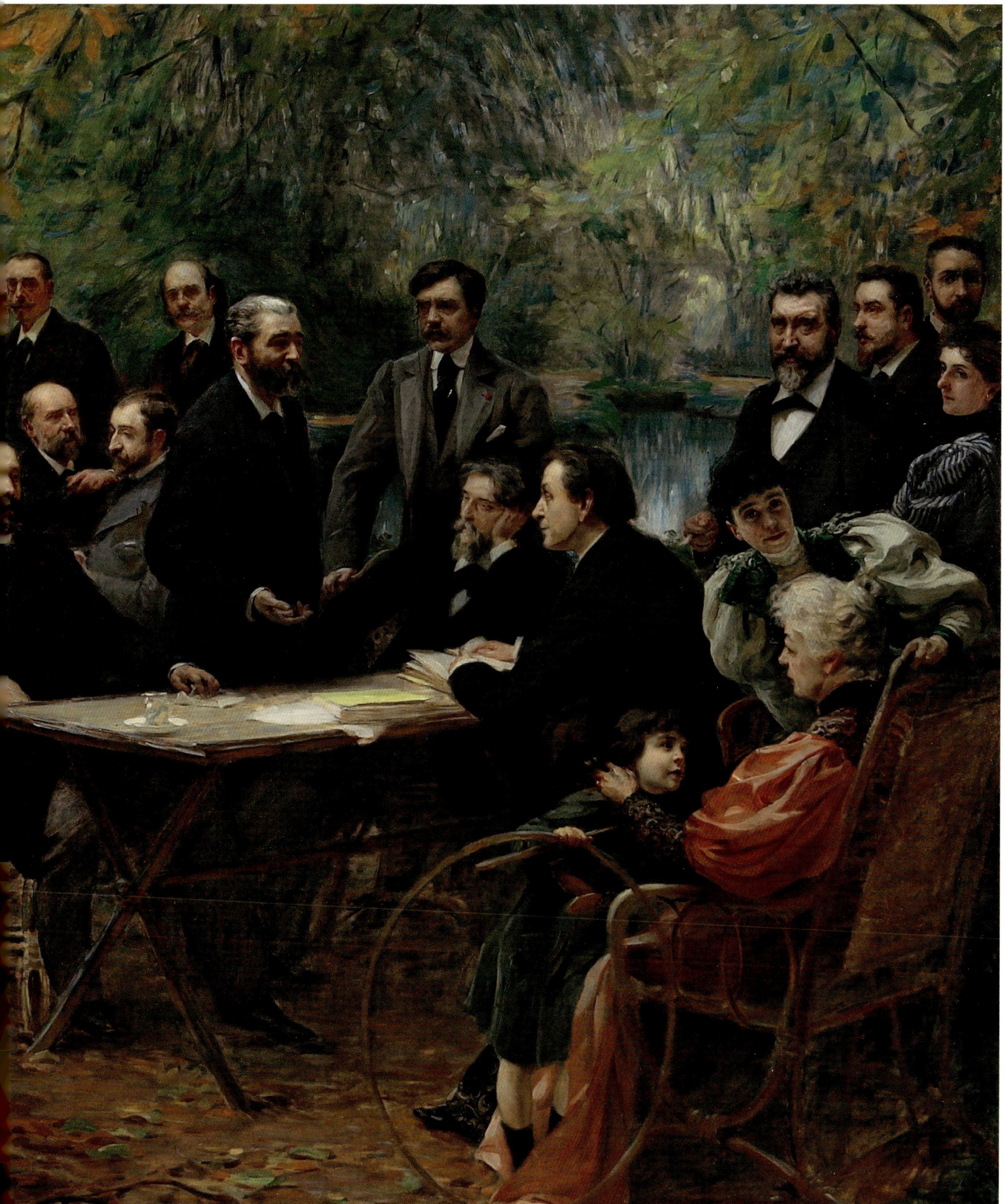

LIST OF ARTISTS